Thought Access

Idil Ahmed

Thought Access

Your entry to more.

Copyright © 2023 by Idil Ahmed

All rights reserved. This book or any portion thereof may not be reproduced or used in any manner whatsoever without the express written permission of the publisher except for the use of brief quotations in a book review.

Cover Artist: Sergey Shenderovsky

Printed in the United States of America

First Printing, 2023

ISBN Print: 978-1-7323885-7-4

Instagram: Idillionaire

Twitter: Idillionaire

Facebook: Idillionaire

Book Club: Idillionairebookclub

Idil Ahmed
San Diego, CA 92037
www.idillionaire.com

Dedicated to your powerful soul.

Table of Contents

Introduction 9

1: Hone In 25

2: Thought Patterns 57

3: It Was You the Whole Time 91

4: Perception: True Self vs. Constructed Self 129

5: True Power: Your Life Force 153

6: Psychological Freedom 181

7: A Message for Your Soul 205

8: Being a Thought Alchemist 225

9: Thought Travel: Past, Present, Future (One) 247

10: Encode 267

11: Access Any State Now 283

12: Thoughts Materialize 303

13: Three Powerful Thought Access Techniques 325

14: Matters of The Heart 355

15: Radiant Inner Energy 373

16: Fifteen Daily Thought Upgrades 391

17: One Hundred Thought Access Affirmations 423

18: Embodiment: Representing Your Thought World ..465

19: You Now Have Thought Access 489

INTRODUCTION

Thought Access is your direct link to the most powerful thoughts, awareness, and vision of all that's within you and all that is around you. You will feel the highest energy while reading this book, and it will take your mind to another level that instantly produces change. You will now begin to receive Thought Access to remind you of your inherent state of being. *Thought Access* operates in the realm of thought—the origin of every single thing you see, feel, and experience. This will give you the power to alter your experience, enter a reality solely created by your thoughts, and live out the version of yourself you truly feel is your highest expression. The power to choose is in your hands. You must remember that all creation begins with a single thought.

The ability to realize that you are powerful comes from having the Thought Access to identify this as truth. The ability to see yourself from this state means gaining access through your mind first. This is what reading, learning, exploring, and discovering yourself is all about: your ability to remember and access what has always been there through reminders and realizations. Nothing changed until you discovered the thought to change, which then gave you access to your potential. This is what Thought Access is: the state of mind, the types of thoughts, and the inner revelations that open up your mind to completely creating, designing, and demonstrating your experience. There are many potential outcomes, and each begins with a choice that takes you to the end result. This is what makes you powerful. You are a conscious being who is able to reflect, observe, analyze, and make the choice to enter the reality you want. With *Thought Access*, you will access insight to illuminate the path of your mind.

INTRODUCTION

By the end of this book, you will KNOW mind power as a natural state. You will understand that life from within was always your true expression. So much of your inner self will begin to activate, and you will feel your supernatural state as an everyday occurrence. You will represent what it means to live from the spirit in the physical. You will KNOW that you are already doing so. The direction you choose from this point on will require you to finally stand in your power. When the layers, concepts, ideas, and experiences all around you no longer allow your spirit to fully operate in its former capacity, change happens. Things get shaken up, and this puts you in a place of vulnerability. In a sense, you experience rebirth as you begin to remember. You shed the illusions that made you forget; and for once in your life, it all begins to connect. You feel understood, as if a part of you that was waiting to be seen is finally coming through. You are activated. All of this is taking place within you right now. This is your rise, and it begins with *Thought Access*. This book is an energy state in and of itself. It's here to empower you like never before. You'll go deeper in your self-belief, exude the radiance of self-love, trust intuitively, and speak boldly and confidently about everything in the knowledge that you have the Thought Access to do so.

The ability to receive anything begins with the realization that it has always existed within you. This demonstrates that your inner knowing believes it to be possible. Where does that knowledge come from? This power begins in your thoughts. You might know this already…but do you, really? Do you know that your access to greater thought begins in the clarity of your mind, the ownership of your beingness, and the understanding that so much is possible? What you believe to be possible exists only in the thoughts to which you have access. When you believe that you can accomplish what you want, you do; but another person might not be able to understand how you do it. The results of your success arise not only from doing, but from your initial thought that it could be done. This is what Thought Access means; you access a thought that ignites within you the certainty that it is truly possible to make your dreams a reality. If you study the thought state of a person who doesn't believe this to be true, it will bring you back to the thought from which their limitation originated. Your potential depends on your Thought Access to your possibilities. This is why people have the ability to change the lives of others through the information they share. The information you learn can alter your path, and the insight you receive from your own spirit can ignite a profound shift in the way you experience your own personal reality.

This is why it was so important for me to write this book. I have received so many wonderful insights that have changed my life in miraculous ways. I understand that differences between human beings exist only in the awareness to which they have access, and my hope is that the insights offered here will move people in ways that bring much-needed understanding of the self for full self-expression. I believe that it is your spiritual birthright to live out your dreams, be at peace with yourself no matter what is happening, and push outside of the realm of the familiar. You weren't meant to be confined in your thinking or to believe in lack.

Belief in what is possible for you is, first and foremost, a mindset shift. This leads to physical results which can then further activate the knowledge that what you want *is* possible. When you have seen it for yourself and broken the mental barriers, you will begin to operate at your own wavelength because you have the Thought Access to do so. This is why *Thought Access* can be such a precious experience for you. It is a vital message I must share to outline specific thought possibilities that will begin to activate your knowledge.

You will see the power of Thought Access by receiving entry to more of yourself. This book is the future in your hands right now. Think of it as a blueprint of the clearest thoughts, direction,

INTRODUCTION

and guidance. You will experience many profound changes that will automatically keep your mindset in a state of possibility. You have Thought Access. Everything will return to the value of thought because you are remembering that the way you see the world, the kinds of thoughts you have, and what you focus on literally create your world.

The most powerful access you can attain is higher thought, which allows you to maneuver any situation, overcome any experience, and create what you want without hesitation. This self-confidence isn't short-lived or dependent upon external validation. It is an empowered you with a stronger mindset, with vison like no other. It starts now.

The only change that actually takes place in your life is change that happens in your mind first. The difference between what you can see and what you can become has everything to do with the type of thought to which you have access. To be able to fully see, you must begin to cultivate Thought Access. The difference between who you've been and who you will become boils down to a difference in your thinking: a single thought.

A single new realization has always opened your mind up first, even changing the direction of your life. Everything is happening right now in your mind, and your greatest access begins there. I called this book *Thought Access* because I know that you will receive your own private connection to a state of mind that will alter your reality, transforming it exactly the way you want to see it. *Thought Access* gives you back the power to decide, to know, and to do what you love.

Below, I will share chapter breakdowns, what to expect, and how to fully use this magical book as a guiding compass.

Chapter 1: Hone In

Before you begin *Thought Access*, you must start to hone in your energy. This chapter will focus on how you can increase your thought power as well as your physical, mental, and emotional energy to direct it any way you want. I see this chapter as a "gathering up" of your energy from unnecessary areas. Whether it's giving your energy away to situations from the past, ideas of limitation, or focusing on things you just know you don't want to manifest, that mental loop will end here, and you will begin.

You'll feel a big transformation in this chapter because you will start to direct your mind by choice. You'll feel more conscious, alive, and in control. You'll start to understand how valuable your mental energy is and what honing in will do for you.

I know how potent the mind is when consciously directed. When you make the choice to stop scattering your precious energy, you start to blossom, grow, shine, and take back the living energy you've always had access to. You'll also unlearn and identify the habits that have been causing you to lose so much of your energy. This creates a turning point for you that powers you up. The more energy you have, the more easily you can express your creativity and passion while building balance in your inner world to align with what you see all around you. This is why "Hone In" is the very first chapter. You'll only gain Thought Access when you are able to consciously direct your energy. Are you ready to hone in?

Chapter 2: Thought Patterns

Your thought patterns are everything. Thought patterns are how you think, how you see the world, and what you believe (which, in turn, creates your world). They include anything you might currently be accepting that limits what you have access to based on the thought patterns you decide to adopt habitually and daily. Until this point in your life, right up to this moment, a thought has always brought you to where you are.

Introduction

Whatever you do, whatever your relationships, however you feel, however the world responds to you…all of this depends completely upon your thought patterns. You can't make a choice without a thought coming first. Identifying the thought patterns playing out in your life and realizing how to tap into your full potential through your mindset begins with recognizing the state of mind you are in. How can you access your full potential when you don't know what is possible for you? This chapter will really expose thought patterns that seem normal, but could be limiting you. It will also break down the power of your thought and the fact that you are a genius just now awakening to your own power. You'll discover how to identify the thought patterns that are limiting you, discover ways you might be self-sabotaging, and access thought patterns that give you more energy, creativity, confidence, trust, and inner knowledge of what is truly possible for you.

This chapter will literally free your mind. You will sense that you are mentally stronger, and you will gain the ability to automatically detect and identify your current thought pattern. Nothing will get past your mental gates without a scan. People will begin to notice how different you are. You'll be much more confident, grounded, and connected to yourself. You'll make intelligent choices because your thought pattern is healthy and on point. This won't feel like much effort, as it did previously. Every word in this book is meant to uplift your spirit and bring you a higher awareness of inner power and self-belief. If you believe in yourself, the whole world believes in you. If you are strong in mindset, reality can't test you in the same ways anymore. You have higher ideals, higher goals, and bigger visions. Getting clear in your thought pattern will be your greatest freedom.

Chapter 3: It Was You the Whole Time

You already are! This chapter will break down the reality that everything starts within you. We'll look at how your inner state of being influences your reality via your mindset, your emotions, and the way you treat yourself. You'll discover that you are already connected and that you already possess the inner access to receive what is meant for you. You will understand how your mind interacts with the thought field so that you can be empowered in your manifestations. You'll become emotionally intelligent and aware of how to use your innate abilities (your own intuition and instincts) to better navigate your day-to-day life. This chapter is solely intended to help you return your attention to your inner world from which everything stems. You'll gain insight about how to understand yourself and optimize your mind and body through mental and emotional harmony.

You'll be liberated from triggers that have previously caused fear or given anyone or anything power over you. You'll see that you've had the power of changing your life in your hands this whole time. You'll feel a surge of energy as each realization frees you, mentally and emotionally. These inner changes will instantly give you the awareness you need to make better choices, find the solutions you need, and balance yourself in all ways. You'll take your power back from anything that previously tried to limit you or tell you what was possible or impossible.

As you gain these powerful insights, you'll recognize that most of what was happening to you before was just a lack of active consciousness and intentionality with your choices. You'll get to know yourself on a deeper level so your decisions gain purpose aligned with empowered action. You're not going to just *think* life is happening to you…you're going to awaken, rise up, and creatively design your experience while at the same time becoming mentally and emotionally stronger. This chapter will give you the tools you need to be your own inner architect so you can build yourself up from within.

INTRODUCTION

Chapter 4: Perception: True Self vs. Constructed Self

You'll go through this chapter discovering your power of your perception and how to easily alter the point of view from which you see reality. As you refine the knowledge that you create through your mind, this chapter will break down any illusions that might be limiting you from seeing all that you are. You'll be elevated, renewed, and restored to a clear understanding of the constructed self as delineated from your true self.

The constructed self is created by society, causing us to act, think, and feel a certain way that's limited to "seeing is believing." The constructed self is controlled by emotions and the world as it appears visually. The constructed self holds a limiting point of view of what is possible and is tethered to the physical alone, thinking the world exists only on the outside. Lack of awareness of one's own nature and reality can make life seem like an unbearable case of ups and downs that exclude the true wisdom of one's own path.

It's time to realize. It's time to know. All of this will be clearly explained in this chapter. Your true self is limitless, boundless, and free. Your true self is your spirit, which knows that anything is possible. Your true self doesn't see people, places, and things as solid; it knows that everything is energy interacting with itself. You true self knows that things can happen now. Your true self believes in your dreams and watches them manifest in the moment. Going on your own path, against all the noise, allows you to operate from a state that is driven by the unknown.

You are a seer, a visionary, and a powerhouse. You are well connected. Your source of guidance is your inner voice. Your trusted compass is your heart. You exist between two worlds: one you can touch and one you can sense. You know and see things before they happen because you are not restricted to your physical state.

Thought Access

This chapter will help you discover how to alter your perception and free yourself from previously limiting thoughts. It will expand your current awareness to see more, feel more, and connect with the unlimited possibilities of consciousness available to you. The way you see the world is unique, but it has also been constructed based upon what you believe, what you have been exposed to, and what you think is possible. You can change your mind. You can be free of any perspective that you feel no longer works for you.

Chapter 5: True Power: Your Life Force

Energy is everything, and everything is energy. You will learn how to harness your life force energy so you can create what you want and experience life more fully. When you are vital, you are healthy, creative, expanded, and open to the richness and beauty of life. Being in touch with your life force means you can experience more on your adventure. You will also learn how to create inner harmony and balance everything through your mind. This chapter will give you the awareness to tap into your own vast life force, removing resistance, fears, and blocks…anything that creates restriction in your mind and body. You will discover ways in which life force can be leaked, and how to switch it up on the spot to further empower and enrich yourself.

Chapter 6: Psychological Freedom

Are you ready to be mentally, emotionally, and spiritually free? This chapter goes into the depths of psychological freedom to bring awareness of mental health, emotional well-being, and spiritual insight for every soul on their adventure to be the best and greatest, as they have always truly been. You'll learn strategies to psychologically influence yourself to get out of any form of manipulation or self-doubt while developing the ability to step into your own power through your mind. You will discover how to create the mental outcomes you want and experience the changes you have mentally initiated instead of wondering why random things keep happening to you. This chapter empowers you with the proper insight and activates your willpower to rise victorious, not only in your own life, but over any situation or circumstance that might present itself from the external world. Are you ready to be psychologically free?

Chapter 7: A Message for Your Soul

This chapter is filled with beautiful reminders for the soul that guide you along your adventurous life as a dreamer, visionary, and awakened spirit. It will move you to tears of bliss and bring you love and reassurance when you need it the most. There will be messages for the rare gem in you, the brave soul, the one who is starting a new chapter in life. Those seeking meaning and purpose will gain direction. Every word in this chapter is meant to ignite the soul's fire and blaze the way for anyone who is ready to see, feel, connect with more.

Chapter 8: Being a Thought Alchemist

Being a thought alchemist is knowing how to take any mental state and transfer it in your favor so you can rise up. You will become a master at choosing your thoughts, directing them, and making them work for you. The goal is to always receive the outcome you want while maintaining a calm, trusting, knowing state at all times. This chapter is intended to make you a master of your own thoughts, which means you have become a thought alchemist. You no longer live life randomly or in a confused manner. You don't wait around, thinking someone or something out there will come save you from the inner misunderstanding or uncertainty of life. You will begin operating from insight now.

You will receive mental protocols for any situation you want to release from your mind and body. This will feel like you are in an inner lab, doing the work of a true alchemist. Once you dive into the mental protocols, I will also share the thought alchemist's mental framework, which will be about stepping into the power of creation. This will teach you ways to work with your imagination and the world all around you. I will talk about codes of conduct for the thought alchemist. This will be about honor, self-value, action, the way you treat yourself, and the kind of energy you put out into the world. It will be about higher values, respect, and representation. Lastly, I will present the thought alchemist's mental tools, which serve as a practical guide for everyday situations and assist you in remaining empowered, connected, and inspired.

Chapter 9: Thought Travel: Past, Present, Future (One)

The goal of this chapter is to expose you to the power of the imagination and the way it takes over the present when we neglect its proper guidance. Some people could find themselves wanting to manifest now while still living mentally in the past. Others could be feeling anxious or fearful of the future. All of this occurs in the present moment.

You are always thought-traveling to past experiences or dreaming up future possibilities. You will learn how to willfully create the past *and* future that bring you healing, trust, expansion, and openness to more. Knowing how to mindfully thought-travel means being honest with yourself about the powers within you. When you don't yet know how you operate mentally or the ways thoughts trigger emotions while creating more of the same thoughts, you might assume this state is normal and that you are bound in that loop.

Breaking free of thoughts that pull you in unwanted directions is what this chapter is all about. You will not only experience what it feels like to choose for yourself, you will also become more creative, energetic, and excited about life because

INTRODUCTION

you understand that your *now* is free for you to make it into anything you want it to be. You will feel a sense of ease in the fact that you no longer need to keep replaying scenes from which you've already moved on. You will develop a stronger trust in all that the future holds for you. All of this will be understood by bringing the past, the now, and the future into this moment to be utilized to the maximum extent possible.

The power of this chapter will also lie in tapping into the highest version of yourself that you can possibly dream up. There is a *you* right now who has what you want, who feels the way you want to feel and is living the life you want to live. The irony is as follows: that *you* is actually who you are right now, but in your mind, that state is still unrealized.

The reality of your truth existing in the moment is fact. We assume that everything is playing out from day to day, but what is actually taking place is far more expansive. Your mental world is a real world that interacts, creates, and responds to all that you see. The potential of what you feel deep in your heart or see in your mind's eye isn't just some random thought; it's insight from a version of yourself that is already living it out. Once you have your mental power back to direct your life, you can start becoming any version of yourself you choose.

Chapter 10: Encode

This chapter will teach you how to work with your mental energy and the power of your voice to bend the field energetically to get what you want. Encoding is about transmitting and producing energy intentionally. You will become a master of words and the master of your reality. Encoding is about creating through your mindset, thought patterns, voice, intentions, declarations, and expectation that it will happen.

Encoding is the opposite of decoding. When you encode, you write the story. You design the experience. You create the outcome. You are so much stronger, more powerful in spirit, and more deeply connected than you might realize. When you begin to embrace your spiritual authority, you stop existing merely as a seeker of external information and you start working with your own internal system. This is what this chapter will teach you to do. Get ready to start entering your dreams in the physical world!

Chapter 11: Access Any State Now

This is the ultimate chapter to help you become your dream now. You don't have to operate in any kind of timeframe to access the state you desire. You can become it now, feel it now, and live in it now. You will be given the portal of access to go into your desired outcome and get the results you need in this moment. There will be seven access states that will fill you with energy to assist you in expanding your mind toward the larger nature of your reality so you can start to see for yourself all that has been possible for you this entire time.

Chapter 12: Thoughts Materialize

Are you ready to manifest out of thin air? This chapter will teach you how to do just that by altering your common beliefs about receiving and the process required for something to happen. You will be encouraged to stretch your imagination so you can feel comfortable with your mind's power and begin to see things happening for you instantly. You'll learn a powerful technique that brings creation out of the void and into physical reality. You will gain high self-confidence and self-belief by putting your mental energy to work. This chapter goes deeper into what is actually possible for the human mind while supporting your path to explore it yourself.

INTRODUCTION

Chapter 13: Three Powerful Thought Access Techniques

The information you learn in this chapter will put the power back into your hands. You will see changes taking place within you that you never thought possible. My goal is to take your consciousness there and give you the access to utilize your own imagination for practical results. These three techniques have worked miracles in my own life, not only in terms of what I have created using them, but also what I have learned about myself through the experience. The wonderful thing isn't just what happens in your life, but what you discover about yourself as you experiment and intentionally alter your own path. I consider these techniques very advanced, and I want to give you a little warning that you shouldn't be startled by how quickly things happen for you.

Chapter 14: Matters of The Heart

"Matters of the Heart" was written to bring you the clearest possible insight to overcome just about anything and bring you back into harmony. You will use this chapter as one of your tools to strengthen your mind, ignite your soul, and find healing. You will notice instant shifts in your life that support your mental health, emotional intelligence, and transformation while bringing actual results. Take your time and be patient as you explore living from an empowered state. This chapter will bring you solace, confirmation for your soul, healing for your heart, and ease for your mind. I want to teach you that what you unintentionally created when you didn't yet know how to fully use your mind isn't the end of the world; rather, it is the beginning of your new life.

Chapter 15: Radiant Inner Energy

This chapter is all about tapping into free energy that is within you and all around you to strengthen your electromagnetic field so you can be healthy, whole, and supernaturally connected. You will learn how to regain your mental, emotional, and physical health through energy system awareness and recalibration of your inner affairs to get back in tune with nature's abundance and your own vitality. You will be empowered, encouraged, and supported with insights that help you liberate yourself from fears and limitations that may have previously weakened your energy field. This chapter is about the new timeline for human advancement in which everyone reclaims what is divinely theirs in the field of unlimited access to real energy for the body and mind.

Chapter 16: Fifteen Daily Thought Upgrades

These 15 thoughts will guide you through a process of insight that reveals your potential, inner power, and ability to create the reality you want. Read one thought a day and feel the message behind it. There's guidance being offered that will nudge you toward your own awakening, bring massive realizations, expose you to your own inner truth, and miraculously magnetize many blessings to you. The goal of this chapter is to create a structure that supports you on a daily basis as a reference point for quick thought upgrades anytime you need them.

Chapter 17: One Hundred Thought Access Affirmations

These 100 affirmations will play a crucial role in your life as they pour real power and energy into you. Every single word was written to help you feel actual energetic increase in your physical body and state of mind. This will be a real natural high that elevates your way of being, the way you think, and the way you feel about yourself. You can tap into any of the 10 unique sets of affirmations at anytime, reminding yourself of the power that flows through you. You can speak them out loud, do them in front of the mirror, or just read them to yourself. The words will have a prolonged and lasting effect as you see everything around you

INTRODUCTION

begin to morph into your new mindset. Everything in your life will literally turn into your own dream world. Be ready for radical changes, unexplainable miracles, supernatural encounters, out-of-thin-air manifestations, high levels of self-confidence, attracting everything to yourself, getting what you need right when you need it, and being your healthiest self. Enjoy the blessings that come with these affirmations.

Chapter 18: Embodiment: Representing Your Thought World

The time has come for everyone to start representing their own thought world. Your physical reality is the embodiment of your inner world. You are your own self-creation. There's no longer space for masks, acting, pretending, or hiding behind a limited perception of self. You are felt before you are seen. The goal for this chapter is to bring awareness back to real empowerment of the self, expansion of one's own perception, and ignition of truth back into every soul. For far too long, people have lived their external lives with no real, true awareness of all that they are…which, in turn, creates everything. This chapter will teach you how to authentically represent your soul's blueprint and what it means to be a super being in this current timeline. You will learn how to identify hidden tricks of the psyche that play on fear, ways to banish false systems that depend on weakness, and how to reharness all of your energy to chart a new path, a new life, and a new world—all through your own body.

Chapter 19: You Now Have Thought Access

Final thoughts and encouragement to prepare you for takeoff!

1

HONE IN

You will now begin to take back your mental power. This means you will start to refine your energy from all places, spaces, people, and things that no longer add vibrancy to your life. Life force and energy are real. You are using them right now to read these words. Your entire attention is constantly constructing images, thoughts, and emotions which play out in the reality that surrounds you. This happens so fast, you might not notice when it occurs, but when it happens in an intended state, you feel a surge of energy that reminds you that you are alive, conscious, and aware of your choices. The most important thing you will learn here is that a potent thought is far more powerful than a million thoughts simply passing by through time.

This is what I want for you: personal consciousness of the potency of your own thought power so you can develop the will to declare any state over your life and see it happen. When you hone your energy and stop scattering it around mindlessly, you stand in your truth.

> *You'll be more empowered when you hone your own energy instead of constantly viewing what's going on "out there" and responding to things of which you may not have full understanding. Focus on yourself and create outcomes.*

This will begin to power you up energetically. You will start to operate from an intended state, and you will choose to see what you tell your mind to show you. Getting to this place will be very easy for you by the end of this book. You will feel so revived, restored, and full of so much energy that you will automatically start seeing what you want to happen taking place. This gives you more confidence, which will be the key that allows you to step into knowing. Your strong inner awareness will speak for itself. Your movement will be about bringing your inner world to life, and this means you're going to start letting your truth shine. Your life will represent your dream, and you will be stronger in the knowledge that you create your reality. There will be no more excuses or people to blame. There will be no past or future that can do for you what you can accomplish right now. It's all in your hands. At every moment, you are making a choice, and this awareness will expand your mind and alter your life in ways you have not yet imagined.

This chapter will be about identifying how you use your mental energy and strategies for honing in on yourself so you can begin to actually see your potential… and use it. If you're distracted from your mind based on what has or hasn't happened, you are letting so much energy go toward something you *know* isn't creating what you want. Honing in isn't only about what you are intending to create with all the extra energy and mind power you'll have; it's also about being the one who is directing your own life, choosing how you feel, how you respond to scenarios, and how long you focus on what *seems* to be happening instead of what *could* be happening.

You are the director of your own life. You will start telling the story you want from a higher mindset, since you have discovered profound freedom of choice when it comes to your mind. Mental freedom is and will be your ultimate success in life. The ability to make that choice for yourself will give you the chance to take back your narrative instead of going on and on about what seems to be happening to you. This will automatically begin to liberate you; you will start to feel a sense of mental freedom that breaks ties with the way you thought things were,

Thought Access

the repetitive stories you have been telling, and/or keeping yourself stuck in one outlook when you really have the freedom to change your mind at any moment.

As your awareness increases, it brings up within you the power of choice. You're not just going with the currents, the narratives, or the way things appear. You're becoming an active creator, consciously making choices, and moving with heightened precision.

Honing in means you will now have the ability to concentrate your mental forces and take back any energy you have been mindlessly spreading. Sometimes, when you are used to thinking a certain way, it becomes a hypnotic state that starts to attract other thoughts to match that energy signature. You must break free from this vicious pattern, which makes it seem like "that's just the way things are." IT IS NOT.

The more you think from a place that isn't helping you in any way, the more vitally important it becomes to start intentionally honing in. Sometimes, when a thought gains momentum, it first starts to show you in the physical world thoughts that match the ones you are thinking. Since you will often start seeing your own thoughts around you whether you are aware that this is happening or not, the thought is reinforced even more. Now you must begin to ask yourself if what you are experiencing is what you want to experience, or if your thoughts are on auto-play, creating for you what you previously accepted as a normal state. This is really where you begin to see what is going on within you and around you. The interesting thing is that you even attract people and experiences that match your core beliefs, repetitive thoughts, and the energy signature in which you consciously or unconsciously operate. Knowing this will begin to completely free your mind to make choices for yourself instead of operating from a perceived/limited self who didn't fully know that *you* were the one who could choose.

When I realized this for myself, I really felt liberated, and not only in the sense that I had the choice to use my energy the way I wanted. I also felt the freedom from the past and wondering how things could have turned out. I discovered that every thought rooted in the past was stealing the present moment from me. I had already lived that time; why bring it into this clear moment?

This self-analysis freed up a lot of energy that could easily have dissipated into a mental scene that existed only in my mind. Another thing I noticed was that concocting that mental state—and the energy spent wondering about it—was really pulling on a lot of my *now* energy, which could have been used in any way I desired. This really helped me to see that not only was I living in the past within my mind, I was also recreating feelings from an emotional state that had already happened. I was using my precious and vital *now* energy to visit some distant memory that had already ended. This mental traveling, as I call it, was, in a way, a mental self-entertainment—which, at times, broke apart what had taken place instead of building up what I could create *now*.

This can also happen if you live in fear of future events or spend time playing out images of things not happening the way you want them to. My newfound sense of self-awareness served a great purpose in my life. It gave birth to the realization that honing your energy starts with the way you are mentally using your energy *now*. The mind creates your experience. The mind is where you imagine your experience. The mind is also where you spend a lot of your energy. Knowing how to hone this energy will bring you back to finer, subtler states which, at times, go unnoticed.

The Subtle States of the Mind

One thing you must know is that YOU have the power, at any second, to change anything in your life in any way you feel will help you understand your own self...what you want to experience or even become. The choice is yours, always, but the awareness must come forward so you can identify what is actually taking place.

I'll share with you a story with you about someone to whom I was giving advice. She was struggling in her relationship of about three years. This relationship ebbed and flowed; there were good times and bad times. She told me that even though she'd been in the relationship for this long, she'd always had a fear that it wasn't going to work out or that it might end somehow. She'd never shared this feeling with her partner; instead, she lived out the fear in her inner life, becoming pessimistic about her future, what she wanted, and how she saw things playing out. This caused her energy to split. She wasn't honed in at all, and didn't realize that she was not giving one hundred percent of herself due to concepts she kept affirming about the destiny of her relationship.

What is even more profound is that she was psychically influencing her relationship based on the mental habit she had developed. She even admitted that a lot of their arguments stemmed from this inner fear, which she never confronted or consciously acknowledged, even within herself. As we kept talking, I asked her if she thought her fear was creating blocks in her relationship or her ability to express herself in the most authentic way possible. She was surprised, as she had never realized that her problems stemmed directly from her fear. What was happening for her on a day-to-day basis had everything to do with her mindset and what she thought about constantly.

This led her to further identify where she had gotten these beliefs and fears about herself in a relationship. Self-analysis and introspection led her back to identify the subtle influences of her mind, which had impacted her outlook. She recalled reading about failed relationships and seeing stories online...even listening to friends who kept sharing doom-and-gloom stories they had experienced in their own personal relationships. She didn't realize that she hadn't been intentionally creating her own narrative and experiences; instead, she was confronted by subconscious thoughts given to her over time which had formed her mind to think a certain way.

As she gained awareness, she was so surprised at how free she felt in the reality that her mindset could really change everything in her life. She never could have guessed that her private thoughts were literally radiating into every area of her life. The events actualizing in the world around her were the direct result of the rays of her mind. She told her partner about it, and he was so grateful she had shared this insight with him. He confessed that his own inner fears and projections about relationships were causing so many restrictions in his own expression to fully love.

Without this realization, the couple would have continued to assume that they had to struggle in love. In reality, they learned to return to inner harmony, exuding that energy in all areas of their lives. They removed so much of the inner junk that wasn't their story, their reality, or even their true thoughts. Once they had purged the noise, they caught up with me a year so or later. When I tell you the light was literally shining from their eyes...I couldn't believe the difference in their aura. It was like meeting a new couple for the first time. They were illuminated by the profound insight of honing their energy and getting clear about the subtle thoughts playing out within them.

> *Thoughts have a magnetic nature and create similar thoughts when and where you focus your attention. Since you're a powerful being and you know this, you command the direction*

of your mental world, which, in turn, creates connection all around you. The change starts in your mind now.

This is just one story from many different experiences I have encountered throughout my time of connecting with others and analyzing myself. Time after time, it all comes back to the energy of the mind. Once you become aware of it, you can really transform in magical ways. You access parts of yourself you didn't even know were there. This is why *Thought Access* is a very important book; it will completely alter your mindset and give you access to a whole new way of thinking by directly exposing the subtle ways you use your mind…and the grand ways in which a honed-in mind impacts your reality. The mind influences the environment, whether you are aware of it or not.

Nothing is really a secret, so it is best to get clear within and discover what is actually happening in your thought patterns and beliefs. The more you know that you are a powerful being, that you are a spirit, that all illusions of lack or limitation are only a blinding thought, the more you will come alive. You become lucid and start to consciously live your life instead of playing out patterns that don't even belong to you. You are honing in and freeing yourself from all thoughts, mindsets, outlooks, and thoughts that don't allow you to see yourself. It is about being authentically *you* now.

You can't wait another second pretending you don't know this. You know exactly who you are and what you truly are capable of. This is in your field, in your essence, and deeply embedded in your soul. This book will help you remember these codes. You will start to feel activated and full of love. An energy of passion will resurface. Your main focus will be living from within rather than "appearing" that you are living a certain way. This isn't about the end results alone (which will be your outcome no matter what), but living with an understanding that your energy will speak for itself.

Hone In

Your energy travels and permeates all spaces. It is felt by everyone. It is subtle communication, which is why sometimes you can even pick up on the "vibe" of people and places around you. There's also an inner knowing. You have no idea how it happens, but it does, and this is where you will start to remember more of yourself as a spirit. This inner intelligence is activated as you become aware of it. We'll discuss this topic further throughout the book.

The more you live authentically as yourself in mindset, energy, and action, the more you start to illuminate and radiate. It will be undeniable that you are shining from within because your energy is no longer scattered or sending mixed signals about what you want or how you act. There will be full inner alignment taking place within you. What you think, what you experience, and how you show up in the world all come into full union. This allows the rise of your spirit to take place.

All of this happens right now, and with every word, you feel a massive change occurring. You will instantly feel a sense of aliveness that comes with a surge of creativity, energy, and a new outlook. The more you get out of the hypnotic "I am used to thinking this way" mindset, the more you will feel like you have a control over yourself, your thoughts, and the choices you make. Hypnotic, trance-like thoughts can end up gaining momentum through a collection of beliefs you've been exposed to. You don't realize it's happening, since it has always been this way over time. As moments go on, you might assume a passing thought to be a true thing, when in reality, it is always open to change depending on what you tune into. You always have the choice to switch it up and open the inner portal, which carries a surge of energy that expands you on all levels.

Start recognizing whether or not you feel like your choices allow you to be in a harmonious state. Do your thoughts align with your actions? If not, look at the thought connected to that

Thought Access

choice. Go even further, and examine the belief that has led to that pattern. The way you can begin to identify this is by not labeling yourself as the result of a past thought. Instead, alter it, remove it, and switch it up. Once you know what is taking place and have made the decision to change it, you have officially started to hone your energy. Awareness alone begins to alter your mindset, and this changes what you attract, manifest, and experience all around you.

> *You'll find yourself naturally gravitating toward people, places, and experiences that resonate with your soul. Be open to what the universe is now bringing in: new ways, new connections, new energy, and a new mindset. It's just your own elevated state.*

A lot of your passion for expression, creativity, and confidence really has to do with this concept, because your mind can create hurdles, blocks, and unnecessary ideas that something "isn't possible" based upon a previous thought pattern. This can be linked to an assumption or fear of a certain outcome. It can then come true because you believed it would. Fear wastes so much mental energy because it creates illusory mental storylines that aren't even happening, have never happened, and will never happen. Fear can halt you from taking action. Remember, this is *your* dream. You must know that the imagined state is your power to create what you want. Imagination is what works in your favor, not imagining what you *don't* want or what you think could go wrong. The mind just creates. It doesn't think that what you want to create is good or bad; it creates what you constantly imagine and feed it.

> *Don't spend too much time judging what's happening or how it's happening. As a conscious creator, you can command more than*

that. You can switch it up. You really hold great power. Try switching your perspective and see what happens in 24 hours.

Creating what you fear only scatters your mental energy and weakens the power of your will to actually do something about it. This habit stops here. This stops now. You know better, so you will move differently from this moment on. You will hone your energy. You will be mindful about what you imagine; you will see in your mind that which is harmonious to you, and you will consciously create your experience. Knowing this starts the process now. Your imagined state will be more positive and reflective of your dreams. You will begin to see change in every area of your life. You have altered your own field, which now radiates trust and knowing all around you.

My Mental Energy Belongs to Me

You must claim this boldly and speak it over your life. Anytime you feel like you are starting to leak mental energy to something you know isn't adding to your vision, healthy mindset, or the direction you want to go, affirm to yourself: *My mental energy belongs to me.* This automatically gathers your energy and causes your mind to start honing in. Even reading these words will start allowing your inner state to automatically clear from your field any unnecessary patterns that don't belong. You will no longer be mindless about your mental energy or the choices you actually have over any circumstance.

Don't spend another moment giving any mental energy away or using it against yourself by playing out mental scenarios of what you don't want. Nothing and nobody can think for you. What you imagine is what you are requesting to experience. Your mind belongs to you, and everything you project is only seen and felt by you…which eventually (or instantly) starts to happen all around you. This is why you must start to hone this energy and

Thought Access

declare to yourself that your mind belongs to you. There's no reason to overthink people or situations, and there's absolutely no reason to waste another second of your mind power in the past or in self-talk that doesn't lift you higher. Instead, imagine from a place where you see it happening the way you want. Use your imagination to create your reality through conscious awareness of what you put into your mental images.

You must always remember that your mind is very valuable, and you are the only who knows what is going on within you one hundred percent of the time. In your entire experience, only you can feel what it's like to be you—and you know what you want. When you really understand this and take it in, you stop letting things take over your mind, and your life force increases. You put in place mental guards that block out what isn't necessary to your evolution so you don't go into a highly reactive state.

You are no longer just a responder, but rather the creator of your experience. Your thought value goes up. You decide what comes in, what stays, and what continues to play out. You feel a profound sense of mental peace, as if you don't even have to try so hard. It won't require a lot of effort. Most of what I have written in this book is meant to bring instant realization that facilitates deep clearing. *Thought Access* brings the experience of something clicking suddenly, and once you realize it, you enter it.

> *You're taking your power back. You're focusing on you. You're rising up. You're starting to come alive to the subtle aspects of who you are, and you're realizing that nothing in your life is an accident or coincidence. This brings you ease, trust, and the knowledge that all is well.*

Honing in is all about taking back your power, your energy, and your life force so you can maximize your own awareness and ability to create potent thought. The power of a single potent thought is more useful than mindless thinking, when you jump from one scenario to the next or travel in your mind from past to future.

Don't play any storyline in your mind about anything that no longer has anything to do with you. This is how you become mentally free and claim your mental energy. This automatically shifts your thinking and powers you up. You will know from this moment on that you will never again give any thought, mental energy, or any part of your powerful imagination to anyone or anything that doesn't allow you to operate independently.

When you claim your mental energy, you literally grab your own life force back from all that was draining you or making you feel down. You instantly feel a physical shift, as if a large amount of energy has come back into you. This happens because you stopped leaking your mental energy. You awakened to the awareness that you never had to let any of it go in the first place. Thoughts are habits you have learned to entertain based on the energy you give them. This stops right now. This ends today.

> *The mind has a way of pulling another thought to you that matches the thought you're having. This is why, if you're good at something or have a passion for it, you get more thoughts, ideas, and visions about it. Thoughts are magnetic. Thoughts are tangible. Think of what you love, and attract what you focus upon.*

You will now become the operator of your own mindset. When you do this, you will be in for a surprise. You will see that so much of what was possible for you was only dependent on the way you had been managing your mental energy up to this point.

Day by day, you will see magnificent changes and profound results. You will be mentally liberated. This is the ultimate freedom. You can't buy this. You can only discover, learn, and

Thought Access

understand by having Thought Access, which lets you know that your mind is yours. No more energy will be wasted, and you will be further expanded as you illuminate from within. There will be an undeniable magnetism about you…because you are honed in.

Walking in your power from within is no joke. It literally reprograms your mind instantly, and can even shift the world around you. Your narrative has changed, your mindset has been uplifted, you have started to hone in, and now you begin to see all around you the results of your dreams coming to life. Greater mental energy in a free state means greater ability to express, create, love, shine, and simply see the magic within you and all around. It all changes now, because now you know. You have Thought Access, and you are honed in. Your mental energy belongs to you.

Now that your mental energy has been freed up, you will realize that your emotions have been freed up, too. Your emotions now respond to your new thoughts, and a new reality has been born. This is where you will start to see that the loop of thoughts leading to an emotion…leading to more of the same thoughts…has been broken. You are free from that cycle, and you are declaring greater for yourself. You will naturally feel content, and a state of joy will energetically flow from you.

A lot of your emotions can be connected to thoughts that don't belong to you. This will be the biggest form of liberation, and it will instantly break any connecting thoughts and emotions that were once "normal" in your body. We sometimes don't understand the ways in which our minds influence every aspect of our lives. This is something I want to share with you so you can stop letting unwanted thoughts and emotions control your life. When you stop feeding thoughts with emotions by constantly reacting to them in an intense or emotional way, you have gained power through awareness to put an end to it.

"I believe" turns into "I know" when you start seeing how things really work. You don't need to

convince yourself anymore. You just start owning your truth as a conscious creator, knowing that everything you want is already yours.

Thought has power when it is given high amounts of emotion (i.e., when you add feeling to it). This is wonderful if you're having the thoughts you want, because it will produce the outcome you are feeling. Ironically, when it is not something you want, you are creating that exact reality from the intense emotion. I want you to start running your own life, choosing your own thoughts, feeling the outcomes you want, and knowing that the changes you're making to hone in your energy will give you back more than you could ever have imagined in your life. It will feel like an unstoppable life force has been accorded to you.

You're no longer someone things happen to…you're someone things happen *for*. You'll begin to feel, radiate, and exude this energy, which will emanate from your entire being. When you get clear from within and let go of all the emotions and ideas you have attached to how something makes you feel, you'll experience a big purge. A sense of release comes with ease, because you have learned that you can harness your vital life force exactly as you wish.

Give yourself the time you need to emerge, grow into your passion, and discover yourself. There's no set point or rush on when you need to have it all figured out. It's a moment-to-moment experience. Embrace the evolution of you. Your season, timing, and expression are unique.

You no longer fragment yourself into states of being that represent any form of limitation. You are emotionally free from the past. You are emotionally free from resisting the unknown or fearing the future. You are emotionally free from thoughts of limitation or lack. You are emotionally free from heartbreak, pain, regret, and doubt. This awareness expands you, opens up your heart, and pours into you. You are revived, deeply renewed, and filled with a newfound hope.

You now know that you are the one who chooses what you feel, how you respond, and what you emotionally hold onto. You are breaking free from the field of the past, and you are lighter emotionally because you don't have to attach so much meaning to events that have occurred. The richness of your life comes from knowing that you have learned, evolved, and understood the power of remaining emotionally free to harness the wonderful life force that is at play now. You don't have to split yourself by sending your emotions in all directions. Hone it in now, bring it back to yourself, and see the surplus and freedom making an impact on your inner world. You will never again be a victim of circumstances or situations because you now have Thought Access. Your emotional energy belongs to you. You can choose how you feel. You are the main character of your life. You are the one the world around you responds to.

I Always Have a Choice

You always have a choice to do better and greater. You always have a choice when it comes to how you use your energy and time. This is your power. This is your ability, and it will help you be empowered like never before. It will be your natural state of mind to know that you always have a choice to alter any aspect of your life whenever you want. This allows you to stop feel like things are just happening to you or that you have no control over them.

Your power to choose gives you back direct power. It is a wonderful feeling to know that you can make a choice today that will give you the outcome you truly want. When someone is not aware of this, they might assume that the situations happening to them will continue to play out. They might even go on adding to the dynamic by making choices from a state of assumption that they have no choice. This creates feelings of regret, victimization, and repetition of the same mindset, which continues to produce the same reality.

> *It's mind over matter. Your situation can change right now.*

Thinking you have no choice in a situation only creates the limitation of remaining stuck in what is happening, which requires a lot of your attention to be focused on the past and/or the assumption that you can do nothing about it. No matter what comes up, no matter what's happening, no matter how things look, you always have the choice to get the outcome you want. Your mind must hone in and go toward the knowledge that you can decide in any moment the way you will react and respond. This gives you authority in deciding the outcome you'll experience based on the choice you make. Knowing that you always have a choice and will make conscious choices in all areas of your life will prove that the power is truly in your hands.

I Direct My Thoughts

As the master of your thoughts, you are aware that you choose their direction, and you see the benefits instantly. Abandon thoughts you don't want and break the pattern right on the spot by switching it up. Live by this affirmation: *I direct my thoughts*. This gets you unstuck from certain thought patterns, as you know you can switch them up at any moment. The most important aspect of our lives is to pay attention to, nurture, and guide our own thoughts.

Thoughts exist just like any physical thing, but they operate in their own invisible realm, which produces all things physical. The thoughts we constantly repeat gain momentum and build into their own external reality. If you look around, you can see

Thought Access

physical aspects of thoughts, since everything was once in someone's mind. Knowing this, you will gain a better understanding of your repetitive thoughts by consciously choosing them. The result will be the thoughts you want rather than the ones that have nothing to do with your dreams, visions, or evolution.

Instead of remaining in a slumber of uncertainty, rise into the belief that you actually can change your mind and create the reality you want. Don't let another moment pass just sitting back and watching things play out without your intentions at work. Honing your thoughts and directing them will give you the exact outcome you expect. There's no denying that the mind will produce exactly what you expect it to produce.

> *Thoughts are always behind physical manifestations. Imagine yourself where you want to be, doing what you want to be doing, feeling how you want to be feeling. You'll naturally attract this way of being, because that's who you've chosen to embody! Dare to be free, to choose, to experience exactly what you want.*

You will now begin to get very comfortable with the fact that you do have the power to direct your thoughts. This energizes you and turns on your inner passion for life. For once, you are aware while you're truly alive, and you know the great gift that is in your hands. Try this in any situation in which you find unwanted thoughts dominating your mind. Stop yourself right in that moment, take a deep breath, and release the thought with the command, *I direct my thoughts.* This puts conscious control back in your awareness instead of just thinking the same thought and going on and on about it. This has worked wonders for me. I noticed that it became easier to direct my thoughts right away, and after a few days of consciously doing this, my repetitive thoughts were no longer on autopilot. I have the choice to think what I want and what I allow to continue on. I have broken my habitual thought pattern by choosing to direct my own thoughts. You'll have great success with this and begin to feel great mental freedom in your thought world.

I Am Powered Up

You'll notice a massive shift in your life with all this insight. You'll notice that you are stepping into your greatest self. This started simply by gaining Thought Access to a new way of seeing yourself and the world around you. Perspective can liberate and free you from habitual or singular ways of viewing your life.

Sometimes, when you have been playing the role of who you think you are, you can become consumed by what it means to be that person instead of realizing your vast potential in your highest and truest state. This is why your have a deep desire to continually improve. It's not that you weren't good enough simply being you; it's that you can now identify unproductive labels, ideas, and concepts. The person the world has told you to be isn't your final state.

You just know there's more to who you actually are. You are always interacting with your spirit and receiving insight. This is why you can suddenly experience massive change and realize there must be a better way. It's the feeling of *this isn't really it, is it?* Internal insights are coming in to power you up. One reminder, one sign, one thought alone can change the trajectory of your life. This is how powerful it is to have Thought Access. You gain insight that opens your mind to many paths, each one holding a different outcome.

> *You are in your own private mental world. Honor yourself, your thoughts, and who you actually are. Know that being this empowered alters your field and the way the world responds to you.*

Thought Access

Being powered up is being self-empowered from within. You are someone who depends on your own inner self for guidance, energy, direction, and clarity. Being powered up from within provides you energy that can never be limited or cut off. It's always there because it is self-generating and self-sustaining.

One of the reasons for a feeling of emptiness or a need for external validation in order to feel joy or happiness is that your sense of empowerment comes from what you receive from the outside. This has caused dependence upon external things, but your real energy source is naturally abundant within you. Understand that when you begin to operate from this new mindset of self-empowerment, you'll experience a magnificent transformation that alters your inner world. Your thinking process changes, your response process shifts, and your emotional processing of how something makes you feel is completely altered.

When you perceive something and react to it, you may often refer to a belief about how you "should" be responding. Your body has naturally gotten used to responding in a filtered manner. This creates a loop, especially if you don't know that you don't need this reaction. This is what I mean by processing your perception, which empowers you instead of allowing you to remain constantly dependent on external reality alone for how you feel about yourself.

Don't get consumed by what others think about you. Only you can think from within you. That's the only voice of value.

It's really draining to need validation from the world around you…constantly chasing energy to feel even an ounce of worthiness and appreciation. Interestingly, you actually become validated, seen, recognized, loved, and appreciated simply by approving of yourself, loving yourself, validating yourself, and believing in yourself. The world then responds to you. People react to your inner declarations, not necessarily their views. This is the ultimate secret you can receive. Stand in your inner thought about how you feel, think, and radiate to the world.

This frees you in so many ways, because you take control of your attention and put it back onto yourself. You gain heightened self-awareness, which fuels greater confidence and allows you to shine brightly. Your effect and impact can only come from a honed-in version of yourself. This gives you the chance to be emotionally intelligent because you have created an inner balance and returned to a state of equilibrium that isn't constantly swayed in multiple directions by external stimuli.

You know who is in control. It's you. You are the one who is powered up now. This is your new state, which you must begin to embrace as natural. You have the codes. You have the access, and you are honed in.

Honing In Brings Massive Changes

Anytime energy is concentrated, wonderful changes take place. You don't want your mind bouncing all over the place, going from one thought to the next. Being honed in is having the ability to first understand that your thoughts are energy. Your mind dictates what you say you want and what you command into your experience.

Anyone who has ever done anything they truly wanted has honed in their mental energy. You'll now have control of your own will, directing the commands and the outcomes you desire. You need to be very aware of how your mind works and how you are engaging with the world around you. All is dictated, decided, and led by your mind. The more willpower you apply to making up your mind about something, the more you will gain in terms of the mental access necessary to bring about massive change.

You hone in your thoughts when you concentrate on getting results or wanting to see a certain outcome. Anything you've put

Thought Access

your mind to has happened for you, will happen for you, and is happening for you. You are, in fact, familiar with this ability, but it might not have been honed in throughout all areas of your life. This knowledge will awaken your ability further and allow you to use it in all aspects of your life, not only when you have a demanding moment or a sudden inspiration. This will be your natural state of being.

> *You'll notice you're getting stronger mentally, emotionally, and spiritually. You're receiving more insights. You sense things before they happen. An inner knowing has been activated within you.*

Be very aware that operating in this state will make you the ultimate human in all ways. When you don't know this, your thoughts can go on autopilot most of the time, which means you're not using your willpower or consciously creating what you want. Think of the days, weeks, and even years that have gone by in this way. There might have been a point once or twice at which you decided to hone in your thoughts.

What happened? You mentally decided on a state, calling in all your energy and using your willpower to get the outcome you wanted. You probably focused on that vision coming to life or even said, *I need to get this result.* No matter what, you have experienced this state many times. However, you may still treat it like an ability that surges inner power when needed instead of your natural ability in your waking life to *constantly* ask, speak, think, act, and will your entire life into existence. There is no off-time for this magnificent giant of creation within you. You have access because you have asked for it.

> *Walk in your truth now, and live by your intention. You'll see your entire life unfolding accordingly, not randomly. The thought,*

feeling, or intention stemming from you is at work, so keep putting out what you want or simply what you are. Let it radiate from you.

Anything that can be given to you, exposed to you, or experienced by you has to come from within you. When you don't use your will, other people come around and make you create their reality for them—or you might use your mind only for entertainment instead of being the main character in your life, living out your own movie. Your will belongs to you, and it is very powerful to know this. The greatest changes in humanity—even the joy of living your dream on the individual level—have started with an inner declaration, willpower, and self-awareness.

This gives you inner freedom. You feel so alive and inspired because you have discovered the power of honing your thoughts and consciously using your mind. This will begin to close the gap between your intention and when you experience the results. You are someone who seems to constantly experience the reality you want because you are awake, aware, and using your mind. You are someone who is moving with intention. You are someone who has decided to actively use your willpower. This is your life experience, and you can't go another day not knowing all that you're capable of. I am truly grateful that you have this insight. You will begin to see for yourself what is possible.

Mental Commands

Your mind is your humble servant. It wants to show you the reality you believe in, and truly knows you are worthy of living out. It is always listening and ready to confirm for you what you command from within. Nobody can do that for you. You are the one who is at the center of your inner universe, and you send the commands to your mind to bring forth the reality you desire.

Thought Access

There really isn't a long process or a how-to; it is simply commanding it and receiving it. This has been done through prayer, asking, and intending. No matter which way you do it, the mind only knows the intention that was put into it, and it must show you the outcome. When your mind is honed in, it operates differently because you have awareness that every intention, every thought, and everything you speak must come into fruition. The time it takes for anything to manifest has a lot to do with how much you simply allow, trust, and know. You must begin to move as an authority over your inner kingdom and speak power over every area of your life.

Your mind is designed to show you what you tune into and are willing to see. It wants to confirm the reality you accept as truth. This can happen instantly or gradually, depending on your state of acceptance of the flexible nature of the reality around you. Choose what you want!

When you don't issue any mental commands, you mindlessly create things you might want and others you might not want. It becomes only a struggle of uncertainty when you don't know your inner power. When you have Thought Access, which is a direct link to greater possibilities, you don't play that game of fear anymore. You don't wonder about *how* or *when*. You don't question the way things end up happening for you. You operate from an elevated awareness that knows the timing. This depends solely upon how fast you release what you have intended. You aren't trying to convince yourself that something *can* happen for you; you KNOW it is happening for you. You have powered up mentally.

Start right now to command your mind to banish confusion, fear, and lack of faith, welcoming clarity, direction, vision, purpose, and results. You are going into a rewiring process that disrupts negative states and pessimistic outlooks. You are being freed so deeply that the person you have become and brought forth from within will be unrecognizable.

Remember that who you are isn't one final state; it's an accumulation of what you have thought up to this point or believed to be true. Alteration of your inner state to something more conducive to your overall wellness must start with cultivating awareness that you have a choice and can actually generate mental commands that begin to rewire your thinking.

There is no reason to doubt yourself. Where did that even come from? This is what I mean when I say, "rewiring your mindset." This process removes limiting thoughts, low self-esteem, self-judgment, living in regret, and staying stuck in the past. These are all conditions that are up for revamping and removal. You don't have to identify with habits, thoughts, or actions produced by your past thinking. Every time you gain Thought Access or receive insight, your life transforms. Your new way of thinking, acting, and carrying yourself must produce the reality of the life that matches that thought field.

You'll notice a whole new shift in energy as far as timelines—how quickly things happen for you and the connection between your thoughts and physical reality. This will become even more apparent, to the point where it is your natural state to recognize miracles everywhere.

When you use mental thought commands, you are choosing to create a new way of thinking. This always shows you a world that reflects your command. It is as easy as that. What seems hard is wondering, *Can it really be that easy?* Yes! Why not? Your mind doesn't always need convincing. You're the one in control here, and your mind is listening to you to make your desires happen.

There hasn't been a moment when I have made a mental command and not seen a desired outcome. You are stepping it up within your thought field, and the realizations you're having will

Thought Access

show you that it *is* possible for you and *you can*. You have a stronger mind now. You feel deeply connected to your spirit. You know the power of your mind, and you are finally using it to work for you. You feel balanced and energized, which is a sign that things have begun to start working. You have rewired your process of thinking with new thoughts that match what you want. You feel more confident because you have Thought Access, which frees your mind from limiting outlooks and connects you back to your own natural stream of hope and possibility. You now represent the dream that has become a reality. This makes you unstoppable!

You Are Now Honed In

You now have received the codes to concentrate your thought field and produce tangible results. Being honed in means you are now someone who values their time, their energy, and their inner world. You are not playing the game of negative thought. You have transcended the narrative of lack and limitation. You have learned to see for yourself what you can produce with your mind—and get exactly what you want.

This chapter will allow you to prepare for what the rest of this book has to offer. Anytime that you start any new path or have a desire to change any aspect of your life that isn't suitable currently, you must start by honing in. This will give you the chance to actually make that change without wondering if it will happen. Your new insight is creating your new reality. Everything from the past was only from previous thought patterns. The only choice that can remain is either a mindset that keeps producing the same actions and habits or a mindset that produces new actions and habits. The outcome will be what you desire instead of random occurrences.

As someone who is honed in and actively using your mind power, you will recognize the many possibilities that are actually all around you. Your ability to see opportunities and blessings really has to do with how you view the world from the perspective of your inner consciousness. You can see in your own day-to-day life how a single mood or one thought can paint life one way, and when you suddenly shift that thinking, you can see it from a brighter perspective.

> *May you experience a surge in revelations, connections, energy, love, and understanding. May you gain clarity, direction, and the wisdom to guide you through. May you feel more in tune with yourself and more magical in all areas of your life.*

This is why it is truly a gift to share this miraculous and life-changing book with you. I want you to be your most powered-up self. I want you to represent possibilities as someone who knows what can happen when you hone in your energy and live your life intentionally. I want you to shine, radiate, and be filled with life.

I know that you will be imbued with confidence, and this will originate from an inner flow. You'll love yourself more, accept who you are, and believe so deeply in what is possible for you. You'll feel lighter as the heaviness of past thoughts is removed from your thought field. You'll find a new passion for life as well as a surge of creative energy. You will be limitless!

You are free. Your past doesn't define you or even limit you. You know how happy and bright you were before that one thing happened, and that only means that your inner state is already your natural state. You are now just removing, rewiring, and recreating with awareness instead of operating from a thought pattern from the past. Your mind only operates in the now. It is wise to be present, as you are going to pull your thought energy from the past *and* the future into the now. You are now honed in!

Thought Access

Key Points to Remember

- *The most important thing you will learn here is that one potent thought is far more powerful than a million unconscious thoughts we simply bypass over time.*

- *When you hone your energy and stop scattering it around mindlessly, you stand in your truth.*

- *There is no past or future that can do for you what you can do for yourself right now. It's all in your hands. At every moment, you are making a choice. This awareness will expand your mind and alter your life in ways you have not yet imagined.*

- *Honing in isn't just about what you are intending to create with all the extra energy and mind power you'll have; it's really be about being the director of your own life. Choose how you feel, how you respond to scenarios, and how long you focus on what seems to be happening instead of what could be happening.*

- *You are the director of your own life.*

- *Mental freedom is and will be your ultimate success in life. The ability to make that choice for yourself will give you the chance to take back your narrative instead of going on and on about what seems to be happening to you.*

- *Sometimes, when you are used to thinking a certain way, it becomes a hypnotic state that starts to attract other thoughts matching that energy signature. You must break free of this vicious pattern, which makes it appear as if this is "just the way things are." IT IS NOT.*

- *The interesting thing is that you attract people and experiences that match your core beliefs, repetitive thoughts, and the energy signature in which you consciously or unconsciously operate.*

- *The mind is where you imagine your experience. The mind also is where you spend a lot of energy. Knowing how to hone in will bring you back to finer, subtler states, which, at times, go unnoticed.*

- *One thing you must know is that YOU have the power at any second to change anything in your life in whichever way you feel will help you understand your own self, including what you want to experience and become. The choice is always yours, but awareness must come so you can identify what is actually going on.*

- *The mind influences your environment whether you are aware of it or not. Nothing is really a secret, so it is best to get clear within and discover what is actually happening in your thought patterns and beliefs.*

- *The more you know that you are a powerful being, that you are a spirit, that all illusions of lack and limitation are only a blinding thought, the more you will come alive. You will become lucid and begin to consciously live your life instead of playing out patterns that don't even belong to you.*

- *The more you live authentically as you, in mindset, energy, and action, the more you will begin to illuminate and radiate. It will be undeniable that you are shining from within because your energy is no longer scattered or sending mixed signals about what you want or how you act.*

- *Creating what you fear only scatters your mental energy, weakening the power of your will to actually do something about it. This stops here. This stops now. You*

THOUGHT ACCESS

know better, so you will move differently from this moment on.

- *What you must always remember is that your mind is very valuable. You are the only who knows what is going on within you one hundred percent of the time. In your entire experience, only you can feel what it's like to be you, and only you know what you want.*

- *Honing in is all about taking back your power, your energy, and your life force so you can maximize your own awareness and ability to create a potent thought.*

- *You will start to become the operator of your own mindset now. When you do this, you will be in for a surprise. You will see that so much of what has been possible for you until this point was solely dependent on the way you managed your mental energy.*

- *Walking in your power from within is no joke. It literally reprograms your mind instantly, shifting the world around you. Your narrative has changed, your mindset has been lifted, you have started to hone in. Now you must begin to see all around you the results of your dreams coming to life.*

- *When you get clear from within and let go of all the emotions or ideas you have attached to the way something makes you feel, you'll experience a big purge. This sense of release comes with ease, because you have learned that you can harness your vital life force to attain exactly what you want.*

- *You will never again be a victim of circumstances or situations because you now have Thought Access. Your emotional energy belongs to you. You can choose how you feel. You are the main character in your life. You are the one to whom the world responds.*

HONE IN

- *You always have a choice to do better and greater. You always have a choice when it comes to how you use your energy and time. This is your power.*

- *You will now become very comfortable in your thought field with the fact that you have the power to direct your thoughts. This energizes you and turns on your inner passion for life. For once, you are consciously and completely alive, and you understand the great gift that is now in your hands.*

- *Being powered up is being self-empowered from within. You are someone who depends on your own inner self for guidance, energy, direction, and clarity. Being powered up from within provides you energy that can never be limited or cut off. It's always there, because it is self-generating and self-sustaining.*

- *You are someone who seems to constantly experience the reality you want. You are awake, aware, and consciously using your mind. You are someone who moves with intention. You have decided to actively use your willpower.*

- *Start right now by commanding your mind to banish confusion, fear, and lack of faith, welcoming in clarity, direction, vision, purpose, and results. You are going into the rewiring process, which disrupts negative states and pessimistic outlooks. You are being freed so deeply that the person you have become and brought forth from within will be unrecognizable.*

- *You have rewired your process of thinking with new thoughts that match what you want. You feel more confident because you have Thought Access, which frees your mind from limiting outlooks while connecting you back into your own natural stream of hope and*

Thought Access

possibilities. You now represent the dream that has become a reality. This makes you unstoppable!

- *You have now received the codes to concentrate your thought field and produce tangible results. Being honed in means you are now someone who values their time, energy, and inner world.*

2

THOUGHT PATTERNS

Your thought patterns are everything. Thought patterns influence how you think, how you see the world, what you believe creates your world, and what you might be accepting that limits your access based upon what you decide to think habitually and daily. How can you access your full potential if you don't know what is possible for you? This chapter will really expose thought patterns that seem normal, but could be holding you back. It will also break down the power of your thought and the fact that you are a genius just now awakening to your own power.

The truth is, everything that you are is your ultimate greatness. In order to allow this truth to shine, you must confront illusory thoughts that have kept you hyper-focused on the limited nature of your existence. Let's say you read my first book, *Manifest Now*, and you manifested your wildest dreams. This means you tapped into what was already available to you based on the thought access offered by the book. The fact that you can manifest has always been your truth, but if you haven't been as successful as you would have liked, a lack of awareness may have been an unfavorable thought pattern you entertained unknowingly. On the other hand, after reading that you could manifest, you may suddenly received a new thought pattern that reminded you of the ability you always had.

A new you wants to come alive.

I know how urgent it is for you to have access to insight that activates you and gets you into a mindset that IT IS possible for you to have what you want. It is very important for you to live your dream. Because why not? This is *your* dream, and it is your right to live from an inner state that is truly empowered, healthy, and vital.

The quality of your life deeply depends upon the quality of the thought to which you have access. If you look at the world around you, you might not be able to really see what anyone is thinking, but you can see what they have manifested through their thought patterns and awareness. Their level of self-belief and self-confidence has to do with their thought patterns. Behavior is completely influenced by the thought patterns one holds. Your reality reflects your thought patterns.

You might be able to manifest what you want because you know it's normal and natural to manifest, but someone else may never have heard about manifesting or even know that their mind interacts with the world around them. They might simply believe that things randomly happen to them, or that they exist in the sea of the unknown without even a say in the matter. They might not know they are constantly creating their reality through their thoughts.

Knowing and accepting your inner power is the key to producing a healthy self-image, a quality life, a peaceful perspective on any situation, and the ability to attract the most magical life you feel is worthy of your experience. You know that everything depends on your mind. You live in your own inner world. You feel what you feel, you think what you think, and you interact with the entire universe based on the thought patterns you are signaling from your mind. This is why I want to bring clarity to the power of your thought patterns—so you can break down, release, and rewrite the ones that no longer belong in your thought-sphere.

The only thing I'm committed to right now is bettering myself. I need to prioritize my mental, physical, and spiritual well-being. I need to step

Thought Access

it up and not be afraid to let go of habits, thought patterns, and beliefs that no longer benefit me. It's time for real change.

This chapter will literally free your mind. You will feel a sense of change. You are mentally stronger, and you will be able to automatically detect your current thought pattern. Nothing will get past your mental gates without a scan. People will notice how different you are. You'll be much more confident, grounded, and connected to yourself. You'll make intelligent choices because your thought pattern is healthy and on point. This won't feel like much of an effort, as in previous times. Every word in this book is meant to uplift your spirit and bring you a higher awareness of inner power and self-belief. If you believe in yourself, the whole world believes in you. If you are strong in mindset, reality can't even test you in those ways anymore. You have higher ideals now, higher goals, and bigger visions. Getting clear in your thought pattern will be your greatest freedom. Nothing can give you this kind of access but yourself, from within. This is the key.

You have to be honest with yourself as you begin to work through this book. You must be firm in the fact that you are ready to activate your own potential. Everything shared here is only meant to awaken what has always been within you this whole time. You are nothing like your past. You are now upgrading those thoughts. The past was only a thought pattern that had created your life up to a certain point, whether knowingly or unknowingly. Who you really are is infinite potential, and at every moment, there is a chance for a new story to be told and a new reality to be created. Getting your thought patterns exactly where you want them will prepare you to enter the world of your dreams. It will literally seem unbelievable that all of this was even possible this whole time, but you are only just now discovering it.

Identifying the Thought Pattern in Which You Operate

To be able to understand yourself or alter your outcomes, you must first look at the kind of thought pattern in which you operate. This will help you see what is taking most of your energy and attention. You must know that right now, all of your life force is in *full potential.* You're alive only in this moment. For your mind to be fully of use and value, you have to know that your thought pattern in this moment will produce what comes next for you and where you will find yourself. You might be physically here, but mentally in the past. To be able to think of the future, you should get into a state in which you see yourself visually in the moment you are headed. The past should only be accessed through memory when you are remembering how something helped you or when you access mental tools from previous experiences. Do you see how that is a healthy thought pattern?

Your mind is being used for specific purpose, not for regretting the past or fearing the future. Identifying thought patterns is crucial because your current state of mind will cause you to choose your future (and everything you decide to do right now). Thought patterns give you access to the frequency you attract, the actions you take, the way you behave, and the person you decide to create yourself to be. To completely alter your life, you must be so honest with yourself about changing your mindset. What state of mind are you in right now? Is it helping you manifest your dreams? Is it keeping you attached to people or concepts of yourself you know deep down you've outgrown? This could literally result in an established thought pattern that makes you feel that just because you have known someone for a long time, or just because you've done something for a certain length of time, you must remain in that energy. You have the power to experience new things, outgrow who you once were, and align with all that is rightfully meant for you.

Thought Access

You have to master your mindset if you really want to understand how life works. It's not about things outside of yourself. It's not about other people. It starts with you first: your habits, your thought patterns, your belief system, and where you place your energy.

The best way to identify a thought pattern is to identify the feeling associated with it and the additional thoughts it attracts. Let's say you feel inspired from within, and you recognize an undeniable urge to make a radical change in your life. The feeling is so strong. Suddenly, you start taking action that follows the inner guidance that called upon you for change. This new feeling attracts greater thoughts, and you find yourself suddenly moving forward. As your change continues, you'll see people or things from your past that want to remind you of who you once were. They may even try to make it seem like your change is something negative. In reality, it only broke your mental bonds to a past version of yourself who no longer thinks, acts, or does what once seemed normal.

You might even experience an old thought pattern resurfacing that tries to make you question if it is even possible. This is good news, because it shows that you're reaching a new level. It shows that you did break free and are currently facing old habits, old thought patterns, and previous connections. It illuminates a contrast with your new thought patterns of growth, and it means you really have risen. Most people assume that if a previous thought pattern or emotion returns, they are doing something wrong. They might even start overthinking why the pattern is resurfacing. This is not something to worry about. You have already broken free. You have elevated. You have risen higher. When you enter evolution like that in your mind, you see what has perished as a form of reflection. Contrast is very important and necessary sometimes, because it gives us reassurance and feedback that we are on the right track.

Thought Patterns

This is why, when you are evolving from within, you might notice your outer reality going through major shifts. It is unexplainable how it all happens. We never discuss much of the mental and emotional world and how it impacts connections, the universe, and the field all around you. We just find ourselves setting our intentions, praying, visualizing, manifesting, and taking mental action to reshape our lives.

Thought patterns provide insight into where you are with yourself. It is so important to allow the mind empower-ment and awareness. To know how your minds works—and to be able to think, create, and live intentionally—will mean that you have truly accessed your own inner power. Nothing can give you this but yourself. The world we see, experience, and feel interacts with the world of your mind. When you stop viewing yourself as a victim of the external world's reactions (waiting for things to happen in order to feel something), and when you stop thinking circumstances are final, you have intentionally chosen to claim your divinity and the gift of belief right now. Your mind already leads, and your body and the world around you follow. This is a powerful thought pattern to have in place.

Mastery over reality is mastery over your mind and emotions. This means you think what you want to see happen. You don't react to what appears to be happening when you know that the world is altering itself to allow you to manifest what you want. You don't react or overreact when something unexpected happens. You just believe things are working according to your highest thoughts and greatest intentions. You live as if it has already happened for you. You aren't afraid of emotions or things not going "according to plan." You know that in any undesirable circumstance, a desirable outcome can always result. You have mastered your own inner world when it comes to your reaction, your response, and how you decide to use your energy. Getting to know yourself will also prove vital when it comes to identifying *why* you have the thought patterns you do…and how easy it is to change your mind. It is so easy to change your mind.

Thought Access

As you cleanse your physical being, spend some time detoxing your mental, emotional, and spiritual energy from anything toxic, whether it's habits, thought patterns, certain people, places, or things that prevent you from reaching your highest self. Be active in your growth.

You don't have to be that person from a past storyline you no longer identify with. You don't have to confine your potential to make others feel comfortable. You don't have to participate in group thinking to feel like you belong. You don't even have to think of what anyone else thinks of you to feel like you're someone. You really are your own powerhouse, your own life force, and your own empowered mind. If you feel great about yourself, you impact many. If you love who you are, you alter your reality. If you trust yourself, you manifest your dreams. If you focus on nourishing, building, and rising up within yourself, you have fully lived. You can only experience life from within yourself. As much as you might want to exert energy to show up for everyone else, it's time to show up for yourself. This is your time to remember, to reconnect, to rise, and to bring forth your gifts.

What would your gifts be if you were fully realized? What would your life look like as someone who has mastered their own thought patterns and chosen intentional living at every moment? You will be surprised to see the outcome of even thinking along these lines.

Understand that your experience is always unfolding. So often, there's an assumption that someone else is making it in life at a "higher" level, and that feeling could cause you to constantly chase a particular state. In reality, you can actively exist in any state you choose at this very moment. Thought patterns may try to make you believe that once you get somewhere or meet someone or do something specific, you will be happy. This causes you to delay your sense of wellness, peace, and happiness *now*.

The enjoyment of reaching a goal is truly in the process, not solely in the outcome. That's why when you get what you want, you end up making new goals and bigger visions. The feeling of accomplishment passes as you venture off into something new. You must choose the thought pattern that you are now accepting your end results in feeling, in mindset, and in attitude. Gratitude and feeling a sense of joy for simply being you are crucial elements. They allow your mindset to start finding bliss in every moment. Rewire your brain to actually take in your life moment by moment instead of delaying gratification. Interestingly, this allows you to manifest quickly, as you feel good about where you're heading because it is already happening. There will be a natural flow instead of a one-day mindset.

Thought Patterns of Self-Sabotage

Right now, there is a dream within you that wants to come to life. There is a vision you keep receiving that wants to be born. There's an inner calling nudging you to embrace yourself, to love yourself, and to feel into the life you believe you can have. You know deep down that you have the potential. You feel that you do. What is stopping you? What is standing in your way? This is where thought patterns of self-sabotage come into play. When you connect with a new sense of power within you, past familiarity resurfaces to cause you to remain where you are—but it happens in ways that seem natural and keep you in your comfort zone.

Change is really a shift in the trajectory of your reality. You literally have the power every single second to make a choice that opens a new path toward your higher calling. You are a natural creative. You have a passion for something, or you even desire better. This comes from the spirit, but thought patterns of self-sabotage arise from memory of what you may have become accustomed to. This reality is not fixed. It's not who you are. It's a collection of thought forms you use to hide behind so you won't move forward.

Thought Access

It's not as scary as you think, but it might feel that way because you're uprooting years of thought patterns or ways of doing things that weren't helping you break free or access your full potential. You have Thought Access now; this break patterns and lifts you into a new awareness. You know you are so much more. You have been feeling like this for quite some time. Your spirit is more powerful than any lower thoughts or regressions. Your spirit, once ignited, banishes all energy in the mental field that no longer works to move you in the new direction you are headed.

This is where your will comes in—the will to be unafraid of your own dreams. The will to just do what it is you have to do. The will of taking action instead of distracting yourself in a hundred and one ways, just to avoid the possibilities of your life instead of actually changing them into what you want. The outcome of following your heart is more fulfilling and empowering than avoiding yourself just to remain in resentment and regret. Most thought patterns that drain your energy come from not doing what you have intended or wanted, then regretting that you haven't done it. So much energy gets wasted this way when you can simply stop yourself right now from living in a mental loop and go for it. Go for what you wanted to do. Start that plan, get that project together you've been putting off, clear your space, follow your spirit, and live more intentionally instead of staying the same in the thought pattern of despair and regret. That isn't you. That isn't your life. There is a force within you and all around you that supports your will to follow through. Tap into yourself; this begins with going forward.

> *After a while, you just get tired of procrastinating and start to want better for yourself. Deep down, you know how much potential you'd have if you just applied yourself. Change your thought patterns and habits. Do something about it. You deserve to live your wildest dreams.*

Thought Patterns

This is why I wanted to bring awareness to the habit of self-sabotage according to past ways of thinking or doing things. So many dreams are killed by self-sabotaging thought patterns. Your spirit knows this is just a once-in-a-lifetime experience. You weren't meant to be afraid or overly concerned with external approval or validation. You were always meant to be powered up from within. Not recognizing how alive you are in the now could cause you to delay your power into the future. This creates a big energy separation between your potential *now* and your idea of *one day*. The divide creates an energy leak that causes you to remain in a state of the sameness while trying to convince yourself that one day in the future, you will follow your heart and live out your dream.

How can you do that if today is the day you are most alive? Today is the day you have all the energy. Today is the day your mind knows you are here, and it operates through your moment-to-moment thinking to create the future you are looking forward to. Don't sabotage yourself. Don't split your energy. Don't be afraid of your dreams. Don't be afraid of your own power.

Don't let anyone waste your time or sabotage your dreams. This can happen when you begin to rise into your power. You might experience people trying to make you question what you're even doing because it is so easy for many to remain the same. Truly living life and intentionally creating the reality you want requires inner access that is very different than what is considered "normal." You'll notice that when you decide to get better in any way, it can throw a lot of your relationship dynamics into question, exposing who actually supports you and who doesn't.

To believe in what is possible is really a special thing. It's very important to know which relationships and connections are sabotaging you through shared thought patterns dictating that it is normal to not follow your dreams or to stay the same. Some relationship thought patterns could have formed before you even gained this insight or awakened. You could have thought it was normal before to waste time, to do things that weren't healthy for your mind and body, or to simply hide from your power because it was okay to conform to the group way of thinking and connected thought patterns.

When you change your mindset, it realigns you with what naturally attract or tolerate. There are many incredible souls who are passionate about life and really believe in themselves. These are the people who inspire you and remind you of the inner beauty that does still exist. This is what you'll begin to attract through your changes. The people who challenge you always give you the power to reflect, to move higher into your inner self, and to want better. Every situation serves a purpose. The moment you know that any form of sabotage is going on, you can create your exit plan from that limitation.

When you switch up your mindset, the old ways of the past are challenged, shaken up, and released.

People know energetically when someone is powered up from within. You radiate without words and without even trying. Going after your dream or believing you can have what your heart is yearning for only means that you are tapped into your spirit's purpose. This is so unique to every single person. Your awakening and realizations happen uniquely, according to your own spiritual evolution and how ready you are to really see what your path offers. You stop trying to conform, fit in, or be accepted; instead, you gravitate toward inner trust, inner reassurance, and inner guidance. This allows you to flourish in a very promising way, simply because you decided it was necessary.

The only place where your entire life can change is within yourself. This is another reason why I wrote this book—so you can always know that your inner access begins with you. You can sometimes wait so long to receive from the external world based on a stipulation someone has set up about ways you can have access. The reality is, you are the creator of your experience. When you KNOW this, you will begin to step forward with an unwavering level of self-esteem, self-trust, and self-awareness.

You're entering a wave of frequency that pulls in what you want to see, experience, and manifest. Your thought patterns are operating at the highest level.

Starting right now, end any form of self-sabotage. Don't complain, play the victim, or wallow in misery. Rise up instead. Show up for yourself. Follow your heart and take moment-to-moment steps forward. Don't feel overwhelmed or try to rush yourself. Breathe, and take one step forward. Every little bit you are able to do is equivalent to the greatness that is taking place and encompassing the grand vision of your story.

Be very aware of your own needs and what they mean to you. Don't accept less when you know everything that is possible for yourself and for others. Don't allow anyone to sabotage you. You only realize what is taking place when you step into your inner power. You suddenly gain clarity. At times, it feels like you are waking up from a slumber and wondering what has been taking place. This is why a lot of people, when they first witness their transformation into awareness, begin to say, "What was I thinking before in reference to my previous choices and way of living?"

The gift of insight also provides visual clarity about what is taking place in your life. You are literally reborn in every sense. All limitations of the mind are banished. You aren't letting people, situations, or your previous narratives about life stop you. You're owning your truth. You're shining your light, and you have discovered a sense of understanding that gives you back your power. This frees you. The most important things that surface from all of this are your voice, your passion, your life mission, and your own proclamation to stand firm in your truth.

Thought Access

Thought Patterns of Distraction

Anything that makes you forget that you are a spirit, that you *can* do it, and that it *is* possible for you is nothing more than a distraction from your potential. You have to own the fact that you are beyond the physical. With this kind of thinking, you don't operate in the five senses alone. You have a higher awareness that trickles down into all areas of your life. This can affect your wellness, business, work, passion, and creative expression. When you don't remember that you are only alive in this moment, you can easily put out your own fire for living and relegate it into the distant future. This causes you to waste energy and time. You don't want to just get by, barely feeling what it's like to be you when you can access the goodness and abundance that come out when you meet yourself rather than avoiding yourself.

So many times, you have received signs and reminders that have called you to remember yourself. These reminders come from your spirit, and they challenge you to own it, be it, and go for it. Listen to this. Trust it. Many things will try to distract you or make you question yourself. This is an illusion. It is sabotage. It causes you to stay stuck in the past, assuming that things might not change. These are doubtful thought patterns that can be banished now. Doubt can't be planted in you; it can only present itself as a thought which you can choose not to acknowledge. You weaken doubt by going for it and trusting yourself, even in moments of uncertainty. You gain confidence when you stop distracting yourself from your own gifts.

> *I am conserving my energy, time, and attention for what expands me, moves me, and ignites my spirit. I am reaching higher levels within myself, and I know my life will never be the same. I am rising upward and forward. I am progressing from within and without.*

Thought Patterns

There are an awful a lot of things that want to gain your mental attention: entertainment, overconsumption of content, fear through information, gossip, and narratives that want you to surrender your power in order to belong or simply get caught up in the latest trends. These are forms of distraction that present themselves as enjoyment or "need to know" when in reality, they require your attention only to give themselves life. As you feed them, you realize that you might be wasting your time, either through worry or avoiding yourself. Your attention is a true energy frequency. It is vital and living. It is always moving and interacting with information, creating images in your mind based on what you have consumed.

Why live in fear? Why tune into something that only causes you to imagine worst-case scenarios? This stops right here. You will vow to no longer give away your attention freely. You will honor the power of your mind and your imagination. You will believe in what you choose and what helps you get better. You will tap into all that is possible. You will start to see what life is made of when you choose where your attention goes. You will find yourself liberated from stagnation and begin to operate in the true flow of your essence. You will not attract the negativity you once did. It truly only gets better and better.

Thought Patterns of Self-Sabotage: Solutions

- Do anything and everything you have been procrastinating on. This will instantly create a positive shift in your life. The way to do this is by simply doing it. There isn't a plan for how to get something done. Waiting on a step-by-step program for this is just one more way to delay yourself from going for it. This applies to any area in your life where you feel a sense of stagnation. It is usually a sign that there is something you're procrastinating on that is much easier to simply do rather than wasting more time wondering how to approach it.

THOUGHT ACCESS

- Cut out thought patterns that try to convince you that you'll do it another day or get to it another time. Remember, you are only alive in this moment, and all your power is with you right now. When you get an idea or feel like there is something you want to get done, follow through. This has so many benefits that increase your energy and activate you to operate as if today is your only day.

- You already are. This just summarizes the vastness of your potential, no matter what it is you want or choose to experience. It is already possible in your field, simply because you had the thought. This awareness will save you so much time by eliminating any mental debate about whether or not something is even possible for you. Questioning if something can actually happen sabotages and delays what is already happening. Telling yourself *I already am,* and move forward instead of spending so much energy contemplating your own possibilities. Don't be afraid of your potential. It is possible for you; it is just a matter of embodying that acceptance and speaking highly to yourself and within yourself. This cuts out the negative chatter and wondering if you are "enough" or on track. Your life is always unfolding, so spending time wondering if you've made it to a certain checkpoint or calculating where you should be vs. where you could be can sabotage how you feel, especially when you already *are.*

- Don't assume that one day of realignment or readjustment means you have regressed into a habit from which you've already evolved. This kind of thinking sabotages your own path of growth. Don't get caught up trying to maintain a certain inner feeling or wondering why things feel different. The greatest changes come with physical, emotional, and mental upgrades that reshape you as a person. There's no reason to assume a positive change is an indication that something is going wrong. Don't get caught up in this type of thinking. Create a positive narrative for yourself, knowing that the outcome you're receiving is part of the unfolding process. This will help you to avoid staying stuck in self-analysis. Instead, you'll operate in a state of high self-awareness that speaks power over any situation that presents itself.

- Identify the thoughts that don't support you; then replace them with ones that do. You'll notice your new thoughts gaining strength, and you'll always follow up on them. This can be in self-acknowledgement for improvement instead of self-criticism for how far you have to go. Constant self-criticism causes you to move backward, which results in a cycle of stagnation/sabotage. You can end this instantly by operating in self-awareness. Notice your improvements, see the areas you are refining, and encourage yourself to keep going. This is a healthy mindset that is also very practical. You will see your inner resiliency coming to life.

- *I am on my own timing and my own path. I am living external reality from my own inner world.* This statement alone will remove habitual thought patterns that involve comparing yourself to others. Seeing how someone else's relationship is going isn't going to do anything for you. Wondering about someone's lifestyle isn't going to do much for you. Your life is your life. You have no idea how many forces are working in your favor in a positive way when you embrace yourself, celebrate yourself, and notice the magic that is happening in your own life. When it comes to comparison, the thought pattern of self-sabotage drains mental and emotional energy while implanting other people's external images into your internal imagination. Your imagination is supposed to be used for *your* life, to see what you want to experience, and to play

Thought Access

out mental scenarios that are in your favor. Don't sabotage yourself by playing the comparison game or overthinking the lives of others. Rest in yourself, get to know yourself, and rejoice in your own divine gifts. There's only one of you in this world. Embrace that.

- Self-acceptance is the most important form of freedom. With it, you won't spend so much time overthinking or wasting your life force in judgement against yourself or being overly critical of yourself. Who you are is precious. These aren't just words to lift you up; they are a true statement. You entered this world in the most miraculous way. It took so much to design and create a being like you. The details of your existence—your mind, your body, your heart, and your spirit—are all operating in wonderful synchronization, and this tells you one thing: You are supported, loved, and provided for. Bring your mindset back to remembrance of your essence and honor yourself. You exist now for yourself. You acknowledge your gifts and walk in this new and powerful thought pattern.

- If you have more mental energy to imagine, believe, and dream, you have more life force to focus on what you want out of life. You're not playing mental games with yourself, overthinking the lives of others or allowing yourself to be consumed by what someone else thinks of you or has said about you. This kind of sabotage ends right now. You are too aware to let it play out unconsciously or unknowingly. You are too alive now, and too purposeful with your energy. You are thoughtful and aware. When an unnecessary thought presents itself, snap out of it and affirm greater. This will cause your mind to retrain itself to magnetize thoughts you want and create momentum in positive thinking. This knowledge alone will automatically clear your thought patterns and end all forms of sabotage having to do with giving away your mental energy.

Positive Contagious Thought Patterns

You are now going to enter a thought field of positive contagious thought patterns that enhance your mindset, outlook, how you feel about yourself, and the way the world responds to you. This is your secret key to high energy, newfound empowerment, and trust unlike ever before. You radiate confidence and creative success. You are a vortex of miracles. This is Thought Access, and it can only be shared from mind to mind, though it can be felt in all areas of your life.

The thought pattern formations I share below operate on a different wavelength—one your spirit already understands and knows. This is why believing in yourself overcomes the opposite thought pattern. Why? Because you have stopped acting and stepped forward into your life. There will be no resistance to change, because your transformation is no longer up for debate. You have now decided to be the embodiment of your spirit in the physical world. You will feel the flow and connection.

Once your thought pattern switches by choice, nothing around you will ever look or be the same. You're consciously choosing. You're continuously evolving into a higher state and breaking down old thought patterns to be renewed and lifted higher. You shed what you thought you knew to experience something completely transcendental.

Your thought patterns represent higher thinking, grander visions, and a knowing that what you want is yours already. You will shine like never before. Thoughts do impact how you look, feel, and radiate. You start to exude what you feel, and this is a magnetic signal that attracts to you many great things. You become contagious in a lot of ways. What you think manifests. You experience miracles constantly. You are at the right place at the right time. You are able to make a decision and get the outcome you want. You attract people and opportunities that are aligned with your mission. People will even show up to help you with your vision or be a guiding light to inspire you right when you need it. You're no longer pleading, begging, or calling upon the universe for a breakthrough. You are stepping into it, instead. You are thinking from the state you desire as if everything is already in place…and it is.

Your life is constantly a profound experience with many insights that bring you all that you need right when you need it the most. You receive information and revelations intuitively that put your mind in awe of how every single thing is connected. All of this happens because you are now operating in a positive contagious thought pattern. You have decided to own your mind and to claim, speak, think, and command every state. You're not letting the outside world take over what you think or who you should be. You're listening to your own guidance, receiving curated insight from yourself based on your access to full awareness. Nobody can live through you or decide for you what your needs are. Only you have full insight to know what your dreams are, what you want to change, and what you yearn to experience. You know what it's like to be you, so there must be high trust in that area…and an even higher prioritization of your inner wellness.

You Now Have a Positive Self-Belief Thought Pattern

You are now going to receive a very important form of Thought Access: high self-belief. This comes first, before anything else. The way you see yourself and trust your inner world/vision brings you everything you need. You will notice that this thought pattern becomes a strong mental state for you as you radiate greater confidence. Anytime you want to go for something or make a decision, do it knowing that the outcome will be what you want.

Thought Patterns

This is a representation of your new thought pattern. You radiate confidence. There is no delay between your thoughts and any form of action you take or choose to experience.

Your level of self-belief comes from within, and it is here right now. You don't have to do anything except remember that. The awareness you are using to read this book is a sign that you are present and ready. You have a preexisting connection to your own consciousness. You will never again be a person that needs anything from the outside to help you believe in yourself. You will just know that it's there, that you are, and that you can. None of this is a coincidence, but it *is* a key part of your path to firmly stand in your inner truth.

Your self-belief is your consciousness igniting and lighting up with innate trust. You were never meant to question if something was possible for you. You were designed to go for it, knowing that you have already conceptualized the image, the vision, and the thought before following up with action. You weren't supposed to be in a mental battle about your own capabilities. Since your natural, innate blueprint supports positive self-belief thought patterns, you are returning to them right now. You feel encouraged, optimistic, and filled with energy from your spirit. It's time to be there for yourself, to represent that your mind is strong and your spirit is resilient.

I unlock my own potential by simply remembering it, owning it, and being it.

Everything you put into your mind is happening. Everything you want is happening. Everything you believe about yourself is happening. You are the one, through your eyes, who uses your energy to see what transpires. Life is experienced through you, and your beliefs design the world you eventually see.

This is why believing in yourself is valuable. It gives back to you in a tangible way. You must be victorious from within to be victorious without. Don't look at this from the mindset that you have to become. With your self-belief pattern, you already are. You are someone with effortless positive self-belief. You are accepting the thought system you want and thinking from that place. You don't have to go backward to remove or replace a thought; that only continues to feed the previous mindset. All you need to do is think right now from your new state of mind and you'll find yourself living life that way.

There is a sense of change when things shift that is usually followed by a profound realization. Once it clicks, it simply clicks. You get it. You feel it. You understand it, and it all makes so much sense. This realization comes from knowing that your positive self-belief was always there. Your previous thought pattern that occupied your mind for so long is not who you actually are. So, this insight is meant to bring you back to your authentic self, outside of any limiting concepts or thought patterns that don't belong to you. It will power you up, bringing you back to the center of yourself so you can acknowledge the truth of your spirit.

You Now Have a Strong Mindset Thought Pattern

Your new mindset functions as a shield from the noise, the distraction, the doubt, the fear, and the confusion. All thought patterns that enter your mind now support you and allow you to see yourself in the highest light. Your mindset lifts you up and magnetizes you to wonderful matching frequencies, connecting you with your highest thoughts and aspirations.

You are a self-sustaining with your thoughts, which guide you at will. Your new mindset clears your mental field of any previous states of mind that don't represent your highest and greatest expression. Start thinking of your mental field as a living space, filled with energy that can be projected into the world based on what you want and need.

Another important aspect of your mindset is that it is a receiver just as it is a projector. The thought patterns you send out always function as actual signals that move through space outside of time. Your thoughts have their own life force. You give this to them as they radiate from within you. This is the unseen aspect of life that isn't usually discussed. It is something with which you become familiar through awareness, manifestation, and experience. Everything connects back to a thought. The thought is a pattern that creates your world for you. This is why, when you have a strong mindset like you have now, it attracts other thoughts that match itself. This creates a strong, propelling momentum in your life.

Be patient with yourself as you're transforming and entering a new phase of your life. You're mentally, physically, spiritually, and emotionally upgrading.

You don't need to spend any more time dwelling in previous thought patterns that you know you no longer associate with. Think of it like this. Do you want that thought to become physical? Do you want to see that thought manifest? If not, pull your life force away from it. Healing from a mindset isn't about dwelling on it or repeating it. Even constantly talking about it feeds it. Your consciousness right now is new, and it is truly free from all concepts of the previous you. You are always brand new. It may seem otherwise; you may think you're living in the linear day to day. In reality, you are a multidimensional being who can shapeshift, renew, alter, and create a new sense of self from a new mindset. I truly believe this for you, as I know how much our inner mental freedom from limiting thoughts, self-sabotage, and fear depends on thinking from a strong and unrestricted mindset.

The new you is mentally free. You have your power back, and you are consciously choosing what you want. No one knows or understands your inner world better than you do. This is your own private upgrade. This is what Thought Access is about. It's lifting you higher within your mental world, feeding you energetically and igniting you spiritually. This alone advances you in the physical world. Thought Access is like having an insight, a key, and the wisdom for everything you need.

This kind of mindset does wonderful things in your life. It opens you up and clears your thought field. It advances your way of thinking, which makes you more intelligent and aware of your own power. You're no longer just a physical being dealing with physical situations. You are a living spirit embodying thoughts in the physical world, which is ready to change itself to match your thought patterns. You are very powerful. You are someone who sees beyond it all. So much of your energy in previous unawareness drained your life force, causing you to focus on things that required you to seek out validation or approval, operating in a space where the unknown seemed scary. This all has ended now.

You know you're not just a physical being. You know your energy only flows out from you, not into you from the outside. You are the carrier of your own light, and you are meant to shine your brightest, not dim yourself by siphoning attention away from yourself in the belief that you'll get it some other way. Nothing can give you energy that's already yours, that originates within you. This kind of energy can't be bought or forced. It's ever-flowing and ever-present within you. This is where it begins, and this realization completely restores your energy, giving you peace of mind like never before.

You Now Have Trust and Faith Like Never Before

You now trust yourself, the universe, and the Source that provides all. You operate in a field of knowledge. You just know it will happen for you. You know it *is* happening for you. You already see it, and you already believe it. Your new thought pattern has now been activated within you. You are someone who goes for it, who follows their dreams, who brings their vision to life, who doesn't need anything outside their inner world to know that their idea is coming to life. You believe everything into existence. You speak it, think it, feel it, and bring it to life, all through your mind.

This higher level of trust and faith is something that comes from within you. Anything you want is within your mind, your spirit, and deep in your heart. How can an inner vision borne of your imagination require external reassurance when you are the one who is alchemically creating with your mind? Your senses shouldn't need to validate for you what is about to happen; your mind does that. When your manifestation arrives in your physical world, you already know that you created it, imagined it, felt it, and believed in it. This is the kind of power you have. You shouldn't let external noise, the past, or even the present moment (the way things appear) take away the power of what is born within you in terms of creativity, expression, and design. You are the keyholder to your imagination. This is all silently happening within, and the entire world rearranges itself to match what you expect will happen.

Your thought patterns of trust and faith are what bring to life everything you have in mind right now. You will never again have to doubt or question how or when. Everything I am sharing with you in *Thought Access* will bring the process of creation back to life within you. Lack of faith comes from your mind being trained in the past to view life as a step-by-step occurrence. Perhaps you became accustomed to seeing things first in order to believe in them. This creates an easily broken thought pattern that the outside world utilized to define what you should think and believe. In fact, it was always supposed to be your imagined state coming to life; you, the dreamer, creating what you want; and you, the observer, experiencing what you expect to experience. It was never supposed to be a battle between your

THOUGHT ACCESS

beliefs and whatever the outer world was showing you in the present moment. You were always supposed to be in a strong, trusting thought pattern, believing in your imagined desire, having strong faith in your inner state of being, and knowing it was happening before it even happened. This faith has now activated within you. The level of Thought Access you have gained through the insights I am sharing with you represents a higher mental frequency. Just reading this reminds you that the entire reality in which we live is actually a mental reality experienced in the physical world.

Believe it to see it. Feel it before it happens. When you have visualized, you know it's already done. Your desired state is coming into existence now, and you did it all through your mind.

With the knowledge that your mental reality creates your physical world, you no longer need to let yourself be weakened by opinions, circumstances, what happened in the past, or what you once did. You are no longer wasting energy, asking, "Can it happen?" or "Will it happen?" That type of thinking is a form of limitation that looks around to determine what is possible. How can you see what is possible for you by looking at external circumstances? You need greater thought to be able to see beyond what appears to be happening. Only through the mind can you determine what is possible. You believe it first; you know it, expect it, and feel it. Then you begin to see it all around you.

The physical world is always responding to you, and this gives you the greatest trust in yourself. You are free of all limiting thought patterns. The possibilities are more in your favor now, as there are so many wonderful ways things can happen. Let yourself rest into this knowledge, and smile about it. You are operating on a level of trust, knowledge, and high faith unlike anything ever seen before. You are making things come to life through your mind, imagination, and vision. External reality operates as response field to whatever you hold in your mind, so be ready to see what you want come to life. This is your dream, and it was supposed to be coming from within you this whole time.

You Now Are Tapped into Creative Thought Patterns

You are a creative being. You can become anything you want, quite literally. Creative thought patterns mean you're operating in your own frequency of expression. You do things in your own unique way, and you follow the urge to express what wants to flow out of your spirit. You'll notice that when you follow this inner inspiration, unlimited creative energy flows through you. The point here is to not hide from what you're good at just because you may have conformed to a previous idea of what the world expected from you. No one can open the inner portal of creativity constantly flowing within you except yourself.

It starts with listening to your inner guidance. What are you being called to express? What feels effortless for you to do? What are your truly passionate about that you haven't yet followed through on, or have kept at bay? You must remember that there is no time limit to you coming alive in the creative sense. The universe only knows *when* you start using the energy that has been given. You feel joy and excitement, even losing track of time as you enjoy yourself through the process of bringing your creative ideas to life.

You have something to offer. There is something you have been called to do. Creative expression is so unique to every single person. Knowing in advance what you enjoy doing or what you can masterfully accomplish will be key. Once you follow this calling, it will feel like back-to-back unstoppable surges of energy. People will start showing up in unexplainable ways to be a part of your vision. Resources will find you, opportunities will present themselves, and the magic of it all is that you simply followed your creative expression to make it happen. The reason it starts happening this way is that when you naturally follow what you are being called to do, you stop resisting yourself and allow. This is huge in the sense of what is energetically taking place. You go from avoiding your creative powers to just going for it. This breaks barriers and resistance, allowing flow to literally take place within your mind and body. It's like the floodgates of your imagination, universal energy, and the life force all conspire to effortlessly flow through you.

This is how powerful following your heart is. So often, when we accomplish this, we don't know how the change occurs, but we feel that it is happening. You feel lighter, brighter, and more centered. You feel connected, confident, and calm. You are a creative genius. This is an urgent reminder to follow what is in your heart, what your spirit deeply yearns for, and what you believe to be your higher purpose. Go for it! You are supported in all ways.

You Are Now Confident and Magnetic

Confidence is a state of being which demonstrates that it is all energy. You can't fake confidence. It radiates out of you. Confidence is how you feel about yourself from within; the world around you detects it through your shine. This is what makes you magnetic. You naturally believe in yourself, effortlessly trust yourself, love who you are, and you do what you love. Accepting yourself and operating from higher values shows your deep connection to your spirit. Remember, thought patterns radiate, which means they can be consciously or unconsciously detected by the world around you. What you are doing is sending a signal of your inner state rather than thinking you can appear one way and feel another. Your inner state operates in the energy field in which we all actually communicate. It is silently felt and heard. I am sure you've been in a situation where you felt someone's energy before they even spoke to you. This is the energy field of communication. We are always sensing people and feeling out the world around us. This is why I always encourage inner self-authenticity—being true to yourself. You're not here to try to convince the world you're a certain way. You are who you are, and you shine that energy truthfully.

You provide great value, and the power of your thought pattern ripples into the universe. Your creativity, magnetism, and light illuminate your path.

You are now confident and magnetic in your thoughts, how you feel, and how you carry yourself. You are confident and magnetic in your creative expression, your business, your passion, and your connections. You have accepted your body, and you honor all it does for you. You send thoughts to your body of love, care, and appreciation. Throughout your mind, every single cell picks up that frequency and begins to shine for you. Accepting your body makes you naturally confident and magnetic because you are sending a signal of radiance, acknowledgement, and blessings to yourself. The body conforms to the mind operating it. Your body is listening, responding, and creating the energy field around you according to the state of your mind. This is why I want you to honor your body, love what it does for you, and send to it an accurate signal of what you want to be, have, experience, and feel.

Thought patterns of the mind show up first in our physical bodies. This is why it is so important for me to mention this to you. I want you to simply be. There's nothing you have to force, manipulate, or try so hard to do. Your body and mind are in sync when you calm down and trust that they are operating in the highest and most intelligent way. No resistance, no rushing, no tricks, no quick fixes, and no destructive energy patterns. You are whole, and you are okay. Rest into this feeling and watch yourself light up. It all turns on when you live from a mindset of ease.

Thought Access

Be open to the energy of massive blessings.

Being confident is living your truth. Being magnetic is shining your light. The world feels you when you feel yourself. The world responds to you when you nurture yourself and live exactly the way you want. Start operating as empowered from within. Start loving yourself no matter what has or hasn't happened. You are alive right now, and you can't live in your chosen state in this moment if you are chasing a future state to "one day" feel. That pattern ends now.

Bring all that you want to feel and be into yourself now, through your mind. Become it first. Feel it first, and shine from that state. You will be so surprised at how quickly people, places, and things rearrange to match your new confidence and magnetism. As we are consciously developing and becoming more aware (returning to our true state), we start to get really good at intuitively feeling out the world around us. As more people remember their primal ability to do this, they will sense energy before they even hear or see what they are dealing with. I want you to know that this is already happening. Being your true, authentic, intuitive self in the moment is so much more important than "appearing" to be so. *Being* it creates your chosen reality faster.

The results of your confidence, magnetic thought patterns, and new state of being will be profound. You'll feel a sense of ease in your body. You'll have faith that you can do anything you want because you just confidently believe in yourself. You'll notice people beginning to recognize your work, your talents, and your gifts. You'll see the world treating you differently because you have effortlessly accepted yourself. You'll see a shift in your relationships and the way people in your life respond to you. So many will be drawn to you to in a positive way that brings more good energy into your life. You'll feel like a lucky person, but you know you're just confident and highly blessed. You'll find yourself at the right place at the right time. You'll see more of your visions manifesting. You'll attract the resources you need in the most unexpected ways. You'll notice abundance increasing in all areas of your life. You'll feel more inclined to make healthy choices in mind, body, and spirit. Your life has literally shifted, and it will feel like you have entered an alternate-reality version of yourself; but really, you have woken up to your own inner power, confidence, and magnetism. Congratulations on this wonderful discovery. I know the results will be unlike anything you could ever imagine now. Enjoy the blessings of your new state.

Your Power of Choice in Thought Patterns

Now that you know what thought patterns are, you can make the conscious choice to operate your own mindset in the way you choose. You will find that it has become easier to identify which thoughts support you and which ones limit you. You'll be able to instantly shift your mindset at any given second to remain empowered, hopeful, optimistic, and positive. All states are available at any given time. It is the mental patterns we give attention to that we enter and live from. Knowing all of this means that you are the one in control. Don't let any thought forms keep you trapped. Don't ever stay stuck. Rise up from it instead. Go higher in your mind, transcending the illusions of perception that try to paint life in just one way.

You have in your hands right now a new and vital insight. With it, you'll be able to direct your mindset, and with your new self-awareness, you'll be able to alter the reality all around you. You'll feel more confident, more trusting, more loving, and more deeply connected to your true self. You no longer allow limiting thoughts to stop you. You are no longer moving through life without the knowledge of the key within you, which has been there the whole time. You are so much more alive, present, and enriched. You feel a surplus of energy, creativity, and passion.

Thought Access

This means that you have entered your desired state, your flow, and your connection. You can make the choice, shift your state of mind, and alter your thought patterns anytime you like. Refer back to this is chapter whenever you need a reminder, reassurance, or a surge of energy confirming that anything is possible for you. I know you can do it, and I know that with this awareness, you'll be much healthier in mind, body, and spirit. Go forward and be your greatest.

Key Points to Remember

- *Your thought patterns are everything. Thought patterns are how you think and see the world; and what you believe ends up creating your world. What you decide to accept either limits or amplifies what you have access to according to your habitual, daily thought patterns.*

- *People often believe things happen to them randomly, and because of this, they exist in the sea of the unknown without even having a say in matters that are important to them. They don't even know that they are constantly creating their reality with their thoughts. Knowing and accepting your inner power is the key to your thought patterns, which are literally capable of producing a healthy self-image, a quality life, and a peaceful perspective on any situation. You attract the most magical life you feel is worthy of your experience.*

- *Nothing will get past your mental gates without a scan. People will notice how different you are. You'll be much more confident, grounded, and connected to yourself. You'll make intelligent choices because your thought pattern is healthy and on point.*

- *To completely alter your life, you must be totally honest with yourself about changing your mindset.*

Thought Patterns

- *Thought patterns provide insight about where you are with yourself. It is so important to me to give mind empowerment and awareness. To know how your mind works and to be able to think, create, and live intentionally will truly mean that you have accessed your own inner power. Nothing can give you this but yourself.*

- *When you are evolving from within, you might notice your outer reality going through major shifts. It is unexplainable how it all happens, because we rarely discuss the mental and emotional world and the way it impacts connections, the universe, and the field all around us.*

- *Mastery over reality is mastery over your mind and emotions. This means you think what you want to see happen. You don't react to what appears to be happening when you know that the world is altering itself to allow you to manifest what you want. You don't react or overact when something unexpected happens. You just believe that things are working according to your highest thoughts and greatest intentions.*

- *Your spirit is more powerful than any lower thoughts or regressions. Your spirit, once ignited, banishes all energy in the mental field that no longer works to move you in the new direction you are headed.*

- *Don't let anyone waste your time or sabotage your dreams. This can happen when you begin to rise into your power. You might experience people trying to make you question what you're even doing, because it is so easy to remain the same. Truly living life and intentionally creating the reality you want requires a type of inner access that is very different from the norm.*

Thought Access

- *People know energetically when you are powered up from within. You radiate without words and without even trying. Effectively going after your dreams and believing that you can have what your heart is yearning for means that you have tapped into your spirit's purpose.*

- *Starting right now, end any form of self-sabotage. Don't complain, play the victim, or wallow in misery. Rise up instead. Show up for yourself. Follow your heart while taking steps forward in the present moment.*

- *You already are. This just summarizes the vastness of your potential, no matter what you want or choose to experience. It is already possible in your field, simply because you had the thought.*

- *Self-acceptance is the most important form of freedom. Don't spend any more time overthinking, wasting your life force in self-judgement, or being overly critical of yourself.*

- *Your thought patterns represent higher thinking, grander visions, and an inner knowing that what you want is yours already. You will shine like never before. Thoughts do impact how you look, feel, and radiate. You start to exude what you feel, and this is a magnetic signal that attracts to you many great things. Your energy becomes contagious.*

- *You have decided to own your mind, and to claim, speak, think, and command every desired state.*

- *The new you is mentally free. You have your power back, and you are consciously choosing what you want. No one knows or understands your inner world better than you. This is your own private upgrade. This is what*

Thought Patterns

Thought Access is about—lifting you higher within your mental world, which feeds you energetically and ignites you spiritually.

- *You now trust yourself, the universe, and the Source that provides all. You operate in the field of knowledge. You just know it will happen for you. You know it is happening for you. You already see it, and you already believe it. This is your new thought pattern that has now activated within you.*

- *You are a creative being. You can become anything you want, quite literally. With creative thought patterns, you operate in your own frequency of expression. You do things in your own unique way, and you follow the urge to express what wants to flow out of your spirit. You'll notice that when you follow your inner inspiration, unlimited creative energy flows through you.*

- *You are now confident and magnetic in your thoughts, your feelings, and the way you carry yourself. You are confident and magnetic in your creative expression, your business, your passions, and your connections.*

- *You have in your hands right now a new and vital insight. With it, you'll be able to direct your mindset. With your new self-awareness, you can alter reality all around you. You feel more confident, more trusting, more loving, and deeply connected to your true self.*

3

IT WAS YOU THE WHOLE TIME

This will be one of the most powerful realizations I will share with you. So much of my life changed in profound ways when I remembered myself. Yes, I remembered who I truly am, and that it was me the whole time. I am the one who initiates the desire for what I want to experience. I am the one who imagines, visualizes, and thinks of what I want to manifest. I am the one who feels and receives what I give my mental, physical, and emotional energy to. Every single part of my reality requires me to interact with it through my attention, my intention, and my mind. Each and every one of us is living life from within. We have our thoughts, feelings, desires, and the contents of our heart. All of this stems from within you, and you are always interacting with reality and the outer world in one powerful way: YOU ARE IMPACTING IT. You, through your mind right now, are impacting every single thing in your life.

Your mind works for you. When you know this, you will be so free, so full of life, and so successful in any way you choose. There isn't anything standing in your way. The only thing that could have prevented you from knowing or realizing this is not having access to the thought that would have given you this awareness. You know now. You understand. I will elaborate further in this chapter upon what it means to operate your life from within, and to allow the world around you to respond to you, align with what you want to see, and create the exact experiences you want.

Listen to the message from within. Your soul is guiding you.

Think of it like this: Your mind is interacting with information all around you. This can be ideas, beliefs, or the way things seem to appear. You, as the viewer observing all of this from within, shouldn't get caught up in the tangible alone. If your mind didn't produce it, then you are interacting with thoughts previously created by others. Everything you see came from someone's imagination, and these imagined thoughts have now become physical manifestations.

We are surrounded by a sea of thoughts that appear to be in a physical state. If we don't remember that it all originated in the imagination, and that what we are seeing is ideas at work, we can assume everything is only "physical" in nature. There is so much more to it all. Your access to this insight indicates that you are now activating vision beyond sight. You are no longer going to think that things are set in stone. Everything is a frequency state that is constantly shifting. The observer decides how they will bend reality to respond to them.

If everything stems from the mental nature of life, then what does that mean for you? What is in your mind? Are you getting distracted by issues or ideas you didn't create? Do you believe that the existing physical reality is the only thing possible? Are you assuming that there isn't an ounce of possibility that it could actually turn out the way you imagined it…or greater? This is where I want you to stop yourself. If you're not acting as the contributor or creator of your experiences, you can easily be pulled into someone else's concept of life. This includes their ideas, their limitations, and even their dramas. You must observe everything as ideas that stemmed from the minds of others. Usually, ideas find attraction through the frequency or energy state of someone who is a match to that idea.

Things are matched up via frequency and energy states.

Remember, life is not merely physical. Your physical nature is being directed by the vast network that comprises your mental state. People in the physical world are all a part of a network of connection and ideas. Thoughts are being shared in spaces and places unseen to the physical eye. This is why *Thought Access* is such a powerful book. It ends the illusion that made you forget that things are more than the physical. It gives you direct access, direct connection, and direct reminders to be self-initiated and self-activated in your own inner power. Nobody stands in the way of who you are and what is innately yours.

The only thing you might have not known previously is an awareness of how it all comes into being. In recent years, as information has become excessive, many people have lost their own innate realization about how to tap in and receive. You are supposed to be a self-sustaining system of body, mind, and spirit. That awareness is yours now. You are free of illusions, limitations, and concepts that make you question yourself or doubt what is possible for you. Consenting to any other state that is not pure inspiration is only misdirected thought. When it first realizes its own vastness, the mind goes into a state of wonder: *Is this even real? What is actually happening?* These are very natural questions that tend to come up as more is shown to you. Insight expands your awareness and shifts the trajectory of your life. As you access more, you become more and receive more.

> *Openness of the mind and heart is the*
> *beginning of interacting with the subtle field.*

Consciousness can only expand at the capacity of the medium that holds of it. You are the medium through which energy expresses itself. As you begin to expand your mind and demand more in your life, your consciousness expands. You gain the information you need, the energy to do all you want, and alignments that you couldn't have planned yourself on the physical level. Think of it as the master creator within that has always been there. It's always working for you and your highest expression…at all times. The whole point is for you to activate your inner vision and trust your inner guidance.

For too long, you watched the outside world alone, waiting for something to change as you remained static within. You never really stepped into your power. This is not about wishing or hoping. It is knowing. It is empowerment. It is claiming. It is about being. The outside world is secondary to our inner world. It's a balance that interacts and dances as it receives from your mind and creates the world around you. This is why I have dedicated this whole chapter to the awareness of your own mind—to return to you the inner richness that guides the outer world in obvious and profound ways. You see it clearly, and you know it.

It Is Possible for You

In order know what is possible for you, we must discuss your true nature. In your essence dwells great power. Even before you developed the world around you and understood the tangible means for receiving things through your mind, you operated from intuition and instinct. For thousands of years, inner knowing was at the forefront of humanity, and dependence upon it was built into our system. We received from within. We inquired from within. We thought from within, and we asked from within. Somehow, we made it this far using the innate ability that sometimes makes itself known to you. You might see it working right when you need it; or you might find yourself in a tough situation, and suddenly, the idea pops into your mind. A way to get out of the situation flows in. This insight is vital, and it is your guiding compass. You know more than you think you do. Your intuition was your gift from nature when you were created and designed. This inner genius knows, understands, sees, and possesses insight beyond what you can imagine. It's

Thought Access

been you this whole time, with the connection to receive.

If your dependency has become about predictability or being able to do everything yourself without insight, you are operating according to what your mind already knows based on experience, not inspiration. This kind of thinking causes you to need to know *how* something will happen or *when* it will happen. You control what you create with certainty by following a path that was paved by others who have already done it. This gives you the reassurance of safety when in reality, your dreams are unbounded, your vision is vast, and your imagination can create out of thin air.

When we go down the predictable path or follow what everyone else has been doing, we become good at repeating or copying what is being done. This is not innovative at all. This is why you might not see many life-changing ideas being created. This changes now as you unbind yourself from the mindset of a limited view and enter the realm of possibility. Anything is possible for you, but like I said previously, consciousness can only expand at the capacity of the medium holding it. *You* are the medium who now believes that anything is possible for you. This opens you up to receive. You return to your original awareness by using intuition, instinct, and your innate guidance. You are free from needing to know *how* or *when*. You are free from needing to see it to believe it. You believe first, you trust first, you imagine first, and you see all of this follow your mindset and enter into reality.

You are the original human. No matter how much we believe we have advanced technologically or gained new access to material things, we still are the same physical human with the same design, and we now yearn to return to this awareness. Excess without sufficient inner empowerment will cause many to seek themselves or want to know who they really are at their core. You know exactly who you are. You are simply removing from your mind the many external voices and things that try to tell you who you are without actually bringing awareness back within.

Too many forces may be trying to pull you in many directions, distracting your mind from itself. All humans, when overstimulation of the mind and/or unnecessary distraction is removed, return to equilibrium. Equilibrium is achieved when your body and mind go back to their natural pattern. This is what people receive when they say things like "I need a break" or "I need to get away from everything." This is their subconscious means of unplugging and returning back to themselves. Within you is the power to always receive from yourself. Self-generation and regeneration make anything possible for you. When you depend on your mind to create the way, it does so in the easiest, most unexpected, most synchronized way. It connects the dots globally and sends the message into the network faster, returning back to you in ways you could never imagine. You find yourself getting more creative, meeting the people you were meant to meet, and getting insight on which move to make next. This was all powered from within.

Everything aligns when you declare within your mind that you are worthy and deserving of the best.

As you start becoming more inner-dependent, you'll notice your confidence going up and your sense of self-trust increasing. You'll start being that person who just knows everything is happening and working out accordingly. You'll never go against yourself. You have an inner intelligence, and you are actively connected back to that flow. This makes so much possible for you, as fears are removed and doubt perishes. The rate at which you imagine something and it manifests actually speeds up; this was all dependent on your inner level of self-trust.

When people don't yet understand this insight, they lose

themselves in the outer world, constantly needing something to give them reassurance that it will happen. They haven't realized that it always works out, and this constant worry only causes delays. Stop your mind from getting so caught up in appearances or the way things seem. You know the physical world represents manifestation of ideas, thoughts, and beliefs. It is also a creative space for us to express the genius within ourselves. Treat it like a world of creation that allows you to express yourself, and *be* more of what you want to see around you. This is what you have access to now—the knowledge that it has been possible the whole time.

Many wonderful things are possible in this life. As the medium, you must believe this and know that your possibilities aren't dependent on what is happening or what people around you *think* is possible. For someone to believe in themselves, they must already know and remember who they actually are. Anyone who limits ideas only sees the physical world as a tangible place that they need to work hard to maneuver. They haven't yet understood their mind, what they believe in, and the fact that what they think always happens. You expect it, then you experience it. Not knowing what you are capable of in this lifetime is truly living in the sea of others' thoughts without expressing what you deeply want at the level of your soul. This is why it is vital that you don't base your possibilities on what someone else views as their own limitations.

We often don't realize that we might be in the same vicinity physically, but mentally, we are in different dimensions. This type of awareness will prevail in the future. The mental aspect of life will be given so much credit, and people will be discussing it more—not just to talk about it, but to empower the inner reality in which we primarily exist before discussing the outer aspect. Nobody will be able to hide behind the veil of the body. Energetically, we will begin to expose the nature of people's thoughts. Before, it was easy to avoid the inner world and focus solely upon the outside and how things appear. As more people awaken, their ability to read energy and see through things will increase. They will be able to navigate their interactions, relationships, and creations much more consciously.

The reason a lot of conversations about mental health are happening now is that we are bringing to light the inner world of human beings and realizing how crucial it is to take care of the inner aspect of ourselves. People are so much more than the physical, and that is very much apparent now. We are beginning to have the conversations and discuss what is needed. I believe the most important thing is giving energy and attention back to yourself, knowing that your mind matters and that you have access to healing now. To be seen and heard is to recognize who you are and how you can express that energy.

Take all that is necessary for you, and center it once more to shine outward with your light. Many people experience grief or the loss of someone they love, for example, and don't have the time to process it. Make the time for yourself. Others spend too much time comparing their lives, as we are overly exposed to images and the lives of others if you find yourself online. You brain wasn't supposed to be used to constantly view and compare yourself. You weren't supposed to have a mental reaction to something you're not even physically experiencing just because you saw it online. This causes a lot of energy loss, and the mental depletion can be exhausting. It's very unnatural, and we find ourselves wanting to be free of it.

> *You're in the middle of your greatest transformation, and you're rising up mentally, physically, emotionally, and spiritually.*

Living in fear of or comparing yourself with others only triggers lack and causes you to feel unmotivated, thinking you're not doing enough. Break free from this hypnotic trance of swiping, scrolling, viewing, following the lives of others, or tuning into information that isn't helping you in any way. No more negativity allowed. No more giving your energy away to anyone or anything that isn't a true representation of where you're headed. No more viewing any form of negativity, drama, or fear-driven information. Tune back into yourself. What do you need? Who are you without all the noise? Returning to yourself means you make space for your rise, your healing, your evolution, and your transformation.

Using the insights of this book will bring you so much peace and clarity, as they bring your mind and body back into equilibrium. The attention I have dedicated to the empowerment of the mental world is very much equiv-alent to a healthy state of mind. You will be provided with all the tools and insights you need to manage your mental world. When the pendulum swings too far in one direction, we yearn to stabilize ourselves and find our peace in a healthy state of mind. This stabilization will allow you to remember what is possible for you, as it restores your mind and empowers you from within.

Self-Awareness

You must have self-awareness in order to be able to recognize that everything exists within you. Self-awareness is knowing you're a conscious being creating your own reality. Your self-awareness and your inner understanding of something more give you deeper meaning and purpose for your life. The flow of energy from self-awareness and honoring who you are is overflowing and constantly pouring into you. When you are self-aware, you know how to manage your mental state, your emotional state, and your physical state. You have discovered that there's a uniqueness to your own understanding of self and the way you process and create from within. The reason I focus on this area is to bring your mind back to knowledge of self, which makes everything you do so much more pleasant. It stops your energy from needing so much from the external world, as dependency trains you to ignore your own inner voice. When you are inner-dependent, you know through self-awareness that you can bring yourself back to balance at will, create because you are tapped in, and express the beauty coming through you abundantly.

Understand that every second, vast amounts of life force are flowing through you. This energy is what keeps you alive, maintains you, and nourishes you. This energy doesn't stop, whether you are asleep or awake. It gives, then gives some more. When you see yourself from a mindset that is unpleasant or negative, you restrict your flow. Sometimes, this can be felt in the physical body, and you might feel tired or like you don't have enough energy. To be able to create, your body needs to be energized, and this energy is what helps you to be optimistic and inspired.

I take my power back on all levels.

Mental states influence the physical body. Through your choices and actions, you drive your mind power to be displayed in the physical body. This means your body is responding to your thoughts on the deep, subatomic level, all the way to the physical structure. Your body is alive and interacts with your thoughts. It hears you and responds to you. With every word you speak over yourself, allow it to be intentional. Allow even your silent thoughts to be empowering.

To be self-aware is to build yourself up from within. Lack of self-awareness is appearing one way on the outside and feeling another way internally that doesn't match the frequency you intend to display. Self-awareness is also being true to yourself, your energy state, and the balance of your inner and outer worlds. This will power you up in the most profound ways, as it means your field is centered. A centered field—your mind, body, and spirit in sync—has great impact. Knowing how to manage, understand, and read your own energetic needs and expression will be key to your self-awareness, as you will know when to give and when to receive. You cannot give from an empty state, so it is very important that you are filled, nourished, energized. Take good care of yourself.

Receiving from the Thought Field

When you operate in self-awareness, you receive most of your insight from your thought field. Your mind guides you, and when you have access to higher thought, as shared in this book, you enter a very sacred unification within the thought realm that connects you to a field of creativity and a stream of visions. Both of these help you in many ways in your physical life. As your awareness expands, you gain more of what you consciously need. The way it happens will be very unique and special to you, as you are the one who knows best what you require. You are sacred, and every detail of your life is precisely designed for you. Greater thoughts produce greater outcomes and creations. I welcome you into the receiving field, as your thoughts are now receptive to what you need. You'll realize that a lot of your normal thoughts will now be of a higher frequency. They'll show you the way, clear your path, guide you, give you what you need, and tell you things intuitively before they happen. You're in the field of knowledge now, and this connection has all taken place within you. If there's something you need to know, you will receive and be shown the way. Rest your mind and breathe, as you are receptive to the information now.

Being in a receptive thought field doesn't require you to learn a technique or practice. It's an available field to which you gain access though awareness. Once you experience it and what it can do for you, you'll never again doubt your own inner power. Have you noticed that you attract more of the same kinds of positive thoughts now? They can be repetitive, as we might not realize we are establishing a thought pattern that ultimately becomes a thought field. From this state, you are fed matching thoughts and ideas according to the frequency of your belief. When someone believes in themselves and knows that something can happen for them, they are usually in a thought field that pulls toward them energy states that act as reminders: *It is possible, there is hope for you, of course you can do it, act on it, here are more ideas, here is the way, follow this path, go after it, it's coming to you,* and *you have so much potential.*

These are some of the many thoughts that may be circulating in your thought field. As stronger mental states overcome weaker ones, older, less productive beliefs eventually get wiped out. This is what I mean by the power of your thought field. It builds upon itself as you stop treating your inner thoughts as if they should be on automatic. If you happen to talk with someone who doesn't believe something is possible for them, you can easily locate a thought connected to that belief. There could even be several thoughts holding them back.

The mental world is a dimension that is alive. This state of mind truly determines the life you experience, what you can manifest or create, and even how much beauty, love, and experience you can share with others. Cultivating wholeness and balance will be key during this time, as we are forging into territories that unite the value of the inner and outer being. No longer will our attention be diverted from the importance of the mental world. It will be supported by physical shifts and changes taking place as more and more people awaken to their own inner power.

> *You might not realize your impact, because we assume we must be known, influential, or have reach in the external world. The reality is, you're a source of energy. Through your mind, being, and feelings, project that state into the world.*

Thought Access

Keep in mind that you're always radiating your thought field. Shine!

You are connected to the thought field, and you influence the world from your mind. If this is where energy must flow to create the world you perceive, then why not expand it, build upon it, understand it, and connect with it? You are the observer here, and you have great power in your hands. Be very aware of this, and be diligent. Remain conscious and concise in your actions. The thought field doesn't judge the state you were in a second ago or even yesterday; it just responds to you moment by moment. You are the one who must create a new moment to produce a new outcome.

So much of what remains unchanged stems from feeding your mind thoughts and emotions from another time. The past lingers only in the mind, even as you continue to repeat what you may not want. When we think of time, we don't realize that our body and mind are always in the present moment. As far as you can tell, you are observing everything right now, and through your mind, you generate images of what you want to see. It then curates that reality for you. This happens so quickly and so subtly that we think it isn't happening. You may not see how quickly it is moving for you. Here is a fun experiment that will blow your mind and make you a believer in how fast your mind actually works for you. You can use this anytime, for anything you need. Say the following to yourself or even write it down. Both ways work, as you are intending consciously.

Experiment: Try thinking of something in particular you want your mind to show you, and write it down in your notes or journal. It can be anything; your mind will locate it in physical reality. Your attention will land upon it, as you have instructed your mind to get to work for you. This is what creates every moment of your life.

Mind, show me _____!

This technique is simple and easy, and it works really fast. You are commanding to be shown what you want to see. However, the most important aspect of all of this is that you are becoming conscious of your mind/reality connection instead of thinking that your thought field isn't constantly at work and showing you what you want to see. This little experiment activates you and creates a surge of energy toward belief in your own influence. We'll go much deeper in the chapters to come, as I want you to be equipped in the thought world so you can have a greater, more pleasant experience in the physical world around you.

Empowered Action

As you become more conscious and aware of who you truly are, what you need, and what you believe is your purpose, your actions and everything you do will change. Don't be surprised at how profoundly Thought Access shifts every area of your life in a positive way. There will be a whole new air to you as you step into the world. You hold the key to be mentally empowered first. We have discussed a lot of the thought realm and how it produces your experience. Now I want to get more into the changes you'll recognize in your actions.

You'll no longer delay action because your mind instantly gives your physical body instructions for what needs to be done. Your thought will be much more potent, so if you say something is going to happen, it will happen. For insight, the reason there was a delay in action before is because you said too many times that you would do something, and this trained your mind to take the response less seriously. You didn't physically act upon what you imagined for yourself.

Let's say there's something you want to do right now. All the means to do it are available, but instead, out of habit, you put it off...and continue to put it off. You train yourself to not take your thoughts and intentions seriously, which creates an unnecessary guilt trip for something you could have just done. This pattern has now broken from your field. You take empowered action because you are so much more aware of your inner power. You know all that you have is right now. You know each moment is an accumulation of your life force to produce physical change.

Start by doing what you want, when you say you want it. Any change you want to make, make it. Any idea you want to bring to life, believe it is coming to life. When you say something, go forward to follow through with it. Be the person for whom words, thoughts, and actions carry the strongest frequency in external production. If there are results you want, and you see the end result in your mind but find yourself doing the opposite in your physical reality, stop the current frequency you're creating against yourself. Let all of your actions be empowered from your mind. If it is all within you; let it flow out of you and into your life. Let all areas be covered by your empowered mind, which produces empowered action.

The most important thing right now is to be the embodiment of what you think. Your energy will start radiating and attracting to you the state you hold within yourself.

Taking empowered action means your every movement is directed by your mind, and you are doing it intentionally. When action happens in this way, the results are spectacular. Your thought is more potent, and what you command in your mind must follow through physically. You banish all delay and laziness from your physical body. You say it will happen, and it does. You make a goal and see it through. You imagine it, and it manifests. Your inner state becomes your outer state.

This will cause you to receive new ideas for any field in which you find yourself. You'll notice a creative flow as your mind and body become more balanced, allowing those ideas to be acted upon. Everything you do will be a representation of your state of mind. This will shine with passion for what you love, creating opportunities out of nowhere. You'll also notice that you attract people who respect your time and energy as you honor the way you use your life force. This is just natural law; your reality will deeply and instantaneously match your new energy. From this state, the world and people around you will begin to shift to match it. This will all be from a positive, intended state, as you aren't plotting or concerning yourself with how to get rid what doesn't work in your life. You change from within, and it ripples out into the world effortlessly, creating bonds that are meant to be. All of your actions are now empowered from within.

Living Out Your Dream

There is something in your heart right now that wants to come out. Your dreams are still alive, and you will live them out. What do you see for yourself in this ultimate vision? What are your dreams? Having dreams is so vital, as it creates passion in your spirit and energizes you to express yourself. Don't hide from your dreams, as they are yearning to come out from the thought world and into the physical world. Bring your imagined state to life.

When you don't actively engage your mind, you forget that you have vast abilities at your disposal. Since we are in a physical experience, we sometimes get pulled into "seeing is believing." This causes you to use less of your mind, as you aren't dancing with the realm of the imagination. The reason the imagined state is crucial is because you go beyond the tangible and operate in your original state as a co-creator in physical reality. The only thing that continuously changes is your mind—what you believe and how you feel. You have power over your perception and your decision to create out of thin air.

The aliveness of your thought field takes up mental energy and brings it into physical manifestation. As you work more in your imagination and see beyond the physical right in front of you, you allow more to flow into you. Your consciousness is highly receptive to expression, openness, and creation. You'll notice more clever ideas, see instant manifestations, recognize how interconnected everything is, and even begin to create your physical life in the image of your dream.

The way your vision comes into your reality requires trust in the unknown. Work with it.

Every single person should have the ability to dream, as it is our innate way of living in the physical world. Dreams should remain alive. Dreams should be encouraged. Dreams should be supported. When you are creatively alchemizing your inner thoughts and feeling inspiration from your spirit to go for it and believe it into existence, you are doing something profoundly possible. You are using your mind to see beyond what is in front of you, bringing that possibility into physical reality and allowing others to gain the light of hope that there's so much more to life.

When someone questions your dream or wonders why you dream so big, it isn't really something to get defensive about. Remember, activation of the mental world requires constant use of the imagination. When someone doesn't use much of their mind to see bigger and imagine greater, it will seem to them like your vision is something intangible, as they can't see it in the moment you are discussing it. To believe in something you can't see, you have to safeguard your ability to dream. This takes courage, passion, and an inkling that there must be so much more to life. As you gain Thought Access, you will begin to place importance upon your dreams, your imagination, and the way you interact with the physical world from your mental state.

Doing this will change you and alter the way you see life. You'll feel lighter, naturally energized, and deeply passionate, with a rush of undefined happiness. You are tapped in. You are a conduit for higher consciousness and awareness.

As you live out your dreams and actualize your alchemized thoughts in the physical world, you will help other believe in themselves through your creations, your embodiment of the creative expression of consciousness, and the blessings you share with the world. Many people still operate in "seeing it to believe it," and this is where you'll gain so much ease—you won't have to convince anyone of the magic taking place within you. You are sacred, and the way you allow the energy of life to be expressed through you will let you expand beyond imagination. The ability of your entire life to evolve into something magnificent will unfold according to how much of this precious flow you accept, allow, and work with. You are an alchemist transmuting some of the finest thoughts and bringing to life what was once just a vision. Greatness can come through you and impact every area of your life, as the force of light gives and gives endlessly to an open medium.

Bring back the state of being you had as a child that knew anything was possible. The world can't steal your dreams by shutting you down. You are awakened, alive, and have the thought access to retrieve your original state…the time when you really truly believed in something more. This is still within you. Time doesn't steal your dreams, either. Limitations don't determine how big you can dream. To dream is to challenge any kind of thinking that tries to put a cap on your expression. To dream is to reclaim yourself, to love what you are made of, and to dance with the universe as you unapologetically shine your light. This is when you begin to live out your dream, when you believe in yourself and accept that it's meant to be.

Thought Access

Shifting Your Perspective

When you know that it was all within you the whole time, you understand how to shift your perspective at any given moment. You won't be limited by thoughts, as you are always looking for ways to see things from a greater perspective. The information I'll share with you in this section will allow you to stop being controlled by the way things appear so you can create your own perception and shift your perspective in terms of how you see it, respond to it, and interact with it.

When someone holds a viewpoint about something, they will often hold onto that view and defend it with their life. If there are so many ways to potentially see life. With a multitude of ways to respond, why choose this one? When you reflect and get to the root of what emotionally moves you and why you think the way you do, this will bring to the forefront what may have been limiting your scope of reality. Ultimately, the ability to change your perspective at will frees you. Remaining open and curious allows you to loosen up and decide for yourself what you want to be a part of. You are an entire field of your own. You are a bioenergetic being who is alive and active, a participant in reality. You are always receiving data in the form of information through your senses and even intuitively. You must know how to shift your perspective at any given time to receive the benefit of insight.

> *Once your mind changes, nothing around you will ever be or look the same. We're continuously evolving into higher states, breaking down old thought patterns to be renewed and lifted higher. We must shed what we thought we knew to experience something completely transcendental.*

The ability to change your mind at will is a superpower all

its own. So many people want to find familiarity, predictability, and certainty, which can, at times, turn on them, as they tend to keep a person in the same sphere of existence and patterns of thought. Openness of mind allows you to see the subtle aspects of reality and the rich tones of life. You call upon greater forces of the mind when you decide to actually use it. As you awaken and fire up the entire neural network of your brain, you attain awareness you didn't even know was possible. You go from a limited scope of life, in which the world seemed disconnected and distant, to one that brings everything to your fingertips through the power of your mind.

You know everything is connected. You know there's so much more to life. You feel like the world is responding to your thoughts as your mind sends electric signals in the form of telepathy. In what field does this operate? One that doesn't require eyes; it only needs the mind to know it's happening. You are always sending and receiving thoughts. You are always sensing and creating from within. Your new perspective must begin to acknowledge that you are so much more. Your abilities are being activated as you start to remember this innate inner power. Remaining open and curious allows you to explore what is possible.

Don't settle on a belief unless you have experimented with what it can produce in your life: wellness, enrichment, expansion, abundance, peace, openness, flow, and a natural state of love. So many people believe in things that cause them to remain restricted. This creates imbalance, as the life force flowing into you isn't being utilized to the max.

You never want to hold two contradictory thoughts. You were created to always have access, understanding, and insight from within. You never have to search for these kinds of answers or do anything unusual to your natural state in order to receive. Are you doing anything extra to breathe the air that is so abundantly flowing into your body? Do you think of what you must manipulate so you can receive more or less? Effortlessness is the way. It all just is. Remembering that will bring you ease. You don't need to force anything on yourself, especially when it is something or someone that tries to dim your light or make you question your worth. Let every belief represent greater for you. If something isn't working for you, uproot it. Go back to the thought from which it stemmed and free yourself from it. Shifting your perspective liberates you!

What You Accept and What You Allow

Your whole being represents your thought field. The things you attract say something about you. Your experiences are all connected and reveal truth. The people, situations, and things circulating in your world are pulled in through your own mind and actions according to what you accept and allow. Every single thing starts within you, and to take your power back at this new level, you have to be very honest with yourself about your own state of being. Personal alignment is more crucial than trying to figure out *who* is causing you a problem or *what* situation has you stuck. Alignment only happens when there is inner agreement in thought, action, and emotional response, which ends up moving the entire world around to set up your life movie. The stage is created, and the characters show up to play out the roles of your thoughts. This is as simple as it gets.

I want you to be empowered from within. I want you to be aware instead of spending another second of your energy trying to decipher the hidden behaviors and patterns of the minds of others. It's not about requiring things from others. It's about stepping into your own divine being and letting the forces of nature align you with your greatest vision. It happens quickly, as you haven't wasted energy overthinking situations or trying to move scenes around by force. You know better now. You take the inner steps first and watch your outer world shift.

When you change yourself, you go to the quantum level and alter your own personal field. This frequency change travels through the unseen and begins the recreation of your new reality with new opportunities and connections. This is the most profound thing you'll ever see or experience. You didn't even have to do anything extra. You simply decided to change your mind and see a new vision for your life. What happens next is that the frequency you are now radiating becomes a calling, and just as it brings plenty of wonderful changes, it also, in the most natural way, removes connections that no longer work, as you are sending a different signal now.

The past state can't respond any longer to the new field, as it has been altered. The original host for those energies and thoughts is no longer the center for the previous attraction. Everything gets rearranged. Whatever and whoever must now begin to match the new frequency, or a quick change will take place that creates a disconnection. You are the host of your own energy, and knowing this makes you aware that you choose with your mind what you allow and tolerate. You choose the signals you send out into the world. You no longer have to explain or go into breakdowns about any situation in which you find yourself. You shift and maneuver onto your new path consciously. New thoughts emanate from you, and this attracts pleasant experiences to match.

There's a bigger purpose for your life. There's still so much within you that's getting ready to manifest.

Your story can change now. Your situation can change now. Your heart can be healed now. Pave a new path for yourself. Be fully present and make the choice. You can longer be emotionally drained by living in a mental world that has already came to an end. You are, right now, in control of your life. You have the power in your hands at this moment to completely create a new life for yourself. The choice you make has no option but to come through you, as you are an intelligent being who is alive enough to actually choose a life filled with peace, openness, and genuine happiness. You can't be swayed by the ebb and flow of reality as it appears to be. You are the center and the point where the light shines out to be able to receive back.

Take really good care of this inner you, and never let anyone steal the hope of your dreams. The promise of your future is right now. So much is possible for you, and you feel this and deeply know that your story isn't over. Right now, the chance of things going the way you want is 100 percent a reality. You never have to carry the mental and emotional baggage of what was. Right now, you can decide what it will be. You are free from it all, and that is the power you have. You choose, and you decide from this moment forward what stays, what enters, and what continues.

The Effects of Remembering Your Inner Power

There are many effects you'll start to notice after reading this book and remembering your inner power. You'll have a new sense of understanding about who you are and what you know is actually possible for you. You will become more mentally aware, and your life will change in miraculous ways as you receive the energy embedded in every word. You'll see actual results. You'll see yourself at peace, without having to do anything extra to be so. You are just in a peaceful state because it is available to you now. You'll see that you don't have to try so hard anymore to bend or force reality to respond to you. It just does, and you know it's always assisting to you. There is ease in your creative process because you are in the magical flow.

> *Believe in yourself so much that you naturally become magnetic to all that you want to attract.*

Most of what you'll witness already existed before we created imagined hurdles to stand between where we are and where we want to be. Old states of being begin to seem so distant, with their obstacles and restrictive ideas surrounding attainment. You don't even operate in that state anymore. You know that what you believe will happen *is happening*. You know you are connected and can manifest anything you want. You know this is your dream, and your entire reality obviously supports it. Your imagination will be free again to create, to dream, and to make what is in your heart come to life. You will be highly intuitive and work with your senses, as many insights will come to fruition right when you need them. The effects of *Thought Access* are very powerful, as it gives you a mental link to the vast possibilities within you right now.

Mental Changes

As you begin to understand your mental world more clearly and discover through actual experience how powerful your thoughts are, you will begin to elevate in your mindset, entering a frequency of thought that is much stronger toward the positive nature of reality. It will seem as if you have finally tuned in, and for some reason, you have become highly aware of the great, the good, and the positive surrounding you and within you. This elevated mental state is solution-oriented, hopeful, optimistic, and trusting. You are a believer in possibilities. You'll be so surprised and in awe to know that small changes in your mind have led to greater awareness and attraction.

You'll become a thought leader, since your mind is connected to the vastness of what is possible. Within your own body, you now hold such consciousness. When you are ready, the capacity of greater consciousness can also be expressed through you. This can be ideas, creative expression, inventions, mass changes, personal changes, and even enriching thoughts for everyday experiences. You'll notice that a lot of what changes in our lives is what takes place within us. You notice every single time that any form of change that has happened in your life was a mental one first that manifested into the physical.

A powerful mindset will be very important during this time. The mental changes you'll experience reading this book will support your emotional health, your greater vision, and the certainty that your dreams are actually feasible. This is your private space to take the necessary time to become your own inner architect. You are the one who builds yourself up. Using this tool, you'll be able to masterfully design, create, alter, and express at will what you feel to be right for you.

As much as we have shared realities, we are also living from within our own reality, which is unknown to others. When you go back in and remember this, you stop wasting so much time trying to be liked, understood, or even forcing any form of connection. You become all that you have dreamed of, and the match to your new frequency finds you. The healthy person who has spent time getting to know who they are and better understand what they truly want is ready to share the beauty with others. Simply being yourself will radiate and shine that light into the field of existence. The effects of your mental changes ripple into the realm of existence. You are sending signals and communicating energetically what you want and who you are.

Emotional Changes

You will find that you have become much more stable emotionally. You have learned how to manage your responses and the way you receive intuitively. You do this by checking in with your feelings. As you change your mental state and shift your entire perspective on your life, you'll find that your emotions begin to serve greater insight, which is about instinctively knowing and intuitively receiving. You're not worried about your response to the world around you; the extra-sensory genius within you signals everything you need to know. If you have been using your emotions to respond to how things appear instead of receiving from your guiding compass within, you'll now remember how to tap back in.

When you get clear about what triggers you or brings up emotions, you'll notice that it is either an insight or some kind of reaction to something you have seen. Reactions are usually programs from the outside that you have attached to feelings/words. Each time you see or hear that particular thing that triggers you, it creates an emotional response within you, and this influences your thoughts to experience more of that state. You can end that loop by deciding to uproot the words that trigger you and/or the behavior that pushes you to the edge. You are so much more emotionally intelligent now, and you know, even better than before, that you cannot be bothered or shaken up by the simple use of a word. You have evolved past your triggers, and you are really, truly reclaiming your inner freedom through awareness and growth.

> *Take it easy on yourself. You're doing all you can. Remember to give yourself credit for how far you've come. You're very strong, and you have what it takes within you to continue to prosper in every way. Just keep believing that it's all working in your favor.*

You are naturally designed to receive insight from your emotions and feelings. A lot of people still, when it comes to gut feelings, know things before they happen, and sense that something is happening without knowing exactly how. This is all inner communication taking place. When we depend upon our inner intelligence to emotionally guide us, we receive the insight we need, and we are shown the way we are supposed to move. We understand the decisions we are meant to make.

Since you know so much more than you think you do, you become accustomed to allowing yourself to receive insight instead of using your emotions to react to external storylines. You'll eventually find a healthy balance between what feels right and what you need to do about it. The answers are all there. You're getting better at understanding yourself and working with your own energy field, and this allows you direct access at any time. Remember, up to this point, you have been using previous knowledge to experience the reality you are experiencing. Any further change will require you to start receiving new insights and thoughts in order to expand your access.

I morph into my desired state by embodying it.

You are coming alive, and this new sense of lucidity and awakening to your adventure is very exciting. You'll start to recognize that much of the way you habitually responded to the world around you in the past kept you emotionally fatigued. It was externally dependent, and not yet guided by your inner power outside of the five senses. You are highly intelligent being, and you may have been accessing only just enough to survive on all levels.

As you start to gain Thought Access, you'll recognize a complete shift in your emotions and the way you process feelings. You'll know almost everything you need to know intuitively. You'll accept that your senses aren't limited to what you can see. You are becoming more open, and this naturally, with ease, prepares you to gain clarity on much of what is happening in your life. You won't be as reactive or controlled by what appears to be happening. You'll observe, and in this way, you'll know what you need to do right when you need to do it.

Much of what am discussing has already started taking place within you, as your mind is receptive right now to every word. This creates a mental change that begins to elevate you emotionally so you aren't still playing in a field of ups and downs.

There's a natural contentment about you now, because you know that ebbs and flows are supposed to be observed. The insight you receive from within in your state of observation is the solution to everything that appears to be happening. The ability to remain centered and calm during your external observation of any situation that might arise allows you to maintain awareness to respond consciously instead of getting pulled into the drama and action taking place.

Don't assume that you are the same person you were before you picked up this book. At every second, you are consciously expanding. This allows you the freedom to be undefined by anything that has happened in your life, previously or even a moment ago. This alone will bring you emotional peace, and, naturally, thoughts that used to be associated with negative emotions will be cleansed. You don't have the same emotional responses anymore.

One thing I will share with you is that right now, you have the freedom, through your mind and your choices, to change your perspective, destiny, and path. Nothing ties you to a certain personality or characteristic or trait. You aren't limited to one form of expression, or even one outlook. You are a multidimensional being operating in the physical and spiritual realms all at the same time. You have awareness that's beyond what you can see, and you integrate this naturally throughout your day-to-day life.

What keeps many people trapped is the idea that they have to remain who everyone thinks they are. Your career can change, your passion can change, your relationships can change, your choices can change; even what you believe in can change. The point of this insight is to embrace the natural flexibility of your mind and inner expression. Don't hide from your gift by remaining the same out of comfort for others or even the spaces you once inhabited. If you feel like this is the time to make a change, go for it. Any inner urge that persistently arises with deep passion, any sense of fire that drives you to be all that you can be...follow through. This is your chance to experience the beautiful effects of being emotionally attuned to your soul's calling.

Physical Changes (Body)

There are great benefits for the body as you experience the effects of remembering your inner power. You'll start to understand and see the link between your mind and body. In previous times, you probably didn't analyze the connection of your thought energy and the way it quickly alters your physical biofield. Your body is intelligent, and it's always doing everything it can to remain in balance. When negative thoughts pervade or pessimistic thoughts enter, you can instantly see how the body moves from strength to weakness. This is why is it so important for you to gain Thought Access, as you will break free from the trance of not knowing who you are and what is actually happening to you. Your mental and emotional changes have a profound impact on your body. You no longer experience restriction, stress, worry, or overthinking. Energy begins to flow throughout your body, and this causes physical wellness that's naturally in harmony with your greater expression. You have already witnessed how optimal you are physically when you are happy, grateful, and optimistic about life.

Your mental and emotional state either pulls in more life force or restricts the flow. You always want to be flowing, expressing, believing in yourself, and hopeful about everything in your life. Awareness of your own empowerment and freeing yourself from unwanted thought forms instantly alter your body, and you feel a new sense of motivation and inspiration to make physical changes. You'll find yourself wanting to eat better, nurture yourself, do more of what you love, tune into the positive nature of reality, and simply let yourself be all that you know you are. There is a balance between mind and body that reflects your vibrancy of wellness.

> *I will direct my attention, focus, and time toward what expands me, evolves me, and grows me on all levels. I am owning my greatness from this moment on.*

Energy is everything, and one of the most important things you'll understand from this book is the power of your entire biofield. You'll know how to balance your energy by allowing it to flow freely through you. You'll prioritize your inner wellness while naturally shifting and elevating to all that you are. Your mental and emotional states influence you energetically, and this affects the strength and vibrancy of your physical body. This is the most crucial change you will experience. As your biofield is strengthened, you will have more energy to manifest, experience life, and create your dream. You will be a center of inner wellness, and this will radiate outward into the field, sending a signal of increased life force. This will attract more of the frequency you're in. You'll begin to make choices that support your overall wellness and health. You'll do more of the things you love, and this will naturally create a stress-free internal world. You are prioritizing your overall mental and emotional health, which trickles down to optimal health for your physical body.

You must begin to look at what makes you feel unwanted states in your body. Is it what you are eating? Is it what you are thinking? Is it fear? Is it how you talk to yourself? Is it a limited perception of your own potential? Everyone knows exactly what they need to change.

Your body has been communicating with you about what you need to quit or stop doing. The communication comes in a feeling of being out of balance. Don't normalize ignoring the signs and signals your intelligent body is conveying to you. The signals you're receiving from your body are biofeedback to let you know what is working and what isn't. Listen to yourself and follow your own signs. You'll see that finally quitting or starting what you have been delaying causes a large amount of energy to enter while clearing out unwanted states from your entire field. Ignoring your own insights is detrimental to your conscious advancement.

This new way of living closes the time gap between your thought and when you follow through with it. In previous times, it seemed normal to experience delays between your words and your actions, as you didn't yet know the great power that you are. This trained your will to be less potent than it truly is. Now, your are highly activated and incredibly potent, so your words, intentions, and state of mind instantly influence your actions, choices, and outcomes. You're not clueless or confused anymore. You are aware and conscious. You are in charge of your inner world and how you manage your mind, body, and spiritual expression. Your inner empowerment will represent the magic of your life.

Embodying Your Magic

The time has come for you to represent your inner world in every area of your life. Embodying your magic will be about living in mental, emotional, spiritual, and physical alignment. You are staying true to who you are and shining that out into the world. The new reality that is emerging from you will be one of inner radiance, one that represents your harmonious balance. You have to know and deeply understand the statement that *you already are*. This means that it was all within you this whole time. Only you can gain access by remembering that everything arises from you. You can decide on anything you want right now by bringing it into your imagination and owning it from within using your entire consciousness. You are the one who creates the reality you want, alters what you no longer deem necessary, and transforms any state of mind at will.

This is what embodying your magic is all about. You take the power back into your hands, as the world you are focusing on and constantly responding to is a projection of your inner ideas, beliefs, and expectations. It is no coincidence at all that your reality has manifested in this way. When you accept this and start to really gain the awareness you need to rise out of the slumber of believing things are "just happening" to you, you take back the very power you have been using to create all of it. You have an inner knowing and a deep desire to be free, open, and filled with passion to change your path. You begin to consciously identify the thoughts that have been running your show and the attitude you have been holding. Go into a state of inner assessment and revamp your inner world so you are prepared to remove the filters that have been creating your images and experiences.

Embodying your magic is being true to yourself and what rises up from within your spirit. Only you know what is in in your heart and what you deeply wish to express. You are the one who can represent who you truly are and how you view yourself. Never let disharmony exist between what you feel is possible and what the world tries to tell you about yourself.

People feel it when someone is awakening to their inner power. They see the passion in your eyes. They feel the dream being birthed from you. They see your energy change, and they feel it. This is what embodying your inner magic does. It speaks to the world that you are standing in your truth and living boldly from that state. You'll never again be someone who can be swayed left and right by limiting views or negative opinions. You'll never again be hurt, bothered, or disappointed by what anyone thinks or says about you.

Thought Access

Being consistently positive eventually turns into a habit. You'll find yourself being naturally optimistic and hopeful no matter what is happening within you or around you.

You are now operating as an awakened being who knows that all is projected outward, and what is heard, seen, or felt on the outside must go through your inner guard to determine if it is worthy of your precious energy. You shall go forward now and claim power over your inner world. You do this by freeing yourself from emotional attachments you have made to words that don't represent how you see yourself. This is the greatest moment of your life, as you have received a vital insight that will save you so much reactive energy. Instead, you will be an attractor of a new way of being. As you start to be all you want to be, your entire way of living and looking at life will be transformed to match your inner view.

Another important thing to know is that your energy will increase massively as you release resistance to your authentic expression. When you're not embodying your magic, you tend to think there is a separation between who you actually are from within and who you portray yourself to be. This can include feeling and thinking one way about yourself on the inside and expecting the world to treat you the opposite of how you feel about yourself. You are projecting that inner energy outward, and people, no matter the distance, can feel what you embody.

Your inner world is constantly sending signals and creating alignments that match what you are embodying. No amount of external pretension can do that. You should be in harmony. This is what creates balance as your inner world matches your external world. You don't want to train your mind to be fragmented. You are a whole being, generated by the amount of energy you freely allow to flow through you. This can apply to many areas of your life. Keeping your heart open is a crucial one, as you don't want past pain to be recreated every day through reaffirmations or memories that are being repeated/replayed now.

I want you to be at peace so you can give yourself the abundance of opportunity that each moment holds. You are free from it all now. A creativity spike will be another sign. When you are embodying your magic and being true to yourself, a surplus of energy flows into your mind and body that will give you inexplicable blessings for your business, passion, home, health, and relationships. Right now, in this moment, you have vast potential available to you. The degree to which you can access it will depend upon how freely you live in your mind and heart. You don't want to hold onto pain, grudges, pessimistic thoughts, or negative ideas about yourself or the world. You don't want to blame anyone or any situation, as you only give your power away when you let someone or something have a say in the way you move. At each moment during the removal of a mental or emotional attachment that represents a limiting point of view for you, you will notice a sense of lightness in your mind and body. The energy is no longer stagnant. You are freely moving and thinking, directly connecting yourself to the vast potential available to you right now.

You now understand the importance of your energy and your mindset. You know that there is an abundance of energy available for you to further tap into as you begin to radiate your light in the most magnificent way. When you're aware, you start to do everything differently. You action is aligned with your mindset and the places you see yourself going. You have inner trust, and it shines out of you while miraculously creating exactly what you need, right when you need it.

All of this originates in your own mind and your own beingness. Being authentically you and living from your heart will allow you to do, be, and experience everything you love. People will start to recognize your light and the undeniable impact you have, simply by being you. This is the blessing of being harmoniously balanced from within. You will find yourself manifesting really quickly, as you believe that anything is possible for you. Everything you touch will be golden as you prevail in amazing areas of your life you never could have imagined.

Key Points to Remember

- *All of this stems from within you. You are always interacting with reality and the outer world in one powerful way: YOU ARE IMPACTING IT. Through your mind right now, you are impacting every single thing in your life. Your mind is working for you.*

- *Everything you see originated in someone's imagination, and these imagined thoughts have now become physical manifestations. We are surrounded by a sea of thoughts that appear to be in a physical state. If we don't yet remember that everything comes from the imagination, and that what we are seeing now is ideas at work, we may fall into the assumption that everything is only "physical" in nature.*

- *Consciousness can only expand at the capacity of the medium holding it. You are the medium through which energy expresses itself. As you begin to expand your mind and demand more for your life, your consciousness expands exponentially.*

- *When you depend on your mind to create the way, it does so in the easiest, most unexpected and synchronized manner. It connects the dots globally and sends the message into the network faster, returning what you desire back to you in ways you could never imagine.*

- *As you start becoming more inner-dependent, you'll notice your confidence going up and your sense of self-trust increasing. You'll start becoming the person who* just knows everything is happening as it should and that it will work out accordingly. You never go against yourself. You have inner intelligence, and you are actively connected to that flow.

- *To be self-aware is to build yourself up from within. To lack self-awareness is to appear one way on the outside but feel another way on the inside that doesn't match the frequency you intend to display. Self-awareness is also being true to yourself, your energy state, and the balance of your inner and outer worlds.*

- *You are the observer here, and you have great power in your hands. Be very aware of this and remain diligent. Be conscious and concise with your actions. The thought field doesn't judge the state you were in a second ago, or even yesterday; it just responds to you moment by moment. You are the one who must create a new opportunity to produce a new outcome.*

- *Every single person should have the ability to dream, as it is our innate way of living in the physical world. Dreams should remain alive. Dreams should be encouraged. Dreams should be supported.*

- *The ability to change your mind at will is a superpower all its own.*

- *Your whole being represents your thought field. The things you attract make a statement about that. Your experiences are all connected and reveal the truth. The people, situations, and things circulating in your world are pulled in through your mind; actions and events follow according to what you accept and allow.*

- *You will find that you have become much more stable emotionally, and have learned how to manage your responses. You receive intuitively by checking in with*

Thought Access

your feelings. As you change your mental state and shift your entire perspective on life, you'll find that your emotions actually serve a greater purpose: instinctively knowing and intuitively receiving.

- *The time has come for you to represent your inner world in every area of your life. Embody your magic by staying in mental, emotional, spiritual, and physical alignment. You are staying true to who you are and shining it out into the world.*

- *Embodying your magic is being true to yourself and what rises up from within your spirit. Only you know what is in in your heart and what you deeply wish to express. You are the one who can represent who you truly are and how you view yourself. Never allow disharmony between what you feel is possible and what the world tries to tell you about yourself.*

4

PERCEPTION: TRUE SELF VS. CONSTRUCTED SELF

Your perception is the way you use your mind to perceive the world around you while creating your own unique interpretation of everything. You are the one who constructs your entire reality, and if you didn't consciously know that up until this point, you'll have a deeply empowered realization that everything begins with you. You will take your power back and own who you truly are. Your true self is free, unbounded; a dreamer, a higher consciousness, intuitive, and instinctive. Your higher self knows anything is possible, and goes after what you want based on the vision you have received.

Your true self is multidimensional. Your true self is a manifestor, creator, and spirit who intentionally brings into the physical your gifts from within. Your true self is your true state. The constructed self is created by society to act, think, and feel a certain way that's limited to "seeing it to believe it." The constructed self is controlled by emotions and the world as it appears to be. The constructed self has a limiting point of view of what is possible and is tethered to the physical world alone, thinking that what is real exists only on the outside. Lack of awareness of one's own reality can make life seem unbearable, a case of ups and downs without any wisdom about one's own path.

It's time to realize. It's time to know. All of this will be clearly explained in this chapter. You will identify the thoughts and

Perception: True Self vs. Constructed Self

beliefs currently running your life. You'll gain Thought Access to an expanded state of consciousness that allows you to see your true state as who you actually are. Your true self is present right now, reading this. When limiting concepts are removed from your consciousness and negative thoughts are cleared, your true self rises up. You become alert. Your awareness is activated, and you become lucid in your experience.

The self you believe you can become is the self you always were.

This chapter will further help you discover how to alter your perception and free yourself from previous limiting thoughts. You will expand your current awareness to see more, feel more, and connect with the unlimited possibilities of consciousness available to you. The way you see the world is so unique to you, but this has actually been constructed *by* you based upon what you believe, what you have been exposed to, and what you think is possible.

You can change your mind. You can free yourself from any perspective you feel no longer works for you. It can be easy to assume that things are just the way they are, or that they might not drastically change in a positive way. The truth is, you can experience something profoundly magical and magnificent at any given moment. When you leave the perception of time and the way it previously operated in your life, you free up the energy of expectation. You untie your mind from that timeline. In reality, everything can happen for you now. You will be stunned to discover some of the wonderful insights in this chapter, as they will take your mind to another level. Remember, what you believe is what you experience on a moment-to-moment basis. This statement will go much deeper as you approach the end of this book and as you begin to see all that will take place around you.

Imagine someone walking through life and not know-ing the connection they have, the spirit they are, or the power they possess. Deep down, they have the code, but something made them forget. Only a reminder can reactivate them in their adventure of life. When they came into physical reality, they were born with this gift, and they were very imaginative, open, loving, and curious. They had great power within them and they knew it. Anything was possible for this soul, and life appeared to be an adventure to take on. There was immense wonder as the body adjusted to the physical nature of reality. They began to interact with the world around them.

The memory this person carried was that they knew they were a soul, not just a body. This allowed great expression of their essence. They knew their mind could create their reality, as the inner world was the main place the outer world was experienced. They knew life was just an experience, and they would journey away to so much more when it all came to an end. Knowing this provided them with peace and acceptance, as they knew they were a spirit in a physical body. They knew nothing was personal or serious, so they always found inner solutions for external circumstances. They were fearless, determined, and full of passion. They never allowed the solid nature of the physical world to overtake their memory that everything was energy at its core. They knew they were multidimensional and that their mind could penetrate the field to create, design, manifest, and experience anything they imagined.

The possibilities of who you can be today aren't defined by who you once were. What you can access in this moment is built from dreaming, visualizing, and imagining what can be, not what was. You can give birth to something completely new, and that potential is just as real.

The possibilities were vast for this great spirit, and so much of life was seen from a greater perspective. This gave them the freedom to alter their own path at will. The change they experienced in remembering who they were allowed healing to instantly take place. They knew they were vast and expansive, so accessing that thought memory allowed them to mentally, physically, emotionally, and spiritually feel a lifetime of healing, forgiveness, and understanding. They had the valuable insight to write their life story at any given moment.

They also knew that change was their greatest tool. As more revelations and realizations occurred, they would return to knowing that they could completely be, do, and experience anything they wanted through the power of choice. They were never limited to any previous timelines, ideas, or concepts they felt they had outgrown or already learned from. They deeply knew all of this, so choosing to consistently move forward saved them energy for new experiences instead of prolonging repetitive lessons and mentally dwelling in a previous experience when they were no longer there physically. They knew that the present held great potential, and that they could decide upon a new outcome right now. This is what made the spirit enjoy the adventure. They had many inner tools at their disposal for any life situation, and they maneuvered through all experiences with awareness.

This is who you are. You are the great spirit. You are the one with all these inner tools and awareness. *Thought Access* is meant to activate this reminder within you so you can go about your adventure as you originally intended. This will be your guide, your reminder, and your gift to start living as a powerful spirit who knows you're so much more. Your memory of your inner knowing will be activated by reading this book, and you will completely take back your attention, your focus, your energy, your mind, and your power to believe in yourself.

The Power of Perception

You currently perceive reality from a state of who you believe

Thought Access

you are. This can be ideas you have about the world around you, what you believe in, and everything you have thought about yourself up to this point. That concept is a perceived reality; every time you change your mind or perspective on anything in your life, reality changes. Perception isn't a final state. It is something that's constantly changing as you are evolving, growing, and getting to know yourself daily.

The point of understanding the power of perception is to avoid being limited by holding onto one way of seeing everything. You are the one who has, up to this point in your life, been observing all that has been taking place. You can truly say that you have remained in a state of being while changing your perception in many ways. A viewpoint you once held is no longer valid to you, because you have discovered a reason to discard one way of looking at the world that no longer serves your new awareness.

The ability to understand that you perceive everything through a chosen scope gives you back the power to change your mind and alter your path to your liking. This insight is meant to liberate you mentally so you don't remain stuck in a fixed mindset that could be tainting your grander vision of life. The true power of perception is knowing that it can be changed. The way you perceive things influences what you see in the external world and creates your experience to match what you desire to see.

Changing the way you see things is the start of seeing things change.

Perception influences everything—not only the way you see the world, but how the world sees you. You can create the perception people have of you by becoming who you want to be and letting that self-creation work in your favor. This can easily become a state of being: living authentically according to who you actually are. You gain the power of clear vision as well as the ability to change your outlook about anything at any given time.

Perception: True Self vs. Constructed Self

Where you give your attention and how you define your focus…these two elements work together to create every perception you hold. You may also have developed perceptions about what it means to be you and what you define as successful. You have ideas about what you consider valuable and worthy, and this creates a perception from which to view the world. Most of the time, there is one area from your past that clouds the way you currently view the world around you. Someone may have shared their negative perception or view of the world with you, and instead of rejecting limitation, you adopted the other person's experiences as some kind of insight for our own path. This is absolutely unnecessary, and it can be identified and changed once you are aware that you no longer have to see life from a scope of limitation.

The core of who you are is magical and magnificent. You have access to a broader view, greater understanding, and deeper connection. You soul already knows. These natural states show themselves to you when you need them the most. When you really need a breakthrough, you receive it. When you ask for guidance, it shows up. When you feel you can't make it through, the light shines for you. When you are pulled out of your outer perception of the world and instead inhabit a place of unity within your soul, you allow natural surrender, trust, and knowledge to take place.

When you stop burdening yourself with the weight of needing answers or demanding change, you open yourself up to greater knowledge, which lifts you out of your worldview and helps you drop perceptual filters. You expand yourself and actually see that there is so much more that can flow in and happen for you. You are the one who is connected. You have to stop playing pretend that you aren't this magnificent soul who actually has the access and the connection. It is just who you are. Your senses can see more accurately through the imagination. Your body feels through intuition. You mind deals with ideas, visions, and thoughts. None of these can be physically seen, but most of your life is spent in these inner fields which correspond with the world around you.

You are asking your own mind to construct for you what you believe. Any ideas you have are going to be true in your world because you hold a belief about them. The world around you matches that energy really fast. Your attention right now is on something, and that one thing you are focused on seems to be gaining more life, as you are giving it actual life force to sustain its existence. You are an energy generator, and this energy is used by you at will according to what you focus on, what you talk about, what you read, what you share, and what you allow to keep going. This can go in a positive or negative direction depending on the results you predetermine.

Seeing Yourself in a New Way

You choose how you see yourself, and you have the power right now to change your image, the way you feel about yourself, and what you believe is worthy of your life experience. You are free right now to write a new story about your life and turn things in your favor. Your mind supports new suggestions, thoughts, and ways of being. You might not realize it, but every change you make within yourself—even a simple thought—creates a ripple effect that instantly begins the alteration of reality. The world around you will begin to work to bring you new thoughts about your life. A mindset of seeing yourself as greater influences the way the field responds to you and wants to give to you. This starts to bring new people into your life who are meant to help you on your mission to follow your own inner calling. Your purpose and passion are revealed to you, which causes you to move differently. It is crucial that you know your own power through your awareness to constantly choose to see life in a new way. You're not stuck or limited. You're not what people think of you or the inner doubts that might make you question your new changes. You are so much more, and with every step forward, you begin to embrace seeing life from a greater state instead of from your current mindset or the circumstances that appear to be happening around you.

> *Things are happening more quickly for you. What you affirm, you receive. What you intend, you experience. What you believe, you manifest.*

You are now gaining inner power and momentum to alter your path at will, and this gives you reassurance that you do have a choice. You can live, feel, think, and do things differently. Before I begin to give you the insight and guidance to remove limiting concepts from your field, I want you to understand what kind of access you are gaining. You are receiving mental freedom to make any choice you want about your life. You are receiving great power in your hands to alter your life in the most conscious state possible. You are aware that you aren't confined, limited, or held by the past. You are aware that you have freedom of choice. You are aware that multiple outcomes are available to you. Choosing to be empowered instantly gives you access to your highest good.

No matter what has occurred in your life or what is happening right now, there is one promise and one vital thing to understand: Everything can change in your favor. You can be lifted from the darkest times and find yourself in a world of unexplainable joy, happiness, understanding, and connection. You can heal your heart, your mind, and yourself from anything through the power of declaration, intention, awareness, and seeing yourself in a new way. You are the signal generator of the new reality you choose to see for yourself.

Knowing this right now has already altered your path. You know you have immense power to make a change. You know that it all begins in your mind and trickles out into the universe, your body, and the field surrounding you, and this literally reshapes how you see things, what you attract, what you begin to think, and how you start to feel about yourself. When you don't understand the depth of this insight, you just become a responder to external influences instead of an active participant in creating your inner and outer state. You can't allow appearances to dictate your worldview or the way you see yourself. You must design, create, choose, and manifest intentionally and diligently.

Affirm: I choose to look for the good, the positive, the opportunities, the blessings, the lessons, and guidance in all situations. My perspective is more important than what's happening. I choose to shift how I see things instead of allowing myself to be controlled by everything.

Seeing yourself in a new way creates the perception the world has of you. What story are you constantly telling yourself and others about your life? What inner state are you projecting, thereby attracting the same to yourself? How do you see yourself? I want you to be in harmony from within so you can live in a balanced state in which your inner and outer worlds match. The way for this to be done is to take control of your narrative, your story, your thoughts, your expression, your wishes, your desires, and your passion for life. You have to stop acting like someone who is merely responding to how things are or appear to be. You must be the master creator, the initiator, the knower, and the conscious participant in your life. Don't leave anything up to chance or assume that the outcome or circumstances are final. You are the one who is using your mind right now, projecting into the world all that you assume about it. Why not assume only best-case scenarios for what you want? Why not be the one who speaks power over every situation, who alters your own path through your own will and choice?

Perception: True Self vs. Constructed Self

Later in the book, I'll teach you many ways to access greater levels of who you are. Access truly depends on what you know is possible. What you know is possible is linked to what you experience, and that starts in your mind. It becomes a ripple effect for mind interaction with matter. This produces tangible results, which, in turn, enhance your trust in your own power to create your reality. Sometimes, based on the needs of your day-to-day life or your primary focus, you can unconsciously keep your life force busy with what appears to be happening all around you instead of the layers of possibility inherent to your own mind and outcomes. This lesson will be of great service to humanity as you step into your inner power. You become free of fear; you are free of being controlled by limited structures of reactions that try to direct your focus in a mechanical way. You are multidimensional. You are more than just your physical body, and with this awareness, you will access greater thought, higher inspiration, and ascended insight.

Constructed Self

You are the one who creates yourself, but when you don't know your true self, you take in what the external world tells you about who you are. When you think of anything limiting that tries to define your life, that is the constructed self. Your true self is free of these concerns, but when the mind is captured by thoughts of limitation, fear, uncertainty, judgement, or anything that removes your power to understand who you really are, that is the constructed self created by the world around you. It only appears to be solid and real.

The freedom of your soul can't be confined by ideas or thoughts. You are so much more, and you are breaking free right now from anything that steals your confidence or makes you doubt yourself. Any form of self-doubt or low self-esteem comes from thoughts that aren't really yours. These thoughts have been handed down by people or experiences that lack any form of awareness of their own true self. The problem is, through conditioning or repetition of a state, we begin to assume that this is reality.

You have great power in your hands, and that is the power to change, alter your life, and create yourself. Without any awareness of how you mentally, physically, emotionally, and spiritually operate, you end up being stuck in what you have seen, which appears increasingly normal through interaction with others. You might put too much value on words alone. What you need to realize is that you can't create yourself from the ideas, thoughts, and beliefs of others. You must go on the path of understanding and self-discovery yourself. You are you for a reason, and when you put yourself in the background and overvalue the ways the world defines you, you operate in a constructed self, not your true self.

Don't internalize external noise. Stay clear, aware, and connected to your own inner guiding compass. Use discernment as needed, and trust that what you feel is a reoccurring sign for you to follow through. You know when you know.

So many different energies are trying to tell you what you should be, how you should act, and the way you should think. Nothing is taking into consideration the core of your existence and the vast potential beaming out of you. Potential can only be externally understood by others who operate in their true self—people who can shine light on you and thereby experience the greater nature of your existence. The constructed self is simply constructed thoughts that say, "This is your capacity, this is your limit, this is all you can do, and this is how far you'll go." It can also be thoughts that define you by saying, "You are a victim, you are your past, you are stuck, you are always going to be this way."

These ideas are not true at all. This is an accepted state of mind from which one can continue to operate without even questioning

PERCEPTION: TRUE SELF VS. CONSTRUCTED SELF

if it is true. So many people lose their dreams this way, remaining stagnant just because of the power of a suggestion made to them at one point in time. When others share a limiting view on the world, they are simply saying, "I operate in a constructed reality in which I see and experience limitations." They are trying to share that lens with you so you will start seeing life from that frame, as well. The truth is, it's just a perspective, a filter that takes over their mind in the illusion that life is "just the way it is" for them. The most crucial understanding is that this perspective isn't reality. The way someone sees the world through their mind and experience does not at all define your potential. Any negativity, fear, or limitation shared by another should never be used to measure one's own potential.

Don't let people tell you to be "realistic" when tell them your dreams. Other people's limited ideas of what is possible shouldn't limit your creativity, imagination, or visions of what you want. What's real is what you believe in, not what others think. Go forward and create.

People easily share their thoughts, opinions, energy, and outlook without taking into consideration the value or impact of what they are sharing. Everyone, to an extent, is impressionable, as truth is often perceived according to what they have heard or been told in the past instead of what they have intuitively felt, sensed, or seen for themselves. When your mind is impressionable, you can be constructed through suggestions, which can happen unknowingly. A perfect example is constantly being reminded that something is "not possible." Initially, the suggestion is made and even repeated; later, it becomes a random thought in your mind.

Suggestions like these in your family, your circle of friends, or in conversation can initially seem innocent until you find yourself operating from that state of mind. This is how mental viruses get passed around. It's just a form of limitation that people don't question and assume to be true.

Nothing is true about limitation. Nothing is real about words that don't expose you to the magnificent nature of your own existence. Your true self is so much more than the idea of something being impossible. The construction of a limited mindset produces limited people, who then go around spreading that idea as normal. Nothing about it is normal. You have the power to know this and be free of it. The whole point of *Thought Access* is to give you the tools to decipher impressions, make your own suggestions, and override all negative thoughts instantly. You will be a mind warrior, a supernatural human aware of your own mental state. You will know how to read energy, run your own show, and live consciously and intentionally. Nothing and nobody can run your life. By the end of this book, you will have mastered your own inner world.

All previous experiences that have constructed you to exist in worry or any kind of fear are now null and void. Anything and anyone that tried to break down your worth or manipulate your self-esteem to construct you as a desperate person is now exiting your mental and physical sphere. All ideas of what you "can't" do are vanishing as new paths begin to emerge in your life. You are seeing much more clearly. You are understanding concepts of limitation and how it all operates. Your freedom begins with your awareness. How far you can go depends on your mindset and what you know. This is what makes *Thought Access* very powerful; the insights shared here are meant to support your transformation, realization, and change. The ability to identify what is actually taking place allows your mind to make links and uproot connections that no longer serve your mental world (which creates your physical world).

The experiences to which you expose your mind have a way of creating a constructed self through content alone. You could

PERCEPTION: TRUE SELF VS. CONSTRUCTED SELF

be watching a story about an issue someone is dealing with, and automatically, on a subconscious level, introduce your awareness to that information. Being intentional with your consumption of information is crucial if you're someone who is serious about creating their reality. Everything outside your inner world is constantly making a suggestion to you, and your mind doesn't treat that information as something you're just watching or hearing. The information directly interacts with your subconscious mind as something you want to see more of. As your mind isn't deciphering your consumption as just content, it is creating a brain that seeks, looks for, and operates from that information, as it is constantly working for you to give you what you *say* you are looking at. This is why it is very important to be aware of what you expose your senses to, as your mind is an intelligent system used for collecting data to relay back to you in your physical world what you are saying you want to see and hear more of. You might even use words and begin to act like the content you have consumed. You might even meet people or have experiences that project this information. Everything is constantly interacting with you to construct an idea of yourself. This is why it is so crucial to be mindful about conversations, content, energy states, and media that is directly trying to connect with your mental sphere.

When you know that you are so much more, that means you are going against a limited, constructed concept by saying, "This isn't it for me. There has to be more to who I am, what I am capable of, and what is possible for me." The light inside you is always talking to you and saying *you can*. You spirit is your true self, and is always whispering that things can change for the better. The constructed self is the illusion and debris collected from the whispers of society.

Once you know, you step into your greatest power and freedom, where you feel completely liberated in the awareness that you weren't any of that noise. You never were what happened in the past. These were just observations of your mind as you moved forward.

Don't ever stay in a mental state from the past. Never for one second attach your vastness to experiences that try to make you feel small. Everything fears you remembering who you truly are. This is where all energy that belongs to you rushes back to you. This is where you become mentally liberated. This is where you recognize that everything that has been happening wasn't your true self, but a bunch of constructed ideas that were trying to define you in the hope that you would fall for their traps. You see, now. You know, now. You are your true self.

True Self

Your true self is limitless, boundless, and free. Your true self is your spirit, which knows anything is possible. Your true self doesn't see people, places, or things as solid; it knows everything is energy interacting with itself. You true self thinks things can happen now. Your true self believes in your dreams and is watching them manifest now. Follow your own path and go against all the noise so you operate from a state driven by the unknown.

You are a seer, a visionary, a powerhouse, and well connected. Your source of guidance is your inner voice. Your trusted compass is your heart. You exist between two worlds: one you can touch and one you can sense. You know and see things before they happen because you are not restricted to your physical state only. You gain insight and data for all your decisions by consulting with your spirit. You know what feels right for you, and you must start connecting back with your ability to sense everything.

So much goodness is constantly being poured into you, and this makes you independent in thought and action. You are supernatural, and you see the magic all around you. No matter what seems to be happening, there is always the feeling that things are good and transpiring in your favor. You never stay in one state. You remain open because you know change is constant. You are playing in your world, never overanalyzing what happened or why something occurred the way it did. You are a master at moving forward and gaining wisdom from everything. You find that your transitions are becoming smoother because you accept that this is all a momentary experience in the grand scheme of life.

> *You are an alchemist. You can take any situation and transmute it into something greater. You are the master at changing any negative circumstance into a positive one. You are a visionary. You are dynamic. You are actively operating as your true self.*

You are your true self right now, and with every single word, you feel your own inner power activating. As you begin to remember, reclaim, and operate in your true state, you will see, feel, and understand yourself in ways you had no idea were possible. You'll follow your heart more easily, listen to your own inner voice, trust your own inner glimpse, and creatively express yourself.

All of what you want from life is possible. As you begin to be activated through your memory and feel a sense of expansion, you'll see that things are meant to be. You'll step into a different kind of power with inner assurance and confidence. You'll know everything starts within you. All that you'll be experiencing after finishing this book will put you in a field of supernatural possibility that would once have seemed like a dream or something out of a fantasy. This is where you'll be. With your mind gaining insight and everything becoming clear, you'll access your true self, not with some special technique or course you

Thought Access

follow for a few days, but through a state of awareness and a state of being *now*. You are your true self now. With every negative, doubtful, or fear-filled thought banished from your mental kingdom, you will realize that your eyes aren't just *seeing* what you see, but *changing* what you see based upon your state of mind.

> ***You have access to the power of your mind, the truth of your soul, and the magic of the universe.***

As an activated being right now, you'll see everything turn in your favor. Everyone will assume you have some magical power, but the reality is, you are tapped in, aware, and connected to the ever-giving. You realize that you have always been connected. People go through life being constructed by the world around them and their thoughts, their level of self-belief, the things they do, and what they think is possible as determined by what they see in the physical sense. "Seeing to believe" trains you to become dependent on known certainty and the things you can accomplish by yourself.

Going through life in a limited scope does have its effects. Everything seems hard, uncomfortable, draining, and a constant uphill battle. People lose their spark, not because they aren't connected, but because they don't even know who they truly are. They have allowed the noise to become their voice. To assume you are just a collection of a few habits, thoughts, or activities day to day ignores the spring that is pouring into you. "Anything is possible" isn't just a statement; it's the truth. What your mind tunes into, believes, and truly knows will happen…will happen.

> ***Anything is possible. Your mind can create it. Your will can manifest it. You heart can attract it. Your soul can materialize it.***

The magical nature of your existence is mostly unknown.

Perception: True Self vs. Constructed Self

You imagine, visualize, and find yourself in alignment with experiences you can't fully explain. All you know is that you had a thought, a passion, or something in your heart that wanted that one thing to happen—and suddenly, in the most miraculous way, you find yourself there. This has always been happening. Your entire life, you have been operating in the magical nature of reality without true awareness. You might have been trained in the past to follow a path based on certainty that you would get a certain outcome. That path wasn't yours; it wasn't your dream, or even something you had an interest in. You only did it because you knew there was some kind of guarantee of success.

Going against your own dreams and real heart-centered passion in exchange for a limited belief of safety trains your mind to settle and be okay with paths designed by others, not your own journey of discovery and exploration. Your true self always wants to shine outwardly, but when you limit yourself, you carry a burden that affects your well-being. The stress of constantly needing to be in control and making yourself do things you know aren't your truth can become overwhelming over time.

The most detrimental aspect of this way of thinking is that you forget your magic. You forget that anything is possible, and that dreams can become a reality. In actuality, what you want *is* possible. Your true creative expression allows your body, mind, and life to thrive because there is no contradiction. You aren't going against your flow; you are embracing it. No one really goes against their flow intentionally; they were just trained to seek certainty, and now the mind habitually looks for that. When the mind seeks certainty, it takes the path of predictability and fears the concept of radical change. However, when you paint your own picture, carve your own structures, and walk your own path faithfully, you embody a sacred connection that is always with you. You find yourself walking boldly in the unknown. You release all fear of uncertainty and embrace the universe, which keeps providing for you. On a daily basis, you receive nourishment and abundance you might not recognize according to where you focus your attention. Take time to really take it all in: who you are, what surrounds you, and the richness of life. This expands you as a person.

> *The new you isn't going to recognize the past you. You're coming out on top—renewed, revived, and reenergized. You'll be more focused on your purpose and prioritize your peace, wellness, and happiness. It is all being shown to you now. The way is being made.*

Every pain of the past or memory of hardship is healed in your body in this moment, as your true self is constantly rejuvenating you on the cellular level. You are being created every second, and every passing moment allows you the chance to release everything that weighs on your heart and mind. In addition to all of your manifestations, cultivating wellness is one of the top priorities of your true self. This is why you always feel refreshed after a good sleep upon waking the next day. There is more to the moment before you wake up every morning. Between the sleep state and the waking state, you just feel at peace before the memory of the physical world returns. The point of transition in awareness from sleep to the waking state is always your true self renewed for the next day, but any memories you don't release can carry on with the assumption that "what once was will always be." This isn't the truth.

Your current truth is on repeat in your mind. Giving yourself the chance for something new is making peace with your emotional state by releasing what could have, should have, or would have been. The freshness of this moment depends deeply upon the clarity of your mind and the openness of your heart. Don't let your past steal from you. Don't let anything or anyone have power over your ability to embrace the newness your true

Perception: True Self vs. Constructed Self

self has to offer you. Repeating memories becomes habitual when you associate yourself with the story of the past. Identifying as the person that happened to is like saying, "This is the final version of myself." Daring to say, "I am so much more" and moving forward with your new energy is really the most powerful freedom you can have.

As you begin to recognize the expansion of your state of being, you see that life has so much more magical and that things really can change for the better. For once, there is feeling of real hope and a chance at magnificent manifestations. You'll begin to see that things aren't as complicated as they seemed, and that you are okay right now. The mind isn't on overdrive with over-analysis. Instead, you are recognizing and taking in everything that you are. You're not forcing it, stressing over it, or condemning yourself. You're not judging, overthinking, or worrying about it. You are simply being, and you can feel your magic being activated. You can feel who you are and see that you have always been this way. A sense of ease covers you as you allow things to flow in. The more you settle into yourself and release the need to go in multiple directions, the more you find yourself in *all* spaces.

You become limitless and connected. Your thoughts do all the alignment for you. You attract what you want. You find yourself where you have always belonged, with the people you're meant to be with, doing what you're meant to be doing. You finally give yourself the power to work with your inner capacity to break free from the constructed world. You create your own life, alter your own reality, and write your own destiny. You are a willing participant in the mental world, which creates the physical world. You are guided by your vision, moved by your heart, and renewed by your spirit. You are a self-sustaining system. You are connected. You are your true self!

Key Points to Remember

- *Your true self is free, unbounded, a dreamer, a higher consciousness, intuitive, and instinctive. Your true self knows that anything is possible. You go after what you want based on the vision you have received. Your true self is multidimensional. Your true self is a manifestor, a creator, and a spirit who intentionally brings into the physical your gifts from within.*

- *When limiting concepts are removed from your mental state and negative thoughts are cleared out, who you are really rises up. You become alert. Your awareness is activated, and you become lucid in your experience.*

- *Perception isn't a final state. It is something that constantly changes as you evolve, grow, and get to know yourself daily. The point of understanding the power of perception is to evade limitation by releasing the need to see everything as one truth.*

- *Perception influences everything—not only how you see the world, but how the world sees you. You can create other people's perception of you by becoming who you want to be and letting your own self-creation work in your favor.*

- *The core of who you are is magical and magnificent. You have access to a broader view, a greater understanding, and a deeper connection. You soul already knows. These natural states show themselves to you when you need them the most. When you really need a breakthrough, you receive it. The moment you ask for guidance, it shows up. Even when you felt you couldn't make it through, your light shone for you.*

- *You are the one who is connected. You have to stop*

PERCEPTION: TRUE SELF VS. CONSTRUCTED SELF

playing pretend that you aren't a magnificent soul who actually has access and connection. It is who you are. Your senses can see more through your imagination. Your body feels through intuition. You mind deals with ideas, visions, and thoughts.

- *The world around you will begin to work to bring your new thoughts to life.*

- *You're not what people think of you or the inner doubts that make you question your new changes. You are so much more, and with every step forward, you begin to embrace the inner state of seeing life from a greater perspective instead of from your current mindset or circumstances that appear to be happening around you.*

- *Seeing yourself in a new way refreshes the world's perception of you. What story are you constantly telling yourself and others about your life? What inner state are you projecting to attract to yourself? How do you see yourself?*

- *The freedom of your soul can't be confined by ideas or thoughts. You are so much more, and you will break free right now from anything that steals your confidence or makes you doubt yourself. Any form of self-doubt or low self-esteem comes from thoughts that aren't really yours. These thoughts have been handed down by people or experiences that lack any form of awareness of their true self.*

- *The most crucial understanding is that perspective isn't reality. The way someone else sees the world—from their mind through their experience—does not at all define your potential. Negativity, fear, and limitation shared by others should never be used to measure one's own potential.*

- *Nothing about limitation is true.*

- *When you know that you are so much more, you go against limited, constructed concepts by saying, "This isn't it for me. There has to be more to who I am, what I am capable of, and what is possible for me." The light inside you is always talking to you and saying, "You can." You spirit is your true self, which is always whispering that things can change for the better.*

- *The constructed self is the illusion and debris collected from the whispers of society.*

- *Your true self is limitless, boundless, and free. Your true self is your spirit, which knows anything is possible. Your true self doesn't see people, places, or things as solid; it knows everything is energy interacting with itself. Your true self thinks things can happen now. Your true self believes in your dreams and seeing them manifest now.*

- *You are supernatural, and you see the magic all around you. No matter what seems to be happening, there is always a feeling that things are all good and transpiring in your favor. You never stay in one state. You remain open because you know change is constant. You are playing in your world, never overanalyzing what has happened or why something happened the way it did.*

- *Every pain from the past or memory of hardship has healed in your body, as your true self is always rejuvenating on the cellular level. You are being created every second, and every passing moment allows you the chance to release anything weighing on your heart and mind.*

- *Don't let your past steal from you. Don't let anything or*

PERCEPTION: TRUE SELF VS. CONSTRUCTED SELF

anyone have power over your ability to embrace the newness your true self has to offer you.

5

TRUE POWER: YOUR LIFE FORCE

Your true power is your life force. It is your energy, your attention, and your aliveness. Life force is what gives you passion, drive, imagination, and inspiration. Living in your most optimal state in health, mindset, and self-belief is a reflection of a strong life force. More energy comes into the body when you are ready to see and experience who you really are. This chapter will expose you to ways you might be leaking your energy and where you can actually tap into your unlimited energetic reservoir to be continuously empowered from within.

You will learn how to convert all energy in your favor. You will see that nothing is actually against you, and this will instantly free up more energy for you to live a life you have willfully created. Life force is the real value, and you will learn exactly how to feel and see for yourself from an expanded state to which you already are connected. Everything is linked to your life force. Everything happens because of your life force. Your entire existence depends on your aliveness in terms of what you are seeing and attracting. You are the center of it all. You are the one in control. You have free will to choose. Nobody can go inside your head and do it for you. You are in your mental and inner world, which is a universe of its own. Every part of that universe wants the best for you.

Affirm: I am the master of my thoughts. I command change in my mindset now, and I know these mental changes will alter everything around me for the better. It all starts with how I see things, the way I respond, and the changes I make.

Your mind is the command center, and you direct your energy where you want it to go. Imagine how much your life force does for you in the seen and unseen worlds. You must start to be aware of your supernatural nature. You can't avoid the subtle aspects of your life any longer. You are a multidimensional being who receives energy every second. The vast energy to which you have access hinges on how much you allow in. Your capacity is limitless, but your state of awareness can sometimes fall into seeing everything from a single point of view. Being unaware of the energetic nature of your existence results in many inharmonious and unbalanced results, which end up becoming a lesson. Equipping yourself with the proper wisdom, insight, and Thought Access allows you to understand yourself without needing to constantly go through it and rebalance. At every moment, your mind, body, and soul yearn to be centered. This is why everyone wants to be at peace. Being in alignment is a natural state.

The more energy you possess, the more you can experience the richness and beauty of life. The more you believe in yourself, the more life force can enter your body. You begin to receive ideas out of nowhere, sudden guidance, and a sense of being activated. Your state of true power isn't just the things you have; it is the wellness you feel inside your mind, and the balance and harmony you attract by recognizing the true value of your existence. Calling back your energy to yourself frees you from mental loops that try to make you see only a small layer of all that you are. The time has come to expand your vision, insight, and connection to yourself.

The access I give in this chapter will activate you. It will all happen instantly, and as the pages go by, you'll start to see power rippling into every area of your life. You are going to be given Thought Access that brings back your memory of your true power. For too long, you have sought ways to gain clarity and peace. You have sought ways to remember yourself, and this desire has been out there in the world, which is in a fluid state awaiting further instruction from you. The external world you see all around you is alive, and it's full of so much more life and energy when you cultivate the mindset and inner vision to see it.

Everything that has already been created by the imagination of other human beings surrounds your physical self as a constructed reality, but below the surface exists the energy field of *all that is* and *all that has been*, which you can access with your imagination. The insight here is to avoid getting caught up in past manifestations as a final form of reality. You are the one with the life force. You have the imagination right now to bring a new vision to life. This vision can be a renewed version of yourself, or even an idea you believe will be more harmonious to nature and humanity. Understand that more life is given where there is alignment with nature's treasures. You are nature's treasure, and you are returning to the realization that the golden key has always been in your hands.

> *Everything already exists now, and the mind that taps into that free energy through openness of the imagination, the freedom to dream, the will to believe in more, and the desire to see it through connects itself to a field that operates nonstop: a stream of consciousness that is always giving.*

You'll learn here not only how to harness free energy available to you, but how to direct it and make it work in your life. Much of the disharmony people experience comes from not knowing who they actually are—not just in terms of identity, but also the way they work as multidimensional beings. You haven't been taught this, as there is no school or system that teaches inner empowerment to a level that unveils the nature of your reality to you. This new information exposes to you all that you are, and all that you have always been.

Life force is what you are using to read this book right now. It is your attention, focus, will, and aliveness. You are the one who chooses what you can do with your time, energy, and mind. Reading this adds to your wholeness, as it opens you up to higher thought and gives you access to limitless possibilities. Everything is a form of investment that either gives back or takes away from you. I'll teach you how to cultivate your highest life force, take your power back from illusion, and be eternally inspired and forever changed. You'll have more potency to do what you want as we dissolve together what has been emotionally and mentally keeping you unaware.

There is so much more available to you—and that statement is a reality. Each time you have made a change in your life or become better than before, you have somehow found yourself in a newer and greater state. You were the one who did this, but the outcome was always a potential reality. Each choice was inherently linked to a mysterious path that eventually led you to a discovery of what is possible for you. This is what makes it all fun; you get to know yourself in every transformation and every manifestation. When you see what you can do, you feel a surge of life force energy. The energy is activated in your body when you are present enough to see and recognize the magic all around you.

Your Energy Field

The fastest way to increase your life force is knowing that you are the observer of your own experience, and that you do not identify with everything happening around you. You are seeing it all take place. Everything continuously changes, but you are the one silently witnessing it all unfold. Each time you recognize this part of yourself, you instantly feel rejuvenated and reenergized. You are not the one things are "happening to." You are a great seer of events playing out. You have always been an ancient intelligence that is both timeless and fully present. This consciousness pulls your perspective back into the energy field that makes you endless and fearless. This energy field encompasses what was, what is, and what will be. It is potential and possibility. It is all now, and you are the one with this awareness, which means you can morph and shapeshift at will into the person you dream yourself to be.

Freedom of being means that you have broken away from concepts that previously limited your being. Anything that labels you in any negative way is an obvious limitation. It is a means of cutting you off from what you have always been, as it is possible to become hyper-focused on a projection of self that was constructed by information and ideas that no longer hold value in your life. All limitations have a feeling of heaviness, including tightness in the body. It can be uncomfortable to live on a small amount of energy when there is a vast amount available to you. Awareness is what frees you. You see, feel, and begin to operate as your whole self, not just a part that plays a role day to day. You live as an expanded, multidimensional being in everything you do. You are the influence, and you do this through the field. You will start to feel a surge of energy as you feel more connected to everything.

> *Your energy craves what is real. Your soul knows the world was meant to be magical. You won't settle or let yourself play the acceptable game. You're so much more, and you're willing to go down your own path to discover it all.*

The energy field is where all creation takes place. You exist through your mind, body, and state of being, which communicate with the entire world. This energy field is the network of the human mind. You are sending thoughts at great distance and picking up on things through your inner knowing. When you have a strong connection with the energy field—and this happens through awareness, being present, seeing the magic in everything, and remaining optimistic, hopeful, and open to the mysterious ways things work—you manifest what you want because you're sure that it is actually happening for you. You know it is working for you, and you are always sending energetic signals to match with your request.

I wrote all about manifesting in my book *Manifest Now*. Here, we go even deeper into the understanding that you are the one already living out what you are looking to receive. Your visualization or intention is a memory of what is to come, not just things that already exist. This is why, when you manifest something, it can feel as if you have already done so. This is how strong you are as a manifestation master.

Creating what you want is recognizing that you are connected to everything. The thing, person, or situation you're trying to manifest is already in the field. You initiate contact by simply sending the intention. Don't overthink it or get too technical. Everything is as simple as you breathing right now. It all just is. You're only beginning to accept the depth of what that means, and this gives you permission to be playful with your intentions instead of giving them too much energy. Overspending your energy on excess worry or lack of trust only drains you, because it's a mixed signal. Be very clear and direct. Everything is at your command.

A portal of possibilities has opened up for you.

Now I'll teach you how to strengthen your energy field connection. First things first: You are always connected. You are connected with every breath. Your knowledge of this process starts pulling more energy to you. The field is one of possibility. It gives you everything upon request, and it doesn't try to figure out which of your requests are good or bad. It operates on requests, intentions, what you consciously or unconsciously speak, your repetitive thoughts, and what you believe you deserve. You strengthen this field through awareness.

You know that there are more layers to who you are and your existence. You're not shocked that your reality can instantly change according to your will. You see magical connections in everything. This includes seeing your thoughts manifest instantly. You recognize that you are so much more. The ability to influence reality at will is a great sign of your strength and energetic connection to the field.

You send a signal, knowing that you will see it. This is a cosmic wink that you're on your path. It instantly pulls more energy to you. One thing to remember when you are operating in this state is that you will already know many things that aren't readily apparent to others. It'll feel like you're communicating with a subtle field that intuitively provides you with insight; and actually, it is doing just that. Things will seem to happen miraculously for you—they always do when you have strong life force energy. This is a sign of your openness.

When someone is judgmental of the true nature of reality or puts too many limitations or negative thoughts on the way things work, they begin to lack life force, which makes it hard for good things to happen for them. They seem to remain stagnant, blocking off better things trying to happen for them in their life. This is why you'll sometimes see an individual create a whole identity around chaos. Don't get pulled into storylines like that. Transformation is an internal affair, and we must be open to going into these territories to witness the parts of ourselves that remind us of our true heritage and connection to the gifts of life. The treasure is received by those who recognize the gift.

This insight will also keep your energy field strong. You may want to bring everyone with you on your inner discovery and share the beauty of seeing how your connection feeds your life. This can only be done by living your life in the grandest way: in full-fledged love, understanding, balance, awareness, celebration, mani-festation, and expression of your creativity and power. The strength of your field alone has the potential to create inner inspiration in someone you might not even know. Change isn't always a conversation or telling someone what to do. Just being and embodying it can send out an energy signal into the minds of many that greater things *are* possible. This is a win-win situation, as everyone subtly receives what they are ready for. We are used to sharing information openly in hopes that it will ignite someone, but we forget the vastness of the energy being generated from our mind, body, and spirit when we are living it. Our energy has immense reach in the field.

Life Force: Psychic Energy

Psychic energy is mental energy. The more life force you have, the more you can willingly direct your mental energy. Everything that has to do with personal development or gaining more awareness in your being can influence the amount of psychic energy you can utilize in your life. For thousands of years of human existence, we have depended upon our inner compass and intuition to guide us. We received from within, which naturally gave us stronger psychic energy. As time went on, we started depending on external information to give us assurances that something could happen for us or that things would work out. Everything started to be predicted in the outer world based on society's habit of developing systems of dependency for certainty. With this new way of living, people lost touch with what it meant to feel, receive, and be guided from within.

With increased dependency on outer-world results, you can naturally develop fear of uncertain situations, which then creates a host of reactions that make you worry for no reason at all. Most of life depends on natural trust, but when this trust turns into only what you can *see to believe*, your psychic energy is drained. It begins to be structured around predictability, certainty, and the known world. Most magic is unknown. Most of what can happen for you is grander and more sophisticated than anything you could put together without it. This is why the miracles or sudden breakthroughs that happen for you have strong divine intervention associated with them.

You may have spent many silent nights in prayer or days requesting of the field that a way be made for you. Results always happen in ways far greater than you could have imagined. This is why you must return to your psychic energy and pull your life force back to yourself instead of leaking or draining your energy. When you use your imagination, you are working with your psychic energy. Any form of mental activity that gives you faith, makes you believe in yourself, or lets you feel that there's so much more to life—this is your psychic energy working at a high level. You are working beyond the five senses, as most of your mental activity is invisible. This invisible energy is alive, existing in its own world that moves through everything. This is why you always find things, people, outcomes, and opportunities that match your mental frequency. People with a lot of psychic energy tend to see and know the things happening all around them; this connects back to the field, as you have naturally always been intuitive. *Thought Access* reignites this reminder within you to awaken and see for yourself.

> *What's shifting isn't the world around you; it's you. You're the one rising into an accelerated state. You're being altered from within. Make peace with that instead of trying to make everyone awaken or get on the wave of energy that's taking place within you.*

True Power: Your Life Force

Many things drain psychic energy: doubt, fear, worry, negativity, judgment, gossip, lack of self-belief, overthinking, constant dependence on entertainment, overuse of social media, and bad relationships. Mental energy is alive, and when it is not engaged in a creative way or in a growth state, it becomes a projection of content and external influences. This fatigues you when you really haven't exerted any physical energy. When consciousness is used in a mindless way, more energy is lost in the mind than in the physical body. This is why you must rise up within yourself and take your inner power back. You will instantly begin to shift. You will sense inner sparks and illumination taking place within you, as every single word written here is meant to pull your energy back to yourself. You will be free from negative thoughts because you believe in who you are. This is not just a statement, but a reality right in this moment.

All negative thoughts wither away and are now cleared from your energy field. This instantly gives you more life force, as you have stopped giving negative thoughts your energy through repetition. You don't have to make it a prolonged transformation. Once your mind has this kind of access, it begins to rewire your system and eliminate old programs. You will intentionally rewrite your mental storylines. You will start to find it almost humorous to think that a negative thought used to exist in your mind, and this playful way of looking at it will instantly give you a boost of psychic energy. Most of what will occur in your life will be deeply supernatural, as these words communicate and connect you to what has always been possible.

Don't be surprised if you wake up with a ton of energy and attract many incredible opportunities. The external reaction to your internal psychic energy increase will be astounding. People will respond to you in a whole new way. The reason for this is that you're no longer wasting inner energy on things that drain you. Instead, you are a walking life force, and the psychic nature of others can detect it without even knowing why they feel this way about you. This insight isn't about what anyone thinks of you, though. It's truly about what an overflow of life force looks like when you see it and meet it.

You will heal many parts of yourself simply by remembering that you are not limited or attached to the ideas, constructs, storylines, or identities of your past. They have nothing to do with the way you currently define yourself. The wild thing is that you are free to completely alter any aspect of your life. It's mind-blowing. This is why this type of insight is so crucial. I wrote this book to give you an upgrade in mindset so a deep transformation can take place that instantly shifts you. Some people need time to clear what they need to clear, but the treasure I am sharing with you gives you the freedom *now* for profound life changes. Each page and every word you read in this book is an actual code of activation. You will experience deep healing, realizations, sudden breakthroughs, alignments, connections, understandings, awakenings, and manifestations out of thin air.

You are starting to stand in your truth. You're moving in a new direction. Something within you has risen, awakened, and is now activated. You are starting to propel forward in all ways.

Great things happen when people are activated in their minds. They gain self-belief, and this creates a ripple effect that alters many areas of their lives. You will become your own energy source, meaning you won't even need to seek validation or ways to feel worthy. You will have healthier relationships, which I'll get into later. I'll just mention here that the expansion of your psychic energy creates a magnetic pull in your field. This helps you attract everything you want as you operate within the realm of possibility. You brain frequency tunes into you becoming a very lucky, blessed, and highly aware being. This state of mind frees you from the psychological patterns that many people live by: viewing the world from a limited perspective.

Mental energy is vital to recognizing the beauty of life. When you have more mental energy, you can be a representation of hope for the planet. You can be a vehicle for inventions and ideas, and a mentor for a new generation of humans. You can lead in your home, community, and business in a peaceful, loving way. You can change your life, liberate yourself from past thought patterns, and free your genetics from repetitive social and cultural expectations. You can give yourself a chance to experience mental wellness by being completely at peace—and not just with one part of yourself. You'll feel a deep peace that envelopes every fiber of your being. You'll no longer need to chase happiness or do a million things to feel an ounce of peace. You are now going to start living in these new states in the normal and natural course of events.

The "chase" always makes things seem like you must do something to obtain them. This is what can make life so difficult. These days, happiness, peace, and mental wellness are often associated with having to do something to get something, especially if there is a product or service involved. Simply being, sitting still, calming your mind, and removing attachment to storylines will do more for you than you could ever imagine. See yourself as the silent observer who has existed within you since the beginning of time. Everything you thought you were going through up to this point now becomes a distant memory. You can let go of any situation, as nothing defines you. Nothing can take your power away. Nothing can steal your shine or the memory that you're not involved with anything negative. This instantly returns a lot of your life force. You are everything, and you will always be everything. Your psychic power is now active.

Life Force: Body

Your body is incredibly intelligent. It is alive, electric, and active. It does everything for you without your awareness of it taking place. Creating your inner sanctuary means becoming really good at listening to your internal signals. Anything that makes you feel more balanced, harmonious, energized, and active is a great sign that you are in healthy homeostasis. When there is imbalance, it starts to show up in your energy, which is why it feels like you might not have a lot of life force. Health is everything when it comes to having and maintaining a strong life force. Life force is a sign of vitality, vigor, and passion for more life. The health of your life force and energy is a great sign that you are truly balanced in mind, body, and spirit. When one area is lacking, it starts to create lack and resistance—which, in turn, begins to affect your life force.

You are always healthy first. Thoughts play a huge role in the wellness of your body. If there are any negative thoughts, insecurities, or self-judgment, they will have a trickling effect, which creates a feeling of resistance. When you are healthy in your mind, your energy field is more open, which allows you to receive. It is a private signal you send to the world indicating that you are full of life force; and this creates a magnetic attraction to you that vibrates at a higher rate.

Be the embodiment of your manifestations. Represent the energy you wish to see all around you. The experience happens in your mind and body first, before you find yourself. By then, it'll feel so familiar and natural to have everything you have always dreamed of.

You are connected to something greater and more powerful every single moment. Don't slow that down by attaching limitations to your body or thinking that everything has a negative effect on you. Every thought is an intention. What is true about anything at any given time is the extent to which you believe in it. Thought is then converted into belief, which says, "That is what I think of something." For example, if someone says a "bug" is going around and they don't feel well, and they start to describe the symptoms in detail, anyone listening could start to play out the same feeling and symptoms in their mind, assuming that what is going around can affect them, too. Words have a lot of power when the imagination is open and susceptible to the physical effect of thought transference. We are very open when it comes to what we *think* we believe, because we refer to shared information rather than independently choosing what we feel, think, and believe for ourselves.

You must have your own mental commands in your belief that you are healthy, that your body is intelligent and will figure it out for you. Once you make your own powerful commands, you will begin to see your body gain a new kind of strength and vitality unlike ever before. You go from needing information that programs you to running your own powerful program in which you choose the healthiest, strongest, and most vital version of yourself.

> *Take very good care of your physical body; your mind will then be so strong and aligned with nature's flow. Everything is interconnected and must be honored, respected, and appreciated. That is the highest form of gratitude for yourself.*

You must always override negative thinking or anything in the outer world that tries to pull your energy down. As I said in the previous chapter, when you first become aware that you need not agree with words, thoughts, or information from the external world that does not support your mental, spiritual, physical, and emotional health, you will develop mental guards that protect you from all forms of negativity. You are a powerful living system. You are the one who can choose at any given moment. This is why I wrote *Thought Access*—so everyone can take their power back in all areas of their life through awareness and insight. You can empower and free yourself while creating harmony in your life.

Everything you think and feel results in a greater life. Don't get used to maintaining a belief system that doesn't show you your true path when it comes to the wellness of your entire existence. Every thought you hold is meant to serve a purpose; it is meant to work in your favor. Start speaking power over your body, your mind, and every area of your life. This is what activates life force to the maximum—when you actually start issuing mental commands over everything happening in your world. When this happens, you begin to instantly create with your words. You are everything you believe you are. There's no other way of putting it.

Many people are still externally dependent on how they should think, feel, and act based on the statements of others. The power of *internal dependency* means you rely exclusively on your inner resources. You are already connected. You know things about yourself that are only unique to you, and you follow your own guidance, which is connected only to you. If you're not used to thinking from this place, this book will activate that reminder so you can awaken inner guidance of faith, trust, and the knowledge that you are supported, nourished, and provided for from within. Once you create mental and emotional harmony by making peace with the past, yourself, and everything else, and you just surrender, opening yourself to greater abundance and life force. This discards the heaviness of any ties that previously linked you to a stuck place. That time has come to an end. You know now, and you are moving forward in a powerful way. The intelligence you have gained restores you on a deeper level, even as you read these words.

> *There are latent powers within you that are being activated. You'll have a deeper sense to who you are, how you treat your body, and what you consume. As you rise up, so will your physiology and psychology. Your harmonious*

equilibrium will alter every aspect of your life.

    The biggest impact on your life force is feeling fragmented, unsure, or confused about your diet, lifestyle, and what works for you. The number one thing is understanding how you feel and the state you're in at any given moment. It will be very obvious what doesn't work for you because your body will give you a signal and tell you how it is responding to the things you consume. You have to start reading your own body, trusting your own signals, and knowing what works for you. Every single body is unique and works in its own unique way. Returning to your relationship with your body means disconnecting from all the excess information that is constantly telling you what to eat, think, or internalize without taking into consideration who you are and what works for you. Life force is drained when you get away from trusting your own self and knowing what your body needs. You have to start listening to your body and all of its signals. Removing all processed and artificial products from your life further deepens that connection.

    You may be surprised to discover the extent to which disconnecting from these things actually gives you back a chance at living your life fully. Your body is the most important location from which you perceive reality. When you are unwell in the physical, it connects with thoughts, people, and places that match that state of being. It's like getting warped into an energy field that pulls you in further because you haven't made the connection to the original cause of the entire experience. Everything has a root, and once you expose it, it pulls you out of every situation you had no idea was so interconnected with subtle changes you've made. Don't be surprised if your relationships, habits, and personal beliefs change, simply because you have uprooted a pattern that wasn't serving your mental and physical wellness.

4 Ways to Stop Leaking Your Energy:

1. *Attention:*

Your attention is your power. Your attention is using your life force to give power to something or someone in order to make it real in your world. When you constantly give your life force away to things and/or people that are only taking, it creates a leak in your energy, which means you instantly feel like there is an imbalance. Usually, your gut tells you, and if you listen, you no longer lose precious life force to unnecessary things and people. However, if you don't detect this, and you sense that you are overextending yourself and losing life force, then you begin leaking your energy, which takes away from your ability to create the life you want.

Learn to master where you place your attention, as this is vital to balancing your inner world. Know that everything around you is attempting to project something onto your inner world. When you aren't aware of this, you may think the projections are what's real, but in reality, only *you* are real. This can create the feeling that something "out there" has power over you, causing you to second-guess who you are and believe what is being projected. *You* are the main character of the world you perceive. *You* are the observer and creator of the world you experience, and all of this happens through the level of attention you offer through your senses.

> *Affirm: I let go of what no longer serves my divine truth. I release any ideas or concepts that are limiting. I am an unbounded soul. I am untethered and limitless. My focus is my power. My attention is my power. I choose to see in every situation the outcome I wish to happen.*

Anytime you feel like something is overwhelming you or causing you to leak energy, stop yourself and really step back from the situation. In this way, you can get a perspective on it without your entire nervous system becoming reactive. You'll notice, through your power of removing attention with the intention of creating more harmony for yourself, that it dissolves the issue. This is the kind of power you have. You'd be surprised to learn that many things desperately depend upon your attention to exist. When you don't know this, you assume things are separate from you, and that they have the power to infringe upon your awareness.

I share this important insight with you so you can stop living your life at the whim of how the world appears to be treating you. Take back your inner power and step into a world in which you never have to be controlled by people, situations, what seems to be happening, or what has happened. With this insight, you are now a different person. You are using your attention to say, "I agree with this, and want to see more of it." If what you are seeing doesn't match what you intend to manifest for yourself, switch it up. This will give you more inner control to influence your world.

The new direction of humanity will require us to start being more energetically intelligent. We must know the causes of the effects we are experiencing. The excuse can no longer be lack of awareness. You will need to start being more active in your inner world so you aren't sidestepping your own guidance just to avoid dealing with emotions or thoughts of change. You can't suppress your evolution by wasting your time or attention on anything that keeps you the same. You are so much more. You don't need to feel suddenly uprooted to reconnect, either. You have always been connected. Anything that is now uprooted or removed was just a mental block or emotional imbalance that caused your energy to be projected or leaked instead of circulated and balanced.

2. Worrying/Stressing/Overthinking

Thought Access

We are constantly creating in our minds, playing out mental scenarios for outcomes we desire—and, some-times, ones we don't, out of lack of self-belief. Your imagination wasn't created to be used for self-destructive thoughts. You were never meant to speak, visualize, or create the opposite of what you want. Your mind only knows how to give you what you put into it. Knowing this, it makes no sense at all to spend any part of your life wondering if something will work out. That's a form of mixed signal you are sending. Believe, and even go so far as to know that it IS happening for you.

Most of life is still a big mystery. *How* things happen and come together is not your business. You aren't supposed to worry or live in anxiety about outcomes. Outcomes are created by you, because *you* know that it will happen. Every situation in which you believe happens. So much life force is lost in the inner world through the chatter of worry, stress, overthinking, and lack of trust in yourself. Own the fact that you can create anything you want. When your nervous system is constantly ill at ease with negative thoughts and feelings that are only happening inside you, you create a lens of fear to view the world. Nothing that is happening to you—and nothing that will happen to you—represents a concern big enough to cause you to live in anything less than a state of well-being. Settle your mind. This creates a ripple effect through your entire body, soothing your nervous system through changes in mindset.

> *How it will happen for you is not for you to worry about. Knowing that it IS happening for you—and holding dearly to your vision—will make the unexplainable occur in such a magnificent way. It will make sense that you've been destined for greatness this entire time.*

When you are on edge within your mind, you send out signals

that reflect this frequency. Stop yourself right in the moment and ask yourself, "What is the big deal? What am I really afraid of? What is the most that could happen to me?" Take the pressure off. The amount of life force that flows into you after you stop allowing negative thoughts is indescribable. You cut the circuit by ending any signals of worry, stress, or overthinking. Many times, the things we know we must stop or change only linger because we never fully commit to confronting what we are afraid of. Sometimes, we overdramatize life and make it a big scary thing, which only puts us in a state of restriction and survival.

It is all flow, and as much as there can be lessons along the way, speed up your insights so you don't become dependent on challenges in order to learn. When you become aware of your own power to change any circumstance, you become an active participant in life. It'll be impossible to be broken by anything or anyone when you know that life flows on. Everything always works out for you. Everything always manifests for you. You heal, recover, and become rejuvenated so deeply that it expands your field in a powerful way. You'll see yourself naturally becoming hopeful and believing in possibilities. Anything can change in your life. Any situation can get better, and things can turn around and become healthier and more beautiful. With this kind of mindset, there isn't one thing happening in your life right now that can't be shifted. Make the decisions you're hardwired to make. Trust that it's all coming together. Let the past be at rest. The future is filled with possibilities.

3. Accountability

The more quickly you realize that you can make the choice to change your life, the faster the things around you change. Stop projecting your power externally, believing that things are just "happening to you" or that people outside of yourself are pulling the strings in your life. You are the sole creator of what you send out into the world. We only discover after the fact that we might not like what we have created. This happens when we choose to make a change.

Taking accountability for every action, thought, feeling, and intention puts things back into your own hands. You'll be surprised to see how many things that happen in your life follow the currents and frequency emitting from you. You weaken the bonds of negativity when you take accountability for your life. You bring light to areas that formerly seemed dim and impossible to overcome. You feel spiritual upliftment and a new sense of inspiration when you decide to stop playing out storylines that ended a long time ago. You won't just fall for the traps of other people who label your life with their limitations. You'll start to actually believe in who you are. Do what is necessary to get yourself back into balance, no matter how long it takes.

Holding yourself accountable helps you stop leaking your life force. There is no one to blame and nowhere to give away your power. Face yourself and become completely transparent. This takes you to another level because you have awakened to the realization that everything can morph into what you want it to be. The thing about accountability is that it exposes you to everything you are capable of. You are put into a vulnerable place initially because it can seem hard to believe that you could attract any type of unfavorable situation. The hard truth always has a sweet ending, however. It shakes you up so you can actually see for yourself that you were in the mental slumber of letting everything around you dictate how you should think, feel, react, and respond. The truth brings you back to a place of knowing your power. This is a very spiritual phenomenon that seems so natural and normal. What makes accountability spiritual is that it shows you the simplicity and beauty of reality giving you what you want, even when you aren't conscious of it. It's a place of creation, a place of communication with the unseen, and a place of surrendering what used to be in order to receive what you want.

True Power: Your Life Force

Take accountability for your thoughts, words, actions, and feelings. The rest will naturally align.

When you take accountability for your words, you start to empower yourself with every word you speak. You no longer say anything mindlessly. You speak with an energetic force that penetrates every field of the universe. The sound from your vocal cords is actual energy that moves at a great distance.

What you say about yourself shows up in your body. Even your cells are constantly listening to match what you are repeating (both internally and out loud) about yourself. Your words have the power to change someone's life through upliftment, encouragement, and positivity. Your words are energy you're sending as an auditory frequency that activates the mind, nervous system, and brain of another to suddenly believe in more. This is the great gift you have in your voice.

Taking accountability for your actions means that everything you do has a thought and intention behind it. Don't just "do, do, do," and learn the lesson afterward. Intend, follow through and see what your creations bring you. In this way, you'll see that you have caused many of the events in your life, and this will give you more confidence in your ability to change your circumstances at will. Taking accountability for what you have manifested is also a great way to manifest bigger and better things. Nothing in your life is final, so at any given moment, everything is up for grabs. This should create a surge of energy in your mind and body that makes you look at life differently. There isn't a certain state for manifesting. Nothing is as solid as it appears. Things can change. You are the one who can change things, and you can do it at any time, at any location, and from any energetic state.

Take accountability for your mindset. This one is so

important. Sometimes, we play thoughts out that don't belong to us because we learned them a long time ago and kept them as beliefs. This pattern can be replaced by thoughts that support your healthy mindset. You don't need to accept negative thoughts as something inevitable or part of your life. You don't need to own any limiting, doubtful, or negative thoughts as your own. You can see what's coming up and choose to replace it with something that supports you. Eventually, you'll realize that these thoughts become your normal state of mind, and what you desire will be done by you. As you move through every page of this book, see your development of a healthier, stronger, more open, and more enriched mindset. The goal is to bring you back to the center of your creation so you can construct the world of your dreams.

4. **Distractions**

Grab your life force back. Stop the excess scrolling and loss of life force to watching other people's lives, overconsuming content, and putting your talents on the back burner. You already know what distractions have done to your life. You can see the results of them everywhere when you don't find yourself where you were meant to be. Gifts can slowly dwindle away when the mind is captured in mindless behavior rather than the authenticity that the soul wants to build and experience.

You have a chance at getting your mind back. This will initially seem hard to do, but when you discover that your inner fire only needs one spark, you'll see yourself blazing away into everything you were passionately meant for. When there are too many distractions from our soul's purpose, things get heavy and foggy. The brain and body start to feel out of sync as you stop listening to your soul's nudges. The forces pulling you in so many directions aren't always tangible. Sometimes, invisible influences you've become accustomed to form into habits that need to be broken. Anything can be rewired, retrained, and returned to balance. People will often feel like they need to detox from the internet and get away from it all. This is the urge of the soul to pull back from meaningless interaction and redirect their attention to meaningful life experiences.

Affirm: I am going forward for a greater reason.

When your soul is yearning for meaning, it returns to wanting to direct its own experience rather than remaining trapped by the digital world or people who keep you stuck in the same habits and patterns. A lot of your next movements will be about returning to meaningful, real, and enriching states instead of letting yourself get glazed over or uncontrolled in the way you use your time. The good news is that your brain, body, and mind can always return to equilibrium. When you stop the distractions, you will initially feel a pull toward the bonds you have broken, because you spent a lot of time in that energy state. When you break free, you will notice that the energy bonds completely disconnect. This gives you the chance to follow your soul's calling.

If you have something you have been called to start, start it. Today is the day. Don't wait for something external to suddenly change to put you in the mood to begin. The distractions are keeping you away from actually going into that sacred place within yourself that pours energy, creativity, and life into you. When your mind isn't active in its own engagement, it becomes a screen to project the world on, and you sit back and watch it like a movie. You, however, are the one who can do the image projection and creating. You are the one who can live the way you want intentionally rather than remaining stuck and energetically depleted.

Understanding how to stop leaking energy allows your life force energy to heighten and your will to grow stronger. You will start to radiate as you get out of restriction, survival, and lack modalities. You will notice your energy becoming more potent. Everything you speak happens, everything you think manifests, and everything you decide to change actually changes. The potency of your energy will reflect how easily you can alter the world around you.

The more of your life force you allow to leak into unawareness, fear, distraction, restriction, and worry, the less you are able to actually influence the field that is starting to respond to you. Your mind will be too busy to see the clear signs, the obvious alignment, and the millions of opportunities and blessings all around you. To see the magical world you are in, you have to cultivate your inner vision. This chapter will help you get back to the world of adventure, possibilities, surprises, gifts, and intentional living. You will instantly notice incredible amounts of energy in many areas of your life. People will even start to wonder what is different about you. Increased life force does change the way you look and feel, even altering your pheromones. This is a signal to the world around you that you are in harmony. In subtle ways, we are always sensing everyone and everything. This will be to your advantage, as you know that it's not just the mask of appearances that matters, but the radiance of that soul that is felt.

Key Points to Remember

- *Your true power is your life force. It is your energy, your attention, and your aliveness. Life force is what gives you passion, drive, imagination, and inspiration. Being in your optimal state in terms of health, mindset, and deepest self-belief reflects your strong life force.*

- *You are the center of it all. You are the one in control. You have free will to choose. Nobody can go inside your head and do it for you. You are in your inner mental world, which is a universe of its own. Every part of that universe wants the very best for you.*

- *The more energy you have, the more you can experience the richness and beauty of life. The more you believe in yourself, the more life force enters your body, providing you with ideas out of nowhere, sudden guidance, and a strong sense of activation.*

- *The fastest way to increase your life force is to know that you are the observer of your experience, not the one identified with everything that is happening externally. You are seeing it all take place. Everything continuously changes, but you are silently watching it all unfold.*

- *You have always been in a state of ancient intelligence, which is timeless and exists in the now. This pulls your perspective back into the energy field, rendering you endless and fearless. The energy field is what was, is, and will be. The energy field is potential and possibilities. It is all now, and you are the one with this awareness, which means you can morph and shapeshift at will in order to become who and what you dream yourself to be.*

- *Creating what you want is recognizing that you are connected to everything. The thing, person, or situation you're trying to manifest is already in the field. You initiate contact by simply sending the intention. Don't overthink it or even get too technical here. Everything is as simple as breathing right now.*

- *Change isn't always a conversation or telling someone what to do. Just being and embodying it can send an energy signal into the minds of others that greater things are possible for you.*

- *Psychic energy is mental energy. The more life force you have, the more you willingly direct your mental energy.*

Thought Access

- *Many things drain psychic energy: fear, worry, negativity, judgment, gossip, lack of self-belief, overthinking, constant dependence on entertainment, overuse of social media, and bad relationships. Mental energy is alive, and when it is not engaged in a creative way or in a growth state, it starts to function as a projection of content and external influences. This can make you feel fatigued when you really haven't exerted any physical energy.*

- *Great things happen when people are activated in their minds. They gain self-belief, and this creates a ripple effect that alters many areas of their lives. You will also become your own energy source. You won't need to seek validation or look for ways to feel worthy.*

- *Your body is incredibly intelligent. It is alive, electric, and active. It is doing everything for you without your awareness of all that is taking place. Creating your inner sanctuary helps you become really good at listening to the signals your body is for or against.*

- *Start speaking power over your body, mind, and every area of your life. This is what activates life force to the maximum. When you actually start issuing mental commands over everything in your life, you begin to create what you speak instantly. You are everything you believe you are.*

- *You have to start listening to your body and all of its signals. Removing all processed and artificial products from your life deepens this connection further.*

- *Your attention is your power. Attention means using your life force to give power to something or someone to become real in your world. When you constantly give your life force away to things and people that are only* taking, it creates leaks in your energy. You instantly feel like there is an imbalance. Usually, your gut tells you; if you listen to your gut, you will stop losing life force to unnecessary things and people.

- *You imagination wasn't created for self-destructive thoughts. You were never meant to speak, visualize, or create the opposite of what you want. Your mind has only ever been able to give back what you put into it.*

- *Holding yourself accountable helps you stop leaking your life force. There is no one to blame and nowhere to give away your power. It's just you, facing yourself and becoming completely transparent. This takes you to another level because you have awakened to the realization that everything can morph into what you want it to be.*

- *When your soul is yearning for meaning, it wants to direct its own experience rather than being trapped by the digital world or people who keep you stuck in the same habits and patterns.*

6

PSYCHOLOGICAL FREEDOM

Psychological freedom is choosing to be lifted up into a new state of consciousness that brings healing, awareness, and expansion to your emotions and mental world while giving you back the power to direct your own life. This chapter will help you recognize how to intentionally be free from all lack and limitation so you can really live your life the way you want. When there is an overwhelming amount of pressure and distraction pulling you in all kinds of directions, you don't get the chance to actually reflect on your state of mind, which creates everything. Any narratives that continue to silently play out, causing a cycle of emotional triggering and attracting more of the same, need to be brought to light. You must understand the way you work so you can become psychologically free and at peace.

This chapter will dive deeper into your inner world and the way your mind works, allowing you to regain your self-awareness as an energetic being who can choose what they think, feel, and respond to on all levels. Who we are is so much more. When you start to understand that, you are not just existing in the physical world. You will begin to feel empowered like never before. You will know the mental space, the emotional fields, the spiritual nature of your life, and how all of this connects together to help you create the life you want. More energy becomes available to you as you become psychologically free of the things that keep you disconnected or focused on only one aspect of who you are.

You're breaking psychological patterns,

programs, and habitual states. You're freeing yourself from constructed external influences to intentionally and consciously create the beautiful life you deserve. You will be guided solely by your own inner voice. You will now start to know and see everything more clearly.

Psychological freedom is knowing that nothing has power over you. It is knowing that you aren't defined by anything, and you are not what others project onto you. Most unhealthy mindsets come from not knowing you're multidimensional and that you are a spirit first. You are a beautiful energy, and this energy is pure, free, open, and vast. When you have forgotten this, you become defined by the external world, and it feels overwhelmingly heavy to bear. Your soul has no limitations, no identity, no pain, no disturbances, and no judgement. When you start operating as a soul in your body, you will be shocked to find out how much discordance, disconnection, negativity, confusion, sickness, and distress leaves your life. We all have a feeling that there is more to who we are. That feeling is real, and many of us have connected back with our imagination and intuition to really navigate life here on Earth. You are becoming the embodiment of your truth. The life you see is far beyond the physical, and when you connect back with your true state, you gain a greater perspective—an overview rather than getting pulled back into everything that has already manifested.

Everything that has happened to you or already manifested has an energy link that originated inside of you. Energy is what creates everything we are looking at, experiencing, sensing, and feeling. You are the energy that chooses what to project, believe in, and create all around you. When we don't acknowledge this, we assume everything is random, and that life is just one confusing place that seems chaotic, unpredictable, and unstable. I want you to start understanding the subtle nature of your

Thought Access

existence so the images you imagine, feelings you have, and the thoughts you create support your entire ecosystem of life. Wellness of mind, body, and spirit depend deeply upon your inner balance, mental awareness, and being the master creator of your world, intentionally and in all ways.

Psychological freedom will be so important because it ends the inner battle that tries to define you, limit you, and make you seem like something you're not. The reality is that right now, anything is possible for you, but the experience for most people is that they think "right now" is their past or even their future. This is caused by repeated storylines that have already ended and/or fear that something that did not work out at one time will perhaps reoccur.

Your psychological freedom is today. Today is a new day, and so is every day after that. The way you show up in every moment represents your level of freedom. Are you acting out emotions that don't belong to you? Are you being defined by a previous shortcoming? Does your belief system cause you to operate from fear? Are you unaware of what is causing the thought and emotional loop cycle that is happening? These questions are meant to serve as a reflection on what is driving your current *now*. Are you actually present, or just playing out a repeated pattern that keeps pulling you into life day by day without understanding the origin of everything you are creating?

> *Being present in one moment can remedy years of living without understanding. That's the power the present moment holds. Feel more lucid in your life, more aware, more connected, and more energetically empowered.*

I'm sure you've been advised so many times to be present or just "be in the now." The reality is, your level of presence directly affects your awareness of everything taking place within you.

Sometimes, we think that just because we are having a certain kind of thought, we should keep going with it. The thing about the mental world is that everything is possible. There is no end or beginning, so you can be in your mind imagining so many things. Thoughts are magnetic. They pull from an archive of thoughts to match the ones you're thinking. This also happens with emotions.

You'll recognize that by the time you, as the observer, become aware of all these thought and emotions, you have the inclination to begin directing them by saying, "I should stop overthinking this" or "I am making all this up right now." We all have had a moment in which our inner observant state gets activated, and we suddenly end the stream of emotions and thoughts that previously played out due to memory and habitual thinking. None of it was ever you. It was all "per usual" thoughts and feelings played out day to day without any kind of awareness that *you* are the one silently observing these things.

When you discover this, you stop letting it all control you. You awaken the ancient overseer that has always been there since you were born. You step into yourself by intentionally choosing your thoughts and feelings to your liking, to match your evolutionary path. You can even choose to silence everything at will and direct it the way you want. It all starts with insight and awareness. You know how your inner world works, so you won't just be *told* to be present, you will *know* what it feels like. At will, with the snap of your fingers, you can command your mind, body, and spirit to be present now. This is the superpower you have as someone who is unidentified, unbothered, undisturbed, timeless, and a forever being.

> *Your biggest realization will be what your mind can actually do. You'll see how important the health of your mental and inner world is. Never go against your own well-being and harmony*

Thought Access

just to do something or get somewhere. Living in your optimal state is the basis of all creation.

There must be a deep deconstruction of your inner world so you can reign supreme over your external world. When you are in disarray, you are controlled by the external world. Without awareness of yourself, everything around you will make you feel clueless, emotionally unstable, and co-dependent on circumstances and situations. You won't feel like you can think for yourself. I haven't seen the depth of the individual understood or adequately explained anywhere, but I have seen solutions to patch up your disconnection from yourself everywhere. There are millions of things in the world ready to please insecurity, confusion, lack of awareness, addiction, and disconnection from self. These will become obsolete once you step into your power. You will not only know what psychological freedom is, but you will *feel* what it is to you. This state of being isn't anything that can be taken from you. This isn't a person that can leave your life. This is unlike anything else out there. It is you. It is *you* who has always been observing the world. Many events have come to a pass, many pivotal moments of your life have come and gone, many people you knew are no longer here; and just like that, everything in life keeps flowing and going forward. You have seen it all take place.

The memories you have collected are but a glimpse. Allowing yourself to be defined, limited, and stuck in what used to be shows that you didn't know you weren't truly a part of any of it. You are an expanded consciousness filled with so much peace, love, and possibility. We choose what we attach to anything. Meaning is created by us. Value is created by us. What means the world to one person might be of little interest to the next. When you know this, it will help you to avoid overvaluing anything else while undervaluing yourself. You don't need to put anything or anyone on a pedestal, because they only depend on you to give them energy to in order to exist in your mind. You, the reader, are gaining valuable Thought Access right now: the freedom to choose what has value and meaning to *you*, and what you feel is worth your energy. When we don't do this ourselves, we are given what we "should" value by default, even if it is a determinant of disharmony in our lives. I will be a doing a thorough breakdown of all the psychological factors that distract you from your potential. I will be giving you the much-needed codes of activation to become a skilled master at maneuvering your experience with the proper tools while remaining in the powerful resonance frequency that matches you with the life you love to live.

Breaking Free: Mentally

Mental freedom is consciously choosing your state of mind. Mental freedom is unique to the individual, but almost everyone wishes for peace of mind, clarity of thought, a strong mindset, and the ability to see everything through. Your mind is actually very powerful. Everything we do in this life depends on our mindset and access to higher thought. Your mentality is determined by your level of self-awareness to a greater extent than the information you hold. Information gets you the things we all collectively see in the world around us, but awareness gets you what works precisely for you and your soul's mission.

Nobody has ever offered to just share the secrets of the universe with you, but in deep moments of thought, or in breaking points when you really needed your spirit to step in through prayer or deep intention, it happened. You switched on your guidance, and it led you to where you were meant to be. This is why things tend to happen right when you need them the most. What you did was activate your true state. You awakened from the slumber of the normal frequency to match up with your true resonance and state of being.

Thought Access

A mindset can be constructed; in other words, you can create it. It doesn't matter how old you are or what you thought about yourself a second ago. You can construct your mentality right now and program yourself the way you want. You can program yourself to be the happiest person in the world and the most blessed person who has ever existed. You can program yourself to be very successful and attract whatever you want. Nothing is off limits, and this insight is for those who are willing to break free from stagnation. Whatever we believe and affirm, we become. Whatever we dream, we receive. The shocking truth is that the physical world is the land of make believe. It depends on your belief to come true. There probably isn't one thought right now in your mind that isn't tied back to something you believe in. Your mentality isn't random; it is created.

Fear can't hold you back anymore. You're aware now, and you're transcending limitations of the mind and emotions. Freedom is using your awareness to choose and create the life you want. You are too great to be limited, and you are awakening to that truth now.

To break free mentally, you must start creating your own mindset. Don't waste another second trying to identify limiting thoughts or figuring out what you want to get rid of. Working through things can sometimes keep you stuck because you keep reliving past events. Talking about them can cause you to get pulled into the undercurrent. Your mind only knows what you expose to it now, and it generates feelings accordingly. When you continuously bring up the past, it makes your mind believe that those things are happening right now. Instead, if you start creating in your mind who and what you *want* to be, you will create a new mindset, a new self, and a new belief system in your favor. This is what you need to choose. You past mindset was chosen for you, and it kept you stuck. This is the dawn of a new day—a beautiful new moment for you to mentally breathe in the illumination of awareness.

Breaking free mentally has become easy for you. You are no longer trapped reliving what was, when what exists now and in your future is so much more promising. At every moment, you choose your mindset, giving yourself a chance to experience life the way you want. I have helped many family members, friends, and clients discover what it is to be mentally illuminated. I have witnessed firsthand someone who was so stuck in their ways light up in their eyes and activate their own ability to get out of the victim/trauma mentality. I have seen instant transformation—and things most people assume would take a lifetime to overcome—happen right before my eyes. Some of the mentality upgrades I have seen have motivated me to add insight into this chapter and all it entails for the reader to enter their own new mindset.

Nobody is a victim, and nobody's life story is over. What we see externally is what people are currently choosing based on their state of awareness. With the right tools, guidance, and insight, a star can be born in every person you see. It is up to them to follow through, decide for themselves, and hold themselves accountable.

> *Your life story can change instantly right now. The truth is, anything is possible at any given second. It is all responding to the choices you make, the words, thoughts, and feelings you send out. You are constantly creating signals for the things you want to manifest.*

To begin the change, choose your mindset. Choose your thought patterns. Choose what and who you want to be. The reality around you will reflect all that you have chosen. If there is a mindset from which you want to break free, choose the opposite thoughts. After you make your declarations, you will notice that everything is lining up to match your new state of mind.

Another thing you will notice about your new mentality is that it will change everything and everyone around you. This type of change is always a great thing. When energetic bonds are upgraded, they weaken previous bonds that didn't support your mindset. Don't worry that this might be a negative thing or something concerning. Energy realignment always happens when a person is evolving at the rate they choose. You might find yourself in a better relationship, a new town, a new career, a new passion, or even a new way of living.

A powerful mindset exposes all limitation and anything that drains your energy. When someone's mind expands, so does their life. It'll even make you a better person because you begin to fully show up for yourself. The transformation period all depends on how much you accept the upgrades and let the process play out. Do everything from a place that is true to your own growth. Don't slip up and allow yourself to be pulled back into mindsets you have already released. People will try to make you feel like something is different about you now, which, of course, it is: You have the gained inner power to move forward. A new beginning is always possible. A lot of new energy and new experiences are taking place in your life.

> *Don't let anything stay too long in your mental field. Think, "Release," and it will start to clear your field. So much good will surround you. You'll feel like you've suddenly gained new access to yourself in a way that is empowered by your own inner command.*

Another important point I want to make about your mental state is the health and wellness aspect. I believe anyone can heal mentally. I believe everyone has a chance to recover themselves. This really, truly depends on what you believe about the world and your place in it. Losing yourself to self-judgement, comparing your path, overthinking your process, believing in negative words, feeling pressured, and being overly critical can slowly diminish your mental health because it makes you forget who you are. You can start to believe in what you're not. Sometimes, societal pressures create a mental burden on people without the right guidance or a way to process what seems to be happening. When none of what has happened to someone gets released, the person could hold that memory in their body, leading to anxiety and worry. Pressure from the external world and inner pain can silently can weigh on a person. This isn't a natural mental state for any human being. To exist in fear when you are not in danger is a sign that your mind is overworked and your imagination is being used in a detrimental manner.

Mental health and wellness are possible for you right now. No matter who is reading this, you can be at peace. Remove the triggers that cause you to feel anxious. Let all the excess noise go. Sometimes, you have to make decisions for yourself just to pave a new path for your mental health. Get back to everything natural and reconnect with your passion again. When you are living your truth and living from your heart, you can do everything that inspires you instead of allowing things to pull you down. This is your time to rise again, breathe again, and be yourself again. Implementing the insights in this book will give you your power back over every situation. As you start to choose your mindset, practice patience to see yourself through it all. This has never been a rush or a destination game. Your timing is truly *your* timing. Slowly but surely, you will rebuild, recreate, reconstruct, and design yourself the way you want.

> *You will find yourself breaking free and manifesting new energy into your life. Positive people, places, and experiences that resonate with your soul and your new outlook will locate you.*

Thought Access

Be open to what the universe is now bringing in: new ways, new connections, new energy, and a whole new mindset. You have entered your elevated state.

Mental manipulation is another topic I would like to mention in this. This chapter is all about psychological freedom, and I want everyone to be free from others who try to control them through manipulation. When someone is mentally manipulated, they aren't a weak-minded individual. They are someone who hasn't gathered enough mental energy, spiritual power, and self-awareness to break free. People only try to control others through negativity, by breaking them down mentally, or by creating a sense of dependency.

First things first: Everyone is free. Second, everyone can create their own reality, which means you can manifest any outcome you want. And third, you can retrain your body to exit overstimulation and chaos, which can manifest as a result of feeling and thinking the same negative thoughts constantly. Sometimes, when people have been manipulated for too long, they become habituated to being treated badly and/or dealing with problems projected by others. They assume that everyone and everything is out to get them.

To see yourself out of a chaotic situation, you will need to see yourself in a new way. Don't deal directly with anyone trying to manipulate you. Don't seek closure or resolution. Go into your own private space in your mind and begin designing a different scenario. See yourself mentally where you want to be. As you imagine it, the universe will find a way for you. The space all around you will start energetically influencing others to fall away from your life while inviting others who align with the mental world you have created. People always think they need to exert energy to get what they want, or even use force. All of these things keep you trapped in their game. When people are truly weak, they depend on the energy of others; but when the one being manipulated becomes energetically empowered, they gain access to a kind of power that weakens any forces working against them.

> *A great sign of your maturity and growth is no longer feeding into other people's drama, games, or negativity. Sometimes, you just have to know how to evolve past what doesn't lift you higher. When you step away from it and step into yourself, you get your power back. Use your energy to become better and attract greater.*

Everything is energy, and the strongest beings are the ones who use their minds to create the life they want. You never need to manipulate or live in a fight-or-flight state. You never have to tell someone your exit plan, or even try to use the energy they are using on you to go toward them. Revenge and grudges never solve anything. Anyone who wants to get out of manipulation or any kind of abuse must immediately replace that with mental power and self-trust to start propelling an inner empowerment that will help them break free.

Go into your place of silence and pour your heart out in your intentions, prayer, and a new vision for yourself. Whatever you need to release, release it, because it is so important in healing and will amplify your command/ request. After that, start seeing yourself mentally in a healthy situation. Whatever the circumstances, use that vision to properly see the new outcome. Keep going about your life. You will discover the way being made for you.

You created in secrecy a strategy you could not have physically accomplished otherwise. This will be a supernaturally aligned breakthrough for you to break free. Everything that came from your mind and your prayer, intention, and vision has been heard. You will see the manipulators leave your life in an unheard-of way. Somehow, they are no longer interested in bothering you or even coming around. Even their attitude toward you will change. They may have broken up with you if it was a personal relationship. You can just never predict the way it will happen, but one thing you will know is that you have mentally chosen the new reality you are living. You created a way out of negativity. All of this is to say, do the work through your mind before you even try to do anything physically. Things always work out when you change your perspective. When you go into your mental world to create something, you power yourself up energetically by linking with the powers that be.

The first place you take back your power is in your mind.

Don't ever play the game of the manipulator. They are lacking life force, and they try to use others to feel empowered. Some people are too kind for their own good, and trust people's words when their actions don't match up. When you see certain behaviors that signal red flags, trust them. Don't over-fantasize about people or make up stories for them. Things are always clear when we get out of our own way and avoid getting pulled into their web.

You'll naturally become very good at reading energy with all the insight and wisdom I am sharing in this book. Your intuition depends on becoming self-aware. It is your intuition that tells you more about people, external situations, and things that will happen in the future. Once again, this is your ancient observer, which has always been present with you. It is your soul. Your ancient observer is timeless, so it knows so much more than you could ever see with your eyes. We will now delve deeper into under-standing our multidimensional states of being, pulling more energy for healing, clarity, creation, and direction.

Breaking Free: Emotionally

Emotions are living energy. When you get over-consumed by one kind of emotion, it is a sign that actual energy has built up and is moving around and within you. This is why, when you feel an emotion, it feels like it takes over your entire body. This can be excitement, sorrow, or anything in between; it is all a form of expression, which ties back into thought and intuition. It depends on how clear the person is and how aware they are of their own body and mental world.

It is possible to learn how to distinguish what you might be feeling or sensing as guidance. The emotions I want to discuss here are the obvious ones that cause you to become overwhelmed to the point that they begin to affect your psychological wellness. When a person is accustomed to playing out a certain kind of thought, that thought always holds an emotional association. This can cause the person to get into a looped pattern of linking the same thoughts and emotions, believing they are being triggered. In reality, this is a response the body has learned.

The psychological freedom you will receive here is that you can end the energy you give away to certain thoughts that come up in your mind. If you have mastered the previous chapters and the previous section on mentally breaking free, you will know exactly how to identify what is running through your mind, where is it coming from, and how it is emotionally affecting you. Since you have understood the mental aspect, you will know that when a thought comes up, you remove your energy from it by disconnecting your emotional attachment to that thought. When you keep feeding thoughts with emotions, more of the same thoughts are created, which produce the same exact emotions. It is possible remain in this state for too long, thinking it's a normal pattern or train of thought. You can end the emotional connection to unnecessary thoughts at will by not creating an emotional response to them. Become the observer again, and you will see that you are not living life on autopilot.

Thought Access

You are self-aware and conscious of what is taking place in your inner world.

> *Affirm: I have the power, the strength, the will, and the choice to change my life. I am dynamic and multidimensional. I am supernatural and superhuman. I have vast abilities and capabilities. I materialize my visions. I see everything I speak instantly. I am the source and the connection.*

When you start to break free emotionally, you also clear your energy field, which means you won't attract experiences that produce the same thoughts and emotions. Everything in life starts on the subtle level before we see the physical manifestation. You never know what is taking place inside anyone at any given time. Everyone ends up manifesting their own material world around themselves.

Getting right within will get you right on all levels. You must know that there are multiple layers to who you are. As you understand the nature of your existence as a multidimensional being, you start treating yourself differently. You gain emotional strength by refining yourself. You will feel emotionally liberated from patterns that were trying to continue to play out within you. You are becoming your own master and alchemist, going into areas of yourself that were hardly ever discussed or acknowledged. You are removing negativity and creating at will everything that is important to you. To be well, at peace, and aware is the foundation of the life. You will create from this place with all the insight you are receiving. Knowing thyself is key.

Breaking Free: Spiritually

Anyone who has experienced deep transformation of any kind knows that something unexplainable and supernatural has taken place. Anything that comes through the spirit will always feel mystical, sublime, and off the pattern of day-to-day life. This is the power of your soul right now. Most of the time, the operations of the physical world seem so solid, so real, and so unchangeable that we become dense and heavy with these frequencies, not knowing that this energy pattern only dulls us to the magical things that are always happening around us.

True vision isn't something external; it is an inner gift to see the world around you more clearly. This is what I want to activate in this section—your ability to remember your supernatural nature and break free spiritually. When you are in a spiritual state, you literally know that anything is possible. You know that things will happen and work out. You feel an inner connection that guides you and reminds you that there is more. You are creative, artistic, and very good at expressing yourself. You know that life will always go on, and this keeps things in your physical body light. At this stage, you have definitely mastered your mental and emotional state, and this gives your spirit the chance to exist unhindered and never misguided by reactions. Instead, you are guided by your own creation.

Your spirit knows you're using your body to experience the world around you for a moment in time, and when you realize this, you gather more energy into yourself. This frees you from the fear of death. When someone lives in fear, they are most likely scared of living life. When you are balanced, you see life as an adventure, a place for you to express and develop yourself. This is your spiritual frequency. When you know that you are truly free, life will become more magical. You will never have to be burdened with lower thoughts that try to keep you in fear and worry. When you are spiritually free, you have an attitude about you that sees everything as a beneficial outcome. You treat every situation as something that supports your evolution, and you have strong trust that things always seem to happen for you right when they're supposed to. You are always thinking and imagining from a greater perspective, which helps you accept your creativity and be open to expression.

When you break free mentally and emotionally, it'll become easier for you to connect back with your spirit, because there won't be noise keeping you distracted from seeing all that you are. All of this happens in its own natural way, in its own natural timing. One reader could read this book alone and receive an instant realization or awaking to an expanded view; another might feel a mental release and start working on things at the emotional level. Still another might experience a blissful feeling that suddenly comes over them. This can bring tears of joy from all the energy coming in, which feels like the ultimate freedom. It can create more energy in your body, allowing you to feel connected to everything in the entire universe.

> *As you gain more awareness spiritually, you will literally start to see yourself as illuminated. You'll glow, radiate, and shine the brightest. You'll start to walk your trusted path. You'll see with your mind. You will know with your heart. This is the blessing of awakening spiritually.*

A spiritual breakthrough is the greatest feeling. It gives you back expanded vision and removes the small perspective you previously attached to everything. It shows you what it means to operate outside of time and space in the realm of thought. It brings you instant healing and wisdom, opens your heart and mind, grounds you, and gives you a feeling of safety, reassurance, and knowledge that you are never alone. You will start to feel love being poured into you. You just can't explain this new peace you have found.

When you are moving spiritually, all the small, limiting perspectives are removed one by one. You might even find yourself completely disinterested in certain things that seemed okay not so long ago. The speed at which you outgrow habits and things that are detrimental to your overall wellbeing will be further catalyzed. This is a time of great change and positive upgrades. Anything you have attached to yourself will come into question, because the new direction that humanity is collectively choosing requires you to free yourself from anything that previously limited you. These things used to seem like part of who you were. They were what you thought you liked, but as your energy increased and your awareness expanded, you realized for yourself that illusion was keeping you trapped and causing you to waste your precious life energy.

Sometimes, when we don't know what we don't know, we can assume that what is happening is all there is to life. In truth, with every small discovery you make and every bit of inner guidance you receive, you will see a richer, finer, more detailed version of reality. Everyone sees the world through their current state of development, and the world around them matches those beliefs. I am sure you have seen this for yourself. Perhaps you changed a habit you shared with another person or group of people, and suddenly, when you decided you longer wanted to do that one thing, it created an energy shift between you. Many times, when we choose to get better, it suddenly influences the external world to break bonds, relationships, and habits that no longer match the new self you feel and see within. This is a change in belief and habit. What follows is a profound shift in your external experience. Anything that stays the same depends on a presence within you calling upon it to remain the same. There has never been a time that you have altered yourself from within when your world didn't alter, as well.

This is a spiritual phenomenon. You are working with the finer energies of your mind and spirit to make better decisions for yourself, even when they don't make sense to other people who haven't yet altered their inner state. The only thing that links us to anything in the physical world is belief systems, habits,

Thought Access

values, and the concepts we share.

The will of your spirit is truly the most powerful energy to break through any situation and overcome any habit.

Be prepared for a massive positive shift to happen in your life when you break free spiritually. You are no longer cluelessly playing the game. You know now. You know where you come from. You know you are a spirit first, and everything you do will come easily and effortlessly. You will naturally know how to flow with the energy of life. You won't be afraid of outcomes or what appears to be happening because you are a master creator and manifestor.

With your will, you can change the way you see things, what you feel about them, and what you expect the new outcome to be. This also means you are no longer controlled by anything going right or wrong. These concepts are the residue of limiting times when life seemed dense or out of your hands. You, as a spirit, know that everything serves a purpose that will be revealed to you when you intentionally ask for guidance and insight. All matters will be resolved in this way. You will use your creative imagination to create everything you want.

You're starting to see with your spirit now.

Always remember that life is happening through your mind, your body, and your awareness. Treat yourself well and do all things gracefully. This couldn't have happened for you at a better time. There is no *could have, should have,* or *would have* that can do what you can do for yourself right now. You are spiritually liberated, and you have psychological freedom to choose the life you want intentionally—from you heart, and at the pace that feels natural to you.

There isn't any rush or urgency, only commitment and dedication to finally experiencing every aspect of life. All that is required from you is to be yourself...listening to yourself, feeling and sensing intuitively, and staying connected to your own inner voice. You don't need to leak, waste, or give away so much of yourself, only to be misguided or told things that don't resonate with your heart. The simplicity and beauty of life is that we already are. We are gently and lovingly returning to the realization that creates the ultimate transformation. Treat the unfoldment like a dance. Take every step forward with precision, and every turn with trust.

I want to conclude this chapter by reminding you of the importance of practicing self-belief, self-love, self-awareness, and self-creation. These will support your mental and inner worlds, which impact every other area of your life. I want you to be the most balanced you've ever been—the strongest in mind and the most loving in your heart. I wish you for you the best in your spiritual unfoldment and in everything that will take place for you as you go deeper into your adventure. When you see yourself living out your dreams, always remember that it was the light of your soul that guided you through—the trust you held, the commitment you made to yourself, and the path you created by recognizing who you really are. You are now psychologically, mentally, emotionally, and spiritually free to be all that you imagine yourself to be.

Key Points to Remember

- *Psychological freedom is knowing that nothing and no one has power over you. It is the knowledge that you aren't defined by anything, and you are not what others project onto you.*

- *Wellness of mind, body, and spirit depend deeply upon your inner balance, mental awareness, and ability to exist as the master creator of your own world, intentionally and in all ways. Psychological freedom will* be crucial because it ends the inner battle that previously tried to define you, limit you, and make it seem like you're something you're not.

- *You awaken the ancient overseer, which has always been there since you were born. You step into yourself by intentionally choosing your thoughts and feelings to your liking, thereby matching your evolutionary path.*

- *We choose what we attach to everything. Meaning is created by us. Value is created by us. What means the world to one person might be of no interest to another. When you know this, it will help you to stop overvaluing everything while undervaluing yourself.*

- *Mental freedom is choosing your state of mind. Mental freedom can be anything for anyone. Most of us wish for peace of mind, clarity of thought, a strong mindset, and the ability to see everything through. Your mind is actually very powerful. Everything we do in this life depends on our mindset and access to higher thought.*

- *To break free mentally, you must start creating your own mindset.*

- *Nobody is a victim, and nobody's life story is over. What we see externally is what people are currently choosing based upon their state of awareness. With the right tools, guidance, and insight, a star can be born in every person you see. It is up to them to follow through, decide for themselves, and hold themselves accountable.*

- *Mental health and well-being are possible for you right now. No matter who is reading this, you can be at peace. Remove the triggers that cause you to feel anxious. Let all the excess noise go. Sometimes, you have to make decisions for yourself in order to pave a new path to your mental health. Get back to everything that is natural and reconnect with your passions again.*

- *When someone is mentally manipulated, they aren't a weak-minded individual. They are someone who hasn't gathered enough mental energy, spiritual power, and self-awareness to break free. People only try to control others through negativity, by breaking them down mentally or creating a sense of dependency.*

- *Anyone who wants to win using manipulation or any kind of abuse must gain the mental power and self-trust to start propelling their inner empowerment to immediately break free. Go into your place of silence and pour your heart out in your intentions, prayer, and a new vision for yourself.*

- *Don't ever play the game of the manipulator. They are lacking in life force and try to use others to feel empowered. Some people are too kind for their own good, and trust people's words when their actions don't match up. When you see certain behaviors that signal a red flag, trust yourself.*

- *When you start to break free emotionally, you also clear your energy field. This means you won't attract experiences that produce the same types of thoughts and emotions. Everything in life starts on the subtle level; later, we see the physical manifestation.*

- *Inner vision isn't something external. It is your inner gift to see the world around you more clearly.*

- *A spiritual breakthrough is the greatest feeling. It gives you back expanded vision and removes the small perspective you previously attached to everything. It shows you what it means to operate outside of time and* space in the realm of thought. It brings you instant healing and wisdom, opens your heart and mind, grounds you, and gives you a feeling of safety, reassurance, and the knowledge that you were never alone.

- Be prepared for a massive positive shift to happen in your life when you break free spiritually. You are no longer cluelessly playing the game. You know now, and you know from where you come from. You know you are a spirit first. Everything you do will come easily and effortlessly. You will naturally know how to flow with the energy of life.

- Always remember that life is happening through your mind, body, and awareness. Treat yourself well and do all things gracefully.

7

A MESSAGE FOR YOUR SOUL

This message is for your soul. If you have ever felt different, off the path of the "usual," or like there was more to you; if you can sense and see what is unseen to many; if you have been called weird, a big thinker, a dreamer, or even considered odd...this message is for you.

Many of the brave souls who have chosen their unique path and felt different most of their lives are individuals who have pushed boundaries outside of what society has told them. They have escaped many boxes and defied many categories. This message is a sign of recognition, acknowledgement, and encouragement, a wink from the universe to let you know that you are not alone.

When someone follows their calling or dares to dream big, they go against everything that seems normal to many people. To be the one who imagines, questions, creates, believes, and dreams big is something exceedingly rare. You didn't go with what you were told to do or accept limitations that only seem real to limited minds. You felt and sensed that there was more, and you followed that feeling. No amount of external pressure ever made you give up. No negative words or fears could dim your soul's vision.

You have always felt like there was a bigger mission for your life. You always felt your own calling, and you went ahead without support from anyone. Your support came from within: that inner voice telling you to go forward, keep believing, and always trust yourself. Everything you were led to do always felt connected, like you were being guided by an invisible force. You always received what you needed right when you needed it the most. You never operated from a place of certainty. Most of what you did was unpredictable, and you depended deeply upon faith to make it through.

Your soul knows what is real. Trust it.

This is what makes you a powerful soul. If you are reading this right now and connect with every single word written here, just know that this message is for you. You are a brave soul who has stood strong while staying true to your own essence. When you are truly alive as a soul, you do everything that is different, unique, and special. People always sense that you are gifted. They might even come to you for advice or guidance. This is all a big part of your light, which is felt by those around you. When you accept who you are, it makes your experience easier. You may have had to face a plethora of challenges due to the fact that you think differently. You may have felt misunderstood.

These challenges were only meant to refine your soul so you wouldn't lose touch with who you are. They weren't meant to shut you down; that would be impossible. When you know, you know. Nothing can take that away from you. You get more inspired to pour from your heart into everything you do. You want to help others. The earlier stages of your growth were about reflecting your place in the world—seeing things the way you saw them and then finding out what everyone else might be thinking. When you initially awakened, you realized you had probably spent too much energy trying to make sense of why other people just didn't get it. Why didn't it seem clear to them?

All of this is part of the process of accepting who you are and just being yourself. When you get to the point in your life when constant questioning about when people will wake up or when they will finally "get it" passes by, you will enter a beautiful state of ease in which you stop trying to make the world see what you see. Instead, you actually start to experience your own beautiful adventure ahead. Everything is part of that unfolding. It is right for you to always wonder, question, and think, because that is the nature of your soul interacting with the physical world. However, as you evolve into your own awareness, you will feel a sense of ease in being different and not needing people to be on your wave of frequency. The wonderful thing that happens after you bask in your own light is that you start to feel it shining into the world by example. Just being who you are is the most magical experience you can have. Everything isn't always about getting everyone onto something. That's like being told to conform when all your life, you have done everything your way.

> *You are a soul on a bigger mission. Don't get pulled into appearances or circumstances. Don't forget who you are, why you started, and where you are headed. Always know yourself.*

You are the representation of a free spirit. You have an open mind, and you probably have many people who depend on you. It is the leader in you and the light within you that attracts people. This is a universal signal that means you are a carrier of great power. This makes you very responsible, dependable, authentic, and trustworthy. People want to share with you, as they are unknowingly looking for guidance or support. When your soul is filled and shining, you get to do more, be more, and impact the world around you.

Everyone uses their gifts in their own way. Some nurture and share love, some become healers, teachers, guides, inventors, writers, or artists. Others put all of themselves into their creative endeavors to express the unique way of their soul. The soul knows that anything is possible, and when you are awakened to that fact, you always find your creativity at a peak because everything has meaning, purpose, and value. You see it because you know. As a soul on your own unique journey, you always understand that life goes on, and this is just an adventure. When you keep yourself in that state of mind, you never overburden yourself. Your attitude is that all good comes from your soul. You know that nothing ever stays the same or in one state. Things are always changing, and you happen to embrace that change.

Many will find solace in the knowledge that they have never been alone on their Earth journey. Everything was meant to be, and you being yourself is also meant to be. There was never a mistake in anything. It all happened perfectly. When you embrace the fact that you have been chosen by the Most Gracious to be a part of humanity's shift, you will understand everything. People sometimes assume that serving as a vital part of the human shift means that everything weighs or depends on them, which creates unnecessary pressure. Just being you is enough. Being well in mind, body, and spirit is enough. Everyone doing their part simply by being healthy, whole, and balanced from within is enough to create a massive impact.

You naturally feel the need to take care of yourself, because that is a part of your soul's path. Anyone who is in alignment with themselves always honors, nurtures, and takes care of their body, as they know they can only live life through it. Many things seem obvious to you, and that is a big part of living from your soul. The things that are usually taught or explained seem obvious and come easily to you. This is probably why people come to you for advice; it is easy for you to share from a place of positivity and hope because you resonate with everything. You naturally gravitate toward nature and animals, and you are in constant awe of the magnificence of the Creator's design.

> *Your energy craves what is real. Your soul knows the world was meant to be magical. You won't settle or let yourself play the acceptable game. You're so much more, and you're willing to go down your own path to discover it all.*

Thought Access

You feel so deeply, and this means your intuition is activated. You pick up on energy for insight but let it go to stay clear. You naturally avoid holding onto things for too long because you thrive on being present. All of this means you are on your chosen path. Take every gift your soul gives you and shine it outwardly. Don't become someone who is easily overwhelmed by your light vs. their level of awareness. That isn't the point. You are who you are because you have a bigger mission. Never spend much time wondering what others think of you, or what *you* think they should think. This is another sneaky way that energy gets lost. This separation is created by the idea that "they are asleep and don't know what is going on, so therefore they need to stay away from me." This only creates restrictions within you. Life wasn't meant to be spent on over-analysis of how people think and the extent to which they should match the state we are in. Stay in the experience of energy, and don't get pulled into the mindset of comparison or wanting to break people free.

The highest way to stay healthy in your mind, beautiful in your aura, and radiant in your beauty is to be, be, be. Don't ever feel the need to force, coerce, or manipulate any experience. Everything single thing requires an energy investment in your life force. Step back instead, and let it flow through you. You already have energy in abundance because your soul is awakened. The only thing that can deplete you is getting pulled into perception games without putting things into perspective for yourself first. Stay present and always go higher, even when you want to go into the battlefield of us vs. them. It's never worth your energy, and most of the time, it's only a mind game we play on ourselves to feel a sense of empowerment or validation of our position of awareness. You just are. You have always been, and you will always be. The rest is a choice in terms of experience and what you want to feel. Choose greater at every moment.

A Message for Dreamers

Your vision isn't random; it is a message from your future. Your dream is being downloaded into you through your soul. Sometimes, your vision might come as a flash, a sign, a sudden realization, a calling, an experience, or a feeling. This is communication from your soul, and it already has the blueprint for you. When you first get a vision or feel like you want to start on a project you have in mind, it all seems perfectly laid out, as the flash actually comes from your future. In your future, you are going to be living it out. It is a probable reality, and the choice you make to follow through with it solidifies that outcome. Your soul is constantly relaying visions to you because they are connected to your dreams. Whatever your desire, feel it in your heart, and your soul will return with a blueprint for its realization.

One important thing I want to convey to the dreamers is knowing how to follow through with the insights of your soul. Sometimes, when you receive a vision, you might automatically feel overwhelmed because it is a big dream. The funny thing is that to your soul, nothing is too big, too over the top, or too hard. However, your day-to-day mindset operates on timelines (how, when), locations (your reach), and fears (seeing yourself doing it). This gets in the way of your natural signaling, which was designed to retrieve the vision (blueprint) and see it through. Every step along the way, you are guided, but you get the ball rolling with your actions based on what you sense, how you feel, and what you are being called to do. Every dreamer should follow through with their visions. Nothing is impossible. Nothing is in your way. Get out of the mental chatter and judgement of your own path. Move with it. Go forward toward it.

> *How else would it happen if you didn't dream it up? You initiate the forces that get you to work with the simplicity of your intention interacting*

Thought Access

with thought. It is all happening through you.

You can't try to predict that you might, later on today, bump into someone who will play a role in manifesting your dream. That person was sent from your soul, as they, too, received a signal to be at a certain place right at that time. For some unknown reason, they came into your life in the most unexpected way. These are soul-guided people. When a dreamer stops using the five senses physical senses alone and starts operating according to trust in higher-power guidance, they are often stunned to know how easily every missing piece of the puzzle can come together to create a beautiful picture (your dream)!

My message to you as the dreamer is to start getting very mystical and magical in your life. Start feeling that you are connected to everything and everyone on an energetic level. Everything that is meant to happen for you is currently being aligned in the world of the unseen, and those who will serve a purpose on your journey are also connected to that manifestation through an invisible link. The point is that you should never for one moment second-guess yourself or the way things are going to happen. Get out of that limiting thought process; it shows that you are closed off from the unseen world. What is in your heart is what is meant for you.

Every person who has manifested their dreams knows what it took, and most of the time, it was a lot of faith and self-belief. The rest was just scenes being orchestrated in the realm of the unknown. You just happened to play a role in every scene, and at the end, your original vision manifested. This is a powerful reminder for you to stay consistent, determined, and, most importantly, tapped in, so you can receive the necessary guidance and take the necessary action.

Every dreamer must know that most of what you are doing is working in the unseen realms. This is true whether you are just coming up with an idea or you are in the middle of your creation. Don't ever, for one second, let anyone who isn't a part of your mental creation speak negativity, limitation, or fear to you. Exposing your private creation means that you are putting it into minds that have never seen the entire blueprint. This can ignite their own projection of what they believe in. How can they see what your soul has shown to you? Don't be tainted by the process of trying to convince them or prove them wrong. This can happen when we are just so happy and excited to share what we are currently working on, only to see that the energy isn't met with the same enthusiasm. This doesn't mean your fire has to get burned out. We have to stop being so overly sensitive to doubters and start being overly empowered by our own soul's mission. Keep your creations private as needed, and let them speak for themselves. Privacy comes from a place of not allowing judgement or external noise to taint your precious process.

This is a sign from your own soul right now to listen up, trust, follow through, finally start your idea, create, get it done, and live exactly how you want. This message is meant for current dreamers; it's also here to revive previous dreams that have lost their fire to awaken at once and restart, dear one. You can, and you will. You have done it before, and you can do it again in a greater way. No matter where you are with your dreams, all that matters is that you have heard the calling and believed in yourself. You are the reason humanity is going to change, and many lives will be impacted. You will give hope to other dreamers, change your family's lives forever, and create from a harmonious place for the planet and yourself. You are the dreamer, the dream, and the creator of it all. NEVER FORGET WHO YOU ARE.

A Message for Brave Souls

You overcame it. You recreated yourself and got out of it. This message is for the brave souls who have made it through. The ones who know they've borne hardship and broken free. Your soul is resilient. There isn't anything that can stop you or make you stay the same. You have accepted your growth, your evolution, and your rise with so much grace that everything seems to bring you where you were always meant to be. Nothing that happened in your past has defined you or even blurred your vision. You knew the benefits of following your soul, and it brought you great blessings.

Being a brave soul means you have used spiritual power to get through everything. When you are being tested, when you're tired and at your wits' end, something suddenly arises within you. This is your soul giving you some light and guidance. You feel an impulse to see it through, and you do. This is what makes you a brave soul. The lessons you have learned have given you a lifetime of wisdom about how to handle any situation that might come your way. You hold the golden key now, and that proves you are unstoppable and fearless. The beautiful thing about anyone who has survived any hardship, trauma, or difficulty is that they find themselves in a better and brighter place without needing to identify with past experiences. You know exactly how to move on and be in harmony. You know how to tap into your spirit for healing, and you know how to write a new story for your life. Brave souls aren't the ones who have been broken; they are the one who have prevailed. They are the ones who have carried on and created a new life for themselves. You too can do it, too, because you are a brave soul.

You feel deep within your soul that you are destined for greatness.

Here's a light of guidance to bring you reassurance, understanding, and hope for the path upon which you are about to embark. Some journeys seem impossible, but those who have gone down paths less traveled will tell you that a wonderful world awaits. When we only see where we are right now, we forget what lies ahead. Don't allow yourself to be consumed by your current narrative, habits, situation, or anything taking place in your life. This is just a scene in your greater life story. This one moment isn't the end of the world or the end of who you are; it is the beginning of something special. Embrace this current state, as your soul is being empowered to be free itself from addictions, habits, lower thoughts, inharmonious frequencies, and limitations.

You feel this battle coming to an end, and your triumph is the knowledge that you never gave up on yourself. What makes you so different in this situation is that you have decided to do something about it. You went against the energetic currents of sameness and said, "This is it, this is the time," and you are doing it so fearlessly. Strength comes from the soul. When everything wants to trap you in the same situation, you are the one who must tap into greater assistance. Each time you go within, you are consulting with your soul and making plans to break free.

Nothing is a coincidence when you receive a sign or feeling about how to do this. The rest will be a process of energetic, physical, and spiritual transformation. It is like a death of the past self and the rebirth of the new self. The way through it is only for brave souls. You'll live through it just to tell the story of bravery, faith, dedication, and the endless possibilities of the soul. Overcoming something does not make you a victim, but an expert on how to be free. Everything will seem possible when you already have the tools to deal with the outcome. You will now reach greater awareness, which no longer needs or depends upon past lessons. You will move with insight, and this will allow you to return to your own true reality.

A Message for the Rare Gem

Remember yourself. You are returning to what it means to be a rare gem, a valuable and timeless soul. So much has tried to distract you and seek energy in ways that didn't feel right internally. You just knew it wasn't right. You knew it wasn't sustainable or long-lasting. What is real is what you are right now…what is in your heart. You have known you were different

Thought Access

for a very long time, and you wanted a life to match that feeling. You wanted soul recognition. You had not yet given yourself fully to your experience thus far because deep down inside, you felt that there was more depth, more meaning, and more value to being yourself in a connected way.

Being a rare gem means living from your soul. Every single thing in nature has already been designed with the codes it needs in order to be all it can be. There isn't something extra the seed needs to flourish into what it was designed to be. You have always been unique, and forgetting that may have caused you to behave outside of your character. We all recognize when we do things that just don't feel right for our soul because it feels inauthentic and requires too much energy. Don't lose yourself in this way. Regret arises from not listening to that feeling when your soul knows what is meant for you. Never settle or do what seems acceptable just to please people while you suffer in silence. Now is the time for everyone to live from a place of authenticity, rawness, realness, and openness. Loving someone for being themselves is a sign that you are connected to your own soul.

You have a special gift, and you know this. It's been making itself apparent recently, and you're starting to own it. You're standing in your truth. You're moving in a new direction. Something within you has risen, awakened, and is now activated. You're propelling forward in all ways.

There are people who naturally carry their light so well. They have embraced their mind, body, and soul. They are highly intuitive and connected individuals. Their connection is their soul, and this is what makes them shine so brightly. When a rare gem forgets who they really are, they start to undervalue themselves and overvalue everything else, which causes many imbalances. This can attract people who try to take advantage of you, not knowing who you are. The time has come to live your truth and live boldly. Much healing will naturally take place when you start to gain your confidence again and love who you are. Healing will trickle down from one thing to another. Let's say you suddenly have a realization that all you need to do is accept yourself and recognize your value. In this realization, you will automatically disconnect any energies that previously attracted disharmonious experiences to you. You didn't necessarily change what you were attracting; you changed yourself, and many other forces went into motion to eliminate irrelevant energy, bringing everything back into harmony to match your new signals.

This is the beautiful thing about seeing yourself in a higher light. When your soul shows you that you are so much more, you stop playing limiting roles that prevented you from accessing the life of your dreams. Always know the gift is in your heart, your mind, and your soul. Every time you need that reminder, put your hand on your heart and feel everything that you are. Close your eyes and take a deep breath just to acknowledge your aliveness. It took so much focus, attention, and love to design all that you are. Nothing was left behind when you were created, and the amount of love the Creator poured into you is something that obviously speaks for itself. Know that you are a rare gem. There is only one of you, and you were divinely created. Cherish all that you are and shine from your soul.

A Message for Those Seeking Meaning

The impulse to find meaning in life provides a way for the soul to return to itself through external things that bring us back to ourselves. It's paradoxical in a wonderful way, because the source is right there within you, but our minds work to find elaborate ways to understand meaning. This is enriching, because it becomes our life's adventure to reunite with the soul. The books we read return us to ourselves. The people we meet allow us to reconnect with the self in many ways we didn't realize were possible. Our experiences teach us. Bettering ourselves gives us more insight and depth to understand how much power we really have.

Meaning allows you to find increments of your wholeness. There is nothing wrong with wanting to find purpose, passion, meaning, and understanding about who you are. That is the symbol of self-discovery and self-awareness. You'll take many paths, only to be led back to yourself; and each time, external negativity will slowly be eliminated from that connection so it can remain unadulterated and undistorted. This is why you keep evolving from every teaching out there. You just keep existing, reminding yourself that it can be so much simpler than this. You return to a pure state of clarity, without hundreds of things showing up as obstacles on the path of reaching yourself. At every stage of growth, everyone is where they are meant to be; and by navigating their own path, will they come to realize their ultimate truth.

The deeper meaning you are searching for is really an understanding of how powerful you are. It is not a search. It is the knowledge that you are. It is a natural state. That's the gift of it all. There is no secret. You just are, and the less you search, the more you start sensing, feeling, and seeing everything all around you.

Knowing how to hear your own inner voice will help you get into a clear state of being and receive proper guidance for your life from within. You can start this by asking your soul for insight and guidance. A simpler way is to ask for an answer to something you need or for the way to be shown to you. As you vocalize your question, say what you need and see how quickly the answer comes. As you get comfortable with this kind of connection, you will start to see yourself as more trusting of your own thought process. Naturally, you will want to test this out in other ways. For example, if you want to manifest something or need answers to events happening in your life, you can use the power of your words to be shown instantly, or within the same day.

As you practice trusting your own soul and connecting to the inner source that wants to give freely to you, you might even begin to stop looking for meaning and start living life from a meaningful place. You will see yourself as the source, pouring into all that you are creating without attempting to study its origin. This is what the creator has designed in you—to always be in the know and connected.

When we think we are disconnected, we operate in unusual ways, acting like we don't know. For this, we use the same abilities to inquire for meaning. This is why nothing feels fulfilling, sometimes; external things are nothing more than manifestations that arise from the original source of the inner world. We can't fill ourselves with "things" to make us feel okay. We can utilize things, but we know we are the source of creation for everything external. All humans do this together, but we don't recognize ourselves as the ones responsible for this creation. Actual meaning comes from the creator of the thing—the source—not the thing itself.

Return to your blueprint. This will initiate a high level of self-trust, inner connection, listening to your own voice, heart-centeredness, and playfulness. Don't get too serious or devoted to one way of thinking. Be open so the insights can flow. Everything else will naturally become meaningful and filled with expression as you creatively draw from your soul.

A Message for Those Starting over Again

Everything you've known has come to an end, and you could be in the vulnerable place of not knowing what's next. All you know is that you *had* to start over again. You had to create in the unknown, with uncertainty, yet you still went ahead with it. Your soul knows what new beginnings will bring you and how they will show you that there is absolutely nothing to fear.

When we are in a place of change, we face some of the most difficult emotions to process, because it causes us to face a crucial question: *What does the future hold?* When we don't know what's next or how it will happen, we can resort to being led by inspiration to go forward or retreat into fantasy about what we have lost and what has come to an end.

Starting over is the best thing that can happen to you. Initially, in the confusion of emotions and the rewiring of the brain from the familiarity of the past habits, it all seems overwhelming to bear. However, you know in your soul that it is serving the right purpose for your path. You asked for this change; maybe you even prayed for better. Every twist and turn blissfully leads us to the life of our dreams. We have to know how to stay faithful to ourselves during those times. The best way to hold yourself together is the promise of a brand-new state of mind and state of being, with the promise of a new life awaiting you on the other side of it all.

> *Many new beginnings are taking place right now, both internally and externally. The energy is propelling an accelerated state. It is you who must make the choices that will let you become free, liberated, and open to more. Some of these decisions will be dire. Choose intentionally.*

When we stay in the familiar and begin to feel uncomfortable there, our soul creates a plan to help us break free. Sometimes, this comes with the loss of something, just so you can see yourself, allow yourself the ability to grow, and solve that initial uncomfortable feeling of being stuck. If something is not for you, or you don't feel your best in it, your soul will find a way out. The way out is starting over. New beginnings bring a lot of new energy when we actually embrace how great it will all be.

As humans, we love what we have always known. We love to be safe, comfortable, and habitual, even if it is detrimental to our own spiritual evolution (or our own well-being). This is why things can start to shake up. Change is required from you so you can be whole, free, and more yourself. The closer you are to existing in harmony and peace, with creativity flowing in your soul, the more you will find yourself living this kind of life for all your years on Earth.

Everything helps us arrive at this kind of place. The more easily we let go and allow change, the more quickly we return to harmony. It is impossible to hide how you feel from your soul. When you want to be freed from chaos, abuse, confusion, problems, and negativity, a way is made for you. What happens next will be about accepting this change, moving toward it, and welcoming the blessings that will come into your life.

Trusting your soul during a transitional period in your life means you know that it all serves a purpose. There was something within you asking for this change. It was all meant to expand your awareness and experience. Always know that new beginnings will bring you what you deserve and what matches your soul's frequency. Trust yourself and go ahead with it. It'll all be worth it.

I hope these messages for your soul resonate with you and bring you back to the internal place where you have trusted yourself the most. These words are full of hope, as they are meant to move the reader into a state of possibility. You can refer back to this section as needed for clarity, guidance, and reassurance. I know many people will experience beautiful energy and find themselves transformed forever!

Key Points to Remember

- *When someone follows their calling or dares to dream big, they are going against everything that seems normal to most people. It is rare to be the one who imagines, questions, creates, believes, and dreams big.*

- *When you've accepted who you truly are, it makes your experience even easier.*

- *You are the representation of a free spirit. You have an open mind. You probably have many people who depend on you, because it is the leader and the light in you that attracts people to you. This is a universal signal; you are a carrier of great power. This makes you very responsible, dependable, authentic, and trustworthy.*

- *As a soul on your own unique journey, you understand that life goes on, and this is just an adventure. When you keep yourself in this state of mind, you never overburden yourself. Your attitude is that all good comes from your soul. You know that nothing stays the same. Things are always changing, and you happen to embrace that change.*

- *My message to you as the dreamer is to start getting very mystical and magical in your life. Start feeling that you are connected to everything and everyone on an energetic level. What is meant to happen for you is currently aligning in the world of the unseen, and those who will serve a purpose on your journey are also connected to that manifestation through an invisible link.*

- *Keep your creations private as needed, and let them speak for themselves. Privacy comes from a place of not allowing judgement or external noise to taint your precious process.*

- *No matter where you are with your dreams, all that matters is that you have heard the calling and believe in yourself.*

- *Brave souls aren't the ones who have been broken; they are the ones who have prevailed. They are the ones who have carried on and created a new life for themselves.*

- *Don't get consumed by your current narrative, habits, situation, or anything that is taking place in your life. This is just a scene in your greater life story. This one moment isn't the end of the world or the end of who you are; it is the beginning of something special.*

- *Being a rare gem means living from your soul. Every single thing in nature has already been designed with the codes it needs in order to be all it can be. There isn't something extra that a seed needs to flourish into what it was designed to be.*

- *When you soul shows you that you are so much more, you stop playing limiting roles that prevented you from living the life of your dreams. Always know that the gift is in your heart, your mind, and your soul.*

- *The instinct to find meaning in life is one way the soul wants to return to itself. This can happen through external things, people, or events that bring us back to ourselves. It's paradoxical in a wonderful way; the source is right there within you. The way our mind works, however, is to find elaborate paths to help us understand that meaning.*

- *Trusting your soul during a transitional period in your life means you know that it all serves a purpose.*

Thought Access

Something within you asked for this change, and it was all meant to expand your awareness and experience. Always know that new beginnings will bring you what you deserve and what matches your soul's frequency.

8

BEING A THOUGHT ALCHEMIST

Being a thought alchemist is knowing how to take any mental state and transfer it in your favor so you can rise. You will become a master at choosing your thoughts, directing your thoughts, and making your thoughts work for you. The goal is for you to always get the outcome you want and the ability to remain in a calm, trusting, knowing state at all times. Every single thing can happen for you. The world wants to serve you a platter of your wishes, dreams, and desires.

Think of it like an invisible ordering system that is live 24/7. All it does, from your mind to the field all around you, is provide you with what you want. That is how this internal system has been operating since ancient times. You can see this very clearly in your life: Everything you have manifested connects back to a thought (or, shall I say, a signal) from your inner world. We don't really pay attention to it because we have always lived this way. The field can only interact with your mind. You are the one who is alive, sending out commands, signals, prayers, and wishes at any given moment. It is such a beautiful thing to know that your thoughts are at work for you.

> *You are an alchemist. You can take any situation and transmute it into something greater. You are the master at changing any negative circumstance into a positive one. You are a visionary. You are dynamic. You are actively*

choosing better on a consistent basis.

This chapter was written to help you become the master of your thoughts, which means becoming a thought alchemist. You don't live life randomly or confused anymore. You don't wait around, thinking someone or something out there will come save you from the inner misunderstandings and uncertainties of life. You begin to operate from insight now.

We all know someone with wisdom and awareness who always receives exactly what they want. A thought alchemist changes their thought patterns at will. They create what they want because they believe in their own inner power to do so. They know that everything depends on their own perception, expectation, and belief that it will be. You are a thought alchemist. Just reading this book has started to give you access to what has always been there with you.

Imagine that all around you, there exists a world in which access happens through simple awareness in order to receive insight and powerful thoughts. This is actually what is happening at any given time. The more you gain realizations and unlock parts of your own mind, the more clearly you can see the vast possibilities, beauty, and energy that is ready to be tapped into.

Being a thought alchemist means you are working with your own mental energy, but also the energy of the universe all around you. You are choosing to positively influence your own life in a way that once seemed unheard of. People will ask you what your new secret is, or what have you discovered that makes you so trusting, certain, calm, radiant, creative, positive, influential, and healthy. This is the result of being a thought alchemist. When you work on your inner world and get to know yourself in such a real way, you activate within you a new kind of energy that flows through your entire body. This helps you clear out negativity, fear, and anything that was holding you energetically hostage (e.g., unhealthy thoughts running on a loop). At this level of awareness, you free yourself from many things on many levels, both visible and invisible.

You will start manifesting instantly now: out of thin air and in the most unexpected and unexplainable ways. Only you will know what happened; everyone else will just see the outcome. Your alchemist self has been in the inner lab for quite some time, harnessing your energy for greater.

Nobody sees the changes you start making initially when you start working in your mental world. As a thought alchemist, this is the silent night of the soul. This is when you are facing yourself. You are being raw, truthful, and authentic with yourself so you can put outdated states to rest. As the old ways perish, you bring to light a new version of yourself.

This rebirth is what I will be going into depth on in this chapter. I will provide you with a step-by-step guide for spiritually transmuting yourself and bringing to life whatever version of yourself you want to be. You are the one who will be doing all of this, and you are the one who will get to see, feel, and experience the beautiful changes. Only you know exactly what your soul is pulling you toward. The guidance is here, but the revelations will be born from you.

Get very comfortable being in the driver's seat and allowing your soul to navigate. The world around you will start to also respond to all the changes you've been silently making, and people will start to notice. Not only will they see in you everything you have seen in yourself, they will also be moved by your energy. True change is borne of the soul, which moves into the thoughts and the mind before transmuting your wishes into physical action and experience. It is all interconnected and intertwined. It occurs in an instant state, which is why we never ponder too much on how we have manifested or created our current reality. If you've read both of my previous books, *Manifest Now* and *Inner Glimpse*, I am sure you understand by now how to consciously create what you want...and the importance of knowing that it all starts with you.

> *You keep getting better! You took what you thought would break you and turned it into a way to thrive. You are a real-life alchemist. You used your inner power to transmute and transcend the situation or circumstance in your favor. You are unstoppable and resilient.*

Let's get deeper into being a thought alchemist. I will begin by giving you a mental protocol you can follow anytime you need to change anything about yourself or your circumstances. Almost everything I share goes back to the mental tools I have been providing. I want you to have the proper access to achieve lasting change you can initiate at any time, no matter where you are or what is happening. You can always refer back to this section of the book, as I am going to lay it out as points you can reference and use to your advantage.

Everything I share here will feel like you are receiving so much energy to support your change. When your mind expands, you feel a rush of hope and a sense of openness. This state is a reminder that you are always connected to all things life-giving and life-supporting. It is, in a way, your own private access that can never be taken from you. Before, when you had no clue about any of this, you may have periodically sensed that there was more—or you just knew, deep within your soul, that a lot more was possible for you. These increments of gaining greater awareness are your soul's way of communicating with you.

Sometimes, we are so stuck in our ways that we forget about this connection and contact. When that channel is utilized and reignited, it starts to pour into you in more ways than you could imagine right now. Everything I share here represents that. I believe everyone should be self-guided and use external tools only as a reminder, not a dependence. Once you dive into the mental protocols, I will also share the thought alchemist's mental creations, which will be about stepping into the power of creation. This will teach you ways to work with your imagination and the world all around you. After that, I want to talk about codes of conduct for the thought alchemist, which will be about honor, self-value, action, the way you treat yourself, and the kind of energy you put out into the world. It will be all about higher values, respect, and representation. Lastly, I will present the thought alchemist's mental tools, which will be a practical guide for everyday situations and assist you in remaining empowered, connected, and inspired.

The Thought Alchemist's Mental Protocol

These mental protocols are for any situation in which you feel that you just want to release energy from your mind and body. They can be used for multiple situations or all at once. This is a renewal space, which means you get to let it all go and make it disappear from your mind, emotions, and energy field. This is all about rising up and being reborn. The beautiful thing is that you will feel lighter and brighter every single time you work through any situation. This section was also created for mental healing. It provides the means for anyone who wants to work through a circumstance that has presented itself. The wonderful thing is that these strategies are for everyone and every situation. The alchemist can take anything energetically and turn it into a favorable outcome.

1. *Identify*

What do you want to release right now? Once you know

what it is, you can start to use your mind power to remove energy from it. Everything depends on mind energy to stay alive in your mental world.

2. *Dissolve*

Thought is energy, so it only exists when you keep repeating it. Each time you dissolve a thought by releasing it or forgetting about it, you notice that you never think of it again. You have naturally been dissolving unwanted thoughts by removing your attention from them for a long time. This is wired in us so we can move on with our lives. Sometimes, life pushes people to move on when they don't do it themselves, and later, they discover how grateful they are that it happened.

Start using this insight to your advantage as a thought alchemist. Your mental protocol is quickly dissolving unwanted thoughts and states of mind from which you want to move on. As you master yourself through awareness and practice, you will see how easy it is for you to dissolve things out of your mind and body. One visual image I see when I am dissolving a thought or feeling is capturing it with a golden bubble. Once you have put whatever you want to let go of inside, say "Dissolve," and you will see it disappear into thin air. Confirmation comes when you see the golden bubble glowing brighter with every release. This works really well, and it helps keep your inner world free of unwanted thoughts and emotions, which are energy leachers.

As you get to know yourself and see how well you are working with your imagination, you will become clever at different ways to let go of what no longer serves you. A lot of what we need to do isn't really about external decluttering alone; it is about revamping the source, where everything is created, so you won't choose misguided solutions. Dissolving unwanted mental states, emotional imbalances, and physical discomfort actually ripples into the greater field, which is unseen by the physical eye. Once the energy link between your mind and the thought is broken, you are actually renewed right away, and this welcomes in a harmonious sense of peace and wellness.

3. *Transmute*

Transmutation involves taking something out of one state and releasing it into another state more favorable to your desired outcome. As a thought alchemist, you must be really proficient at this mental protocol, because in life, there are always unexpected things coming our way. As we deal with many different people and situations, we must know how to transmute negative thoughts to positive ones right on the spot. This will help you the most when you feel a sense of doubt, fear, or worry. Stop yourself and lift that thought higher, transmuting it into one that works in your favor.

We often think we are somehow required to entertain our current thoughts and/or engage their energy when it is clear that this might not support our vision, direction, or mental balance. To change this means you must regain control of the thoughts that receive energy, the thoughts that are being transmuted, and the thoughts that will instantly be dissolved. Understanding this insight is crucial for you because things happen in life, and we don't want to get caught up or brought down by what happens. We have to know how to move through everything with awareness so we don't lose ourselves in unnecessary problems.

4. *Rise*

Every time you perform these mental protocols, you will rise into a new state. You will feel good about yourself, and you will know that you are the one who accomplished it. This is what will empower you further as you gain the power to make a difference in your life. After every win follows a great rise. The small changes you make on a mental level help every other area of your life, and you will slowly start to notice your light shining even brighter.

This brightness means your confidence has reached a new level. Inner confidence is no joke. When we know that we can be free by actively applying ourselves, we surpass all that has kept us in the darkness and rise out of what once seemed like our end. You hold the key to your new beginning, and you are choosing to RISE!

The Thought Alchemist's Mental Creations

As a thought alchemist, you will be great at these four mental creations because of how naturally the process comes to anyone who knows the world responds to their self-belief, visualization, and state of being. When someone knows how to create their reality and see firsthand their own manifestations, it gives them spiritual confidence and expands their mind in the knowledge that anything is possible. Inability to create the reality you want only comes from not knowing. You are always creating, whether you've just realized this or have always known. The point is to do it intentionally and consciously so the outcome is always in your favor. When a thought alchemist taps back into their own mind, they know how to begin the creation process through their imagination. A thought alchemist knows that the way they feel is crucial, and whatever they constantly speak functions as real energy. Use the four mental creations below to get anything you want.

1. *Image to Reality*

When you imagine something, it becomes a real outcome in your physical reality. When we picture or visualize something in our minds, we often assume we are just leisurely entertaining mental scenarios. What we are actually doing is reality shopping, and when the image you see is repeated, you are creating that reality in real life. This is the reason vision boards work—you are constantly looking at photos that represent what you want, and reality literally prints it out as a scene. Suddenly, you find yourself in it.

The first thing you need to do as a thought alchemist is treat your imagination like the real world. The world in your mind will match the world around you. Without too much concern about how this happens, simply repeat the mental images and be at ease with yourself. You will be so surprised to see how your mental image becomes your reality overnight. You don't need to do any special rituals or buy external things to support your mental creations. As a thought alchemist, all you need is your mind. This will also help you build self-trust, which will be crucial to creating the reality you want.

2. *High Self-Belief*

A high level of self-belief equates to trust in your spirit. You live life from a place of awareness, as you know you are not merely physical in nature. All of your creations that you imagine, visualize, and step into through your mind will require you to REALLY believe in yourself. This is a high level of self-belief, which means it all depends on you, and you alone. What you feel in your heart and know in your soul can only be experienced by you, because these are subtle energies within you that require you to trust. When you trust yourself and apply a high level of self-belief in the direction of your dreams, they always end up manifesting. Every image becomes a reality.

Your secret as a thought alchemist is that you train yourself to believe for no apparent reason. You believe before you see it. You feel it before you have it. You just know that it will happen 100 percent of the time— it always does. There's no amount of proof you need to sit around and wait for in order to start believing. High-level believers in the self understand that the proof comes after you have committed the price of faith. It is a form of transaction, and the exchange is simply believing.

Believe, even when you are in doubt. Believe, even when you are in fear. Believe, even when you want to think you are just making it all up. The fact that you are choosing to go against the current of a normal, "acceptable," predictable life is proof enough that you are ready to step into your role as a thought alchemist who intentionally creates a magical life from within.

3. Being It

Your mind believes you when you start acting like it. Get comfortable with the idea that you are living in the magical world you have created in your mind. If you want to be the greatest writer or the best in whatever field you choose, start owning that title. Start saying, "I am the greatest at writing" or "I am very talented at singing" or "I am a creative genius with life-changing ideas pouring into my mind." You will notice that you might suddenly want to write more, or sing unexpectedly well, or receive creative ideas that change humanity forever. You might even become the next best inventor, or any other worthwhile purpose you dream up.

The point is, we must be overly confident in our mind and allow our body to download the ability to express that creativity and talent. This is where *being it* comes into play. We assume that we have to go through some kind of external rigorous training in order to become an expert in any field. The truth is, you can convince yourself first that you are good (or wonderfully great) at something, and then you will notice your mind and body beginning to change to match the state of mind you initiated.

Being it isn't always about faking it to make it. It is about conditioning yourself to the point that it feels so natural and real to you. An external manifestation will always follow. Whatever you want to do, be, or become, always expose your mind to that state of being by speaking those talents into yourself and letting the untouched energy of that talent flow through your mind and body. Your daily self-conditioning begins to be seen, felt, and heard with every fiber of your being. Your energy field will now start to take form in your physical world. As a thought alchemist, you must always make *being it* a part of your creation protocol. We can only become what we condition ourselves to be.

4. Living It

The way you start to live will almost feel like you are in your own movie. You might find yourself smiling a lot or laughing more, because you see how you are working with the forces within you. You just can't explain how you have found yourself in this positive new life. What makes your current state so positive won't be about what is happening in the world all around you; it will be about what is taking place within you. Only you will know the inner changes that take place to alter every aspect of your life for the better. All you can really do is share that beautiful energy in the way you feel is right for you. Your highest and greatest honor will be nurturing your own wishes and following your own heart. The rest will take care of itself.

A thought alchemist will always know how to live it up. The weight has left your shoulders, your soul feels light again, your heart is softer, and your energy has been unified. This coming together of yourself naturally makes you central to the universe in a way that is both healthy and whole. You center your own energy and pour out from there. This means what you share will be from a pure, clear, and direct state. There will be no confusion or misrepresentation of yourself, as you have done the inner alchemical work to understand who you are.

The Thought Alchemist's Code of Conduct

This section will bring clarity about how you should treat yourself and take care of yourself in addition to insights about the power of your words/actions. You will take your energy back in all ways, as needed. Being the greatest representation of yourself is all about embodying what you want to signal to the world. How you feel, the kinds of thoughts you have, and your silent inner thoughts all function as a signal to the world that turns into energy "aroma," or what we sense with our pheromones. When we know there is a light shining brightly, all things of the universe will naturally gravitate toward it. This signal for more life is a sign to be inspired or to grow and expand. This is similar to the balance and energy of nature. We are attracted to flowers, trees, animals, and the beauty all around us because of the clear energy they represent. This energy vibrates at a harmonious frequency with which we naturally want to become one.

The one thing I always emphasis to anyone I personally know or work with is how to represent themselves authentically and harmoniously, as the world can feel, sense, and subconsciously pick up on our biofield signals, which are the sum of our emotions, thoughts, and bodily health. People who are "detectors," as I like to call them, are always sensing other people's energy. They can exercise this gift by reading spaces, bodies, and the energy of anything or anyone. As more people free themselves from the mental and emotional cycles of responding solely to physical-world signals, they elevate their state of awareness to show them more. We all naturally do this, and everyone has, at least once, sensed or felt when someone's energy was not right or incredibly beautiful. This is our primitive superpower at work, telling us what is good for us and what we should avoid. The code of conduct I will share with you involves taking yourself to the next level in terms of inner harmony and awareness of the ways you use your precious energy.

1. *Feeling Good About Yourself*

Feeling good about yourself is connected to the thoughts

Thought Access

and emotions you habitually play out in your body. It is not natural to remain out of balance. Sometimes, things happen that shake up our natural equilibrium, but only for a moment. We are supposed to bounce back, and we do this in the way we perceive and respond to events. Feeling good isn't a "becoming" state or trying to make yourself feel good; it is a natural state first. External things are what trigger or pull you out of this state of being.

Something I constantly teach in my books and share with my family and dear friends is the importance of checking back in with yourself when anything pushes you out of line. When you successfully identify the cause, most of the time, you'll find it relates to a fear that something is going wrong or defensiveness to protect yourself from others. When you know how to avoid internalizing and personalizing things, that awareness automatically returns you to feeling good naturally. When you don't fear others or what could go wrong, you settle down and return to your natural state. The point I am getting at is to never be bothered, disturbed, or put in a place where you lose energy or get thrown into a mental or emotional loop.

The best way is to keep perspective in every situation so you don't get pulled in or drained by it. Choose higher thoughts, and think of solutions anytime you feel like you can apply them. Don't get into the game of power or think you need to be right. Sometimes, you just have to let go instead of proving a point. This is an important determinant of your peace, energy, and ability to feel good about yourself. Do what makes your heart the happiest, with the people who make your life the brightest. Whatever presents itself, you will know how to handle it as a thought alchemist. You have the tools and proper guidance here to turn any situation in your favor, all while remaining balanced within yourself.

2. Taking Care of Yourself

Taking care of yourself in the manner you feel is best for you is a sign of energetic balance. Making time to get to know yourself is a matter of really checking in with your emotions, state of being, and overall wellness. This commitment to nurturing yourself puts you at the forefront so you can create an energy overflow to ripple out into your expression, love life, family, friends, and creative work. Being centered brings you back into alignment. With all of life's demands, people forget how to check in on themselves. Constantly giving without acknowledging your own energy can take a toll after a while, making you forget that more energy is available to you so you can snap back into yourself.

A vital aspect of a thought alchemist's life the ability to put oneself first. To be something more, and to share yourself at the highest level, you must do this from a place of balance, wholeness, and connection. Do what it takes to avoid living in constant overdrive. I believe *doing nothing* is a necessary part of life. As we settle deep into ourselves, we surrender the noise and the constant need to be in control in order to gain an outcome. This can be a tricky thing sometimes, because we assume we need to do a hundred things to gain the benefit of wellness.

The trick is, you will need to constantly make the commitment to get that outcome, and this can be a struggle to keep up with. *Doing nothing* is a form of energy rebalancing, realignment, and clearing in its own way. This could be staring off into the sky or watching the stars at night. Just *being* is a big part of taking care of yourself so you don't feel like you need to suddenly have a to-do list for self-care. Always do what feels right for you. Slowly, you'll start to embrace the richness of just being, and a flood of energy will cover you.

3. Higher Values in Words and Action

Be the one who puts the most valuable energy behind their

Thought Access

words and actions. You're doing all of this for yourself, to show the universe that you mean what you say and will see it through. As I discussed in "True Power: Your Life Force," believing that your energy is next to nothing will have you speaking things into existence with no basis or care about they happen or not. When you weaken your own vocal power and the way you transmit energy through words, you don't allow your will to travel very far into the field. This causes you to lose energy for no reason. It always connects back to lack of follow-up after the potency of your words has been lost.

It's time to start recognizing your voice as a form of subtle energy transmission. Every word you say has value behind it. It is heard in the field, and it is at work. People will know that when you say something, it is done. You are speaking power over your life. As a thought alchemist, you understand that your words and actions are everything. You can create whole worlds with just your words, and you can have many people moving into action just because of the frequency they feel as a result. If I ever say something is going to happen, it does. If I take any action toward something, I see it through.

Breaking free from a lack of value in your words and actions starts now. Break the hypnotic bonds of the past by choosing something different right now. If we only assume the same, the same gets recreated. If you say, "Right now, every word I speak has power, and it moves through the field to bring what I intend to life," this instantly starts to work. You might even get inspired action that matches your intention. Always follow through.

The cycle of speaking and acting upon what you want shows that you run your life the way you want. When the power of your voice is weakened through unawareness of the fact that your voice is an energy transmission, you might say negative things for no reason, without realizing that everything has an aftereffect and/or reality creation to match the transmission you're putting out. With this insight empowering your words and action, you can start to have higher value in your conversations, self-talk, manifestations, and even your own self-belief. This is an important code of conduct, as it supports your deeper connection with the world around you, giving you the confidence to connect it back to your mental creations, as well.

4. *Always Take Your Power Back*

No matter what kind of situation you find yourself in, it is all just an energy exchange. When you feel like you're being overwhelmed in your thought process or emotions, stop yourself right away and take your energy back. When you become aware that everything is an energy exchange on all levels, you stop losing so much energy. You stop becoming drained by the mere thought of the situation or person you're imagining. To be able to do more in your own life, or to just be at peace, we must remember how to work with our energy. You can't just assume that overthinking a situation or person "is what it is." You're sending so much of your energy in that direction, and you're creating the feeling of being drained simply by remaining unaware.

When you have Thought Access, you know exactly how to take your power back. Insight and awareness are of very high value in this life, as they help you operate from your soul while at the same time mastering your physical world. This is something we are always getting better at, and when we gain the proper guidance and open our channels of inner communication, we grow stronger and become better able to manage our energy.

We also stop playing the game of losing ourselves in preconceived mental scenarios. It will become very easy, knowing what you now know, to stop and say, "I take my power back right now. All of my energy returns to me instantly." This will automatically break the hypnotic state of thought followed by an emotional loop. It even dissipates the images associated with your

Thought Access

mental scenarios. This is a very powerful technique I see being used by my family and friends all the time. It almost seems like night and day, the way I have noticed people change through proper management of their mental affairs.

Nothing and nobody has power over you. It's all about energy management. The code of conduct presented here is an insight you can apply to practically any situation—even if it has to do with pessimistic thoughts, other people, something from the past, or a situation that has taken over your mind. You can always take your power back, and it's wonderful to feel your energy rushing back to you.

The Thought Alchemist's Master Tools

Practical mental tools will be provided here for you to tap back to. It's all in your state of mind, from which everything stems. To be a thought alchemist, you must always refer back to this sacred ground for solutions, guidance, insight, and awareness. Everything else will follow once you have regained your mind to fully express your spirit. No matter where you are in life or how much you have evolved, these master tools will always come in handy when you need them the most. They serve as a reminder that you can do it.

1. Always Ask for Guidance

This has been the most important thing in my life in terms of receiving insight and tapping into a more expanded awareness. When we live life according to what is physically in front of us, we dull our inner vision and guidance. We become trained to "seeing is believing," which connects back to the need to control external outcomes out of fear. When you open the channel of communication to your inner all knowing, you will be guided. Your master tool, no matter what is happening in your life or which answers you need, will always be asking for guidance. Your questions can be about anything. There isn't a good or bad question. You'll never sound silly or bizarre in the inner world. You can even ask to be shown things or for more insight to be revealed to you.

2. Direct Your Thoughts

Don't ever assume that a thought is just a thought. It is energy that is being presented to you as a transmission of some sort. When you receive it, do what you will with it. Don't be controlled by your thoughts; choose them, replace them, uplift them, and banish them according to your liking. You are always the observer in every situation. Don't become the thoughts or the feeling; be the observer and make choices according to what you like and want to create in your world. This will be helpful for those strengthening their mental health as well as those who are building their thought world into a flourishing field .

3. Create Using Your Imagination

This master tool is one of the most important of them all. Imagining something, or visualizing, is a true parallel reality that you are getting ready to step into. What you imagine and construct in your mind isn't just some random image you're playing around with. It is a world of its own, and as the engineer of your reality, you are technically shopping for potential realities. The ones we end up in are the ones we have held in our mental world over and over again. We believe in them so much, they appear in the physical world as the field adjusts to match your powerful imagination.

For anything you want, imagine it over and over again, as this is a world coming to life for you. The reason they keep telling you to "believe as if it has already happened" is because in the world of the imagination, it already has. It moves into the physical through scenes you intentionally set out. People are being aligned. Experiences are being altered. This could only have started in the imagination.

Someone who is really strong at image creation will feel like their life has turned into a dream, and they will use their willpower to make the physical world bend to their imagination. This is a powerful insight, as nobody usually explains the imaginative world in this kind of depth. We are told to believe and visualize, but what does that really mean? When you have the insight of knowing that you are the observer creating through the real and unseen world of your imagination, and you know the response is already in creation mode in the physical world, you will automatically begin to see the world around you for what it really is: a land of creation governed by your mind. This will give you so much energy that you will naturally believe in yourself, because why not? Everything will become obvious to you, and by then, you'll be living it in your dream.

4. *Be Playful*

Always keep things light. This helps your mind and body stay resistance-free and helps avoid the creation of energy blocks. When we are too serious and think everything is so rigid, we alter the way we receive energy. We tend to do things based on how they will be seen and judged rather than how we feel and want to express ourselves. After years of domestication in both behavior and movement, we shun the thought of allowing ourselves to be free, playful, fun, and joyful.

The energy of laughter is playful because you are taking things from a lighthearted place. Dancing, running through nature, swimming in the ocean, going for hike, and having a good time with those you love always keeps your energy open. Playfulness isn't just an act; it's how energy moves through you. Unrestrained energy is the byproduct of being playful. This will also increase your creativity and open your heart even further. A lot of healing will happen naturally here, too. You will feel an energetic weight leaving your field, so don't be surprised if you also feel an overwhelming amount of love for everyone and everything. This will assist you in forgiving yourself and others. You will even see how precious the time is that you have on Earth. Instead of remaining closed off, you become more interested enjoying every moment of your life.

You will now start to feel illuminated and connected to higher access. As a thought alchemist, you know how to apply this insight. Instantly, you will notice that a shift has occurred in your energy field, mindset, attitude, and state of being. You will see the world around you in a greater light, and this will inspire you to share in the overflow of energy. It'll almost make you want to shout from a mountaintop with joy to know and feel yourself as alive as you are right now. With so much energy available to you, you can do practically anything. Use it as you will, and enjoy the benefits that follow. The goal is to always be self-aware, connected, and in tune with your soul so life becomes the magical place it was always meant to be.

Key Points to Remember

- *Being a thought alchemist is knowing how to take any mental state and transfer it in your favor so you can rise.*

Thought Access

You will become a master at choosing your thoughts, directing your thoughts, and making your thoughts work for you.

- *Being a thought alchemist means you are working not only with your own mental energy, but also with the energy of the universe all around you.*

- *Nobody sees the changes you initiate when you start working in your mental world. For a thought alchemist, this is the silent night of the soul. This is when you are facing yourself. You are raw, truthful, and authentic with yourself so you can put outdated states to rest. As old ways perish, you bring to light a new version of yourself.*

- *When someone knows how to create their reality and see firsthand their own manifestations, it gives them spiritual confidence while expanding their mind to know that anything is possible. Inability to create the reality you want only comes from not knowing. You are always creating, whether you just realized it or have always known.*

- *The first thing you need to do as a thought alchemist is treat your imagination like the real world. The world in your mind is the one that will match and predetermine the world around you.*

- *A high level of self-belief allows you to you trust in your spirit. Live life from a place of awareness with the knowledge that you are not just physical in nature.*

- *The best strategy is to maintain perspective in every situation so you don't get pulled in or drained by anything. Choose higher thoughts. Think of solutions anytime you feel like you can apply them. Don't get into a game of power in which you only want to be* right. Sometimes, for your peace, energy, and self-concept, you just have to let go instead of proving a point.

- When you feel like you're being overwhelmed in your thought process or emotions, stop yourself right away and take your energy back.

- *"I take my power back right now. All of my energy returns to me instantly."* This will automatically break the hypnotic state of the thought/emotion loop. It will even dissipate images of unwanted mental scenarios.

- When you open the channel of communication with your inner, all-knowing self, you are guided. No matter what is happening in your life or which answers you need, always ask for guidance as your master tool.

- Imagining or visualizing something is a true parallel reality you are getting ready to step into. What you imagine and construct in your mind isn't just random images. Never assume that you're just playing around with images in your mind.

- Always keep things light. This assists your mind and body in staying resistance-free, and helps avoid the creation of energy blocks.

9

THOUGHT TRAVEL: PAST, PRESENT, FUTURE (ONE)

What if I told you a secret about yourself? One that has been latent in your DNA during your entire existence on Earth? One that connects you with your true power and purpose as a human being?

You come from a lineage that has always known that the past, the present, and the future are all happening in this moment. There was never a fragmentation of the self, but rather a unified being that never wasted their energy on past affairs or worried about what was to come. Your lineage knew how to create the future and move on from the past, and it was all done during every waking moment that you were checked into the *now*.

The awareness you are using right now to read this is the same exact awareness you use to imagine your future and your past. The thought world is a creation world. The thought world has no limitations. When you live only through memory of what you have always known as experience, you remain at the threshold of that creation point. Creation depends on how we use our minds. Your ancient linage knew this power of creation, and our ancestors did wonders with their minds. They interacted with everything in the universe and created everything they imagined.

Each time you create from your imagination, you are using your ability to thought travel. You are seeing something that is invisible to many, and you are bringing it to life. The secret insight you have right now is that you are no longer controlled by past habits, what happened to you, or fear of the future. You are choosing a new mindset, a new attitude, and a new perspective that actually works for you. Every time you think in the past, you are thought traveling. Each time you think of the future, you are thought traveling. We never think of it that way, because we assume that imagining scenarios is just something we do mindlessly. What you are really doing is bringing that vision and experience to life right now in your body; as a result, your body assumes that you are in that state. This is why you can get lost in a thought and be so physically removed from the world around you when you are imagining, daydreaming, or playing out a mental scenario. I will share with you the insight and gift of knowing how to stop losing energy to anything that happened to you in the past or fear of what comes next in your life.

Dreams inspire the imagination to see outside of the timeline. You travel through your mind to a wonderful vision you imagine and bring to life.

Literally anything is possible for you, and you must get used to feeling empowered in a natural way. When you understand the processing of your thoughts and how you respond to them, it gives you more power to direct them instead of being the victim of every flowing thought that manifests in your mind. One thought alone can brighten up your day or make you feel like something is wrong. The difference between the brighter thought and the one that negatively influences your mood is how you respond to it.

Understand the freedom of your mental world. It has no confinement or limitations. You can travel into the past by revisiting memories, or you can use your imagination to dream up a whole new life for yourself. Everything is happening right now. You are only using your current now to recreate the past or create a new future. The power of this chapter allows you to tap into the best version of yourself you can dream up. There is a *you* right now who has what you want, who feels the way you want to feel and is living the life you want to live. The ironic thing is, that self is who you are right now; but in your mind, that state is still unrealized. The reality of that fact in the moment is a real thing.

We assume everything is playing out from day to day, but what is taking place is far more expansive now, because your mental world is real. It interacts with, creates, and responds to all that you see. The potential of what you feel deep in your heart or see in your mind isn't just some random thought; it's insight from a version of yourself that is already living it out. This can occur in your future, as well. You are receiving downloads and reminders of what you should be doing right now to arrive at that state. This arrival isn't just going off into another world; it is literally seeing the world around you morph into your dream because you believe in the version of yourself you have dreamed up.

When you have a passion, a calling, vision, or sudden inspiration, this is just a sign from a newer version of yourself that has already realized that state and is sharing with you all the energy you need to accept it. My goal is to assist you in opening your mind to your own self and becoming more connected to your own truth. You are a very unique being who senses, interacts, and creates the world around you.

Nobody will feel the depths for you but yourself. You are the one inside your body living it all out. Giving yourself a fair chance at actually playing the game of life means taking back your power so you don't get sucked into concepts of yourself that fragment you into many layers without an awareness of how you work or who you actually are. Every foundation from which we build depends on what we have been told about the way our mind and inner world work. Without a proper blueprint and guidance, we are pulled into the demands of every moment with no time to really reflect, understand, and connect back with ourselves.

> *Something will suddenly guide you to do what you need to do. A passion will be ignited. A vision will be sparked. A calling upon your soul will be experienced. You'll receive insight about how to do it, and be invisibly guided to where you were meant to be. It'll feel so energizing, and you'll be filled with so much life force.*

We are always getting closer to being brave enough to fully allow ourselves to experience life. Experience isn't just what we go out there to do; it is also the way we get to know ourselves. I believe the most important thing is the unfolding of who we are as we journey into our soul and bring to the Earth the vast potential buried within us. You are the carrier of this seed, and it has been flourishing within you for a very long time. The comfort to blossom comes from recognizing that you already have it, not spending your life trying to defend your truth or make someone else see. Those who stand in their truth right now, against all odds, against all disbelief, and against all naysayers will get to know a world within themselves that doesn't require many eyes—just the one observer.

You are the observer of your world. You see, feel, and know all that is taking place within you. For your truth to be heard, it will need to come through your natural expression and creativity as well as the way you move, love, and project your beingness into the world. You are the one who will break mental barriers and bring inner freedom to the Earth. You will do this through your family, your business, your community, and your mind. You are the change the future awaits. Understanding this will assist you in accurately seeing time. When we thought-travel into the version of ourselves we want to bring to life, we are working with this moment while also seeing what the future holds. If limiting words steal your dream, how else will you be able to bring your dreams to life?

Everything depends on having access to your true self so you can bring forward the version you believe was meant to be born. The impulse to be the best you can possibly be isn't just an external motivation for personal development; it's a reminder from your spirit that there is more to who you are. Our evolution happens in increments, and we play different roles at different times to get closer to ourselves. At every moment, you are unfolding, and the feeling that yearns for something magical and profound serves as an inner glimpse of your soul's vast power and potential.

I believe there can be multiple outcomes and probable realities at any given moment, just waiting for us to step into them. Every choice unlocks this ability. When you give yourself the chance to use your thoughts and let them work for you, you begin to step into a greater version of yourself. Everyone is evolving at their own rate, and that depends deeply upon how connected they are to their inner truth. Self-awareness is key during this time, as you will need to know how to project your desired reality into manifestation in the knowledge that you are the sole creator of your experience. The depth you attain will help you go higher. You will move from the emotional bondage of past traumas into the liberation of expression.

All past thoughts keep you tied to those timelines, and that steals from your current *now*. Negative mental and emotional states can be recreated by the individual who is mentally traveling. You are choosing to visit through your natural ability to thought-travel to a mental image of things that happened to you previously, and this creates a feeling that makes the past moment seem so real. The hardest truth is that we self-perpetuate versions of ourselves from which we should have moved on a long time ago. Since our mind collects memories of past experiences, we don't usually look at the memory as something that happened that one time; instead, we look at it as *that is who I am* or *that is my past story*.

The most profound thought, and a truth I have seen with my own eyes in the people with whom I work, is the way they have created a new version of themselves no longer bound by thoughts, feelings, or awareness of the version they used to be or what they have experienced in the past. It is so unbelievable to even explain that we are filled with this many possibilities. We not only recreate ourselves, but build a completely new version of who we are.

> *It's already written. The story was already imagined by you. You play a role in your own creations because you have designed your experience that way. If you could see to the end, it would all make sense. Let the magic and memory fill you with ease. You will have it all and more.*

When you use thought travel to work in your favor, you will alter your past by creating a path you feel is worth defining in terms of who you are now. Simply repeating a memory is the same as recreating it today. However, if you see yourself overcoming something from the past, use that strength and awareness as the gift of your resilience. The past can only be tapped back into if the memory of it still empowers us today. Healing can be instantaneous or it can be prolonged, depending on how much you understand your emotional and thought processes.

You are free to be healed today while giving your body and

THOUGHT ACCESS

emotions the mental command to catch up with your new state of being. Say to yourself, "I am the version of myself I am creating right now, and this version is optimally healthy in mind, body, and emotion. I am completely renewed, revived, and regenerated. My cells change instantly to match these words. My emotional world is cleared out and space is made for a new pattern, which I create through harmony and balance." Repeat that to yourself as you need, and you will start to change your subtle energy field, which will then reflect in your entire world.

The blessing of knowing that you can change your mind is understanding the place from which you think about your life. Are you in a memory from the past, or are you imagining the future? All of it happens in the now. You are signaling to yourself the state in which you want to exist and the state you want to attract.

At times, we may have live life based on what was needed from us or what was expected of us according to external societal ideals of how one should live. These external influences create excessive chatter in your mind. This throws your passion temporarily out of balance, but your true self goes against the expectations and boundaries being put upon you. This is what makes people rebel. They aren't necessarily that far out in their thinking, but they want to have individual, unique expression in a world of conformity.

The individual has the power to make a change by working with their own mental world, emotional system, and overall bodily well-being. The ability to free yourself from constantly being pulled in all directions starts with learning that you are always using thoughts to see where you want your current to go. You weren't meant to be confined or limited by thoughts. These things only happen when we give power to thoughts rather than the observer who is actually choosing them.

You are the observer weaving the world all

Thought Travel: Past, Present, Future (One)

around you through your imagination.

Always see yourself as observing your thoughts rather than being the thought. As you select a goal, start choosing your thoughts in this way. The ones you choose will start to influence where your imagination takes you, and you will be deeply empowered by what comes out of you. Your future happens right this second. It doesn't matter what you have gone through or what happened before. Nothing can define you or limit you. What matters is that you see your own potential. This is where you will feel a high level of energy rising up in your body—when you believe in yourself and know that so many beautiful blessings are possible for you.

When your energy increases, that is your spirit being inspired. Don't let anything steal your shine or your energy…not even your own thoughts, imagination, or fear of what is to come. It's all a mental game, and these mental states create emotions in us that either make us stay the same or inspire a deep desire to do better. Anything that limits you inspires change; that is the spirit's way of returning to equilibrium. Everyone has a chance at every moment to come alive again. We are so resilient; it is beyond words to explain. Sometimes, a fear that things are "just okay" can cause us to try to manipulate *how* things can be okay. This is just a way to feel in control, but the feeling is momentary. It will always require you to perform another trick in order to stay in control. Cultivate a state of feeling fully at ease, in acceptance that everything is really okay and that you are always being renewed.

Harmony is happening every second because every-thing, in its core state, is in harmony. "Trying" to feel good causes you to rush yourself, and this can make you anxious for results. I like to see it as a rhythm. When you settle into yourself, you will notice your own rhythm, which will show you that everything is perfectly fine. Initiate the change first, then begin to allow yourself to be brought into complete balance.

Thought Travel: Past (Memories)

You will discover in this section how to recreate favorable memories and how to break free from limiting ties of the past. The past was meant to be a reference point of what we have learned, and to provide tools that can further assist us as needed. If we have overcome fear before, we already have the tool for how to overcome it again. If we know that believing in something makes it happen based on a past time when we found ourselves in a difficult situation and it worked, we have the tool with us now to believe in ourselves no matter what.

These (and many more) are reference points we can access to remind ourselves that we can do it, and simply go forward. Everything you have grown and learned from has made you better, and the ability to make it through will remain as an inspirational reference point you can tap into as needed in the future. When we don't think of it this way, we can start to live in a past time in our mind, which pulls us back to a state that has already happened. The energy devoted to this timeline creates the impression in the body and mind of the same thing reoccurring right now. This kind of thinking is a hypnotic, trancelike state because you visualize scenarios, replay things that have already happened, and feel like you're in it all over again. It captures your consciousness because the mind is a virtual reality of its own that pulls you into the images you are playing out.

If you have gained this insight, you know how to break the hypnotic trance of thoughts that try to go into your past and make you feel badly or overthink things. Stop yourself instantly, and break the pattern by taking your mind back from those imaginings. Bring yourself into your current location and tell yourself, "I am no longer in that mental world." This will also help you cease to identify with it.

Breaking links to the past brings so much healing and power to you now. The more mental energy you free up, the more easily you can become the director, creator, and writer of your story. You will come to understand that it's not a real feeling or a real place you are at, but one that you are imagining. This will bring clarity to unfavorable memories while breaking bonds that could have made you think, *I am forever connected to it*. You are only connected to anything because you believe you are. If this is the case, you will continue to perpetuate thinking and emotions that tie you to the experience. The truth is, you are who you want to be. You can make peace with what has happened—that is another way to break free from it.

Another powerful thing I want to share with you is creating memories of yourself with the abilities you want. Let's say you want to be really good at something or have a certain kind of talent or gift. Start remembering yourself being good at it. For example, imagine yourself performing it or doing it with such excellence that it becomes downloaded into your body. As you imagine yourself as someone who has always been a very successful person or has always been healthy, you bring that energy state into your body. This is a real state. Don't be surprised if you start to notice the talent you have remembered flowing through you in such an easy way.

The reason this works is because we imagine what we believe we are. When you go into your past, you are bringing that memory up because you are remembering yourself in that state. Why does it have so many feelings associated with it when it is "just" a product of your imagination? You could be 100 percent happy now and find yourself visiting a mental story you didn't like from the past. Suddenly, your mood changes. This is all happening because you can influence yourself to imagine something, causing the feeling to become real in your body now.

You will realize your own power to influence everything according to the capacity you can handle. You will see how quickly and inexplicably things can happen. Remaining open is crucial to dramatically (or even slightly) altering the way the universe responds to you.

I remember a time when a friend of mine asked me to help him with his science research. He wanted to know if he could see actual physical changes based upon mental images he created himself. He came to me because I am the friend who believes anything is possible. We devised a plan to play with the imagination to see what it produced. His goal was to look very young, change his hair color, and gain recognition for his research. He did this alone just to experiment with how he could influence himself without physical products or external aids. He wanted to use his imagination.

I found this experiment to be fun, exciting, and something I already believed could happen. I was there as mental support and someone who could co-create with him by visualizing him in his new state. The first thing he did was start remembering himself with dark black hair (his hair color was brown), very youthful skin, and people telling him, "Wow, you're looking younger every day." Every time we hung out, I would affirm to him only the state he desired. We would just laugh at the whole thing, but truthfully, I started seeing him that way. He kept at it every morning. When he looked in the mirror, he imagined his new hair color, his vibrant skin, and giving a speech about his research findings. From 30 minutes to one hour at a time throughout the day, he would imagine the mental images of himself already that way. He used his imagination to go into a memory of himself already being whatever he wanted.

He did this for six days, and by the tenth day, he called me, telling me that everyone was repeating his affirmations to him. People were saying, "Wow, you're looking younger and younger every day." Someone even thought his brown hair had been dyed when his black hair started to grow in. Having not seen him for

Thought Travel: Past, Present, Future (One)

20 or so days, I was not surprised at all…but truly ecstatic to see the physical changes. He looked like a whole new person, in a way I could only describe as someone who had gone through deep rejuvenation. His hair had grown out black, and he had gotten a haircut to let the memory of the previous color go. The thing I noticed the most was what had happened to his eyes. They were brighter, more alive, and more piercing…as if his spirit had awakened.

I think when someone is able to see their own mind power at work, it activates something deep and profound within them. My friend's character and way of being had changed. He had gained confidence and spoke with such determination. He even said he felt healthier because he had imagined himself as young and vibrant. He didn't do anything else differently; he just used his mental state to produce physical results. He was so stunned by this, but in an overwhelmingly happy way. About two months later, I received an invitation to a ceremony recognizing the fact that he had received funding of $1.3 million and a new lab to further expand upon his scientific research. To see him giving his imagined scene speech in real life was just another example of how we can all become what we mentally imagine, focus upon, and give our energy to. It always feels like a whirlwind to see it happen. I smiled, looking up and thinking of all that was possible for him, myself, and everyone else out there.

Everyone deserves someone who believes in them and can imagine with them what they wish to become. We are all creating our worlds in our minds. When someone wants to do something that seems very unusual, it is the perfect time to say, "Hey, go for it."

My friend and I never thought of how, when, why, or what the point of it all was. We just started being it, feeling it, and speaking it. He imagined everything for himself, but I was there for reassurance that he was already embodying it. This is what I

THOUGHT ACCESS

want this book to be for you—a personal cheerleader of sorts that is always there for you when you're living out your wildest dreams and imagining greater for your life. You'll know this is possible every time you read *Thought Access*. The blessing of being there for someone is sharing the energy of hope—not just in a sentimental manner, but in the very real way of picturing them already in their imagined vision. I always believe in people; that has been my deepest truth. I can only see what is possible and what can happen, which helps me lift people up into their expanded state.

> *The day has come when you no longer associate yourself with anything that has happened to you in the past. You feel a freshness of the present moment with a clear mind and an openness that right now, anything is possible. You feel your aliveness, your presence, and your vibrant spirit.*

What you can do right now is start actually using your mind—not just repeating affirmations, but going into your imagination and seeing mental images like scenarios. The mind imagines in images, not words. Words, when you say them, have a visual counterpart, but when you create mental scenarios and *feel* each image in your mind, you really start to create reality. This also happens when you make your new imagined state a part of your day rather than just repeating the same old routines. When you see yourself in the mirror, start seeing the image of the person you are becoming—who you see yourself as. When you are walking, walk with confidence toward your desired state. When you are eating, bless yourself, your food, and your body to enter your most optimal state. Every moment can be used to connect powerful energy with the way you are living.

You are always using your mind to see yourself in some kind

of way. Why not begin to see yourself the way you want? You might be surprised to find out how responsive your imagination is to your body, your look, the way you feel, what you attract, and everything you experience. You will return to reimagining in your mind and walking through the mental scenes you have created for yourself. If you will be doing all of this from now on, how much time do you even really have to visit unfavorable past experiences? You will be so empowered, inspired, and motivated to live fully that nothing can take your mental energy away anymore. You are far too aware now to be mindlessly bothered or emotionally disturbed. You know how to direct your mental energy, and you do everything intentionally.

Thought Travel: Future (Possibilities)

I am not sure how the future turned into something we fear when it holds so much power to be anything we want it to be. When we use what we believe is currently happening to imagine the future, we are using information of the decaying past to try to spring up a powerful thought of change. The reality is that everything is constantly changing, on a subtle or obvious level. Our ability to imagine greater depends upon the health of our mindset right now. If you are mentally a strong believer that your story can change, you are the perfect person to imagine a better future. Your mind isn't hijacked by dread, problems, or the limitations of things remaining the same. You have a fertile, healthy imagination, and you can choose the best for yourself right now.

Make it an inner law that everything has the potential to be far greater than you can see right now. This will leave so much room for growth and magical things to happen in your life. When you are set in the ways you think and see the world, you remove the magic from life. You stop seeing all there is and all that can be. To be an inventor, you must see what is unseen. To

Thought Access

be a creator, you must believe in what is unseen. To be able to live life fully, you must trust that tomorrow will come.

Everything depends on connecting the future to the now. We exist in this imagined state. We bring the *now* to life by continuously imagining a better tomorrow. Don't be robbed of change by exposing yourself to people who think from a place of limitation. Every conversation is an energy exchange. Everything you view is an energy exchange. You are either lifting yourself up or being made to believe that there is something wrong. Your brain can be retrained to see the brighter side of life while knowing that you are living fully now with acceptance, forgiveness, and love in your heart.

You don't have to continue any thought pattern or habit that no longer serves you. The previous state is just playing out because of mental and emotional repetition. Take an inner stance, make a firm choice, and decide right now that you are ready to break free and pave a new path.

When the mind is exposed to one narrative for too long, that way of seeing the world becomes the filter through which you see everything. This is why it becomes hard for people to change their mind. They believe their mindset is who they are instead of looking at it as something through which they are choosing to see life. You are just observing everything happening, and you are choosing favorable thoughts for your now and your future, which is taking place in this moment.

The future is everything you choose now. The future is the mindset you have now. If your mindset changes today, your future also gets upgraded. Your mindset is your access to a better version of reality. All creators, especially if they are artistic, are constantly imagining their craft. The mind is open, active, and full of hope for a better future. They use their craft to inspire the imagination

Thought Travel: Past, Present, Future (One)

(the mind of today) to see the world in a brighter way (the mind of tomorrow).

The best way to start thought-traveling to the future you want now is to mentally *be* everything you want to see happening in your life. Imagine it as part of your day, just as you would perform any kind of action. Your vision of your future in the now will make your mind and body believe you are already there. You can also do this by looking at images of the life you want or the way you see yourself being. Don't limit yourself at all. Dream fine dreams. Feel it, and walk into your imagination. That is what it will feel like when you show up in the setting of what you have created with your mind.

This activation of your imagination will do something profound to you. You will start to link up with a stream of thoughts that will guide you and give you ideas. When you don't use your imagination and instead do physical activities all day long, your mind starts to depend upon doing in order to receive. However, when you start to use the power of imagination by getting better at visualizing, seeing mental images, and playing out favorable scenarios, you start to pull in those matching energy states that later become your mindset.

You can see this in the life of someone who has overcome hardship or survived the unimaginable. If you ask them how they did it, they will always tell you they believed in themselves, changed their mindset, or felt a deep inspiration that more was possible for them. Knowing this will help you to start seeing yourself as an inspiration for many possibilities. You will see yourself creating your future today while using your past as a reference point to be the best you can be. The wonderful thing about it all is that you will experience what it really means to be you, not just a disconnected version of yourself or someone who sees only a small scope of your full abilities. You will know, and you will see what it means to know. Everything will be results-based. Manifestations will be tangible, and you will start mentally printing into the world around you everything you have imagined it to be.

Doing It All Now

Your sense of presence will magnify when you understand that you are willingly and consciously thought-traveling in the now to create what you want instead of not knowing what is happening. Your mind will feel freer. You will feel more content and calm. You will also know what to do, exactly when you need to do it. The present moment will feel richer for you because you will not live in the dread of unknowingly existing somewhere mentally that you did not intend to be. Thoughts will no longer pull you in all kinds of different directions. You are the one who will choose your healthy state of being—in the now, by knowing how to thought-travel at will.

Everything will be more responsive from the energy state you are in, instead of trying to be outside of your mind or feeling unnecessary emotions from uncontrollable mental states. You will feel, for the first time in your life, that there is a sense of true balance, harmony, and awareness behind your state of being. The precious gift of the now is the ability to allow yourself to feel so alive, so connected, and so present that you can direct your energy the way you want. You are just at peace with yourself, with everything and how it will all play out. You know what you know, and you will allow the manifestations of that insight to energetically play out in every area of your life. You are not resisting, forcing, or trying too hard to make anything happen. You have reached a greater awareness of how all things end up taking place, and this gives your life a sense of clarity so you can be more relaxed and trusting. You are the initiator of beautiful changes, and you know in your soul that greatness springs from you. BE IN THE NOW and imagine it all!

Thought Travel: Past, Present, Future (One)

Key Points to Remember

- *Each time you create from your imagination, you are using your ability to thought-travel. You are seeing something that is invisible to many, and you are bringing it to life.*

- *The potential of what you feel deep in your heart or see in your mind's eye isn't just some random thought; it's insight from a version of yourself that is already living it out. This can be in your future, and you are receiving downloads and reminders of what you should be doing right now in order to arrive in that state.*

- *You are the observer of your world. You see, feel, and know all that is taking place within you. In order for your truth to be heard, it will need to come through your natural expression and creativity: how you move, love, and project your beingness into the world. You are the one who will break mental barriers and bring inner freedom to the Earth.*

- *Giving yourself a fair chance to actually play the game of life is taking back your power so you don't get sucked into a concept of yourself that fragments you into many layers without awareness of how you work or who you actually are.*

- *Always see yourself as observing your thoughts instead of being the thought. Just as you select items in the physical world, start choosing your thoughts the same way. The thoughts you choose will start to influence where your imagination takes you, and you will be deeply empowered by what comes forth from you. Your future is happening right this second.*

- *Breaking links to the past brings so much healing and*

Thought Access

power to you now. The more mental energy you have freed up, the more you can become the director, creator, and writer of your story. You also will know that the past is not a real feeling or place you are at, just one you are imagining.

- *Everyone deserves someone who believes in them—and also someone who can imagine with them what they wish to become. We are all creating our worlds in our minds. When someone wants to do something that seems highly unusual, that is the perfect time to say, "Hey, go for it."*

- *When you see yourself in the mirror, start seeing the image of the person you are becoming or what to see yourself as. When you are walking, walk with confidence toward your desired state. When you are eating, bless yourself, your food, and your body to be in the most optimal state. Every moment can be used to connect powerful energy with the way you are living.*

- *Our ability to imagine greater depends on the health of our mindset right now. If you are mentally a strong believer that your story can change, you are the perfect person to imagine a better future.*

- *Every conversation is an energy exchange; everything you view is an energy exchange. You are either being lifted up or being made to believe that there is something wrong. Your brain can be retrained to see the brighter side of life with the knowledge that you are living fully now with acceptance, forgiveness, and love in your heart.*

- *Your sense of presence will magnify when you understand that you are willingly and consciously thought-traveling in the now to create what you want*

Thought Travel: Past, Present, Future (One)

instead of not knowing what is happening. Your mind will feel freer. You will feel more content and calm. You will also know what to do right when you need to do it.

10

ENCODE

Encoding is your ability manipulate the energy around you to produce real results. Everything around you is alive, active, energetic, and full of life, possibilities, and untapped powers of creation and expression. Your ability to encode is very different than what you have been doing so far in the world around you, which is decoding. Decoding is seeking external information to approve of your innate abilities. This can be "seeing it to believe it" instead of believing it first in order to see it.

When you don't know that you are always creating the outcome you want in a literal sense, you may start to need a lot of external proof to decode what is possible for you. The most powerful tool we have is encoding everything through intention, willpower, words, imagination, and state of being. The way we feel is not externally dependent, but internally encoded by us when we awaken from the slumber of not knowing.

Lack of insight produces so many unwanted outcomes that you feel trapped by it, since you can't link the effects to their original cause: the way in which you are mentally, emotionally, and psychologically structured. The beautiful thing is that change is now. Being empowered is now. Being awake is now. The fact that your entire life can start to change today is the power of being able to encode a new wave of energy. You are the one creating an acceleration and propelling everything forward. You will learn some easy, fun ways to get results through your thoughts and imagination. These outcomes will serve as proof of the small glimpses of everything that is possible.

A lot of energy is coming into your mind and body to support new beginnings, massive positive change, and your willpower to break free.

Encoding is about creating, through your mindset, thought patterns, voice, intentions, declarations, and simply expecting it to happen. Encoding is the opposite of decoding. When you encode, you write the story. You design the experience. You create the outcome. You are so much stronger, more powerful in spirit, and more deeply connected than you might realize.

When you begin to embrace your spiritual authority, you stop acting as a seeker of external information, and you start working with your own internal system. Every single person is designed differently. We think in different patterns. We have different levels of self-belief and self-awareness. When you bring your energy back to your own body, you start to hear who you are. You start to gain a sense of freedom, because everything has been right there with you from the start.

This is what this chapter is all about: exercising spiritual authority over every area of your life. With the power to encode your reality, you will also learn to see how energy moves through your mind and body. We don't realize that when we are watching something inspirational, we assume we have already accomplished that through our body because of our exposure to it. As helpful as this may be, it can create external inspiration that didn't spring from your soul. When things aren't in a synchronized flow with your inner state, it ends up just becoming mental entertainment to feel a certain way, not the ability to dwell within it as a normal, natural way of being.

When you start to encode your reality intentionally, *you* will be the inspiration. *You* will know how you feel, where those feelings are stemming from, and ways in which you can choose different outcomes that match where you see yourself. When simply being *you* becomes all the power of the universe in your hands, you start to really feel expanded. This expansion can make you feel a state of bliss and give you solutions, creative ideas, instant manifestations, out-of-the-blue breakthroughs, and sudden miracles. When someone owns that they are the point of creation from which everything radiates, they exemplify it in every area of their life.

To encode, you will have to start stepping into full spiritual authority. You can't blame anything on anyone. You can't live powerless, thinking there are forces against you. You can't attach power to external things, and you can't live life without awareness of yourself. To encode means that you are in the know. You know what you possess, you know what the source has given to you, and you know that you are an energy generator. You produce. You create. You imagine. Being able to think like this will draw so much energy back into your body. Without awareness, too much energy is lost to superstition that something "out there" is controlling your life.

Many spend years of their lives blaming the system or being drained by one thing that happened to them in the past. They repeat the narratives given to them, spread the same energy of confusion, and hope that one day, something out there will change. Everyone is responsible for their internal state. Everyone has to step into their power *now* and own that they are co-creating with the world around them.

This is a powerful time for the rise of the individual. This puts responsibility for yourself back into your hands while unraveling your own inner mysteries. Accountability brings higher energy, giving you inspiration to change the world all around you. You have to emerge now. The time has come for you to remember yourself. I wrote this book for you—to activate you. To assist you in remembering the greatness of your soul. Reading this book will make you feel like you have received a key to a treasure. It is meant to be that way, as you were meant to find this book for a reason. You are ready, and it is time to begin.

> *Writing the script of your life is your superpower. Treat everything like a dream, with no limits, no rules, or concepts. Everything is already a story, and this experience is your dream. Make it your finest adventure.*

The first thing you will do to encode your reality is begin to see yourself as someone who gets everything they want. Stop your mind if it tries to make you question that statement. A lot of how we process what is possible is based on past experiences that try to dictate from a previous lack or limitation that it might not happen.

Besides sharing all these life-changing insights, I also want to break down behavioral and thought patterns that try to paint the world for you in one particular way. When someone has spent most of their life being told something is not possible, or they weren't given the natural secrets of the soul, they assume everything externally. They become externally faith-based instead of spiritually faith-based. When you need to see something to believe it, it trains your brain to start seeing life from that perspective, which turns the internal guidance down a bit until you can't hear it as clearly.

You are never disconnected from your guidance, but you can create a system of perceiving everything through experience. This makes you spend a lot of time decoding how the outside system works. It will require you to gather a lot of information to get ahead in the way that seems to be taught. This has no soul in it, so the internal person's wellness, spiritual connection, and instincts aren't taken into consideration. When there is a sense of imbalance in this way, we feel overwhelmed by the duties of life. The pressure becomes all about how to "make it," what to manipulate, how to compete, and even how to force.

The soul connection always makes the life experience much easier. There is a knowing available to you and a natural trust for things to turn out the way you want. There's a spring of energy that gives to you, since your flow of receiving, processing, and creation is working in harmony. This is what encoding is all about. You depend on your own spiritual system for everything in life. This can be for healing, creating, knowledge, guidance, manifestation, and insight. When you accept this, you can put the energy into the universe that you want to get back. This makes your flow smoother.

How to Encode:

Mind:

You will need to accept that your mind is limitless. You can change anything about yourself: your story, your looks, your state of being, your financial status, your relationships, your health, your attitude, your personality, and even your what you love to do. To encode, you need to have an open mind. This will make it so easy for you to mentally think something and see it happen. The more open you are, the easier it is. I have seen people receive changes they wanted within three hours or less, simply because they decided to mentally start living from the images they put into their mind.

We are absolutely living a life of mystery. We don't know how powerful our mind is in terms of capacity, but we can, in our lifetime, get a glimpse into a vast world of possibilities. This is what you will be doing when you start to encode what you want into the field all around you. Start by choosing in your mind what you want for yourself. Choose without thinking about *how*. Just choose it. See it. Feel it. When you tell your mind what you want, it starts to work for you.

There's an invisible world all around you that is aligning everything. How else can we explain miracles and prayers being answered? These are real energies at work, and when you have no awareness of them, you are at the whim of other people's belief systems. You may even think from a place that makes you feel disconnected. You are connected to the invisible, and this is what comprises your inner world. You can't see your thoughts in your mind now, and you can't see your feelings, but you can see what they manifest. This is where the link can be found. Your mind is your humble servant, and for better or for worse, it shows you want you ask it to, in the assumption that this is what you want to see. Your mind doesn't say, "I don't think he or she really means this." It just says, "Okay. Here you go." We know what is good for us and what isn't, so when we give our energy and attention to what we want and the things we want to manifest in the world, we are in harmony with our expectations and reality matching up.

Open your mind to a reality in which things instantly happen for you.

To be able to encode, you need to accept that you are a powerful being who can live the life of your dreams in true health, genuine happiness, real peace, and openness to always receiving in all positive ways. Encoding is not just knowing mindpower; it is using that living energy for your growth and self-discovery. You think intentionally when you are encoding. You feed yourself with powerful thought commands by repeating in your mind what you want to encode into the field. This is something you always do anyway, but when you don't think of yourself as a powerful being, you just go into thought patterns that don't represent what you want to see.

If you are unaware of your thoughts to the extent that you think they may not be doing anything, you will continue to create from a space of randomness. Intention has fire and real life force behind it. When pure intention is present, you will awaken. A plan is sparked into motion. You have probably seen this happen when you were deeply desperate for a breakthrough or needed an answer instantly. Urgent energy forces the spirit to awaken, and emotion usually pulls these forces to work faster because your will and desire for an outcome is higher. You don't need to wait to get to a place of hardship or breakdown to get answers. You can activate that state now by becoming intentional about all that you want…and asking for it all. There's no trick to it, and there isn't a long ritual you have to perform. Success can be found in operating in spiritual authority through knowledge of who you are.

You are the change the universe has been waiting for.

You may be the first in your lineage to live the power of the spirit through mindset, action, and way of being. You will create a life unlike anything that has been, because you will be choosing from a state of awareness to pass on and share with the world. Everything will change for you in the most supernatural way because you have discovered your supernatural connection. This makes miracles naturally occur in your life. You are the one creating it all; you have decided to put out thoughts in their highest expression, which is simply what you want for yourself.

To be well is our natural birthright. We get in the way only when we start to get taken over by learned negative thoughts, which attract habitual actions that manifest unfavorable circumstances. These are all effects arising from an inner cause. When you decide to think for yourself, you are breaking free from a line of thought that tries to make you feel unseen, unheard, and misunderstood. Choosing to represent a greater life for yourself is a sign that you are living what has always been meant for you.

Aspiring to greater things is part of the human spirit. Some people are highly activated to follow their soul's calling because they are aware that there is more to life. This is how you will be proceeding when you decide to encode through your mind the life you want for yourself. Right now is your new beginning. Right now is your chance. That is your real power—to suddenly know and to begin propelling and projecting a new image into existence.

Begin by using mental images of yourself in the scenarios you want to encode. This is a real signal you are sending out to instruct the image to come to life. It is not about being good at getting a clear image. It is about getting to know the advanced technology within your own mind. Every time you visualize your mental scenario, you are turning on that ability further. When someone doesn't imagine very much, they get distracted from the image and return to whatever is happening around them. This is just a habitual thing you will break as you start to see the results of all the mental scenarios you encode into the field to manifest for you.

You can create any mental scenario you want. You can even do it by seeing yourself already with the result you want. Anything goes, so don't limit what you imagine for yourself. The mental scenarios will manifest really fast because you are seeing yourself already there. You can imagine as much as you like. There is no setpoint. Everything is about training yourself to see in images so the pictures get printed right out of your mind and into the surrounding space.

Someone might come into your life to assist with this type of manifestation. Something might happen to get you the outcome you desire. Things might even come out of nowhere. It all gets to you one way or another. If you imagine health for yourself or someone you love, you will see yourself making better health choices, feeling lighter in your body, and overall just being well. If you want to share beautiful energy with someone else, you can visualize them sharing good news with you about their health or business. Whatever it is, you can see any outcome you wish simply by seeing the end scene play out in your mind. Have fun with it, and construct the reality as you like. You will be surprised to know how much you can alter with your mental scenes.

Voice Power

Use your voice power to encode and command outcomes you want. This is speaking things into existence, but not just when you need to get results—all the time! If you feel your throat right now and make the *ahhh* sound, you will feel a vibration, and this is actual energy hitting the field to literally make things happen. You can create with words, or you can destroy. You can build up, or you can break down. Everything you say to yourself becomes signals you are sending to your body.

You can become more beautiful by saying beautiful words to yourself, about yourself, and about others. We assume radiance is just how we appear, but we are actually enveloped by the energy of our mind, which shows up on our skin, in our aura, in our pheromones, and in what we project in our bodies and our lives. You can speak encouraging words to someone and the trajectory of their life will change, simply because voice power is energy codes hitting their brain and upgrading them. Voice power is actually energy that is always at work, whether silently or loudly.

You can see who someone is by the way they speak of others, themselves, and the world around them. You can see the results they have gotten based upon what they have done with their voice power. *When you know, you will literally have a hard time speaking any form of negativity.* It will actually become difficult to have such thoughts or to speak in those ways. This is the power of awareness and insight that I share throughout *Thought Access*. I want you to be so empowered that you feel the surge of energy all over your body, along with a high level of self-belief that your dreams are right in front of you. It is all here, and the beautiful thing about it is that you already know.

> *Your voice is a powerful instrument that vibrates into existence what you speak habitually.*

Encode into the field the words you want to experience more of. Let's say you want to be wealthy. Speak words of abundance, not just in finances, but in every area of your life. Abundance is recognizing the never-ending energy that allows you to be who you want to be in this life. Abundance is the rays of the sun, the sky, the stars, the animals, the ocean, your breath, the electricity of your nervous system, the real things of the Earth that are continuous and eternal. This is what you are connected to.

When you speak, speak from this place of abundance, because you see it all around you already. Never mention limitations. (Why do such thing? It requires energy to speak of lack.) You don't want to create that. When it comes to conversations, speak the reality you want in all ways. People might not understand why you're so positive and optimistic, but they will see that you carry the activation of knowing how to encode and use your voice power. They will ask you your secret, and wonder what it is that gives you so much energy.

Every second is a chance to encode healthier words into your field. You will see things become easier because your words aren't working against your vision, direction, passion, or lifestyle. The one thing people do that creates energy confusion is wanting one thing, but speaking negatively about it by making it seem as if it is impossible to attain. Stop cancelling your own dreams by putting any kind of limitation on them. You never have anything to lose when you speak positivity or use your voice power to create what you want. This shows that you have developed and trained yourself to be aware of where your energy is going and the outcome it is producing.

> *Speak power over your life and the lives of others. Use your voice power to change outcomes. Amplify the energy you want to attract, and manifest it all by speaking it into existence intentionally.*

One thing I love to do is speak power into other people. I command my voice power into action by knowing that my frequency is deeply felt when I speak. I remember doing a call with a family member who was in the hospital. Choosing to speak to him as if he were healthy was my priority for the call. I didn't want to bring his mind to the state he was in. I took him far away into his imagination and brought back beautiful memories to him in which he was vibrant and living life joyfully. I knew the memory would bring the feeling back into his body. Our bodies believe what we are imagining, no matter what is happening physically. Laughing, we talked for an hour and almost forgot about the time and what was going on.

I could feel something shifting energetically in the conversation. He entered another state as his mind forgot where he was in the moment—not in the literal sense, but in the spiritual sense. This allowed him to leave the hyper-focused state of his condition and opened him up to memories already known by his body. I called on two other nights, as well, to imagine with him and to share more laughter.

I asked him to go hiking with me on the weekend at the end of one of our calls. He laughed at my optimism, but I told him that by the weekend, we should plan a hike. I did that to put his mind in a healthy state and to make him feel that things could instantly change for him. I wanted him to feel enough strength in his body to even imagine himself hiking. Something deep within me knew that this was all going to happen, and that I had to use my voice power to encourage his mind to accept that it could take place.

Not to my surprise, he was discharged the next night. He energized himself at home and contacted me three days later about the hike. We went hiking, and he kept telling me how every night when he was in the hospital, he would feel a surge of energy from our conversation. He even had a dream about the hike. This helped him see that another version of a reality was available to him already.

Knowing that my words can heal, empower, encourage, and put people in their most optimal state, I used that information to get him back to life, to get him to see himself in a better state. It all happened, and he's healthier and stronger than he has ever been. Everything has to do with the power we have and how we use it. If I see a greater reality for someone, I speak that for them by energizing their mind and empowering their spirit. You will be very surprised to know how much someone can accomplish when their spirit is empowered. You can do this, too, by always using your voice power to command greater for your life and everyone you encounter.

Write It

You can also use writing to encode your reality by keeping a journal in which you write out the story of your life. Let's say you want to see yourself in a loving relationship. Write a little story in your journal about this. Treat it like a movie script. Who is your person, what are you doing together, what does life feel like for you, where do you want to go with them, how do they treat you, and what kind of life do you want with them? Be as detailed as possible. Connect feelings and energy to it. Include funny moments and make your characters come to life. You will be surprised to find how this works to create everything you write. You can do it for abundance, physical goals, health goals, career goals, and everything in between. Go into your imagination and just write it all into existence.

I remember a time when my friend, who writes movie scripts, told me she always sees the scenes she has been writing playing out in her life in unexplainable ways—like seeing someone who looks exactly like the character she is imagining for her movie. Another friend said he encountered something from one of his own novels. Most people who live in creativity are in their imaginations, which means they are always bringing something to life. Writing a life story that you intentionally want does the same thing. It puts your mind at ease and activates your imagination to dream everything into existence. I have seen it myself, through writing down what I wanted to happen and seeing it take place right away. It is truly unexplainable, but fun to do. This will help you open yourself to more and turn your life into your own magical dream.

Key Points to Remember

- *Encoding is about creating through your mindset, thought patterns, voice power, intentions, and declarations, simply by expecting it to happen. Encoding is the opposite of decoding. When you encode, you write the story. You design the experience. You create the outcome. You are so much stronger, more powerful in spirit, and more deeply connected than you might realize. When you begin to embrace your spiritual authority, you stop being a seeker of external information and start working with your own internal system.*

- *To encode, you will you have to start stepping into full spiritual authority. You can't blame anything on anyone; you can't live powerless thinking there are forces against you; you can't attach power to external things; and you can't live life without awareness of yourself.*

- *The first thing you will do to encode your reality is see yourself as someone who gets everything they want.*

- *The soul connection always makes your life experience much easier because there is knowledge available to you and a natural trust that things will turn out the way you want. There's a spring of energy that gives to you when your flow of receiving, processing, and creating is working in harmony.*

- *To be able to encode, you need to accept that you are a powerful being who can live the life of their dreams in true health, genuine happiness, real peace, and openness to receiving in all ways. Encoding is not just knowing mind power; it's using that living energy for your growth and self-discovery.*

- *You will need to accept that your mind is limitless. You can change anything about yourself: your story, your looks, your state of being, your financial status, your relationships, your health, your attitude, your personality, and even what you love to do.*

- *Begin by using mental images of yourself in the scenarios you want to encode. This is a real signal you are sending out to construct the image and make it come to life. It's not about being good at getting a clear image. It is about getting to know the advanced technology within your own mind.*

- *Voice power is actually energy that is always at work, both silently and out loud. You can see who someone is by the way they speak of others, themselves, and the world around them. You can see the results they have gotten based on what they have done with their voice power.*

Thought Access

- *Never mention limitations. Why do such thing? It requires energy to speak of lack. You don't want to create that. When it comes to conversations, speak the reality you want in all ways.*

- *You never have anything to lose when you speak positivity and use your voice power to create what you want.*

- *Use writing to encode your reality by keeping a journal in which you write out the story of your life as a script or novel-style.*

11

ACCESS ANY STATE NOW

This chapter is a portal, in its own way, to access any state you want. You can feel one way and come out completely transformed, in any state you desire. Entering states has to do with your mindset, beingness, awareness, and simply reading the intended message as offered. Many powerful states will be offered below to help you travel into the beingness of what you want to feel or attract. This automatically shifts your energy, helping you magnify and magnetize that state.

We are energetic beings. We are spiritual, and we are in a constant state of change. We are limitless, and we can be anything we want. Your current state is only happening because there are so many emotions and thoughts going toward the outcome of who you are. What this chapter will do is pull you right out of that, neutralizing how you feel and transmuting the previous energy to maximize the new energy you're about to enter.

States of being are just concentrated energy of what you think is happening to you. The good news is that everything can change toward the positive: your thought patterns, how you feel, what you think about what you feel, and the outcome it is producing. The greatest blessing is discovering how quickly you can change any state, even helping others access the greater reality that is always available to them.

A portal of possibilities has opened up for you.

Accessing any state now means choosing to walk through a

portal. You know that when you enter it, you will come out the other side downloaded into the new state you desire. You will leave behind past states, emotions, thought patterns, and stories. You'll be doing this willingly, knowing that a greater reality is possible for you. You won't have to live in a memory trap of pain, lack, or limitation. You won't have to repeat the same habits or cycles of learned behavior.

Things can instantly change when we decide it is time. Most of the previous reality you are leaving behind was nothing more than a constructed world of responses, behaviors, and emotional triggers from the mindset that kept producing those states. You have the freedom now to create something new. Years of "who you thought you were" can be transformed if that is what you want to do. Whatever you don't like can be changed. Whatever you love can be amplified.

Everything is energy in motion and at work. Our greatest is still within us, and as we keep unfolding more of ourselves, we can witness the richness of life that our soul holds. We are entering a new level. The time has come, and we are starting to make choices not from repeated patterns, but from the conscious awareness that life can be so much more. You are the one breaking free from conditions, and you are the one who deeply knows in your heart that it was always meant to be this way.

When we encounter our soul, we reach a point of expansion and sometimes need guidance. We get pulled into an expanded state that unveils your life—not according to your role in society, but from a greater viewpoint that encompasses your existence as a whole. You feel accepted, loved, and open, and negative events dim in their power to control your emotions and point of view.

When you expand, you feel otherworldly and connected, with a great a sense of peace—a return to what you have always been. You get better at knowing your soul's mission and seeing life as a space to express your innate abilities. You go from life happening *to* you to mastering your own energy to make life into everything you will it to be. The whole point is knowing that you are creating, playing, getting to know your mind, expressing your soul, feeling what it is like to be human, and bending atoms of energy to construct the world you wish to manifest.

The states listed below will help you step into a greater version of yourself. The words are meant to activate you and bring power into your life to propel you forward. You will instantly feel a change and start to see it all around you. You can come back to this section at any time to enter the portal corresponding to the state you want to embody. Know that this is automatic, and once you read the words, it is done.

Access High Energy Now

High energy is available now. It's around you. It's within you. It's a state that is already here. By accessing it, you come into your awareness, your mind, and your body. Knowing this, right in this moment, you feel a surge rising up within you. You feel it in your mind as if you have connected to a power grid that feeds you in an unlimited way. This energy is high, and it soothes you, energizes you, and fills you up.

Higher energy is a natural part of life. When your awareness is on it, it comes to you. It becomes one with you. Start by recognizing that it is here. You would be surprised to know that all the natural energy you need is right in the air. It is always there, and always has been. With this knowledge, you can use it as you were meant to do: by breathing it in right now and filling yourself with the golden lights of energy balls that seem invisible, but are quite visible to those who can see.

You will know that higher energy is here, and you will feel revitalized. This higher energy brings the body back into balance and increases even further, giving you a supercharge to use as you need. This higher energy also clears out negative states, unwanted thoughts, and imbalanced connections, making you superhuman.

Being superhuman is a natural state in which we sense energy, pull in energy, balance energy, and alter energy to work with us. Energy bends to your will. When you command that you want to access high energy now, your body starts to absorb natural air and Earth energy to be utilized by your body to the maximum extent.

This will allow you to start utilizing the free energy your body already knows about. Treat every breath like a surge of energy charging every cell of your body. When you need it, always say, "I breathe in through my mouth, my nose, my skin, my feet, my hands, and the top of my head the highest energy of the Earth, the ether, and the field to charge my body. I feel a sudden boost. I feel a sudden change. I feel fueled. I feel the currents. I feel connected. This energy stays within me and gives me access to higher outcomes that are natural to my mind, body, and soul. I feel so different already. I feel so alive."

Be aware that this energy will naturally impart a euphoria that can feel exciting because you get to experience an expanded state of awareness of all that is available to you. When you can work with the natural elements surrounding you, you feel empowered in the knowledge that you don't need much in order to be all that you can be. It is all just a state of mind, awareness, and higher Thought Access to the reality that more is available to you. Use as needed and when necessary. You will learn by utilizing this energy that you can be charged up for activities, creativity, and expansion—or simply fill yourself with the natural energy the universe has to offer.

Access Spiritual Insight Now

You will know what you need to know right when you need to know it. Spiritual insight access opens up that channel of receiving when you say, "I want to know my truth, my spiritual nature, and my connection." This alone will start to generate thought connection that seems to come out of nowhere. You will get the answers you need and see signs that are connected to your questions. You will feel guidance within you and all around you. You will feel like you have tapped into something which has truly been there with you this whole time. You mind was just busy with life and searching, so you probably didn't always think from a state that everything is here and now.

When your mind knows it is all here right now, you engage by asking the all-knowing a question. You close your eyes and see—not from the perspective of the stories taking place in your life, but from a bit higher up. You see yourself outside of your body, looking down at yourself living out a whole way of being from your greater perspective. This greater perspective can see things that you, living inside your body, can't fully know.

With this means of accessing spiritual insight, you get to stop being taken over by the current affairs in your life and begin to see it in the way you would guide yourself to live if you already had all the answers. This is a real state that you can tap into by being present within your body now. Say, "I know there is more to who I am. I know I am not any of these storylines or what seems to be happening. I have a bigger mission, and my soul is timeless, grand, and eternal. My life isn't just these moments. I have always been, and will always be. I want to download into my mind right now greater perspective, spiritual insight, and liberation for my soul in this physical body. I want to be multidimensional while I am in this body. I want to feel what it feels like to know myself, to receive proper guidance, and to always be connected to my authentic state. Give to me. Share with me. Pour into my mind. Flow through my entire system. Walk with me on every path. Lead the way. Increase my imagination. Allow me to see depths. I am one with you, and I am witnessing myself as I come alive. My awareness is increasing. I already feel so different. I already feel so spiritually gifted. I am in the know now, and I embrace my new access to greater spiritual insight."

This is very powerful, so get ready to receive download after download. Life will become so much richer and more beautiful. You will see and feel a beauty beyond the physical world. You will be the embodiment of eternal life. Everything makes sense this way, because we are so much more. This will become quite obvious, especially with the process of birth and death being so apparent. We are continuous and forever. Use these new gifts to enhance your life and the world around you—your family, community, and friends. As you tap into this never-ending energy, you will spiritually impact many lives.

Access Health and Healing Now

You will step into your healthiest and most healed state. These states are versions of yourself that have already gotten there. Everything starts at the level of energy. Your mind believes that your physical body is the healthiest it has ever been. Somehow, your change of mindset begins to heal your emotional state, as well. You feel that you are in an inexplicable state of peace, as if you suddenly no longer have the same attachments, thoughts, or energy connections. All of that has left your awareness. You feel a sense of aliveness you have never felt before. It feels like a breeze from the ocean, light in your heart and on your shoulders as if something has been lifted off of you. You feel like you can actually take deep breaths that reach the lower part of your belly. Your thoughts are light. You are emotionally at peace. A sense of forgiveness overwhelms your body with joy. You feel free from any attachments related to harboring, holding onto, or resisting old energies being cleared from your body and mind.

You have forgiven yourself. You have forgiven that person, that one situation, and what didn't work out. You have released so much that a new energy of vitality, life force, and health has entered every cell of your body. You have shifted. You have stepped into a parallel version of yourself that is mentally, emotionally, physically, and spiritually liberated. All of this instantly heals you. It goes into every area of your body where you previously held onto years of unresolved emotional blockage, and suddenly, it all melts it away. You feel it all dissolving; you feel lighter and lighter.

You feel healthier and whole. All resentments, regrets, grudges, and stagnation evaporate. Your field is stronger because there is no longer imbalance or confusion. There is clarity within you. Your body will follow your state of being within your mind, and you will feel aligned again.

Most of this access is already within you. The align-ment happens in the mental world and the spirit world. It all trickles down into your physical body, where it begins the rejuvenation process that makes you feel healthy and whole. Always say, "I am emotionally healthy. I am mentally healthy. I am whole. I am liberated. I am the healthiest version of myself. I healed a long time ago. Every cell of my body is renewed every second, so new, healthy, healed memories can be stored in this way. Mental and emotional weight has been lifted off of me. My heart has discovered everlasting peace. My mind has discovered how to access these states at will. I am now in command of my reality, and it feels so good to speak what I want, think what I want, and feel the way I want. I am being intentional with what I create, what I accept, and what I allow. I am all that I have always dreamed of being. I have permanently accessed health and healing now."

Access Supernatural Abilities Now

It is obvious that there is more to who you are. You see signs connected to your thoughts. You think of someone, and they contact you. You speak something into existence, and it happens.

You manifest what you want. You can even feel things before they happen. You can sense energy and pick up on how other people feel. You know things, and you can't explain how you know them. These are just a few of the supernatural abilities you have within you. There are a lot more, and as time goes on, you will understand how things happened and realize what a wonderful thing it is for you to be extra-aware in the way you consciously exist.

We are multidimensional beings. We are energy. We are spirits. We are everything…and so much more. When we acknowledge the expanded state of who we are, we think outside the parameters of the physical body and know that we are connected to all that exists. When you see everything from the physical body alone, you tend to associate your abilities with things you can see and touch. However, with heightened awareness, you can tap into expanded senses that you just can't explain.

Welcome to the reality of life. You are not alone in these supernatural abilities. You are just gifted at unwrapping the human treasure, and your attentive energy allows you to notice everything. Accessing supernatural abilities means putting your expanded senses to work. Say, "Show me a dark green rose," and your eyes will find many. Say, "Show me many people smiling at me all day," and you will see a big smile on all the faces you encounter. You can say, "Show me" for anything, and you will see it. Why? Because your supernatural ability is to find in the world all that you wish to see.

The main thing is getting to know how you are interacting with the world around you and the fact that you can make things happen through your mind. This is about becoming confident in your influence: your words, state of mind, and what you want to see happen. You will discover that there is and always will be more, because we are limitless and filled with possibility. We get to experience as much as we are open to.

Always be curious and explore. You will start to see that much of life was simply waiting for you to influence the outcome. The more you live in your spiritual authority, in the knowledge that everything is energy, the more you become a magical being. You start to attract to yourself what you are ready for. If you are good with your intuition, you know what is in your favor and what is not. If you are good at trusting the thoughts that come into your mind, you can feel what someone is thinking or what they are not trying to tell you openly. If your words hold power, you can speak things into existence. I have already discussed voice power in a previous chapter, so that will strengthen this ability, as well.

If you can visualize, you can materialize. Everything is about deeply trusting yourself without any kind of doubt, overthinking, or questioning whether you're doing it right or not. Whatever you think is whatever it will be. Always say, "I have many supernatural powers now. I have tapped into my ancient codes, which have always been within me. I can read energy. I can sense what I need to know. I make the right choices in my relationships and connections by nurturing needed energy and dissolving energy that is unfavorable. I have insights into all of my life events before they happen. Everything is shown to me like a flash: a thought, an image, or a feeling, depending on what is right for me and what isn't. I save so much time and energy by trusting my intuition. I have voice power. I have telepathic abilities. I know these are natural states, and I speak them into life in order to further develop them. I manifest everything I want. All of this brings back memories of who I have always been and who I am meant to be. I operate from an empowered state now. I feel supernatural, magical, and divine."

Access Strength Now

You can tap into spiritual power within yourself for strength. When we feel supported in any way, we believe something is there with us, telling us we can. This can be through others or through your own inner guidance. Strength, for me, is cultivating spiritual energy and knowing who I am. In these kinds of states, you are beyond the current moment alone, and this gives you solutions and guidance from a greater perspective.

Inner strength is an attitude and way of looking at life that protects you from words, other energies, and how things seem to be happening. You don't let yourself become weakened by an accumulation of unprocessed energies, which can make things seem exaggerated. You are strong—not just physically, but in the powerful knowledge that you can pierce through anything negative you might be feeling or going through in the moment. You have spiritual strength now, and you always have; you are just becoming aware of it all in a deeper way. During trying times when you kept believing, your spiritual strength was telling you, "It's okay; you can make it through. You have used this power many times before in your life, and you can use it again right now."

There is unlimited energy within you that powers you up, makes you internally stronger, and gently pushes you forward. Nothing within you is broken or damaged. Whatever has happened in your life or is happening, there is a way to see through it, knowing that you have invisible support encouraging you to go forward. Say to yourself, "Every cell in my body is stronger. I am emotionally stronger. I am mentally stronger. I am a believer in invisible power and guidance. I am supported in ways I can't imagine or see. There's help within me and assistance all around me. I see beyond the now while remaining present. I don't get caught up in any noise or lose myself in fleeting moments. I stay centered. I stay calm. I stay connected. My energy multiplies every time I believe in myself because I am going higher and seeing greater."

No matter what your path, you can call upon spiritual strength in any part of your journey. Anytime you need it, just say, "Give me spiritual strength now." You will feel the arrival of massive energy that encourages you from within. You have accessed strength now.

Access Your Truth Now

Start hearing your own inner voice to know your truth. At times, you just have a strong gut feeling that is that says *listen to this, instead.* Your truth is your truth. Nobody has the same inner guidance system. Your body, spirit, and energy field know you in such a unique way and want to work directly with you. So many external influences constantly try to tell us what to think and how to feel about ourselves, which can make us co-dependent on external guidance.

Who you are is *one of one.* What you're made of is uniquely crafted and designed. To put your own guidance system in the background causes your inner truth to go unheard. This is why we so often have experiences that work against our own inner guidance. How many times have you experienced a gut feeling about something or known something just wasn't right, but gone ahead and done it anyway—and it later turned into a life lesson about contradicting your own body and spirit's intelligence?

You must understand that you know so much more than you realize. When you are unaware of your own connection, guidance, and personal truth, you enter external dependence, which isn't fulfilling because the external world isn't focused on your personal needs or care. Your mind, on the other hand, only sees the world from within yourself. Your whole energy field is working for you at all times. It doesn't think about "out there" because everyone (and every mind) is being personally catered to by their own guidance system.

Your spirit is your spirit. This expanded way of seeing yourself allows you to access your truth anytime you need it. It is there with you 24/7 for the rest of your existence. Accessing your truth starts with bringing awareness back to who you are. You are the center of your creation and your own universe. Managing this inner universe creates external harmony with everything. Mismanagement of the inner universe creates a ripple of imbalance from every individual who isn't connected back with their own self.

Give yourself back your power by saying, "Everything starts within me." When you acknowledge that you are already everything all at once, you will suddenly feel a connection to yourself. As you become whole within and start to seek guidance internally, you will feel warmth pouring from your heart and begin to activate your truth.

We all have felt our truth many times in our lives. It can come as a feeling, a knowing, even in a blunt or obvious way. It's now time to access that voice again so you can understand what is truly for you. Start by asking yourself questions. Say, "Guide me in this situation," or "Tell me what I need to know about this one thing." You can even ask, "What is my purpose or my truth?" Asking yourself might feel new, because we have all been encouraged to seek outwardly, look externally, and ask others. How can someone really know all that you are and what you need to know about your path? For it to be a lasting solution, people can only guide you back to your own inner system. All you really need to do is ask yourself the questions, because you are already tapped into your all-knowing state. Your body isn't all that you are limited to, either. You have insights you can receive right now simply by asking for them.

As you get comfortable with receiving from within, you will see all around you that the answers pop up in the form of thoughts, images, and signs, often in the most obvious way. Everyone is unique in how they get their answers. Some receive a direct answer instantly. People will start speaking things you were meant to hear. Everything will turn into one big orchestra of unfolding truth.

This is how it was always meant to be. Losing inner connection means losing your inner guidance, which goes back to losing your truth. As you strengthen your own self-trust, you will feel the freedom of oneness with yourself. It will feel so liberating to know that everything has always been within you. This will assist you in every other area of your life, even empowering your relationships with others and the world all around you. Seeing everyone accessing their own truth and being healthy, balanced, and genuinely connected to their own guidance system will take humanity to the next level collectively.

Accessing your truth will now be easier for you, as your mind provides the way and creates external unfoldment linked to what is meant for you. Just as this process is unique to you, so is the timing of everything meant for you. When you seek your truth, make sure to listen and follow through. This will help you believe in yourself further and build your own self-trust that everything is divinely happening for you.

Speak this to yourself: "I have been given direct access to my truth, and I am one hundred percent using my own guidance system to know what is best for me, meant for me, and good for me. Truth is exposed to me in a flash of thought, a sudden realization, a deep revelation, a sign, another person, a contact, within my own mind, and/or in any other way that is necessary for me to know. I am patient and I trust myself. My truth access is activated!"

Access Self-Love Now

Self-love is a state of being, a radiance of your soul, a connection to your heart and truth. Self-love is trusting who you are, getting to know yourself again, and representing your own wellness. Self-love is being at one with yourself, living in the moment, forgiving yourself, acknowledging your inner state, and nurturing every part of yourself.

Sometimes, it takes an event to help you see yourself more clearly. Everything it takes to bring love back into your heart is worth it. This section is about magnifying the wholeness of your being, which is filled with a natural state of love. To me, self-love exists in a natural state of bliss, which is energetically filled with life. This doesn't have much to do with something you *do*, but rather embracing who you are, which is love. Your existence is enough.

This can be a process for some people as they learn to rediscover what it means to just be themselves, to hear their own voice again and settle past thoughts peacefully in order to connect with their own essence. Everything you have been through can sometimes make you forget what you have always been. We carry the memories, the stories, and the unfulfilled wishes of the past as if that is who or what we are. This is just a layer that covers the love inside you. All of this is now revealed to you in a way that is energetically enriching.

Love isn't just a person, a thing, an experience, or a wish fulfilled. Love is your beingness, your aliveness, your breath, your electricity, and your essence. When you start to change your way of feeling love and receiving it, you begin to feel it pouring out of you, surrounding you, and finding you. You become love without even realizing it, and it can all be felt from within.

Anyone who wants to access self-love now needs to start settling into the feeling of life itself flowing through them. This will instantly remove thoughts that try to say otherwise and the narratives that try to put you back in a story of when love wasn't in your life or what you did or didn't do to experience it. Learning that this has always been true can feel unusual initially, because people have been trained to assume that they have to do something in order to get something, which is tied to an exchange.

Thought Access

Inner wellness, self-love, and a healthy mindset are energy states. You accept yourself as who you are before you even experience it in your body or the world around you. Accessing self-love is acknowledging that you *are* love already, completely, just as you are. This gives you healing and natural forgiveness because you go higher than simply confronting parts of yourself that require attention. I believe accessing a positive state can override many unseen processes because we go into an expanded consciousness that heals, unifies, enriches, and makes us whole again. We stop being fragmented by thoughts that say, *You will get self-love if you do this or that.* This is a trick that makes you feel like you have to fight off past identities and ways of looking at yourself instead of just accepting the new state, which then trickles into every other area of your life. If you feel that access to self-love is as normal as breathing, you make that awareness a part of your existence, which realigns and balances other areas without you having to focus on each one of them separately.

The beautiful thing about self-love access is that it will work within you 24/7 for the rest of your life. Even when you're not thinking about it, you will feel a warm energy of support and love. Even when you are sleeping, the powerful energy of love flows over your body. It pours into you so that each morning, you wake up peaceful. It will often feel like you are handling situations in a more level-headed state. You no longer feel imbalanced or overtaken by your perceived worth or value, or what you think someone should do in order for you to feel a certain kind of way. You have graduated to a higher way of living, and have discovered your endless self-love. Always say, "I am in a new state every second, and every breath I take is filled with the real energy of love. This energy of love showers over me and recharges every part of my body. I feel loved. I feel supported. I feel at peace. I am free of my past states, simply by accepting access to self-love now. I never have to wait around for validation or approval. I never have to give my attention to other states from which I have already moved on. I only give my attention to the state I want to feel and experience now. I choose self-love. I welcome self-love. I am self-love."

These states are written here for you to tap into at any time. Don't treat this book like something you are merely reading through. *Feel* every access point, integrate it, and let it become activated within you. Every word is powerfully charged so you can start to see instant changes throughout your mind, body, and environment. You will truly become good at spontaneous change and become known as a shapeshifter. You will leave the world in which you had to live through the dread of memories, welcoming instead the newness and aliveness of every second. You will command specific states to become a part of your world, reality, and life. You will notice that you can't explain why you have changed as quickly as you have. People are used to prolonging their states, working through them for years without realizing that the attention they have been giving to the problem keeps it alive.

You hold a different kind of treasure: a key to a field of wonderful, magnificent possibilities that allow you access to a new narrative, new thoughts, new feelings, and new memories that are all in the favor of the direction you are going. This is what *Thought Access* is all about—giving you a higher level of access that bypasses the usual means of processing thoughts. We are entering it and being filled by the desired state. Our minds and bodies know only what we feel as truth *now*, tell as a story *now*, remember as the past *now*, and repeat as normal *now*.

For today to be new, and for you to have another chance at claiming a new experience for yourself, you have to intentionally direct your mind to the world of your dreams, not stories of what you want to release. This way, your mind says, *Oh, this is our new reality, this is our new story, and this is our new direction.* This will instantly free you from being stuck in memory or recreating it by reminding yourself that this is your story. Liberate yourself from it all, and discover the vastness and greatness of your soul. You are everything you say, believe, and claim yourself to be.

Key Points to Remember

- *Accessing any state now is choosing to walk up to a portal. You know when you enter it that you will come out the other side downloaded into you the new state you desire. You will leave behind past states, emotions, thought patterns, and stories. You are doing this willingly, in a state of mind of believing that a greater reality is possible for you.*

- *You don't have to live in the memory trap of pain, lack, or limitation.*

- *High energy is available now. It's all around you. It's within you. It's a state that is already here. You are accessing it to come into your awareness, your mind, your body. Knowing this, right in this moment, you feel a surge rising up within you. You feel that you have connected to a power grid that feeds you in an unlimited way.*

- *When you command that you want to access high energy now, your body starts to absorb natural air and Earth energy to be utilized in the most optimal way. This will allow you to start utilizing free energy, which your body already understands. Treat every breath like a surge of energy charging every cell of your body.*

- *Spiritual insight access opens up the channel of receiving when you say, "I want to know my truth, my spiritual nature, and my connection."*

- *You will step into your healthiest and most healed state.*

These states are versions of yourself that already exist. Everything starts at the level of energy. Your mind believes that your physical body is the healthiest it has ever been.

- *You have stepped into a parallel version of yourself that is mentally, emotionally, physically, and spiritually liberated. All of this instantly heals you. It goes into every area of your body where you have been holding onto years of unresolved emotional blocks, suddenly melting it all away. You feel it all dissolving. You feel lighter and lighter. You feel healthier and whole.*

- *Accessing supernatural abilities can come about by simply putting your expanded senses to work.*

- *The main thing is understanding how you are interacting with the world around you, and how you can make things happen through your mind. This is about becoming confident in your influence through your words, state of mind, and what you want to see happen. You will discover that there is more, and there will always be more. We are limitless and filled with possibility.*

- *Strength, for me, is accessing spiritual energy and knowing who I am. In these kinds of states, you are beyond the current moment alone, which provides you with solutions and guidance.*

- *Your truth is your truth. Nobody has the same inner guidance system. Your body, spirit, and energy field know you in such a unique way and want to work directly with you.*

- *As you get comfortable with receiving from within, you will see the answers pop up all around you as thoughts, images, and signs, sometimes in the most obvious way.*

- *Self-love is a state of being, the radiance of your soul, connection to your heart and your truth. Self-love is trusting who you are, getting to know yourself again, and representing your wellness. Self-love is just being at one with yourself, living in the moment, forgiving yourself, acknowledging your inner states, and nurturing every part of you.*

12

THOUGHTS MATERIALIZE

You can make things appear out of thin air when you learn your power to materialize thoughts. You have been doing this all along, but you have done it at a rate that is comfortable for your mind. When you are manifesting something, you are doing what you believe you need to do to make that thing come into your life. The thoughts and the outcome are already here. The process includes accepting the fact that everything you want can't materialize simply by thinking, *I need to repeat this set of affirmations* or *I need to use a vision board*. The processes I am outlining here give you a much stronger level of self-belief, which is no different than making thoughts instantly materialize.

Many have forgotten this ability because of the way we have been taught to view the process of receiving. In reality, there are ancient secrets buried within us. When we assert power over our lives, we reawaken these abilities. We wholeheartedly accept that we have influence over our physical experience through our thoughts, intentions, voice power, and energy states.

The current teachings tend to only share what you can do without actually putting the power back into your own hands. You can manifest, but the nature of who you are at the moment is what's actually manifesting. Knowing what is truly happening empowers you to stop battling doubts, questioning if something is even real, or wondering if it will even happen for you. These are signs of forgetting who you are. To begin thought materialization and to understand this topic, I want you to start operating from spiritual power, automatic self-belief, and encoded self-trust to see that you are supernatural and multidimensional.

> *Anything is possible. Your mind can create it. Your will can manifest it. Your heart can attract it. Your soul can materialize it. The magic is you, and has always been you.*

The greatest reminder of this phenomenon is seeing that life exists beyond the physical body. Being present here and now can only mean that there must be some magic to who you are. This can be utilized to make your visit here what it was intended to be. Many things will help you to remember this, and this is why I wrote this book—to reawaken the power within you so you can remove the many processes that function as obstacles to yourself.

When you are, you just are…and you have always been. This knowledge can be activated within you simply by being reminded of it. Sometimes, this understanding comes through your own soul. You are given guidance and told what you need to know. To even get into the next level of manifesting and understanding the deeper teachings of this natural state, an individual must accept their spiritual authority and be ready to alter their physical reality.

The source of life has given us this gift and shown us the way by making it possible for us. If this innate knowledge wasn't in you, you would never have found this book. This is why life is a very spiritual experience. The teachings of letting go and surrender get you comfortable with the invisible world and how it works. In the end, releasing (or just living) will help you let go of learned behaviors such as needing reassurance, confirmation, or proof of what is already known. The truth is, you can manifest out of thin air. You can say something now and see it right now. You can envision a desired outcome, and the path to it becomes a part of your life. This is about activating and seeing that you are limitless. Through many possibilities and in many ways, anything can happen for you. This chapter on thought materialization will delve deeper into what we normally think of as manifesting.

You can start to exercise supernatural self-confidence. You know already that you will see everything you have willed into existence. By the end of this chapter, you will be able to imagine something and see it instantly. You will be able to speak something into existence and see it happen. You will have the power to heal, empower, positively influence, and make things turn out the way you want. You will experience an energy upgrade with every word of this chapter because it will assist you in restoring your power to simply *know* instead of constantly trying to convince yourself that something is possible. You are entering your next level, and you are ready for it.

The Physical World Is the Mental World

Everything around you in the physical is a thought which has already manifested. You are even manifesting right now, simply by knowing your thoughts will materialize. If you look at everything you possess and are surrounded by, there is 100 percent chance that it started with a thought. You always imagine something before you get it. You always mentally plan everything before it happens.

If we take it a step further, we can see that the items you purchase originated in someone's imagination when they were first creating them. We are living in a world created by our minds, and many minds are at work manifesting the lives of their dreams…or using stuff that has been dreamed up by others. You are now going to be the one who is consciously and actively dreaming up your reality. You will start adding to the world. You will use the power of your mind to get anything you want. The physical world responds really quickly to mental energy. Not just mind power, but the amount of energy you hold within yourself.

Thoughts Materialize

Anything that previously stood in the way of your instant manifestations was the illusion of someone telling you that something wasn't possible or a lie that something couldn't be done—or maybe just forgetting about your gift by not using it. If you look to the next person for all that can happen in your life, you will be capped at their level of self-belief. This is why you don't need anyone to believe in your wildest dreams. All that is needed is your mental energy to make anything happen. People who live from their greatest potential are the ones pushing humanity forward. You are going to be the future of humanity with this insight. Your self-realization leads to a highly confident, empowered, loving, strong being. Greater power must be unlocked within you so you can know what this feels like, looks like, and acts like. Becoming that person is what this book will bring out of you.

> *I have the power, strength, will, and choice to change my life. I am dynamic and multidimensional. I am supernatural and superhuman. I have vast abilities and capabilities. I materialize my visions. I see everything I speak instantly. I am the source and the connection.*

The physical world you see through your eyes is projected outward by you. You are the main source of creating this projection, experience, and awareness. You are using real energy to create real manifestations. You are a supernatural being.

When you weren't aware of this, you lived life from a state of reaction, response, and repetition of what seemed to be out there. Nobody taught you the depth of your soul. You were just being shown how to *maybe* trust yourself or believe in yourself, not the truth that *you* are the main creator of real energy through your mind and body.

Thought Access

Your mind influences the physical world, and this will instantly start to show you real results. You don't have to wait anymore or project your manifestations/creations into the distance. It is all here right now, and you are being pulled directly to it. Patience is practiced by those who are trying to convince themselves that it will happen. Of course, this is a good thing, and it is helpful, but we have to go to another level.

You are entering a new level now—the level of knowing. You understand that it is here now. You know it is meant for you. You know that you will see it today. This harnesses all of your energy to go to work now. You aren't in the future or the past. You only exist now, and when you think and feel from this place, the world gives, responds, and supplies what you need right now.

You are getting to know your true self again, and you are whole, powerful, and a commander of universal energy. Everything bends to assist you on your path. See yourself as the center of these creations, and start becoming familiar with your ancient gift. You will realize that much of your previous way of seeing life had to do with losing energy, projecting yourself into the future or past, trying to convince yourself about manifesting, and constantly searching for new information to try to make yourself believe. Those days are now over.

Your new self knows that everything is your mental energy at work. You know that everything is taking place now. You understand that the physical world isn't as solid as it appears, and anything can be changed, transformed, and brought to life. The new you also knows your voice power. You have infectious self-confidence. You walk as if you have millions of higher forces with you. You live from spiritual authority. You take responsibility for your life and accelerate your own healing through the awareness that you are everything, you are eternal, and you are just visiting Earth to see how much you can remember of your true self. You are learning to create, to love, to see it all, and to share that energy with others.

We can clearly see that the physical world, and even our physical bodies, are something we experience through our soul. We have seen many people we love transition out of the physical, and this can help us remember that we are so much more. We must really feel, live, and express all that we are now.

> *You have always been a master of the realms, a seer of the beyond. Your treasure has been unlocked. Your command to claim your power has been heard. You are becoming ALL that you have always been destined to become. It's time to see yourself.*

As your mind and body grow lighter, released from the dense information the world tries to place upon you in the form of barriers and fears, you will feel reawakened, as that place was a distant land. What's actually happening is that you have activated everything has been latent in you. You begin really seeing everything as it was meant to be. As you see the world through your mind, your mental space must become healthy, strong, expanded, and aware.

This reawakening of yourself gives you a glimpse into a vast world in which you narrate your own story, create the people you want to enter your life, receive the opportunities you feel are worthy of your valuable mind, manifest pretty much anything you can dream up, and receive as you please. You know everything is mental energy at work, and you are putting it all to the test.

These energies love to serve you and get things done for you. These energies are your mind. If you were able to see thoughts with your eyes, you would see hues of electrical energy. The same goes for your feeling states. How you feel at the core of your body is living, moving energy. This is why teachings instruct you to feel as if it is already true or feel it into existence. If you uncover the deeper state, you will see living energy moving throughout your body and into the physical world to create the shapes of your manifestations. In this way, the energy signals you hold in your mind and emotions are turned into objects, experiences, and states matching the signals you are already sending out.

When we don't think of our thoughts and feelings as alive, we don't use them in our favor. This is why your thoughts can just run in multiple directions, and your feelings keep changing without you choosing them. The only reason negative thoughts exist in the mind is because we have made it okay by interacting with them as if they are something happening to us, not something created by us. You have to take an authoritative stance over your mental world. Your past lack of awareness has shown manifestations of unwanted thoughts, experiences, and feelings that don't match the direction you wish to go.

> *Don't give power to anything that drains your energy or makes you doubt yourself. This isn't a reality, but a state of mind you're tuning into for a moment. Switch it up. Snap out of it and remember that you always have a choice for higher-quality thoughts and emotional intelligence.*

This has to do with seeing your mental and emotional space as a world in which you can begin to speak, think, and feel different things into your invisible spaces. You now choose with awareness. This is when those voices change up. You will naturally develop an encouraging, positive mental voice without even trying. It just changes into one that says, *You can, it is happening, how about trying this? Of course it is working out, you are a genius, you are smart, you are strong.*

Everything positive will be heard and felt by you. Even your emotions will assist you intuitively, as it was meant to be this way.

Once your mental and emotional states are recalibrated as naturally healthy and positive, you will see that life is so much more, and that you are now supportive of yourself. Acting against oneself and battling oneself happened in the world of the past, when people had no idea about the great power they were or how their inner world worked. People pick up belief systems that try to define the world around them *for* them—which, in a way, is magic in itself, as you then start to see everything that belief system says you should see.

If people lack self-belief, they are easy to control and manipulate. They are susceptible to unfavorable conditions because they weren't the ones who created them. They end up adopting mental beliefs that say these conditions and problems are a normal and part of life, and you should just obey them. Anything that strips you of your pure, natural state of mental wellness, emotional balance, deep con-nection, and intuitive intelligence is only misleading you through fear, confusion, and imbalance. Anything that even tries to say anything negative about the world or your potential is a form of mental virus. This is why we can feel energy as repulsive or contagious, because our higher state, if we are sensitive to it, will naturally guide us by attracting those who are good for our soul while disconnecting from those who lead us astray.

> *Suddenly, it all clicks. Your life begins to feel like a dream. Things begin to happen for you in ways you can't explain. You feel power surging through you. A transformation has taken place, and you are free to fly.*

All of this will lead you to the freedom of influencing the physical world through your mind. You have become free. You know now that your mental energy is connected to your physical manifestations. You also know that what is coming into your life depends on just asking for it, feeling it, being it, and energetically welcoming it. Pull it toward yourself, and have fun doing it. You can even manifest for other people by sharing your strong self-belief with their minds. It's up to you…whatever you want to do with it.

I believe everyone should learn all of this and manifest their lives for themselves so they don't become co-dependent on anyone in any way. We should only be sharing insights and awareness to expand each other. Anything is possible, and it gets much more interesting when we share the journey, go on the adventure of life with others, or even do it ourselves.

Everything is the way you want it to be. When the insights go deeper, we discover that we have built a magnificent inner world that becomes our physical world. All of this is to say that yes, you have strong energy to bend reality in your favor. No, the physical world isn't the only space in which you exist. Yes, you can make every outcome the way you want it to be. Yes, you can solve problems that seem difficult by receiving spiritual insight for them. Yes, people will respond positively to your new energy, which you hold as your truth inside your body. Yes, a way will always be made for anything. Yes, your mind is powerful enough to heal yourself. Yes, you can find the love of your life and live happily ever after. Yes, you can change your body, habits, mindset, and what you attract, all through your mental energy. Yes, your story can get better. Yes, you can live in bliss, harmony, and peace.

All of this and more is possible if it is what you wish for. If you can stretch your imagination, you will see some of the most incredible things happen in your life. Knowing that your physical world is responding to your mental energy, you will become intentional and direct when it comes to receiving.

Another major blessing I have noticed from cultivating deeper awareness is this: The way things used to emotionally affect you also changes. You will naturally understand how to respond to almost any situation with centeredness, calm, and trust in the outcome you want. Even if things seem to appear one way, you know that appearances only lead to your outcome; they always have, and they always will. Keep this in mind as you start to materialize in the physical world. Energy shifts to instantly realign you with what you want to receive.

A lot of energy is coming into your body and mind to support your new beginnings, materializations, and massive positive change.

Start seeing everything around you as energy. See yourself as energy. At first, your mind will show you signs of this being true. You will begin to see the influence of your mind on physical things. Initially, you will become comfortable with sudden manifestations and how quickly your thoughts are produced in external spaces.

You can already see this with technology; something you've been thinking about shows up on your phone or what you are looking at online. These are things you haven't even spoken. They are just thoughts matching up with the energy field of thoughts that are already all around. The internet is no different from physical-world manifestations. You can manifest something online, digitally, just as you can in physical space.

The whole point of thought materialization is for you to get comfortable with the subtle nature of the manifestations that are instantly happening already. You are becoming a master at this because it is natural to you. The reason it doesn't always happen suddenly is that we have created many beliefs about how things happen. If you are shocked by something appearing suddenly, or someone showing up in your life who matches everything you have been thinking about as the kind of person or partnership you desire, this just means you aren't used to this path of creation.

The truth is, what we create depends on how comfortable

we are with the power of our mind. I have seen people manifest out of thin air in the most unexpected ways because they weren't attached to lengthy process-thinking. They believed that all is now, and they made unimaginable things show up in their lives.

When I work with people who are just learning about manifestation, and I tell them, "Let's make something show up in your life this week." We start off with what they feel comfortable with—something that is believable for them. One woman chose that her neighbor would offer to mow her lawn, and another chose someone spontaneously bringing her a gift in a blue package. All of this materialized for them within the same week. These were test experiences for them, because they thought it was completely unusual for someone to do that—especially the lady whose neighbor mowed her lawn, since they weren't on good terms (or so she assumed!).

The process started off with me asking them to imagine their end reaction or better, then calling me to tell me the news. The first woman saw her neighbor smiling at her and asking if she needed some help with the lawn. The second just imagined the blue gift bag in her hand and saying, "Wow!" These were the simple mental creations they came up with. I just added the part where I said, "Now, imagine rushing to your phone to calling me, saying, 'WOW, IT WORKED!'" This was fun experience for me. I always love seeing how people's lives change when they manifest something strange and unexpected for themselves. Both women said they never thought they could make a difference with their minds or create outcomes like we did together.

I do believe people with strong self-belief can help others realize what is within them—not by telling them, but by encouraging actual experiences. People need to see for themselves in order to believe. This begins the activated acceleration of true power and self-confidence. The truth is that everyone has a preconceived idea of everything around them. Naturally, people don't think someone will give them a gift out of the blue, because the mind has been trained to need a reason for why something like that would be done. It shouldn't have to make sense, however. All that matters is what you want out of your experience.

When I empower people, I come from a limitless mindset, and that means going beyond barriers in thinking and expectation. As the woman received her gift in the blue bag, she at first found herself in a somewhat bewildered state because she hadn't known how her specific outcome with all the little details could possibly unfold. When it did, it stretched her imagination, and it actually energized her. She felt something deeply spiritual: She had the ability to create the world she wanted. She had never known about her true power to materialize what she wished. The wonderful thing about both of these stories is that both women were new to manifesting, and still got very quick results. They have been unstoppable ever since. I get calls sometimes from them, saying, "Oh, you won't believe what I materialized the other day." It's truly a delight to see how one fun experiment turned into an adventure of creation. Anything is possible, in the most literal sense!

> *If you choose to live your truth, make sure you are ready to operate outside of constructs that limit human interaction and behavior, as most people are looking for mirrors of familiarity instead of mirrors of possibility. Some things will require you to break free so you can move forward and stay true to yourself.*

Start by getting comfortable with your own power. You will realize just how much structure you have built up around receiving, and the more you work through this book, the more you will accept that you are a master of materialization despite illusory limits that only exist in the mindset.

Whatever the mental world believes in, it projects into the physical space. Your mental reality matches up with your physical reality in every sense. The only hope we have is taking our power back from any kind of uncontrolled thought, going even deeper to break down belief structures that try to explain away the unexplainable world around us. You can see this everywhere simply by examining different people and the different outcomes they create. The only difference between people in the physical sense is the mental world they all uniquely occupy.

I wanted to break this down so you could have a stronger foundation to be able to grasp out-of-thin-air materialization so it makes more sense to you. When we allow our full potential to take over our lives, we become deeply transformed and access more energy. There will be a day when you see yourself materializing everything you want, and that will be your normal state. Just as many people are now having the conversations about manifestation, it will also be normal in the future for someone to say that they can materialize out of thin air. Humanity is always advancing, which for me means that we are removing learned, limiting concepts in order to bring life back to the physical world the way it was always meant to be. If someone is told they can do it, that it is possible, that of course it can happen, and that they have great power to positively make a difference in the world from childhood onward, what do you think would happen to that person's life experience? You could be that person right now, through your own ways of implementing strong self-belief as natural and normal for you. It is very easy to create a new mindset, outlook, and reality. All that matters is that you remember this truth, live to your fullest, and see it for yourself.

Materializing Out of Thin Air

Materializing out of thin air means there's no logical way

something should "make sense" in terms of how it happens. It just does…in the most unusual, unexpected, and miraculous way. You can't reason it away, explain it, or try to understand it. This has probably happened to many of us a few times or even many times in our lives. There've been moments when you materialized something you needed urgently, or spoke of something and it happened to you. It is sudden, quick, and always feels like you're in the twilight zone.

What is happening is that when our mind produces something we want, it takes pathways that go outside of our normal expected belief system. When this happens, it shakes things up within you because it takes place outside of what is normally believable to you. This is why the feeling is intense with excitement, high energy, surprise, and stunned gratitude. It brings you right into the moment.

This is a normal state, and it also helps people catch a glimpse when they experience events that exist outside of their current mindset. There are so many things we can't explain. The mystery of the universe means so much because it is here in order for us to learn. I believe *we* are the greatest mystery. We spend our lives unraveling our own selves and discovering more about our souls. If you're reading this book, you are naturally operating in an expanded state because you attract everything you connect with and are ready for.

I know this next level of your adventure will only bring you closer to something that is very familiar to you already. When you can't explain it, explore it. The first step in materializing out of thin air is accepting that you are magical being and that you are always receiving. Get this feeling in your mindset and in your body. You are a receiver first. On an energetic level, this means you believe that you are connected to something that provides for you.

The second factor is how you see the world. This means you

see everything as energy coming into your life, everything as alive, moving, and working nonstop. See the world as filled with trillions of opportunities, forever abundance, limitless connections, and so much beauty. See the life energy in you and all around you. Don't put physical things above yourself. See it as normal and natural to have, to receive, and to utilize the materials of the planet in the most balanced way. This changes the power we give away and the stories we make up. There's nothing in your way. There's nobody against you. To even think in a negative way requires an energy investment. You will start to see thoughts as real energy moving around. You'll become pretty imaginative, which will instantly help you end unwanted thoughts and reinvest that energy into supportive thoughts.

The third factor is openness and flow. You must be open to what doesn't make sense to you. You might get an urge to contact someone, and that call could completely change your life or give you an answer you needed. This urge is something that doesn't initially make sense. *Why do I need to contact them?* These are the kinds of questions that can cause invisible barriers, since you are always looking for reasons for things to make sense. The out-of-thin-air mindset means you follow urges, instincts, intuition, gut feelings, and/or callings for you to go somewhere, contact someone, or make a connection that links you to your greater purpose. Openness and flow work more with energy instead of making stuff up in terms of the real insights your spirit is giving you.

Fourth is getting used to your new life. You are someone who has taken back their power to reach new heights of self-discovery. Every time you have an out-of-thin-air experience, the energy of your physical body will increase because you start to instill a higher level of self-belief. This is uncommon in our society. This type of energy is very attractive, as it is closest to nature's expression. Flow in the body allows more to become possible through that person. It will be up to you to decide how you share or explain to others what is taking place in your life. It will be very clear to everyone that you have discovered something. It's all energetic, so explanation isn't always needed. You have entered embodiment now, and everything you do will have heightened magnetic energy.

> *The more you trust yourself, the more energy, momentum, and life force you generate.*

Now that you are ready, start working with your own body's energy and the field all around you. Think of something you want to materialize, and feel its energy state instead of just thinking about the physical aspect. See that it is really just air or atoms arranged in a certain shape. When you think of air forming into atoms and turning into a physical shape, this will help you see what it really is instead of it just being solid. When we think in terms of air or energy first, we stop feeling like something is so difficult to receive. Microscopically, you yourself are energy first; and if we go deeper, we are back in the void. This is the point from which you will be materializing.

First, see emptiness, and pull the structure energetically of what you wish to materialize, giving it a physical form. Create an energy link between yourself and your materialization so that it can locate you instantly. This is a very advanced technique that will show you unimaginable, miraculous, wonderful results. What it does is get your mindset out of the physical alone, placing you in your endless lab to materialize. You can create anything in this space, and the match in the physical world will suddenly show up in your life. It will be an exact carbon copy of what you have imagined it to be.

The energy link is only a locator. It has a magnetic charge that pulls what you are manifesting into your physical sphere. All creations start off in the energy world (the mental world of creation). You can materialize out of thin air because you create what you want in the energy world first. See it as such, and you will see it into being. You can even use this awareness to make changes in your life by imaging a new look for yourself, better relationships with your family/friends, greater ease in sticking to habits you want, rearranging your personal and business life to be more wholistic, and making situations in general healthier and more favorable.

Go into your mental space, as it is the void. This is the first step in energy creation. Start the energy construction, the physical details, and the energy link. For example, design your new look by materializing in your mind the changes you want. Don't be surprised if you notice same-day physical changes. It will start as a feeling first, and in the mirror, you will see the reflection of what you wanted to look like. I share this example because people seem to always want to feel good in their bodies. Usually, a change in mindset helps them to truly accept and create the feeling first, followed by looking their best as a reflection of their mental creation. This just one example of the many strategies you can start to play with. You can even get favorable positive responses from people around you or people with whom you want to make things work. Get very comfortable going into the mental world to construct the physical counterpart of all the things you want to materialize. Results happen instantly, so be sure that you are ready for what you want.

Materializing Is Easy for You

Your self-confidence will build when you know you can get the results you want. You don't need much…just your own mind in order to do just about anything. This is why materializing is so easy for you. It's free, it's natural, it's available to you every moment. You wake up every day and use your mind to think the thoughts you're currently thinking, feel the state you're feeling, and talk about your current storyline. All of this takes the same amount of energy and investment as simply "switching on" what you want to see come to life, the ways you want to feel, and the conversations you want to have.

Since being who we are feels so natural, we never take into account what actually builds our perception, *why* we feel the way we feel, and what makes our experiences repeat. When you're out there living your mental projections, it's a new thing to be able to self-analyze your own outcomes, experiences, and ability to make improvements. We are taught throughout our lives to just bury everything and keep going as we slowly forget our superpowers. As you take a step back and see what this version of yourself has created in the now, you can identify ways to optimize your experience by going back into the void or creation point and beginning to switch things up. This is when you start to remember that you can materialize, and that thoughts do come to life through your own awareness, not just from some quote "out there." You will be living proof of this.

> *Being in harmony with yourself attracts higher energy all around you. The spiritual nature of reality awakens and moves toward you. It wants to give to you. It brings you everything because you believe that it will, and you are constantly grateful for it.*

You won't need to make yourself feel any particular way in order to materialize. It is just as natural as breathing. You can be in any state and use that energy toward your vision. All emotions are just energy that can be utilized to your advantage. Release your focus on *am I doing it right? Do I feel positive enough for it to work?* Release having to raise your vibration first. The truth is, everyone is always creating, no matter what state they are in. The goal is for you to get comfortable with your own powers through experience. This instantly gives you energy and strength to rule out doubt, fear, and uncertainty of the outcome.

It's usually a lack of firsthand experience that causes unwanted thoughts or states to come up. When you convert any kind of energy toward the outcome you want, that new focus becomes the main focus. If, however, you feel like you *need* to be ready to start materializing out of thin air, you are only creating

Thought Access

an invisible hurdle: the illusion that you will need to perform extra acts to eventually reach the same goal.

I want to remove these limiting beliefs so you don't play tricks on yourself that prevent you from just going for it. As you reach this greater understanding, you won't need to battle negative thoughts or question if something is even possible. You'll just go from exactly where you are and how you are feeling. You will be surprised to find out that the past *you* no longer looks or feels familiar. It wasn't even a battle. You just set your mind on your mental creations and got results, which gave you real physical energy.

As you play with this concept and materialize what you want, you will feel different, more energized, more connected, and deeply trusting of yourself. This is why this experience is so easy for you: You are always doing it. A lot of high energy in your mind and body means you will attract more peace, self-love, people, experiences, and blessings that match this energy state. Even if you see something that isn't at your level, you won't have judgement; you'll just know there are people out there who just haven't tapped in yet.

One thing I noticed about being in this state is that miracles just become a normal occurrence. You open yourself up to the flow of things naturally happening as you intend. It will look like you're a lucky person or have a special gift. The truth is that you know who you are, you know how important your mindset is, and you know exactly where to go (within) to get results. There will be so much good coming into your life, the lives of those around you, and everyone connected to your energy field. When someone is activated and walking in their soul power, it holds real weight. You don't have to do anything but to be real with yourself. An authentic soul can expend less energy and get maximum results.

We assume that appearances are all there is. The truth is,

energy is constantly communicating at the highest speed, and everyone can feel and read beyond appearances. When you remain true to what is in your heart, the universe bends to your will. You will use these insights to better yourself and the world. You will be a representation of what is possible in the human experience. Do everything with love and honor. Enjoy your materializations!

Key Points to Remember

- *You can make things appear out of thin air when you learn your power to materialize thoughts.*

- *To begin thought materialization and to understand this topic, I want you to start operating from your own spiritual power, automatic self-belief, and encoded self-trust while witnessing the fact that you are supernatural and multidimensional.*

- *You are entering your next level, and you are ready for it.*

- *Everything around you in the physical world is a thought that has already manifested. You are even manifesting right now, in the knowledge that your thoughts will materialize. If you look at everything that you possess and are surrounded by, there is a 100 percent chance that it started with a thought.*

- *If you look to the next person for all that can happen in your life, you will be capped at the level of their own self-belief. This is why you don't need anyone to believe in your wildest dreams. All that is needed is your mental energy to make anything happen.*

- *The physical world you see through your eyes is projected outward by you. You are the main source of creation for this projection, experience, and awareness. You are using real energy to create real manifestations.*

Thought Access

You are a supernatural being. When you weren't aware of this, you lived life from a state of reaction, response, and repetition of what seemed to be out there.

- *The new you knows that everything is your mental energy at work. You know that everything is in the now. You understand that the physical world isn't as solid as it appears, and anything can be changed, transformed, and brought to life. The new you also understands your voice power. You have an infectious self-confidence. You walk as if you have millions of higher forces with you. You live from a place of spiritual authority.*

- *Start seeing everything around you as energy. See yourself as energy. At first, your mind will show you signs of this being true. You will begin to see the influence of your mind on physical things. You will become comfortable with sudden manifestation and how quickly your thought is reproduced in external spaces.*

- *Start by getting comfortable with your own power.*

- *There will be a day when you see yourself materializing everything you want, and that will be your normal state.*

- *Materializing out of thin air means there's no logical way something should "make sense" in the way it happens. It just does...in the most unusual, unexpected, and miraculous ways. You can't reason it away, explain it, or try to understand it. This has probably happened to many of us a few times (or even many times) over the course of our lives.*

- *The first step in materializing out of thin air is accepting that you are a magical being and that you are always receiving.*

Thoughts Materialize

- *When you can't explain it, explore it.*
- *There will be so much good coming into your life, the lives of those around you, and everyone connected to your energy field.*

13

THREE POWERFUL THOUGHT ACCESS TECHNIQUES

What you'll learn in this chapter will put the power back in your hands. You will see changes taking place within you that you never thought possible. My goal is to take your consciousness there and give you the access to be able to utilize your own imagination to get practical results.

These three techniques have worked miracles in my own life, not only in terms of what I have created using them, but also what I have learned about myself through the experience. The wonderful thing about this book isn't just what happens in your life. It's also what you discover about yourself as you experiment and intentionally alter your own path. I consider these techniques very advanced, and I want to give you a little warning that you shouldn't be startled by how quickly things happen for you. This will assist you not only in accepting your own powers, but also the degree to which you will begin to receive instantly. I believe you are ready for these kinds of insights, and I know you will use them to better yourself in the highest way possible. Again, you are to do everything through your own mind, as you are the most advanced technology that has ever existed.

Everything is possible through you, and everything begins within you. As you start to accept this and express it, so much within you will come alive. It will feel like you have awakened from something, and the truth is, you have. You have awakened to

Three Powerful Thought Access Techniques

yourself, and this heightens everything around you so you can see the mental, energetic, and spiritual links to everything.

These three techniques will further encourage your self-awareness so you can feel more confident in your own ability to receive while influencing yourself to operate in your divine truth. You can use these techniques once and get fast results, or you can repeat them to continuously get more results. The point of each is for you to actually see for yourself what can happen when you start to use your own mind.

I am big on everyone experiencing what is possible for themselves. In this way, we can move on to higher and greater creations. If you feel confident, assured, and trusting in your own ability to create what you want, you will feel empowered, expanded, and even more open to all the greatness life has to offer.

1. *Creating Any Version of Yourself Technique*

This technique will teach you how to download into your mind the codes for the version of yourself that represents the state you want to be in. These are real versions you can create of yourself. Just as you can decide to change one habit and feel like a whole new person, you can also better yourself in higher ways through the mind. Your body follows these changes. This will help your transformation from a deeper level instead of battling a version of yourself that may already be playing out unfavorable habits or patterns.

To understand this technique, you must also know that who you are right now is also a version you have created. This slowly happens through our ways of thinking, feeling, and attracting. As we repeat certain actions and replay certain thoughts, we construct who we believe we are. This attracts people into our lives as well as possessions, the way we feel about ourselves, and what we are willing to tolerate. Everything is learned. To be able to see the connection of your mindset with the version of yourself you have currently created, you need to look within to discover the origins of those ideas. This will prepare you for the powerful technique of choosing who you want to be.

Sometimes, this way of being just happens to us, as the body and mind readily adapt to states over time. What the world thinks of you can sometimes solidify into a version of yourself before you are even able to recognize the fact that it is just something you are expressing, not the entirety of who you are. This is why we are about to recreate ourselves, change our lives, and become greater. The ability to accomplish this shows that there is more within you. Now that you have the idea that you can create yourself to be anything you wish to be, we can dive deeper into the practical side of the technique.

You're becoming the greatest version of yourself.

Creating a new version of yourself starts with choosing who you want to be. There is no limit to this. For the first change, we will be working on the mental side of things, allowing you to naturally flow into your chosen physical version of yourself.

You choose everything you are through your mind first. You speak to yourself in your mind about who you are all the time, and this repetition creates the version of yourself that you allow to continue to exist. Let's say there are certain habits you are just done with, and you really want to change them in some way. You have to start downloading, through your mental state and energetic body, the new version of yourself with new habits. You do this by no longer mentally or emotionally associating yourself with the person who does those things. Instead, you become the new self with the habits you would like.

The reason I want you to start becoming this version of yourself in your mind first is so you can create powerful energy circulation within your body by entertaining these new thoughts.

Three Powerful Thought Access Techniques

This circulation of new energy is a way of downloading and bringing to life that version of yourself. You will start to feel different from your previous habits and all they attracted. You will almost instantly begin stepping into the new version you have created, not by battling habits or forcing things, but through embodiment via energy changes.

We only change through our mind, and then this inner alteration starts to take place in our body's chemistry. We are pure energy, and as we shift our perception of who we think we are, we start to bring to life within us the person we believe we can be. At some point in the past, you may have become fed up with a version of yourself or a state of being that didn't represent who you were. That version came to an end because the inner you wanted better and knew deep down that it was possible. This is the kind of energy we are working with when I say *creating a version of yourself*.

> *Be so busy becoming the best version of yourself that you don't have time or energy to involve yourself in negativity, drama, the past, or things that drain you. Define yourself by what you do, not what others have done to you. Don't give anyone power over you.*

This technique can be used to change all unwanted habits, behaviors, aspects of your personality, and ways you feel about yourself, creating a version of yourself that is healthy, successful, at peace, in love, whole, and highly aware. You can use it to create a version of yourself with specific talents, creative abilities, and forms of expression. You can create yourself to be anything you want to be.

My main goal in this technique is to assist you in knowing that all versions of ourselves we play out in life have been learned in some way, either from external influences or through

Thought Access

something our soul has expressed. Soul expression manifests as higher ideals of freedom playing out through your body—the way you feel in terms of what you believe to be possible through expansion of your mind.

We are either guided from within or created by our past experience, which tries to say, "That is all there is to you." The truth is, you are the main observer who sees the many different experiences you have had throughout your life. The observer is all that you have been, from the start of your life up to this very moment. The different roles you have taken on have all been momentary, which is why you keep changing and developing new interests, relation-ships, and ways of being. These are easily changed, because we are playing with physical creations based on what we know is possible.

If you knew you could become anything you wanted, who or what would that be, without any limitations of the mind? This is how far you can expand yourself. The only thing constantly changing is your mindset, and this is the most important part of the technique.

Create yourself. Literally create who you want to be. Download talents into yourself. Feel gifted within your body. No matter what your dream, there is a version of yourself who, right now, has realized it already. This version is an energy state you allow into your mindset. You welcome this state of being and tell yourself that this is who you are. It is you, and only you, who chooses what you want to play out. Nobody has a say in what goes on in your mind and body when you are choosing to upgrade your thinking. This is a private space of creation which remains unseen as it comes to life.

Three Powerful Thought Access Techniques

Creating Any Version of Yourself Technique

Phase 1

Start by choosing a version of yourself you want to become. Write this down, listing what this version of yourself looks like, feels like, and what you are doing. Keep in mind that you don't have to consider the current version's states, because when you are creating a new version of yourself, the past is invalid in terms of the possibilities of what can be. So, you will not need to think in terms of lack, but rather potential. When you are writing, be so free that it almost feels surreal. This pushing of your imagination wakes something up within you.

This space of creation is free for you to dream your wildest dreams. The version you are creating can be literally anything: healed version, more successful version, more talented/emotionally balanced version, a speaker, writer, dancer, singer, highly creative, spiritually aware, a great communicator, a magnetic person, someone who always manifests what they want, a fast learner, highly intelligent....the list goes on. Anything is possible here, and you will download this version of yourself into your mind first, then your body, and then the physical world.

This is about you. You know what you want and what you feel is your highest expression. Writing it down is the first step in the activation of your creation. Once you write down the details of the new version of yourself, take some time to read it. I like writing new version creations like a story. Treat it like a mini-script of your life, all about the new way you will be living, thinking, and feeling. The story element helps with imagination and makes it more real. Start with a list, then create a story. Title the script of your new life and read it to yourself.

Phase 2

In this phase, you will get into the imagination phase of your life script. You will need to imagine scenes playing out of the story you created in your mind and feel them in every part of your body. Only consider yourself as the new version. This will even change your habits, because you are no longer the same person who did things that weren't in your favor.

The secret I want to share with you here is that once you make a true mental image of your new self and the version you wish to become, you alchemically alter how your body responds to your current self. This means that all forms of anxiety, fear, doubt, overthinking, uncertainty, and stagnation are removed out of your actual process of thinking in a wave of new energy. The version of yourself you create literally alters your energy field. You will feel exceptionally vibrant, energized, strong, trusting, aware, tuned in, fearless, limitless, and expanded. This can only happen through mental changes, which is what I am teaching you here.

I have seen miraculous things happen instantaneously when someone has accepted a new version of themselves. Don't spend another second of your life trading your valuable creative mental energy to go to war against a past version of yourself. Don't even think from that perspective. The newness that you are intentionally creating is doing all the work.

The moment you read your story, imagine it playing out, and feel it to be true, you welcome that energy to be downloaded in a literal sense into your body. This can be a rush of energy for some people; others might cry tears of joy because something profound is taking place in the mind and body when we mentally embody a greater version of ourselves. It is as if a deep portal of insight has been opened, and when you feel more of your expanded state, you will feel so much energy coming into your body as unwanted states that were previously holding you back

Three Powerful Thought Access Techniques

simultaneously perish. It will be like giving birth to a whole new self. You can imagine at any time of the day, no matter what you're doing. Just see and feel yourself as that state. You only need to do it once to see changes—that is how powerful it is.

Phase 3

The first thing that will happen with this technique is that you will feel empowered, different, and activated. You'll notice things aligning to your new version and manifesting: a certain kind of person coming into your life, other people beginning noticing your changes, and more. You are manifesting out of thin air to match your new-version thoughts. You just naturally feel calm, trusting, and relaxed. You have a different way of being now, and this will reflect in your relationships, habits, and the way you think.

These changes bring so much good. They also create a vortex for attraction. This can be such a great time of change in your life that associations with the past version of yourself will suddenly come to an end. This is a natural part of your rebirth. Anything that is not energetically aligned won't go with you into your new life, and that is a normal step on the path to greater good. You will know what works and doesn't work, what is healthy and what is naturally not good for your soul.

This is a beautiful time. The rearrangement of your energy state always leads to better and greater as it removes blockages while renewing and restoring you. Prepare yourself by knowing you're entering a new life that is far greater than you could have imagined. You did it for yourself by creating this new version and stepping into it, just like a scene out of a movie. Welcome all the blessings that follow your new state, and allow all energy that wants to exit, as well.

The grace of allowing helps us to receive far more than we can ask for. It's time for you to get what you want, live the life you dream of, and enjoy what you have created. Have fun with this technique while achieving any result you desire by simply creating a version of yourself that is already aligned. Find time to celebrate your mental success by doing things that remind you of your power to change your life. Honor yourself in the highest way. It is you who did it, and it is you who *can* do it.

2. *Suggest It to Yourself Technique*

You have the power to positively program yourself through suggestion. Your mind is listening to you at all times: the way you speak about yourself, what you think of yourself, and what you believe to be true. All of this is a form of suggestion and results in self-influence at the highest level. You have to start taking your power back and believing not only in yourself, but also the potential of your mind and body. Each time you say something about yourself, whether negative or positive, your whole body, environment, and universe conform to this energy influence.

Suggestions are the core of your life, both in creating your world and in molding the next generation. Every word we exchange matters as we influence each other to think greater (or do the opposite and spread limitation). Suggestions are very powerful. You can see the way someone is living and how they feel about themselves based on the kinds of suggestions they make to themselves. If you say you can do something, your mind and body feel that anything is possible. If you say you are good enough, you start to feel and think that way.

You have to begin to take control over your mind and body by looking at what is influencing your creations and attractions. Everything is making a suggestion to us at all times, which then influences us to act and think a certain way. The kinds of people with whom you surround yourself, the music you listen to, the streams you tune into, the books you read, the things you watch, the way you spend your energy, and the things you say about yourself are all suggestions that influence you. You might see yourself buying something, not because you really want it, but because it is something you have seen or been told to purchase. Marketing and ads are suggestions, as well. What I want to really focus on is self-influence so you can receive the creations you want, not the ones created *for* you during the times you were unaware.

> *Build a better relationship with your inner self. Your inner conversations, thoughts, and feelings influence everything you do. Be kind to yourself. Encourage yourself. Believe in yourself.*

Self-influence is the creation of inner beliefs that support you. Speak in all ways from a state of what is possible for you, with faith that great things can happen. Tell yourself that you can have those things. Tell yourself that the results will work out. Tell yourself that you are strong, beautiful, healthy, balanced, aware, and connected (and many other powerful words you can add and speak over your life).

What you really need to know is that you are constantly in a state of potential. This means that you are either ready to renew yourself or repeat what has already taken place in order to keep recreating that. Every moment holds a magnificent chance to turn things around. Understand that energy is a very real thing, and it molds you. It is easy for you to actually become all that you want. It is just a matter of changing up what you suggest to yourself.

If you are able to see what I am talking about, you will see every word constructing you and magnetizing everything to you. At the subtle level, what is taking place is that you are changing your aura, your biological energy field, your heart's magnetic power, and your soul's illumination. Every word is building you up and making you into who you wish to be. If you notice, in most people who don't really have strong self-belief and don't trust in themselves, you can locate something someone said to them in the past (or that they said to themselves) that dimmed their light. It's not that they can't do it—they've just bought into the suggestion of what is possible and believed someone else's projected insecurities.

This is how powerful suggestions are. Just as they can help someone become their greatest self, they can also cause people to lose themselves due to repeated suggestions that implied they weren't worthy or good enough. In reality, all of that is a lie, because everyone is special and has a gift. They only lose themselves for a moment, until that guiding light comes back to them and sparks hope back into their hearts and minds. Once you regain your own power to not believe in negative suggestions, you start to actually see that it is all just words, and it was not the true reality of all that can happen for you. This helps you begin your new life in which you don't give away your power to anyone simply because of the suggestions they are making. You don't easily fall for weak tricks of word manipulation. You are a sovereign being who now knows that you can self-influence. *You* can suggest powerful words, higher thoughts, and grander ideals to yourself.

You'll realize your own power to influence everything according to how well you can handle it when things happen quickly and unexpectedly. Being open is crucial to dramatically or even slightly altering the way the universe responds to you.

We give away too much power when we listen to the words others suggest to us and take them as a truth. In reality, words are just words unless they make us believe or think something. We can change how we feel about what others say to us when it doesn't support our mental and emotional health. How many dreams have been shut down by naysayers and people who make negative suggestions? How many people how forgotten themselves just because someone spoke less over them? How many relationships came to an end because of lack of care, respect, and encouragement?

Everything revolves around words and how they make us feel. When we start to understand this, we decide what we agree with, allow, and even accept. We stop giving our power away and start defining ourselves. Someone could say something so negative to you, and it would probably make you laugh once you have gained access to a stronger inner world. You have left the reality in which you were triggered by words, people's opinions, thoughts, and negativity. You know that everything requires your agreement in order to gain validity or enter your bio-field.

Your body and mind belong to you. The way you feel belongs to you. Everything external that doesn't support your growth, development, and positive change should always be reviewed before you allow it to influence you. You have every right to not accept negative influence or people suggesting problems. You have every right to deny anything that tries to put your self-esteem down or make you question your worth.

You are entering a whole new state of being.

You can start to influence yourself today by making suggestions to yourself about yourself. This suggestion technique is about intentionally making yourself feel a chosen state, through your own mind and with your own words. You are going to start to understand that when you say something about yourself, it is not just words, but rather an alteration of your energy to believe something about yourself.

The mind does what you suggest in just about every area. If you look at your current state of mind or what you believe about yourself, there is a 100 percent chance that it is linked to a suggestion you're making about yourself or what you think will happen (or even what you think won't happen). Every suggestion produces many outcomes at once, and gaining this insight will help you avoid being controlled by negative suggestions or external influences that strip your power just so you can be co-dependent.

The goal of this second technique is for you to understand that you have the ability to literally suggest to yourself what you want. Your body listens to you intently and responds to what you are suggesting. If you say, "I can do it," your body conforms to that suggestion. If you say, "I am healthy," your body conforms to that energy state. As I previously mentioned, everything we know thus far has been taught to us. When we stick to unfavorable or inherited words, thoughts, belief systems, and ways of being that don't honor our true potential, we continue in a hypnotic trance state, repeating those learned states as truth, living life oblivious to the fact that we are being influenced to play out roles and operate in repetitive, knee-jerk responses without ever wondering how we arrived there.

Becoming aware of the connection between what you are attracting, how you are feeling, how much you believe in yourself, and the suggestions you are constantly making to yourself will free you from the slumber of unawareness and all its attractions. When someone tells you something negative, they are asking you, in a way, to accept their negative suggestion as reality. When we are aware that anything someone might say isn't necessarily the truth, but rather a filter through which they view the world, we free ourselves from adopting other people's limiting views and perceptions of the world. This can also happen in a positive way: When someone gives you insight or shares encouraging, uplifting words with you, they are expanding the way you see yourself and giving you the inspiration needed to break free of previous ways of feeling and thinking. When you are aware of how things constantly influence you, you take your power back to influence *yourself* by making highly charged suggestions that support the way you want to live.

Three Powerful Thought Access Techniques

Suddenly, it all clicks. Your life begins to feel like a dream. Things begin to happen for you in ways you cannot explain. You feel the power surging through you. The transformation has taken place. You are free to fly.

Many people will free themselves by having this book and reading these words. They will know and understand how to get themselves back, scattering away unwanted views of life. You will now be able to change anything about yourself, your life, your situation, and the way you feel, which is the most important state when you are starting to speak power over your life.

The suggested technique is for you to speak of everything you want as truth to yourself, even when it initially feels unnatural to do so. The reason it can sometimes feel like you're making it up, or you're unsure about whether or not it will happen, is an inherited response from your old program. The way you used to think of life was that you wouldn't dare make up the world you want for yourself because you needed to be certain about how things were going to happen. I am sure you have heard people say, "You're just dreaming. What are you really doing all day long? You're making things up and dreaming up worlds other people want you to." The only reason this seems so real is because a path has already been paved by the ones who want you to follow. The reality is that you are a unique individual, a soul with your own mission and vision. You know you can't walk other people's paths or live their lives. You want what makes sense for you, feels right for you, inspires you, and makes you feel most alive. This is why, when you are paving a new path for yourself, you have to make up the way as you go along. This triggers people's fear of the unknown, which is why conforming and thinking along the lines of acceptability is favored by society.

When you make a suggestion to bring something new out of yourself and you actually believe it, you must chart the path of the unknown with the faith that it is already done. There is no way to explain *how* it will happen for you. You can't try to make sense out of the mystery. You will just find yourself living the suggested reality you created through your own mind. You are already doing this daily, but this time, you will do it the way *you* want, and you'll get the results you suggested.

Suggest It to Yourself Technique

Phase 1

For Phase One, you will be making suggestions that represent the opposite of unfavorable suggestions that may be currently running. This will be good practice before we move on to Phase Two, which will go into more depth. Pay attention to the suggestions running in your life now. Each time you spot an unfavorable suggestion, thought, word, or feeling, suggest the opposite—something with higher energy that feels good to you. This will start making you aware of what is running on a loop when you didn't realize it. It will also help you become more conscious of your own thoughts and what you allow in your inner world.

This is an important phase when it comes to program-ming yourself with the energy you want in your life. You can do this phase for about a week so you have enough time to see for yourself the power of suggestion and what it has been doing in your life. You will also see the new/opposite suggestions you make in the face of the previous/unfavorable ones beginning to take effect all around you and within you.

You can do another very powerful thing in this phase, which is to cancel out any negativity someone projects or shares with you. The way you can do this is to speak greater in that instant to yourself or to the person. This makes you a force of positive change, which will influence them to think greater while at the same time causing negative energy to disappear from your field. This tip will also help you avoid being mindlessly programmed by other people's opinions and perspectives on the world. After some time, you will naturally know how to handle unfavorable suggestions and words with ease and confidence.

Phase 2

You are now ready to make all the suggestions you want to yourself so you can influence the field to get the outcome you want. You have to start realizing that you *are* everything already. If you can think of yourself in the greatest way possible, everything you have imagined about yourself in the moment is a real, true state. This is what this phase is all about: being the embodiment of your own highest imagined self.

You will start by suggesting the reality and state of mind you want to yourself. If you have already finished Phase 1, you will notice faster results at suggesting new states for yourself. Let's say you want to feel more love in your life. You suggest that you are the energy of love, you are the universal representation of love, and that you attract all love in the universe. Suggestions can initially feel like you are just saying things, but isn't everything you are usually saying just "saying things," too?

The point is for you to start saying and feeling that which will support your human experience from an expanded mindset. You have to actively suggest to yourself that everything you feel in your heart is true for you. Nothing external can initiate this state in you; it is born in your soul, and you alone can project it. Tell yourself that you are mentally healthy, that you attract great opportunities, relationships, success, blessings, and miracles. Tell yourself who you are and what you are worthy of. If you don't make any suggestions to yourself, there will be many things trying to influence your mind and how you "should" feel, which puts your essence in restriction.

Thought Access

Your life force energy is supposed to flow freely through your body so you can bring more to life. When someone has been made to believe they aren't all that they truly are, they live life from limited self-perception and attract worlds that match those limitations. You are being liberated here. You are being freed so you can be the one who changes your narrative on command. You are the one who is making powerful suggestions over your life. Anything you feel like you need or want to bring into your life, bring it into your mind.

You can do this in conversation, as well. You can paint the greatest image of yourself and move into that world. It happens because you are creating it right now. There is truly no difference between what you want to step into and what you are already in, because it's all energy configuring to produce exactly what you will experience in this life. The difference now is that you are the one intentionally and consciously doing it.

To suggest anything, start by defining who you are and how you feel. Make yourself get into the mindset that sees life from a greater perspective. You are a master at altering your perception to get the outcome you want: how you respond, react, and create. Everything is just responding to your self-image and how you deeply feel about yourself. The point of suggesting something new is that it takes you out of the trance state of "this is just the way life is" or "these are the things I am supposed to be going through." That doesn't let you identify what created it or what you could say now to change it.

We sometimes think we are stuck in a mindset and identify too much with the inner world of what we have learned. You will be deeply and profoundly stunned to hear that there is a vast array of versions of yourself that you can tap into, and these versions depend on your current state of being. Versions signify expressions of lifestyle, aspirations, inspiration, self-belief, goals, and creative expression. These are all possibilities within you, ready to be called upon through self-suggestion. Having Thought Access is gaining the mental awareness to step into the version that is the highest expression of who you are. This is something you will choose, and this is something you will experience.

Phase 3

As you begin to become more open, connected, and aware of your ability to self-influence through suggestion, you can begin to positively influence the world around you by using your voice power to suggest to others what is possible for them. Words make or break. Words create or destroy. Words pave new paths or block dreams. Knowing what you know now, you can be of the greatest contributor to the change by building up the people around you from within. This isn't a duty; it's simply a natural expression.

When people are in healthy balance, they speak from a higher place. You are always talking anyway, so when sharing with someone, you can practice releasing positive, life-giving suggestions out into the world. As you do this, you will see that it becomes easier for you to feel and think from this state. You really can change the whole trajectory of someone's life with your words, suggestions, and belief in them.

I remember telling a friend of mine that I saw her getting married to the man of her dreams. When I initially told her, she laughed, saying she was single and wasn't really looking. She had, at a prior time, told me that she was open, but for her, it was only a dream to meet someone like that. The truth is, I knew she had so much love within her. Sometimes, people shy away from thinking they can have their dream union because of the way things seem now. They assume many unfavorable suggestions about what isn't possible, when in reality, the field is just waiting for them to say, "You know what? That is what I want, and I can have that." This could be your experience, and you are able to receive that. We sometimes block off what can happen for us by being afraid of the dream itself—not the actual dream, but it being realized. So, in that state, we tell ourselves that maybe that wasn't for us, even though we wanted it. This is how sneaky unfavorable suggestions can be. We create another story on top of the limitation just to mask fear of the unknown.

Back to my friend's story. She was used to living her life on her own, but I felt within me that she was going to be with someone straight out of her dreams. Why? Because she could, and she deserved to have her dreams, too. I asked her to tell me what her ideal partner would be like and what she wanted. We spent one evening almost unintentionally planning the wedding. That was how far our conversation got. I kept telling her I saw myself dancing at her wedding, and she was full of so much happiness and love, and her eyes had a new glow. I sensed it, but only through my words of encouragement was the suggestion planted within her to even consider the possibility of something like that happening.

We stopped treating it like a probable reality and started making it real. It seemed far-fetched to her, but we can all sense what someone deserves, and to ignite that flame requires dream creation and suggestion on the soul level. I kept suggesting to her, "He is already here on Earth, and he's locating you." I even did a ritual with her in which we created the space to welcome her union. She cried so much that evening in overwhelming joy, telling me she saw him in her vision.

We laughed all night and just stared off into the stars. It wasn't surprising to us that we saw a shooting star that night. It was one of the biggest confirmations for her that it was done. Fast forward to a year and a half later, and we were celebrating her wedding. Everything happened exactly the way we had imagined it. It gives her chills to this day.

All of this was made possible by igniting the power of

suggestion and possibility within someone. She could have kept her mindset in a place, assuming she wasn't worthy of that dream. I came in and mentally, emotionally, and spiritually put her in that dream. There was no other way around it except sharing my voice power to help others get their dreams, too. This is what I mean when I say that you, too, can start to impact, influence, and change lives in a positive way.

We are energy generators and we are life changers. We already have the ability to shift the world into a greater place by reminding others that so much more is possible. Every dream realized generates more energy in the field for even more life to be expressed. Every person who is transformed by a dream realized will always know the magic of life. Be it so others can become it!

3. *Ask Your Mind Anything Technique*

This is a powerful technique when it comes to getting to know your own mind. It not only teaches you to tap into a vast field of answers and guidance, it also allows you to begin to feel highly confident, in deep trust that you are connected to your own all-knowing perspective. We have all experienced receiving answers suddenly as a download in our minds—a feeling, a sense of knowing, or the clarity to do something at a certain time. This is just a small percentage of your mind working with you. A sense of needing to know or deeply desiring an answer finally allowed your controlling mind to settle and let something greater come in.

The controlling mind wants to be certain that something will be happening. This side of yourself only sees a small scope of reality and tries to make things work by force. This sense of needing to control everything has trained many minds to only trust paths they think are promising. This is usually a very predictable path that has already been paved by the dreamer who came up with it.

The originality of who you are is unique to you, so when you ask your mind to guide you, you aren't necessarily using memory of what you have always known. Instead, you are using a part of you that has insight into everything, that knows your past and the future you will create. Your spirit is timeless and unconstrained by current emotions, timelines, and what you seem to be solely focused upon at this time. There is so much to who you are, and you have vast access to insight, understanding, guidance, and new ways of seeing life. You have to allow yourself to be lifted into these states where you stop seeing your mind only as a response mechanism or data-collection tool. You are generating energy to create everything you see all around you through your mind. You are pulling atoms together to create the images and live them out.

> *Ask to be guided, and you'll never have to worry again. Speak powerfully in your prayers, meditation, and time alone for answers, clarity, wisdom, and freedom from all burdens. Feel yourself getting lighter. Remember your spiritual essence. You can ask for anything, knowing that you will receive.*

You will know what you are ready for based on your willingness, state of being, and how much you want to access or allow. Sometimes, people can fear their own inner power and ability to alter reality so much that they slow down the process and the amount they get to see by choosing to call it coincidence or luck. You really are the actual miracle creating miracles. These lucky or miraculous moments happen when we let our own power shine and breakthroughs begin to happen. When we operate from inner knowing instead of a place of control, we let go of the need to force things to happen.

Forcing is resistance and lack of self-trust. There's different

Three Powerful Thought Access Techniques

energy being used by your body when you have the willingness to see something through. You just feel that it will be. This is called being in the flow, but the truth is, your energy is flowing through your mind and body unrestricted. This causes changes to happen faster because unification with the field is sensed.

We assume that what we do outwardly is all that is happening. What is actually occurring is that a world within you is producing the world all around you. This is the invisible world in which everything is being created. If you think of your mind, can you see it? If you think of your emotions, can you see them, as well? What about all that you're imagining? All of this is the invisible world, which comes to life in the outer world and interactions all around us.

Every time you believe in yourself, you are not just doing an affirmation or suggestion; what you really are doing is altering your biochemical and energetic field to get into a resonance that aligns with the entire universe. This is where many blessings are experienced. Usually, this resonance occurs in unintentional states when people are praying passionately about something or are in a blissful state of enjoying their creative endeavors.

We get a peek into a vast world of possibilities when we are energetically aligned for that experience. When I say aligned, I don't mean there's something you need to do to get into that state; the truth is, confusion, resistance, fears, doubt, and lack of self-belief are unnatural states people are beginning to unlearn in order to get back to themselves. Many people are gaining their own voices again, their own spiritual authority, and their own guiding compass to maneuver life on their own terms.

When you refer back to this technique, I want you to have an understanding that your mind is so much more, and that asking your mind for things isn't something new—it's just something that may have been untapped. What you will be doing is tapping into your original intelligence, which has all the answers. Everyone will have different questions, different needs, and unique outcomes. Everyone is different, and that is why your own mind and body know you more than anything or anyone else out there. The future will remember our advanced biological technology, which was used in the past and is being used now by those who are aware of it. Your mind, with its own access, its own connection, and its own expression, is capable of altering your own life forever. By the end of your implementation of this technique, you will be self-sustained and self-aware with high self-belief.

Ask Your Mind Anything Technique:

<u>Phase 1</u>

Instead of searching for answers, ask your mind for an answer. Start practicing this now, since you might not be used to it. It can be done in conversation form with your mind or with a simple question. People do it all the time when they are praying for something. It is a kind of communion, opening yourself up to answers, guidance, and clarity. Ask yourself a question: *What is the answer to this problem?* or *Which path will be best for me?* You will start to feel the answer, get a flash of insight, or see a sign connected to your question. It's kind of fun doing this, because you will see how everything is really interconnected to bring you what you intend to see or want to see.

The first phase is all about getting really comfortable with your own mind and how you actually speak to yourself. You may never have done something like this; if you have before, the technique may seem familiar to you. No matter what your situation, you need to know that the answers are within you right now. It doesn't really matter how far-fetched the questions are or what you need to know—the answers will be provided.

For example, if you are working on something and want to

Three Powerful Thought Access Techniques

access more creative energy, ask your mind to inspire you and give you greater creativity in your self-expression. You will find that doing this creates an energy shift within you that suddenly feels more energized, inspired, and creative about your work. This will be natural and unique to you. Another example would be requesting guidance to make a big decision in your life. Ask your mind, "What is the best choice for me? What is the best choice in this situation to support my best outcome?" You will find yourself feeling good about the decision that is meant for you. This will all bring reassurance so that you won't try to settle with the least when the most is possible for you. Try it with almost anything, and you will be surprised by the extent to which you are being guided, supported, and loved by your invisible world.

Phase 2

During this phase, I will teach you how to go from asking for guidance for help with your circumstances or current situation to becoming timeless and getting insights for your own spiritual development. Once people feel balanced and confident with inner trust, they want to explore the natural world. This can be your own purpose, mission, and reality. The funny thing is, you already know this. First, we deal with the day-to-day affairs of our lives, which require a lot of energy and focus. We yearn for the unknown, meaning, truth, and the freedom of our own soul. We know there has to be more, and to feel that sense of expansion, we connect with things that inspire us moment to moment. In this way, we keep that link to the mysteries existing within us as we live out our lives.

We live according to demands, but are inspired partially by the inner thirst of wanting to know ourselves. When you enter Phase Two of this technique, you will stop fragmenting your life into duties, self-care, and demands, and enter a wholistic balance of knowing that you have the essence already, the truth already, and the gift of the supernatural. You will turn your life around with the knowledge that self-awareness has freed you from previously created worlds, releasing you into a new and intentionally created life. This is when the bigger questions come in, and they will always change according to your current phase of life and what you need to know. You can access the blueprint for your life; it is available in your mind right now. You only receive incrementally based upon what you are currently able to process and utilize, but eventually, the bigger picture will become the entire blueprint.

This is the perfect time to start asking your mind, "What is my purpose? Show me my highest expression. Give me spiritual insight. What is my ultimate vision? Give me more awareness to know myself and all that I am capable of." You will be inspired to start new ideas, meet new people, find a new way of expressing yourself, or even change everything about your current life. We have to remember that the way we are living was created by previous mindsets: how we once felt, what we once knew, and what we thought was normal. When you start to transform deeply, you might want something different for yourself because you are consciously making the choices. Before, you may have been unaware (or less aware) of yourself on that level. Be sure to allow yourself to pave a new path, if necessary, and do it without worrying about the unknown realms of what is next for you. You already know the answers are there within you, so always ask inwardly as you begin your adventure.

Phase 3

This phase we won't be about asking to receive answers, but asking that a current state of being change within you. Let's say you want to become better at your talent. What you will do is ask your mind to download within your awareness and physical body the ability to become better at that talent. If you want more creative energy, for example, tell your mind to open up an unending stream of creative energy. If you write poetry, tell your mind to open up inspiration to see the world within you and all around you—a place from which you could write your finest poetry.

Whatever your interest, your spirit can spark up many ideas and allow you to express them. Inspiration opens within you the ability to see the link between what you encounter and the message is behind it. With the knowledge that energy, inspiration, and life come from within you, you can become great at practically anything. Everyone has different passions to focus on. If you had a passion previously you didn't tap into, use this technique to reawaken that gift.

I had a friend come up with an invention this way. He was working on something within the stem cell field and needed a breakthrough for one of the problems he was trying to solve in his lab. We were casually talking and catching up, and as he was sharing his idea with me, I asked, "Have you thought about just asking yourself for the answer?" He was bit confused, because he was under the stress of forcing himself to figure it out. I said, "You already know your idea is there. You see the bigger picture of what it will do for the world. How about asking yourself for the answers while you're on a walk outdoors?" I specified that it should not be in the lab, because I wanted him really get out of the space where he was trying to force creativity. "Enjoying yourself as you are asking the question will naturally bring the answer in," I told him. He did think it was bizarre to not be working directly on something and still receive the answer. However wild it sounded to him, he followed my simple instructions and went for a swim, asking for the answer to be given to him. He also went for a few walks while pondering the question. He traveled to a lake, where he became captivated by a flock of birds. In the middle of his awe, as he watched these blue birds fly in a circle, the answer dropped right into his mind. He rushed back to his lab to put a few equations together and called me right after. I wasn't surprised; I was ecstatic to know he had made a breakthrough.

My friend's story is no different from millions of stories out there of people receiving divine intervention. The reason I believe in doing things you enjoy as you ask your question is that you let yourself wind down and de-stress from the mindset that is trying to force and control things. Enjoying yourself in nature creates a resonance of alignment; and being in a state of awe helps you get out of overthinking and enter a natural state of just being. Seeing the blue birds flying in circle was a sign connected to his question. This is quite similar to the shooting star my other friend witnessed after her wish for a greater union.

These are all signs that happen at the right time. The myriad ways in which nature works with you are unique. You will see the world around you perform for your benefit in a way that opens up your heart and mind to remain true to the rawness, aliveness, and power within us and all around us. I wish these experiences for you, as well, so that you can know more of yourself. Ask to be shown, ask to be guided, ask to receive, and ask to have the state you desire. All will happen in the way that is most magical for you.

These three powerful techniques are meant to assist you on your adventure and give you a greater access to yourself. You can use them anytime; and with every read, they only get more powerful. Give yourself the time necessary for each section and phase so you can fully receive the results. I want you to see for yourself what is really possible for you, not only through inspiration, but through tangible energetic creations. These understandings will naturally become a part of how you use your own mind as your body begins to return to its own self-trusting state.

I do believe this will bring many wonderful ideas to the world. So many people will create their dreams, knowing that they are tapped in. I consider this section of my book a portal of energy, creativity, and access to a higher power and greater connection. There will be an overflow of energy for everyone to know that they can do this, and that it is all right there within them. As you receive, the energy will continue to circulate into the world, and abundance will be created for everyone who encounters it.

Key Points to Remember

- *Creating a new version of yourself starts with choosing who you want to be. There is no limit to these changes. The first change we will be working on is the mental side, so that it can naturally flow into the physical version of yourself. You choose everything you are through your mind first.*

- *The truth is, you are the main observer who sees all of the experiences you have had throughout your life. This observer "you" is all that you have been, from the start of your life up to this very moment. The different roles you have taken on have all been momentary. This is why you keep changing and developing new interests, relationships, and ways of being.*

- *Nobody has a say in what goes on in your mind and body when you are choosing to upgrade your thinking. This is a private space of creation. It is the unseen coming to life.*

- *The version of yourself you create literally alters your energy field, and you will feel exceptionally vibrant, energized, strong, trusting, aware, tuned in, fearless, limitless, and expanded. This can only happen through mental changes.*

- *Anything that is not energetically aligned won't go with you into your new life, and that is a normal part of*

Thought Access

- *being on the path for greater.*

- *Everything is making suggestions at all times that influence us to act and think in certain ways. The kinds of people you are around, the music you listen to, the streams you tune into, the books you read, the things you watch, the way you spend your energy, and the things you say about yourself are all suggestions that influence you.*

- *Self-influence creates inner beliefs that support you. In all ways, you speak from a state of what is possible for you in the knowledge that good things can happen. You tell yourself that you can have them. You tell yourself that the results will work out. You tell yourself that you are strong, beautiful, healthy, balanced, aware, and connected, along with many other powerful words you can add and speak over your life.*

- *The mind does what you suggest in just about all circumstances.*

- *Pay attention to the suggestions running in your life. Now, and each time you spot an unfavorable suggestion, thought, word, or feeling, suggest the opposite—something with higher energy that feels good to you.*

- *We give away too much power when we listen to the words others suggest and take them as a truth. In reality, words are just words unless they make us believe or think something. We can change how we feel about the things others say to us that don't support our mental and emotional health.*

- *No matter what your situation, you need to know that the answers are within you right now.*

Three Powerful Thought Access Techniques

- *The originality of who you are is unique to you, so when you ask your mind to guide you, you aren't necessarily using memories of what you have always known; instead, you are accessing something with insight into ALL, a sacred presence that knows your past and the future you will create.*

- *Every time you believe in yourself, you are not just doing an affirmation or suggestion. What you really are doing is altering your biochemical and energetic field to get into a resonance that aligns with the entire universe. This is where many blessings are experienced, and usually, this resonance occurs for people in unintentional states—when they are praying passionately about something, or are in a blissful state of enjoying their creative endeavors.*

- *Ask to be shown, ask to be guided, ask to receive, and ask to have the state you desire. All will happen in the way that is most magical for you.*

14

MATTERS OF THE HEART

The experiences of life shape our emotions, thoughts, and expectations. We begin with a clear state, and over time, we slowly start to reshape our own clarity through what happens to us. We are created by this collection of experiences and forget our original self.

With that said, we were never meant to lose ourselves to the trials, tests, and lessons of life. In reality, you aren't what happens to you; you are the overseer, the observer, the soul watching it all take place. Give yourself guidance through positive reminders, encouragement, signs, and invisible connections to steer yourself forward. Part of you knows that what happens to you isn't *who* you are, but a set of experiences that helps you return to yourself. It's like walking through a labyrinth to return to the center. Everything that has happened to you has only brought you closer to yourself, your truth, and your soul. You were always supposed to see the bigger picture. For many people, the stories they have lived have altered them, causing them to forget their power, voice, soul, and vision. They have forgotten their resilience, the adventure they signed up for, and the unwavering strength they hold.

Nothing can really harm you, because you are more than just a body. Nothing can really take away from you. All that can happen is that you can be distracted from your light, and this can make the world appear to be a certain way. Your light, however, can't be stolen. Your mind can be distracted, your vision can be tainted, and your emotions can be riled up, but nobody can steal your light, nobody can shut you down, and nobody can create your life for you.

Everything is about mental state. People sometimes lose trust and paint the world as full of untrustworthy people. Some go through heartbreak and become identified with the pain. Judgements are made from previous experiences in order to determine what's next. All of this comes from limiting experiences trying to overtake your mind into thinking that this is how the world is. The truth is, we can learn to process experiences without identifying with them. Experiences aren't who we really are, but they end up molding our lives by creating the idea that just because we have experienced it, it is the definition of our lives.

> *No matter how far down a path you've gone or how bad things appear to be, it can all change now. It can get better. A spark can be ignited in your heart. A vision can be given to you. A miracle can suddenly happen. A way can be made. Don't settle into a narrative and think it's over.*

What happens when you live according to memories of past shortcomings is that you create an identity around those experiences. This identity can become your way of viewing the world; but before that one thing happened, you never saw the world that way. Events and experiences play out through our nervous system in alignment with the way we feel when we are going through something. When emotion is high, we store the memory of what happened more easily to create protection against ever having to go through that again. Signals get created, and we begin to think, *These signs mean this outcome.* The highly charged emotions of unfavorable experiences can be reprogrammed when we look at them from the perspective of *why* our body might have

Thought Access

created that signal to protect rather than limit us. We must never block off our hearts from new love, our minds from new adventures, or our souls from new journeys.

Forgiveness also creates a powerful energy change when you decide to release things from your memory and body. When a thought comes up and your body begins to feel the emotions all over again, you can say, "I forgive myself. I forgive that situation. I am free of it." What you are doing in that moment is creating a new memory of how you feel about that one thing that happened. Instead of being triggered by it or just reacting to it in your inner world the way you always have, you intercept the usual signals and create a calm, open, loving space. This brings ease to your heart, nervous system, and mind while at the same time intentionally altering your past memory in terms of how you respond to it.

We spend all of our lives in our mental and inner worlds. Knowing how to manage this sacred space is the most important part of your physical experience. Finding peace isn't just a set of affirmations or something you do externally to feel peace; it is how you nurture your soul, clear your emotional blocks, open your heart, and understand yourself. This is such a private space, and only you know all that it takes to be who you are. Nourishment of your inner world will clearly give you more confidence, assist you in attracting the life you deserve, and teach you more about the world. You will feel more, see more, and connect with the unseen nature of yourself.

Healing the hearts and minds of many people is so important for me because I know what is buried inside them. I know they aren't just what has happened to them. I want to lift you higher, as well, so you can have a new vision, a grander perspective, a deeper connection, and continuous energy pouring into you. I know that once you feel the rush of warm, healing energy from every word written here, you will connect with something you understand.

Matters of The Heart

Everything you are releasing is freeing you.

This chapter is about bringing you solace, confirmations for your soul, healing for your heart, and ease for your mind. I want to teach you that what you unintentionally created when you didn't know how to use your mind fully isn't the end of the world, but the beginning of your new life. When someone doesn't know that everything they are thinking, feeling, and doing is constructing their world, they live unconsciously in terms of how their thoughts influence what they attract.

Let's say someone never knew that everything they thought, felt, and believed actually manifests what they create in their life. They just assume that life happens to them, and that every experience is filled with ups and downs, which all seem so uncertain. They have belief systems within them that propagate fear, limitation, negative thinking, and lack of awareness when it comes to true self-love. What will this person then manifest? Who will they manifest? After the manifestations come, what will that further prove to them? That what they think of the world is actually what is happening. These confirmations unknowingly cause them to keep seeing the world from this perspective.

With emotions built up and unresolved, with thoughts running rampant and self-esteem low, we can feel like we are in an uncontrollable state and assume it to be destiny or just bad luck. Some may even believe that this is just the way life is. I have seen people awaken from this slumber and get out of toxic spaces, relationships, workplaces, and connections by waking up to the truth that they are so much more and they deserve better. When one awakens to their potential, the first step is that the environment gets confronted. The reason relationships end, business or personal, is because they are the tangible manifestation of a previous thought one no longer agrees with. The person is now thinking intentionally and consciously for themselves. These things happen all the time. When someone is controlled through fear, their self-esteem and self-belief are lowered, causing them to no longer receive the idea that just maybe, they *can* break free from the trance. This is why any change is possible. Once that awareness sparks, nothing and nobody can stop that individual's change.

> *You must keep rising. Even in moments when there are a lot of fears surfacing and discordance trying to present itself to you, keep rising. Keep operating from the heart. Don't go into defense mode or feel like you need to expend too much energy just to get your point across. Relax and surrender.*

Anything that keeps your heart closed, your mind in turmoil and unaware, only leaches off of your energy as a way to keep you controlled. A free person can heal, help, and become better. The freedom I am referring to isn't just social liberation, but personal liberation by which one mentally becomes free. Once the mind is liberated, I know what will happen in the physical world of that person. Life changes. Life expands. Life has vibrancy and color again.

The first way to return to your original nature is to start understanding that your choices, outcomes, and current/previous manifestations are linked to your self-perception. All that really matters is how you feel about yourself, your own soul connection, and your understanding that the affairs of the heart run deep. Your first freedom begins inside of you. People can detect when you lack self-belief, not because of the clothes you're wearing or how you appear to present yourself, but because of the energy signal coming off of your body. We radiate real energy through our mind, body, and field. These signals are picked up by those who can sense your energy (knowingly or unknowingly). What truly protects you is to be whole within yourself and have strong self-belief, trust, and connection to your own soul so you don't even manifest negative situations.

Cultivate a powerful mind full of faith, resiliency, and supernatural energy. You will realize that every time you change, so does who and what you attract. We have lived untrained about our inner world and unique signaling system for so long. We focus so much on external cues to determine who someone is, but the biological, primal system has always used senses beyond what we normally are accustomed to. Many of us can pick up on energy, read other people, and know what they need. You can save yourself a lot of life energy when you work with your intuition and senses. In this way, you can avoid many unnecessary encounters that turn into unwanted experiences just by trusting what you sense already. If you feel it, trust it.

When you start to know that your life is just momentary and that you're developing your mind to go beyond it all, you will stop being consumed by the regrets, storylines, pains, heartbreaks, discouragement, and endings of situations. You will instead remember that this is your one life, this is your experience, and this is your journey. The harsh moments and dark times never last.

Some silent nights of the soul awaken us and remind us to return to our path. We get guidance in those moments, and we are reminded that we can make it through. In everything you have gone through, you have made it through; you have discovered yourself, and you have reached new heights in your inner world and physical reality. We all have a chance to be reborn, to get closer to meaning, and to discover our soul.

You have reached the moment in which you'll discover your true home and your place of rest from the world. This revival is your return. No matter what your story is or what has happened to you, it can't steal your light or make you forget your soul. Fears and problems want you disoriented, indecisive, and confused. These energies aren't real states, but they become a mental reality for those who feed that world. Regrets make you believe that you could have, should have, or would have done better if only you had returned to that state. This is just a mental loop trying to trap you in a clever way by making you entertain scenarios of a past you're no longer a part of.

Discordance between people continues on in the mental world because trust was lost, hearts were broken, or someone took advantage of someone else. Things always end in the physical world, but we must now end them in the mental world first so we can cultivate new soil from which to build a new life. When we mentally disconnect our energy from things that have happened in the past—regrets, disharmony, problems with people—what we are doing in that moment is rising out of the field of disturbance and regaining ourselves again. Replaying previous states is a mental habit. The mind goes back to images it has been exposed to over and over unless the person discovers that this is just a habit, not really what they want to do.

To stop this, you can interrupt negative mental scenarios and images with favorable ones by saying to yourself, "I have moved on from that." Keep saying, "I have moved on from that already. I have a new life now." This will intercept the trance state of mental replays to end them, and then you will see those mental states leave your internal world. It will feel so good to know that you can do this. You realize that your mind complies with new impressions when you intentionally do this instead of remaining on autopilot.

> *Sometimes, events bring you to a place so you can break out, not break down. Your actual breakthrough comes from the moments that test you because you've gotten so busy with limiting yourself that it confronts you. There are no more excuses. You can't hide from yourself.*

We give people too much power over our lives when we think they can dictate how we feel and how we should see life in the inner world that belongs only to us. *You* are the primary mind experiencing your life from within. The debris of mental lingering, thoughts of others that repeat themselves, and negative self-judgement aren't who you are. They were just caused by events, and after weeks, months, or years or replaying them, you suddenly assume that you are linked with them. In truth, this is just a mental link that you, as the primary mind, can choose to release. It's not a real state now; it just feels real because there are emotions connected to mental images. Replaying them only brings up those emotions, and, in turn, more mental images.

You can end the cycle right now. It's very easy, actually. The mental world can be molded when you become aware. Lack of awareness is the real trap, not the mind itself. The mental world is our humble servant that loves us by giving us what we have given to it. It assumes that we want to see what we are choosing to see. When we speak up and say, "Not anymore," the mental world also says, *Not anymore.* It begins clearing, and you start rebuilding yourself from within. The fact of your mind being in order allows more of your real energy to flow through you, and this gives you a new glow.

This change could have only happened with you breaking away from mental cycles and emotional loops. After these come into harmony, you heart opens up, your mind rests (which welcomes higher thoughts), your energy field is cleared (which attracts new experiences), and your overall mood changes (which helps you be content with yourself). Everything has effects underlying the initial state, if we are still in it. This is why you'll see mental clarity resulting in your skin glowing and your health getting better. Release of emotional blocks brings layers of healing which you really had no idea were interconnected. Just know that everything will make you better in some way.

You are an important part of the universe. The fact that you made it here, expressing yourself

Thought Access

in your current body, living, breathing, and operating in the most magnificent experience, shows you that you are a multidimensional entity. This is just a small part of your bigger journey.

Our soul's mission always has a bigger plan for us. The mere fact of you reading this book right now is a sign for greater insight so you can find your own hidden treasure. We are miraculously guided to what we need right when we need it, and we are transformed deeply in order to start our new story. If you stay focused on the real meaning and purpose of your life, you will know that you were meant for so much more. This is your safe space to connect with your expanded self so that more of what you need can flow in and through you.

You are living a life of expression, not repression. You are allowing yourself to remember that you can recreate yourself, you can shapeshift, and you can switch up the narrative. Your story is written by you and lived by only you. You hold the mental power to alter your path. Nothing that has happened in your past can dictate your life, but it can expose your supernatural resilience. It's in the way you rise out of the ashes like a phoenix, the way you blossom out of the cocoon like a butterfly, and the way you adapt to new strategies, just as nature has designed you to do.

You are a part of a bigger system—not in this realm, but in many unseen worlds. You made this mission to come here and to bring the gift you carry in your heart back to life. Before that one thing happened, you were an innocent light, and after that one thing happened, you are still that innocent light. The hardest times can't break you because your soul is nonphysical. Your body adapts to change, and the downtimes are just readjustments to realign with your greater purpose.

We have to stop being so afraid to feel, chasing only one facet of our multiple means of expression. There will be days that are overly happy, some content, others nonchalant, and some in a rejuvenating state. We are constantly integrating ourselves and building a stronger foundation, creating bases to stand upon that won't get trampled upon or easily break just because of how things might seem. Chasing moods will have you always chasing moods, because you are telling yourself that the state you're in now is unnatural, and that you should be feeling something else.

Of course, you can process feelings or things happening, and that in itself doesn't mean something is wrong. You are clearing and releasing on levels you don't even realize. We have to stop micromanaging every emotion and being so controlling. We need to release the worry of trying to make sure we are being positive enough all the time, and the worry that releasing our feelings is somehow a negative thing. That just puts us back into the mental chatter. Release is the most peaceful feeling, as it provides you with healing and clarity while renewing your soul.

Start living authentically the way you are. Don't listen to people who try to mechanize your behavior. Instead, go with the moment and see what you need. Personalize, honor, and pay close attention to what your soul is communicating to you. One moment of self-unification can bring more progress than years of self-avoidance, neglect, and playing games with yourself. You can't trick yourself. You know yourself more than anyone else. Live intentionally, authentically, and holistically.

Embracing New Beginnings

One of the major things that causes us so much resistance is fear of new beginnings and change. You will leave your previous life, change your passion, start a new life, overcome breakups, move to a new city or country, advance your career, even quit everything and start over somewhere else. You might pick up a new hobby, discover a new talent, find new ways to nurture yourself, and do things that finally feed your overall wellness. The

Thought Access

soul desires what the soul desires.

When the calling comes, it can't be stopped or avoided. You must always be ready to embrace new beginnings. Matters of the heart will be lighter if we don't let our perception of the familiar ruin the possibilities ahead of us. When we don't embrace new beginnings, it manifests as stagnation in our lives. We just feel like things aren't working out the way they used to, or they aren't changing as quickly as we'd like. Stagnation can even show up when something is overdue in being released, so unnecessary arguments start up to free you. The way has to be made, and it can be harsh, because some people will hold onto the familiar until they are holding on by a thread.

This is where the initial nudges turn into a dramatic push forward. You literally get shoved into the change. In the beginning, when you were being called upon to start transforming, you were shown a sign, you got a feeling, a circumstance arose that caused you to analyze things. If you didn't get the hint about your new path, you may have been put into uncomfortable and difficult situations in order to face the reality of embracing change. This really helps you to finally get going. You do what needs to be done, and the energy that opens up in your life is unexplainable. It feels as if pent-up progressive energy is being released into your life to help you get where you need to go. Suddenly, your health improves, your mind seems to clear, your new career is promising, your business is growing, your talent is taking off, a person you were meant to really be with shows up…one thing after another affirms your path until you are reminded of the energy that is flowing back into your life. Stagnation is lifted, and everything begins to accelerate.

You can always start over. You can always get what you want. You have to embrace the unknown territory, the uncharted paths, and the life awaiting you on the other side. Getting comfortable with change will show you that nothing is as bad as it seems. You are always supported. Even the shakeups, sudden misfortunes, and endings lead you to a divinely guided breakthrough. Always embrace new beginnings!

Finding Yourself Again

You are coming alive again, rediscovering the greatness of your soul, hearing your own voice, and remembering that this is *your* life. You had a little moment, but it couldn't get rid of you, it couldn't take the timeless essence you carry, and it sure couldn't make you forget everything you are. You're finding that spark again, and this time, it is coming from your own mind, heart, and soul. Your passion is developing again. You find yourself wanting to try new things. You start being creative and taking care of yourself the way you should have all along.

This is your personal reunion, and you are doing it with so much love. You are giving yourself time and investing that energy to grow in all the ways you feel are necessary for you. You're spending time with yourself again, and it feels good to get to know the parts of yourself that needed you. You're loving unconditionally again, and your heart is open. You are embracing new people and nurturing the relationships of those you love. You have found balance, and this is all happening to guide you to get in touch with more of who you are.

Nobody could have predicted that you would return the way you have. This is the greatest arising for you, and the people in your life may never have seen you like this. You have gracefully collected yourself and moved on with your life. Nothing that has happened to you can be recognized, detected, or noticed in your energy because you have healed yourself, released it all, and recreated a new version of yourself. You have built yourself up. You have worked on your mindset. You have communed with your soul. You are now unified and unstoppable. You are ready to live the life you have always dreamed of.

Thought Access

Overcoming Regret, Betrayal, and Disappointments

Some people will try to make you lose faith in humanity and even lose yourself in the way how they treat you or the things they do. You must understand that under fear, survival, and lack of self-awareness, people can play a very vicious game of lies to continue to plant, spread, and create confusion in others. We have to step back to fully assess what is taking place. If you respond with an overwhelming amount of emotion and react the way they want you to, they pull you into their web of misfortune. Everything is an energy state.

We want to see the good in people, but some people prove otherwise about themselves. The experience of encountering situations such as these causes you to question yourself and wonder, "Why is this even happening to me?" It can be hard to pinpoint the original thought, state of mind, or emotion that attracted this to you. We always forget how it all started when it is ending. The truth is, people will represent the energy state they are in, the current point of the evolution of their soul, and the amount of work they need to do on themselves. Some people will never change—not because it is impossible, but because they will need to actually go deep to discover the discordance they have created in their own life and the lives of others.

The wonderful thing about *Thought Access* is that it provides everyone with the tools to create a strong energy field that nobody can penetrate as far as projecting negativity or causing you to lose yourself in overthinking. People do the most unusual things because they are trying to control everything in their lives, even going to the extreme of manipulating and acting as if they didn't do anything to you. You have to be able to see things through by refusing to absorb their behavior or energy into your mind.

The greatest thing you can do is instantly disconnect yourself from that chaotic connection, rebalancing yourself so you can create a space for new energy to be cultivated within you. You have to see through the masks, the charades, and the theatrics. To see through them, you must never personalize or give too much of yourself trying to play detective, figure someone out, or turn them into your project to help save them from themselves. That's one of the tricks that keeps you stuck. To avoid feeling your own truth, you start coming up with stories for them and how they need your help. In reality, you can't go inside someone else's body and think for them, feel for them, or alter them in that way. You just need to free yourself and look at the blessing you have been exposed to so you can actually get out. You'll realize that with this level of understanding, you won't consent to putting all their energy into yourself by questioning what you could have done or thinking something was your fault. Nothing is your fault.

Now that you know, you can start creating a new energy field that blocks unwanted energy-seekers looking to spread their fears. A lack mindset and fear create the worst behaviors in people. Avoid this at all costs, and go higher when you see signs of something unusual. Our greatest protection is our mindset and what we think/feel within. If we are strong and aware enough, able to sense energy, read people, and keep our hearts open, we can be saved from these situations by virtue of our own spirit. Life does get better in these states. We make peace with the past, ourselves, and the challenges we have encountered so we can experience more of who we are instead of being restricted by circumstances.

Forgiving Yourself

Take a moment to look in the mirror and repeat *I forgive myself* until you feel completely at peace. You will know you have forgiven yourself when you feel a rush of emotion or tears, or break into a blissful smile. You will look into your own soul and tell yourself you forgive yourself. Feel it. Whatever you need to forgive yourself for, do it in the moment and let it be done. I love looking into my own eyes in the mirror and speaking power, love, and encouragement onto myself. This is one of the most healing, deeply moving, and spiritually transformative things you can do at any time. In each moment you forgive yourself, you become lighter in your body, and you stop carrying regrets and burdens. You will no longer keep negative things in your mind, and you will remain at peace with yourself.

Spiritual Strength

Anytime you need guidance for the matters of your heart, contact your inner guidance. Ask for spiritual strength to be given to you. Ask for a way to be made for you. You will discover something pouring into you that refreshes your spirit, bringing you back to the center and adjusting your perspective. Sometimes you need energy from within, not just from words. You need to be still with yourself and let your heart be healed by the warmth of love from your soul. Let your mind rest as you are revitalized by this energy.

We receive what we ask for, and this happens instantly. With any feeling of overwhelm, heaviness of the mind, or reaction to loss, ask for spiritual strength to be poured into you. You can say it anywhere, at any time: "Give me spiritual strength now." You will always feel a boost of energy and balance in your body.

As I mentioned before, we aren't used to communicating with our body and mind in this way. We assume we need to go through tribulations for strength. We think we need to talk to someone else or read many things to lift ourselves up. What you really have the power to do is command a state of being. Your body immediately starts responding to your mental energy. Use mental communication, as if you are sending a telepathic message to your body. A lot of uplifting energy will come in, and you will be inspired to tap into it when you need that extra support.

This chapter is meant to bring you the clearest insight to overcome just about anything and bring you back into harmony. You will use it as one of your tools to strengthen your mind, ignite your soul, and be healed. You will notice instant shifts in your life that support your mental health and emotional intelligence as well as transformations that bring you actual results. Take your time and be patient as you explore how to operate from an empowered state. You are ready now!

Key Points to Remember

- *Nothing can really harm you because you are more than just a body. Nothing can really take away from you. All that can happen is that you can be distracted from your light. This makes the world appear as if it is only one way, but your light can't be stolen. Your mind can be distracted, your vision can be tainted, and your emotions can be riled up, but nobody can steal your light. Nobody can shut you down, and nobody can create your life for you.*

- *I forgive myself. I forgive that situation. I am free of it.*

- *Have a powerful mind full of faith, resiliency, and supernatural energy. You will realize that every time you change, so does who and what you attract.*

- *Finding peace isn't just a set of affirmations or what you do externally to feel peace. It is how you nurture your soul, clear your emotional blocks, open your heart, and understand yourself. This is such a private space, and only you know all that it takes to be who you are. The nourishment of your inner world will give you more confidence, assisting you in attracting the life you deserve while teaching you more about the world.*

- *Anything that keeps your heart closed, your mind in*

turmoil and unaware, only leaches off of people's energy as a way to keep them controlled. A free person can heal, help, and become better. The freedom I am referring to isn't just social liberation; it's also a personal liberation through which you can mentally become free. Once the mind is liberated, I know what will happen in the physical world.

- You are allowing yourself to remember that you can recreate yourself, shapeshift, and switch up the narrative. Your story is written by you and lived by only you. You hold the mental power to alter your path. Nothing that has happened in your past can dictate your life, but it can expose your supernatural resilience to you.

- We are miraculously guided to what we need right when we need it, and we transform deeply to start our new story. If you stay focused on the real meaning and purpose of your life, you will know that you were meant for so much more.

- Live intentionally, authentically, and holistically.

- The soul desires what the soul desires. When the calling comes, it can't be stopped or avoided. You must always be ready to embrace new beginnings.

- You are coming alive again, rediscovering the greatness of your soul. You are hearing your own voice again and remembering that this is your life. You had a little moment, but it couldn't get rid of you. It couldn't take the timeless essence you carry, and it sure couldn't make you forget everything you are.

- Our greatest protection is our mindset and what we think/feel within. If we are strong enough and aware *enough, able to sense energy, read people, and keep our hearts open, we can be saved from these situations by virtue of our own spirit. Life does get better in these states.*

- *Anytime you need guidance for matters of your heart, contact your inner self. Ask for spiritual strength to be given to you. Ask for a way to be made for you. You will discover something pouring in that refreshes your spirit, bringing you back to your center and adjusting your perspective.*

15

RADIANT INNER ENERGY

Vibrant, magnetic energy has everything to do with the electromagnetic field of your body. The health, flow, and connection of your entire system is deeply connected to how in harmony you are emotionally, mentally, spiritually, and physically. Radiant inner energy is source energy that is flowing through you. Everyone is born with an abundance of this energy, which was meant to support you and prevent sickness, negativity, imbalance, and disharmony.

As a person grows up and opens themselves to the world, they adopt from external experience ideas, concepts, projections, and belief systems that try to weaken their magnetism through exposure to limitation, judgement, questioning of their worth/value, heartbreak, past trauma, and/or holding onto grudges or shortcomings. We normally don't assume our state of being is self-created. We may believe that what we think doesn't really define our personal world, but when we listen to words and believe them, we are confronted with a choice. Should we be altered by what we experience, or remain true to our own inner knowing?

As we face experiences, we slowly become altered by them, changing who we are to recreate a version of ourselves that we believe is better than what has happened to us. Many of these changes influence our self-perception, and that really affects our radiant inner energy. We go from projecting so much life force, light, and hope to questioning our own worth and who we are while being confronted with our own level of self-esteem. This also impacts our healthy magnetic field, creating imbalances that result in the manifestation of physical health problems.

If we have never viewed our outcomes as a result of energy mismanagement based on self-perception, we may start to wallow and blame ourselves, taking on the energy baggage that was projected onto us and identifying as the person who went through that experience. You have to know that experiences do not define who you are. You don't ever have to rebuild your identity on a foundations of shortcomings, trauma, or disharmony. Your story is beyond what has happened to you. It is who you always were, before that one thing happened. Who you are is vast, limitless, grand, and unidentified. You have so much potential when you uproot reliving the identity of the person who lived through that experience. Instead, you can choose to go directly back to the person you have always been.

You are on the cusp of something so life-changing, it will alter every area of your life in a positive way.

Radiant inner energy is becoming free again. This starts with your mindset, attitude, self-perception, how you feel, the way you treat yourself, what you think, and the love you allow to flow through you. Stress, confusion, chaos, indecisiveness, anger, jealously, and negativity all weaken the body, which weakens the magnetic field of the human. This is why, when one thing is going wrong, it creates a catalyst for more of the same energy. A lack of awareness to stop, reflect, and release these states causes one to perpetrate the emotions surfacing instead of confronting the thoughts and solving the disturbances.

Energy works really fast, and everything is changing at every moment. When we recalibrate ourselves by working through our state of being and come back to our center, we become free of the hypnotic states that manifest the same type of energy continuously. People tend to assume that the prolonged emotions they have been feeling are unchangeable; they have become so familiar with them. The truth is, you can free yourself and break out of the hypnotic trance of any problem. If you start to observe yourself when you are in a certain mood or when you feel like you are being challenged, you can literally change the course of your own destiny in one second.

We often don't really look at the power we have in the moment and our ability to gain a new perspective on life by halting the circulation of unwanted energy. You can literally change your life forever and get back your vibrancy, vitality, illumination, and radiance. A glow comes through your body because your inner affairs are in order.

People often don't have time to process what has happened to them, and they cope with situations without knowing their power of self-awareness. Accumulation of unprocessed emotion leads to buildup of negative creation that results in manifestations you don't even want. Sometimes, people create from a place of limitation because of what happened to them in the past. At one time, they believed anything was possible for them, but challenges or shortcomings, small or large, may have stolen that strong sense of self-belief. Look at just about anyone whose life has been very challenging. They could tell you how something is not going to happen, or how another thing is not possible. When you follow the trail of their statements, it leads back to layers of experience with which they have identified instead of reflecting and rereleasing. Staying in your power means relearning the possibilities of your soul.

> *You have to stop being afraid of your own potential. It's confronting you every day so you can get out of resistance and get into your power. You are the greatest mystery unraveling.*

Anything you can release or let go without identifying with it will help you stay lighter in your mindset, clearer in your emotions, and more balanced in your body. When we allow overaccumulation of energies that are prone to negativity, we start to see negativity all around us. Our outer world is really our inner world. We see what we feel in the form of people, situations, experiences, and what happens to us. If we are going to walk in our divine state, we have to know who we are and what we are made of.

Your body emits electromagnetic energy, and your inner state radiates that out into the world. You were born with powerful, radiant inner energy surrounding your body, your organs, and the space all around you. Knowing who you are and how you function allows you to become illuminated while projecting immense energy into the world around you. You are a powerhouse of source energy, healing yourself and the ones you love.

We are moving into a whole new timeline, and this time around, we the people are standing in our power through awareness, accountability, and owning our truth, living in harmony with nature, confronting our fears and limitations, working through what needs to be worked through, and being authentically who we are. This is one of the most important times of your life—purging the illusory layers that have kept you trapped and confined. You no longer view the world from a limited perspective of who you are.

Being controlled emotionally by your past and replaying stories weakens the imagination from seeing the potential of what could be. This is a trick of fear that uses your memory to keep you stuck. In the mental world, we can entertain practically any kind of thought we want, but the unlimited nature of the mind can sometimes be used unknowingly to keep us stuck in the fantasy of past experience instead of the hope of what is next and

Thought Access

possible for us. As you start clearing up your emotional state, open your mind, expand your energy field, and release what was taking your psychic energy. Looking at yourself from within, face yourself as you would a mirror, and work through it. The more you free up your mental energy, the more you can experience yourself.

We can't call repetition of unwanted thoughts *life*. Freedom is the clarity of mind to design the life we dream up or be present for the one we have. Any thought that pulls you out of the present to forsake your aliveness in the now, only to land in fear or worry, is stealing from you. Put a stop to it instantly and regain yourself. The ability to be fully present according to your will has to do with how much you have purged out of your mental field and the extent to which you have released the debris of hypnotic thoughts that try to make it seem as if life was better before, or that remaining in a negative situation was what you should have been doing.

This is kind of mental addiction is something we don't even consider an addiction, because we don't usually talk about the affairs of the mental world. You could be physically present with someone, and they might not know anything about you. Verbally sharing who we are is the only real way to disclose the vastness of all we are within. Mindsets, just like anything else, arise from habitual training. We experience the same thoughts because we are thinking the same thoughts. That doesn't mean, however, that those few thoughts are all there is to life. When we see from a greater perspective, we expose ourselves to different variations of who we can be. When you are in harmony, your radiant inner energy becomes self-sustaining; it supports you with positive thoughts, heals you, nourishes you, attracts matching frequencies, gives you solutions, and opens you up to a wider field. We expand when we are in harmony and retract when we are in resistance and restriction.

The next phase is about bringing in more energy to your body. This is why you are probably gravitating toward taking care of yourself more, quitting energy-depleting habits, doing things you love, ending what needs to end, moving forward, and listening to your own heart.

The secret is that you are a powerhouse of life force energy. When you work with, understand, and calibrate that energy, you can do wondrous things human beings have yet to understand. We have always been designed and created to exist in harmony with nature, which is why we feel so connected when we are in unaltered environments. We magnetically connect with that energy field, and it helps our entire system return to harmony in the presence of it. This happens unknowingly, but we feel transformed by it. Humans thrive in nature, with nature. Live your life as close as possible to what is real, alive, and radiating with life force.

The sun is a representation of that same radiant energy interacting with our body. All health comes from our Earth, and utilizing the harmonious energy of our planet will assist everyone to return to true and vital homeostasis. The physical aspect of your life must be honored, nourished, and supported with healthy foods, living your true purpose, connecting with nature, loving your body, and resting your soul.

The mental aspect will be supported in many ways throughout this book with life-changing insights, but the knowledge I want you to really focus on is living authentic-ally within as you do without. When we are true to ourselves, we eliminate mixed signals and get clear about what we are projecting into the world. We take ownership of our own personal creations, analyze all conditions, move with grace, build a stronger self-image, exude natural confidence, and start to shine brightly.

Harnessing More Magnetic Energy

People sometimes think magnetic energy is the concept of trying to get something external to draw people to you. You can't force, however, what you haven't naturally built up from within. Magnetic energy is so much more than manipulating outcomes; it is real energy. You can't artificially create the energy concoction that your brainwaves, blood flow, heartbeat, hormones, and radiant inner energy accomplish naturally. All of this is what you naturally become when you are at peace with yourself: open minded, trusting, imaginative, creative, a believer, and embodying your truth. Magnetism is what you become when you have discovered yourself. It is a part of life itself, and it is a signal your body creates to remind the world of possibilities: more life, more energy, and the expression of nature within you. It is a primordial signal for fertility, abundance, creativity, expansion, and hope as well as a source of guidance. These signals are naturally occurring, and they draw everything to you through the representation of life energy. This is not a trickster's tool, but nature's mastery.

Everything must be done authentically by existing in harmony with yourself. Desperation or forcing things alters the signals of your body and the way energy flows through you. It creates resistance rather than alignment and flow. You have to let go of the past, when everything you did was motivated by what you could get out of it. This is scarcity thinking, fear running rampant, and lack of self-belief. Everything is abundant in nature and also within ourselves. When we think from scarcity, we feel out of balance inside and play games that try to make it seem like we have it all together. We don't realize that we can't beat nature's inherent system of signals.

Anyone who can sense energy or is good at picking up on

things can always see through the facades and masks people wear. This is why I am saving you the struggle of following the very difficult path of fear and welcoming you to the beautiful world of possibilities. Here is where you harness your own life energy and create through your own body what you want. It doesn't have anything to do with anyone or anything else—just yourself getting right, centered, and clear. Harnessing more energy means claiming it within yourself. It is already here, and the reality is that you can instantly shift your energy right now. My entire book is meant to assist you in reaching your next level. Every chapter deeply shifts your energy so you can automatically see the difference taking place. It gets very supernatural, so be ready to amplify your gratitude for all that will be given to you.

The first step is claiming more energy in your mind. Let it saturate your entire body; feel currents of energy flowing through you. You will eventually become aware of the abundance of energy around you and within you, but first, we have to know that it is all here right now, and that we are going to start tapping in. This is a fear-free zone, so keep your mind open and allow yourself to receive in unexplainable ways. As you become more open, so does your access to a vibrant life. We see more around us because we now have the vision to do so.

Throughout your own transformation, you will be able to connect with the abundant energy you start to harness. You must be a mental warrior when it comes to slaying unwanted thoughts. The good news about building stronger magnetic energy and activating more of our radiant inner energy is that we get real protection. The only time we don't have protection from external influences is when we fall into the trap of thinking in an automaton-like way and react negatively to everything because we are told to think and feel negative. We never choose our state when we are followers of the external, which wants to decide how we feel.

This is one of the reasons people regurgitate "what's going on" without thinking of the energy behind the information they are spreading and how it weakens their body, energy field, and overall mental state. After multiple exposures to negative content, we open ourselves up to more of the same kind of information, and all things become moving energy currents. Just by hearing something, you are using soundwaves in the form of information to process them through yourself. Your eyes' photoreceptors take in energy signals in the form of pixels processed as light codes. All of this is constantly happening, and any lack of awareness of how you use your data collectors (senses) causes energy transmission of signals you don't want to associate with.

Fear can't hold you back anymore. You're aware now, and you're transcending the illusions of the mind and emotions that limit your full expression. Freedom of thought and harnessing your magnetic energy will consciously help you navigate your life. You're too great to be limited, and you are waking up to that.

The future is all about how we manage our own energy field. In society, when the pendulum swings to extremes, everyone starts to seek out solutions to rebalance themselves. Escaping the world of overstimulation will become a movement, and new trends for unplugging will start—not because people are tired of the information overload, but because of the fatigue created by unnecessary emotional reactions, responses, and the overexposure to discordance.

As you start to move toward what you need to do for yourself (because we all know what it is we need to do), you break free from spaces that weren't regenerating your energy. You can't lose that much energy, only to get so little out. You have to expend the bare minimum—close to nothing—and still get more out of it. This happens when you start to harness the energy all around you and within you. You become one with it by removing what drains and weakens you.

Any sign of energy loss that has you feeling drained is a signal to step back and gather yourself. And really, it's also a sign to bring that pattern to an end. Just because you have done certain things your whole life that drain your energy doesn't mean it has to go on. Sometimes we continue patterns because we believe they are normal, even if it is to the detriment of our wellness. Refreshing your thinking is one major way you can harness more magnetic energy. You won't be drained or weakened by external factors anymore, which means you will have time to heal and become stronger. This strengthens your radiant inner energy and magnetic field. Quit what you need to quit so you can have a chance at a healthy, balanced life.

Stop judging yourself, comparing yourself, forcing things, rushing things, overthinking, and worrying. All of these states create misalignment and signal confusion in your body. There's really nothing to fear or lose yourself to. We all have seen wreckage of emotions, both in the body and on the face. If you remain in one state for too long, it recreates itself on your face as a signal to the outside world.

Signs of internal health can be seen in many ways, and these are nature's signals of what is going on within. This is why we are moving into internal and external balance—to harness more magnetic energy. Always remain centered, poised, present, gentle, calm, direct, and clear. When you are true to yourself, your energy grows x 100. When you are empowered, your energy radiates. When you are in harmony, your energy is very attractive. Always speak powerful words to yourself, build yourself up, love who you are, and cheer yourself on. Don't take anything personally, don't argue over petty things, and stay connected to what is real. Once you embody your own greatness, you will see what it means to have magnetic energy and all the beautiful things it can do for your life.

Living the Radiant Life

After you fulfil the states of liberation and free all your energy, the next phase is the mystical phase. This is where you start to see the magic of life all around you. The wonderful thing about having more real energy in your body is that you become more in harmony with the universe all around you. It's as if a cloud has lifted from your mind. This is the world, both seen and unseen, linking up to create magnificent things for you. You will be a walking, life-changing energy force. People will sense it. Everything you are a part of will thrive. People will have good luck and blessings just from being in your energy field. This means you can uplift people, shine your light, and give hope. It is very contagious energy, and automatically, they will want to know what you did or how have become the way you are. This isn't something associated with needing to be known for this; it is just a natural state. I am just sharing the side effects of living the radiant inner-energy life.

This will also be beneficial for your overall wellness because you will understand how energy flows through your body and the environment, giving you stronger health and a better mindset. You will unlock many inner levels for yourself. This is unique for everyone because we all have different paths, adventures, and visions when it comes to how far we want to go. Some will bask in the bliss of just being, and others will extensively explore their own creative capacities.

You will also start to notice that you are becoming more energetically sensitive to insights, revelations, dream exploration, and other people's energy. You will know what you need to know about anything that is necessary for your path. It will be like a flash of thought, an inner glimpse, a calling, a gut feeling. Another thing I wanted to share is that when your magnetic field becomes stronger, you will naturally not want things that cause disharmony or make you feel out of balance. You won't even have to think about it; it will just be a strong feeling against these types of experiences.

You will see yourself transforming faster than ever before. You are living the radiant life, and things just happen as they are supposed to. You don't have to obsessively worry about trying to protect your energy, or do special things to clear it. When you are built up properly from within with awareness, you have many positive forces naturally at work for you, and you don't consciously have to think about any of them. If you attract someone, it is because they align with your energy field. The only place you find protection is through your inner world as you calibrate your energy to align with harmonious experiences. Also, people can't influence you negatively, steal your energy, drain your energy, or bother you because you really don't play in that kind of field internally. You are past those kinds of thoughts—worrying if someone is sending you bad energy or causing you problems. Just the thought alone propels that kind of energy, and the only person that needs to understand your experience is you. So don't bother with all the excess focus on protection or needing to keep the evil eye away. Whatever you believe is whatever you experience. Whatever you are focused on is whatever you are bringing into your field. You are always benevolently supported, guided, and covered.

> *Mentally picture yourself radiant, strong, at peace, in love, happy, full of joy, and full of life. See yourself moving upward, toward an increasing brightness and loveliness of energy. See yourself progressing, expanding, thriving, growing, evolving, and succeeding at everything you do. You're entering your next level.*

Thought Access

As you move upward in your thinking, energy management, awareness, and balance, you will start to think greater thoughts and feel called to follow your purpose much more clearly. You will feel a sense of guidance and love always within you. This is a great sign that you are in unity with your own energy. Don't be surprised if your relationships start becoming stronger, your business success increases, your ideas get many supporters, your wishes manifest, and things happen for you out of nowhere.

One of the blessings of living the radiant life is how supernatural your entire life becomes. You go from thinking of how and when to knowing the way is always made. You move in a new way. You think higher, you love deeper, and you are passionate about everything intertwined with your soul's mission. Everyone who lives the radiant life will heal the world with their energy. You are a vital part of this change, and the greatest thing you have is the Thought Access to believe in yourself, know it is possible, and see it through.

Always know that you are powered from within first. Your changes will start with the energy shift you receive from this book. Words are codes, and they activate a person in a way that alters their life path and awakens them to take back their power. No matter what your situation, you, too, can live a radiant life and have the energy to create your dreams. Don't think things happen randomly, or that it is just coincidence. You are living a magical life. Once you are open, you will see many fascinating things. The mysteries of life will be revealed to you. You will know that you are not just a body, and that things aren't just solid. You will know that you can command more energy, welcome a renewed perspective, and be deeply revitalized. The dance is between you and the universe. Nobody else can live your life or feel your feelings from within your body and consciousness. You have to take care of your inner self and bring to life who you truly are.

This will become a way of life when you see that your

energetic changes affect the trajectory of your future lineage. You carry the seeds to plant new hope in the world. We never really take in how important healthy humans are for the future, the present, and our planet, both mentally and emotionally. As everyone focuses on their health, rebalancing their energy, taking care of themselves, getting rid of stress, discovering who they are, and returning to harmony, we can reach further toward a better life.

We can't exist in a state of burnout with bare-minimum energy. It's time for everyone to come out of the darkness and reignite their own soul. Be bold when doing this, because you are literally breaking energetic barriers that have been running your life. Change can initially seem like an uphill battle as your body undergoes energetic transformation, but the truth is, this is your rebirth, your rise, and your return to the person you were meant to be. As we are liberated, so do we access greater energy. When we don't get our bodily energy in order in terms of how we think, feel, respond to the world, and manage our own health, we reflect that on a mass collective level, signaling that we aren't ready for free energy or the ability to tap into it. *As above, so below* is a real statement. Most of what we want to see in the word will exist in what we see in ourselves. We can't wait for someone or something to come save us; we have to save ourselves. This puts the responsibility back in our hands and makes us the key players as we transition into the world we dream up. This is the right time to start.

> *An inner portal of energy has opened for you: a surge of life force, magnetic energy, creativity, trust, connection, and awareness in all areas of your life.*

Your radiant inner energy will demonstrate that your body is energetically aligned. This creates a strong electromagnetic field around you and within you. This is why people give compliments like "You are radiant!" or "You are glowing." This is the natural glow and radiance coming through your body once you have become healthy and whole. Energy can be seen in our bodies, and the way we feel is a real signal being projected out into the world. When you start living the radiant life, you live your-highest quality life from within, and this self-image is projected onto the world around you holographically. The internal always represents the external, and vice-versa. People must be ready to recreate themselves, be free again, and live life without unnecessary programs of limitation and fear. This is your playground, and this is your adventure.

You should always take the high road in every situation and live your life as your highest self. Your life has now transformed into a surreal experience. You feel more energy in your body; you are automatically starting to heal inner energy that has been stagnant for years; you are returning to real peace; you are manifesting what you want; the things you need show up; your encounters become extraordinary; and the level of creativity you possess has quadrupled. This was always meant to be normal. Now you have received the insight to see for yourself all that is possible for your life. Enjoy this new energy, and have fun with the secrets it continues to reveal to you.

Key Points to Remember

- *Vibrant, magnetic energy has everything to do with the electromagnetic field of your body. The health, flow, and connection of your entire system is deeply connected to your level of harmony: emotionally, mentally, spiritually, and physically. Radiant inner energy is source energy that is flowing through you.*

- *Your real story is beyond what has happened to you. Your real self is who you always were before that one thing took place. Who you are is vast, limitless, grand, and unidentified. You have so much potential when you uproot reliving the identity of the person who went through that experience in favor of returning to the person you have always been.*

- *Radiant inner energy means becoming free again. This starts with your mindset, attitude, self-perception, how you feel, the way you treat yourself, what you think, and the love you allow to flow through you. Stress, confusion, chaos, indecisiveness, anger, jealously, and negativity all weaken the body, which weakens the human magnetic field.*

- *Accumulation of unprocessed emotions leads to buildup of negative creation, which results in manifestations you don't even want.*

- *Staying in your power means relearning the possibilities of your soul.*

- *Humans thrive in nature, with nature; and we have always been connected to it. Live your life as closely as possible to what is real, alive, and radiating with life force. The sun is a representation of that radiant energy interacting with your own body. All health comes from our Earth and the harmonious energy of our planet.*

- *Magnetic energy is so much more than manipulating outcomes. It is real energy. You can't artificially create the unique energy concoction of your brainwaves, blood flow, heartbeat, hormones, and natural radiant inner energy. All of this is what you naturally are when you are at peace with yourself: open minded, trusting, imaginative, creative, a believer, and someone who*

Thought Access

embodies their truth. Magnetism is what you become when you have discovered yourself.

- *Harnessing more energy means claiming it within yourself. It is already here, and the reality is that you can instantly shift your energy right now.*

- *The future is all about the extent to which we can manage our own energy field. In human society, when the pendulum swings to extremes, everyone starts to seek out solutions to rebalance themselves.*

- *Any sign of energy loss that leaves you just feeling drained is a sign to step back and gather yourself. It's also a sign to bring that pattern to an end. Just because you have done certain things that drain your energy your whole life doesn't mean that has to go on.*

- *Stop judging yourself, comparing yourself, forcing things, rushing things, overthinking, and worrying. All of these states create misalignment and signal confusion in your body. There's really nothing to fear or lose yourself to.*

- *The only place you can find protection is through your inner world, as you calibrate your energy to align with harmonious experiences. People can't influence you negatively, steal your energy, drain your energy, or bother you anymore because you really don't play in that field internally.*

- *We can't exist in a state of burnout with bare-minimum energy. It's time for everyone to come out of darkness and reignite their own soul.*

- *We can't wait for someone or something to come save us; we have to save ourselves. This puts the responsibility back in our hands and makes us the key players as we transition into the world we dream up. This is the right time to start.*

16

FIFTEEN DAILY THOUGHT UPGRADES

These fifteen thoughts are meant to give you daily access to sharpen your mindset, strengthen your self-belief, and assist in increasing your confidence in the knowledge that anything is possible for you. A powerful mindset starts with awareness and access to thoughts that help upgrade you in the mental world. Everything is all about the thoughts you have access to and the awareness they can ignite in your own imagination. The mental world is a real place that generates the tangible, physical world all around you. These fifteen thoughts will guide you through a process of insight that reveals your potential, inner power, and ability to create the reality you want.

Read one thought a day and feel the message behind it. There's guidance being offered to you that will nudge you toward your own awakening. It will bring you massive realizations, expose you to your own inner truth, and miraculously magnetize many blessings to you. The goal of this chapter is to create a structure that supports you on a daily basis so you can create a reference point for quick thought upgrades anytime you need them.

Thoughts have a powerful energy current behind them. In the same way that you see a physical being or object, thoughts, in their own unique way, exist in a network within the ethers, which is always at work. Thoughts can upgrade you, give you access, evolve you, and make you a better person. At the same time, they can have the opposite effect, depending on the mental world you have cultivated. Just as you physically end up where you energetically invest your life force, in the mental world, you align yourself with people, places, and things that match your thoughts.

The process is so precise in matching you up with your belief system that it almost seems surreal. We usually don't think of the mental world as a location, or of thoughts as being alive. We tend to focus solely upon the physical aspect of what the thoughts have manifested. The reality is, this world is a sea of thoughts that have come to life, but the creators have somehow forgotten that they are the ones imagining the entire thing into existence. There isn't one thing you see that doesn't have a thought connected to it. There isn't one moment in which you aren't thinking something up.

The blessing of these fifteen daily thoughts will be to keep your mental world renewed and in a state of continuous positivity that helps you upgrade yourself in what you experience, attract, and call upon in your own life. It is not random or a coincidence that you find yourself in this situation, or that you are living the outcomes you have manifested. At any given point, the real transformation happens when you transcend your own limitations, negative self-concepts, and unconscious creations that try to associate you only with your physical self alone. You are beyond it all now, and as you build up your mindset, your true self will begin to remove all energy blocks and illusions while helping you break free of the lower natures that try to drain your energy. You will feel deeply moved, enriched, and revitalized at the core of your soul.

The results of the fifteen daily thought upgrades will be an increase in your own physical energy, unstoppable determination, supernatural experiences, daily miracles, a healthier mental state, more trust in the unseen world, connection to your own soul's wisdom, and confidence to

Thought Access

overcome just about anything. You hold greater power when you allow yourself to be upgraded mentally.

Don't ever settle or keep yourself in one state too long. You have every right to decide to change, to choose better, and to initiate your own breakthrough. Thought upgrades help you become lucid in your own dream in the context of the physical world. You have every right to know who you really are, what you can do, and all that is possible for you. With the proper guidance and inspiration, you can be anything you want to be. Every word is going to provide you with spiritual energy that supports your physical life in magnificent ways.

For fifteen days, read every thought upgrade once a day and sit with it. Let it enter your field, then use that inspiration as your guide for the day. This gives you enough time to integrate the inspiration so you can be transformed by it while at the same time receiving from it. Each daily thought will upgrade you on a mental, spiritual, and physical level, so prepare yourself to witness many areas in your life changing all at once. You can always go through the fifteen daily thought upgrades as much as you like. Alternatively, you can repeat one with which you deeply resonate as needed. May your soul come alive, and may your life be forever changed.

Day 1

Things work out supernaturally for me.

Your current situation is not permanent. It will pass. You will come out on top. Watch what happens for you. It will all seem supernatural, magical, and unexplainable. You'll be in awe, filled with so much gratitude that magic and miracles have arrived in your life. You can feel the supernatural shift taking place. You have surrendered the need to force, overthink, or worry. You are now in deep trust, knowing that all is working out for you.

Repeat Daily:

I am a supernatural being.

Things happen for me out of thin air.

I think it, feel it, believe it, and it all happens.

*I take responsibility for my inner state
by choosing to believe in myself.*

*Miracles come into my life
because I believe they are a natural and normal thing.*

Things supernaturally work out for you because you know that you are beyond the physical. You have stopped concerning yourself with the world around you, as it has already been created. Just hold in your mind what you want, and deeply feel it to be true. This starts the creation of your vision. Take your mind's power back by going supernatural. You know everything is already a mystery, and you know that life is already a miraculous experience. Your new perspective creates a new life for you, and this connects you to a field greater than anything you have known before. Out of nowhere, things just work out,

Thought Access

and this is why it all feels so supernatural and surreal to you. You have left behind the world of worry, concerns, and needing to see it to believe it. You have entered a super-natural state of believing it into existence and working with the powers of your own mind to influence the world all around you. You have stopped waiting around for things to randomly change. You are the one creating the ripples now. You are one who has become supernatural, and you are the one who is making all the change happen.

Anyone or anything that tries to tell you you're not great is a lie. It is an illusion. Deep down, you know better than this. You know how divine you are. You are beyond the physical. Accept yourself completely, and remember the little things you worried about so much that they actually ended up working out. Remember that one situation you thought you couldn't get through…and you did.

Looking back is a way to become inspired by your own resilience. You are supernatural. You are superhuman. You have so many abilities once you just stop, breath, release, and allow yourself to just say, "I believe in myself." Miracles happen daily. Things can turn around for you right now. Claim it. Believe it. Overthinking ends when you start trusting yourself and trusting the unknown and life's uncertain moments. Think about how vast life is, how grand it all is. Cultivate a greater perspective daily so you can snap out of it and restore your own power naturally.

I'd rather believe than doubt. It's all the same energy. Where are you directing yours? Feed your faith. Your self-belief will grow stronger every day, and you'll look at any situation that tries to test you from the perspective of "It will work out!" This is where you are now. Each word brings power into your life. You are pure greatness, and nothing defines you because you can shape-shift, alter, and recreate yourself every second. You have choices. It's a new day for you. Feel empowered!

Day 2

I honor myself in the highest way possible.

Feel good about yourself. Love who you are. Look at all the effort you continue to make on a daily basis. Even when things don't go according to plan, don't give up on yourself. Allow a new path. Accept the change. Believe in yourself. You are so strong, and you might not even recognize it. This is a reminder that you are a miracle! Thank you for being alive and for being a big part of humanity during this time. You are celebrated!

Repeat Daily:

I accept myself.

I validate myself.

I love myself.

It is all within me.

Everything changes when you begin to love yourself. You no longer send out the energy of desperation or need to be filled from the outside. You become a powerful source within yourself that aligns the frequency that matches your inner state. The more you love who you are, the less you seek validation and approval. Just because someone doesn't recognize your value doesn't mean you aren't worthy. Loving yourself and respecting your time and energy actually shifts the way the universe responds to you.

You are sending the signal that you deserve so much more from life. Everything starts with you. People will treat you the way you allow. People also feel the energy you put out and the way you carry yourself from the inside out. The experiences you attract have a lot to do with how you feel about yourself. Your standards set the tone for how others treat you. Don't belittle

Thought Access

yourself by accepting behaviors that don't resonate with your life goals. You know what you want; believe that, you will get it.

Most people fear that something great won't enter their life, so they settle and accept mediocrity. They think just because they've "wasted time" or spent years in relationships, there is no longer hope for greatness. Know that change starts with you. Send the energy signal that you deserve the best in your life by taking the right action and becoming better! Start elevating. Start loving yourself. Start investing in being the best you can be, and allow the universe to remove, replace, and connect you with what you deserve. There's no loss—just lessons that help you realize your worth.

Day 3

I am creating my own breakthrough.

I am the one who is initiating my own breakthrough by making greater choices, acknowledging who I am, stepping into my power, and trusting myself. May good things happen for me to confirm that. May I experience the breakthrough I have been waiting for. May I receive healing energy, unexpected blessings, an overflow of love, and spiritual insight. May all that my heart desires manifest for me.

Repeat Daily:

My soul is liberated.

My inner power is activated.

My mind is open to more.

My dreams are becoming my reality.

There is a blessing in what you are currently going through. It is forcing you to break free, even if it means your belief system or the way you once saw the world is getting challenged. You're not who you used to be, and this means you need the space to stretch your energy potential in order for things to get more supernatural and real in your life. Many things happen when you take a stance to operate with more potential. You stop hiding from all that you can become by actually following your calling, moving on, and daring to break free.

In familiar states, we remain the same. We release the same neurochemicals of what we have known. When you start rewiring yourself, attachments associated with past states are challenged. Will you enter all that you can become, or will you feel everything you have always felt? These are the things that come up when you decide to move in a supernatural way. The limitations that have confined your soul's potential are revealed to you, and it is from this place that you will be given options to transform your life. This is where radical change happens. This is where things get supernatural. This is where miracles become a daily thing.

As you start to operate from your soul and claim your supernatural state, things will work out so quickly and so inexplicably, it will make you question why you even waited so long to move into your own power. This is why *now* is the time for you to step it up and step into it.

Day 4

I am mastering my own energy.

I feel stronger than ever before. I am no longer wasting my energy, my time, or my precious life force focusing on things that have nothing to do with my evolution. I am becoming better at managing how I feel: what gets to stay within me and the ways I work with my own soul to know when it is time to let go and enter my higher state.

Repeat Daily:

I have mastered myself.

I am evolving at an accelerated rate.

I am reborn every second.

My path is clear.

This is the time when you must be very patient and gentle with yourself. Constantly forgive and move forward! You have a choice in what you give your mental and emotional energy to. You can decide to tune in and allow positivity to live within you when you become an observer in situations that test your patience. You might be working on yourself and evolving past dramas that once pulled you in. Certain situations might return to test you just so you can see that they no longer affect you. When we're learning to master the inner self, we can see clearly what triggers us, and those situations are the ones that require us to grow. So be thankful when things come up. You now know exactly how to work through them instead of overreacting or overthinking.

Mastering yourself is an everyday experience that helps you get better at being the best *you*. You'll realize you no longer have the energy to play along or react so easily. You'll find yourself

Thought Access

investing your time in what adds value to your life. Your focus becomes living a more enriched life because you know that anything else is only draining your precious life force. Ask yourself, "Is it even worth giving my precious life force to something that happened in the past? To someone who doesn't deserve it? To a situation I outgrew?"

Remember, your attention and your focus are your power. The scenarios you overthink and constantly replay aren't evolving you. Stop the self-judgment and just forgive yourself. Decide now that you're going to better manage your energy. You're going to think, feel, and do what evolves you. You're going to make peace with what has happened and anything you can't change. Starting today, you're going to take back your power by consciously deciding where you place your energy. Don't allow anyone to thrive off of you feeling low or down about yourself. You have the power to manage your mental and inner world, and this will reflect in the way you handle your everyday life. Things will get clearer for you.

Day 5

I am becoming who I am meant to be.

I am destined for greater. My entire path has been paved in such a way that I can fully realize this, accept it, and operate from it. What I am currently experiencing is part of the path that's leading me to where I am meant to be. I am unraveling and unfolding my soul's own light. I will allow things to flow, and I will trust myself even more. It's not always about the go, go, go, but the restful moment when I just breathe and connect with myself. I am receiving energetically, spiritually, physically, and mentally. I am integrating and upgrading. I allow today. I trust today. I receive today. Subtly or tangibly, it is all here now.

Repeat Daily:

I am a supernatural being.

I think it, feel it, believe it, and it all happens.

*I take responsibility for my inner state
by choosing to believe in myself.*

*Miracles come into my life
because I believe they are a natural and normal occurrence.*

You are being deeply transformed—mentally, psychologically, spiritually, and emotionally. You are feeling a rebirth, and the process is revealing yourself to you. This is your RISE. Believe that it is all working itself out. There's so much happening for you. Don't for one second think about giving up or questioning if this is even possible. You're probably wondering, *when will it turn around?*

It already is. It already has. It's all happening right now. Everything you're experiencing is moving you forward. You're being elevated as you evolve. You're learning so much about yourself. You're discovering your inner powers. You're clearing out a lot of the past and transforming. This can all happen at once, and that can be bit overwhelming. All kinds of emotions can arise. This is why it's important to keep believing deeply. Rest if you need to. Take a moment to consistently remind yourself that everything will work out naturally. That can bring you so much peace. That can bring you ease right now. It's not so much about *when* and *how;* it's more about faith and trust. Surrender, as you are doing all you can.

Faith will get you through the darkest hours and restore your vision. This is why I believe in you. I know that you, too, have immense inner power, which, once reawakened, can ignite and bring about miraculous changes. You must hold on. You must stay strong. Ride the wave and allow yourself to come out on top. You're going to start feeling lighter as you shed and release. You're also going to become more aware as you discover that you have choices in each moment. You decide everything. Keep your energy high with self-belief, affirmations, and positive thoughts.

You are so great and so whole. Don't forget this. You are truly special, and a gift to this experience. Your existence means so much to the universe. You are supported, so stay positive. Love. Be lifted. Don't hold any grudges. Keep yourself cool and a believer in possibilities. Watch miracles start presenting themselves to you right now because you have the mind and eyes to notice them. Feel that bliss. You are too powerful!

Day 6

My mind creates everything out of thin air.

It's all here. Everything you dream of exists. All that you desire is already here. Imagine it as yours already. Imagine that it is in your hands, your environment, and your life. You are a magnet pulling yourself toward all of your dreams. All alignments to make this happen are working for you now. Not someday, but in this moment. It is all here. Nothing is as solid as it appears. You are engaging with the ever-changing space of possibilities. What you assume to be still is actually filled with subtle energy. You are always interacting with everything: your thoughts, your body, the environment, and your mind are all in sync. See and feel what you wish. The choice is always yours. Don't doubt your abilities. You can make a big decision right now that will alter your experience exactly the way you want. Create a shift today.

Repeat Daily:

My mind is a powerhouse.

I influence the atoms in the air.

I am magnetic to all of my blessings.

Things happen for me suddenly and miraculously.

I am connected to the source of the universe.

I enter the state with my mind first. The reality reflects what I imagine, hold as truth, and feel deeply within myself. This is why I choose to imagine living peacefully, doing what I love. I am resilient. I am strong. I am filled with so much wisdom to share, create, and express. Everything I do represents the highest expression of what is possible. I know great things will align for

Thought Access

me. I have a strong positive feeling about it. I feel a great energy that's pushing me to express my ideas and create the reality I want.

My manifesting ability is at an ultimate high. I believe in the power of my mind. Everything I imagine has the potential to be my reality. The clearer my visions are, the faster I experience them. Connecting my emotions with my visions works as a catalyst to receive what my heart desires. I have to feel it. I have to believe it before I see it. I know everything around me stemmed from a single thought. I trust the process, because I know the law of gestation states that everything planted grows to a state of fruition.

I'm starting to spend more time understanding how my mind works. There is truly a vast power within all of me, and the only way I can tap into it is to go on an inner journey. I am not my mistakes, my past, my shortcomings, or anything that makes me feel low. The point is to vibrate higher and increase my energy to just be at peace. The pain and confusion come from forgetting who I truly am. I am a magical being with vast power. My thoughts, imagination, and the way I create through my vision are enough to know and believe that there's so much more than I think. I have to be committed to understanding myself and learning to heal, be open, and access my own heart.

Day 7

I am so good at receiving.

You will start to notice yourself receiving more now. There's this unstoppable energy that wants to give, give, and give to you. Everywhere you go, you receive. Everything you do, you receive. You have become so good at receiving that people and things are naturally drawn to give to you. This is your ultimate power, and knowing how to receive when things are flowing toward you is a divine sign that you are universally connected.

Repeat Daily:

I am good at receiving.

I easily and effortlessly receive.

I am open to surprises and gifts from the universe.

The more open I am, the more I allow to enter my life.

It's time for you to see the results. You have been doing all the inner work. You have invested in your ideas, vision, and mindset. You are ready to receive now. You are ready to manifest your dreams right now. Give power to yourself in this moment. Feel charged up, electrified, full of life, and completely trusting of what's next. Today is your turning point because you have declared power over your life, your situation, your business, your family, your dreams, and your blessings. This is where you claim it as your truth. We are no longer living in the distant future, hoping that one day, things might turn around. Not anymore. Today is the day. Now is the moment. Breathe a new breath. This feels different. Your faith is restored. Your mindset sees a whole new world of possibilities. One of potential. One of miracles. You are everything! You are so gifted and so special! You can ask for it. You can instantly receive! Let's get your energy up. You are full of life now, so grateful to even be reading this, and filled with joy just as you are. *You being you* is what life supports. You are so loved. You are being guided. Trust your heart and declare this moment as your turning point!

Day 8

Nothing and no one can stand in my way.

Nothing can stop your energy, where you are headed, and what you want to do. Nobody can get in the way of someone who knows who they are and what they want. You are the main person who can believe anything into existence. No matter what others say, do, or think about you, only you have the power over your own life to make decisions that support your vision and direction. All that is required is to believe in yourself and go forward daily.

Repeat Daily:

I am unstoppable.

I am dynamic and determined.

I believe in all that I am becoming.

Nothing can get in my way.

Once you speak it, it's on the way. Once you think it, you have already energetically created it. Once you let it go, it shows up. This is the power you have. Move right now as if you know it's coming. You know it's here and has already happened. You have already spoken so much power over your life. Your manifestations are completely in formation, and they are entering your reality right now. There is nothing and no one that can stop what you have created in your mental and emotional realm. You felt it within and thought of it within. This is your sacred space of creation. It is beyond anyone's control. Your vision is your private world. It's something you go inside to bring to life. There's no force that can stop what's meant for you. Fate is in your favor. It's already done. You have believed, spoken, and visualized it all.

Thought Access

You might have moments that literally make you see how powerful you are, because you are recognizing your conversations as they become reality. You see what you hear. You notice your thoughts coming into the physical. It might seem so surreal, the way it's all happening for you. You are truly a gift. This brings you so much joy and reassurance that you're onto something great. The power of your mind can build worlds, turn thoughts into tangible form, and manifest your wildest dreams into reality. Believe in yourself. You are very powerful.

Day 9

I am at peace now.

Prioritize your peace. Practice being calm when you feel like you're being challenged or tested. Overreacting only creates regret. Take a few hours or days for things to clear out. Be emotionally intelligent so you can be in the right state of mind to make better choices. You're about to overcome something you've been dealing with. Your mind and heart will soon be at peace again. You're going to start feeling lighter. Things are about to get clear. Breathe through it. Be patient about it. Trust that you will make it. Everything will be okay.

Repeat Daily:

I make peace with it and I move forward.

I release all energies out of my field.

I am more centered and grounded now.

I am at peace within myself.

You deserve to be at peace with yourself. Don't wait for circumstances to change to accept the peace that's present within you right now. The "someday" when you think you'll have peace and calm is today. Right now, you can mentally, emotionally, physically, and spiritually claim peace and calmness. This is the beginning of things shifting externally for you. Too often, we let our inner world become clouded by what we see on the outside, which usually tries to control how we think and feel. This is no more. Banish anything that attempts to claim your mind or tries to gain power over how you react and respond.

Your growth is in claiming the states you want to feel as your truth right at this moment. Get out of the waiting game for

Thought Access

things to change by claiming blessings, peace, joy, calm, and happiness over your life. So what if things are the way they are? What are you going to do with thoughts and feelings that reaffirm a negative state? Nothing! They don't help, and they can't change anything. You're better off thinking, "What if it does work out?" You're better off fanning the energy of hope.

Simply believing that things can change is a big shift. Your mental state needs to be lifted! Higher and higher we go as we stop being reactors. Things happen, but that's not the end of it. Nothing is final. Why marinate in anything that's not feeding your good energy? Why allow anything or anyone to get a piece of your life force through your attention? You've thought about it too long. You've felt it. Now try something new. Claim peace instead. Here and now.

Today, we claim the state we want to enter as our truth. You are very powerful! You are very special and gifted. Anything else is disrespect to yourself. You don't like anyone doubting you, so don't do it to yourself. Let's reclaim our mental state and see something brighter for ourselves. You are a visionary for a reason. You have an imagination for a reason. CLAIM A NEW STATE!

Day 10

I break all barriers.

I break all mental barriers and fears. I pave new paths and dream up new worlds. I am free from social constructs and thought patterns that don't serve me. All illusions are officially removed out of my life. Blocks and barriers have been broken. So much is happening for me on a spiritual level, which I'll start to see immediately in the physical now.

Repeat Daily:

I am free from societal pressures.

I don't conform to limitations.

I keep my mind and heart open.

I overcome all fears.

You can return to what is real, authentic, whole, and true. Everything that doesn't represent your soul's mission will be challenged. Anything that limits your scope of self-awareness, self-love, self-esteem, and deep understanding will be called out. This is the time for you to rise. Many illusions will be revealed so you can see more clearly. The person you are becoming is who you have always been internally. The subtle nature of life must be acknowledged. You can't live in a masked state internally while thinking and feeling something different externally. Balance is needed. Truth is needed. Anyone or anything that has kept you unaware will be removed. You will be healed, restored, and reenergized. A lot will come to an end as newness comes into to your life. As your physical energy increases, so will your soul's ability to express greater love, creativity, beauty, and happiness as a natural state.

THOUGHT ACCESS

You don't need to try to be this; it is what you are. You just have to nurture and embrace yourself as is. You are a new human being with new energy and new power to make a difference, in your own life and the lives of those around you. It's time to claim your freedom and your true heritage, acknowledging that who you are is so much more. You will feel free from this moment on. This is your activation and acceleration.

Day 11

I am a dreamer.

I am someone who is naturally optimistic, a strong believer, and a dreamer who brings things to life through my imagination. I see things before they happen. I construct everything in my mind and lay out the full blueprint so I can make it come to life in the physical world. I still have so much life ahead of me. So many trips to take, places to see, books to read, people to meet, and adventures to go on. There's still a chance to live the life of my dreams.

Repeat Daily:

All my dreams come true.
I keep going no matter what.
The best days of my life have yet to come.
I end up where I belong.

You're already living something you once wanted. In the same way, you'll soon be living an experience you're currently dreaming of. The point is to never give up, to never stop dreaming, to never stop manifesting and imagining greatness into your life. Believe so deeply and passionately. Bring into being all that you think and feel. Manifest your visions into reality. Doubt and fear are just feelings that come up to test your comfort zone. Your wildest dreams are valid. Your greatest vision is real and tangible.

Just like that, a new feeling and new way of thinking can be your push forward to strengthen your faith today. No adversity, challenge, pain, or obstacle can stop someone who believes. We have the natural ability to imagine for a reason. We go into a mental space and see what can happen for us. It feels like a glimpse,

Thought Access

sometimes, of all your potential: *Wow, I truly can, and that is possible for me.* This is your spirit, unbounded by space and time, giving you a glimpse into all you can be if you decide to accept who you truly are today…if you decide to take that action…if you decide to go into the uncharted territory of possibility.

The actions you need to take are obvious. You know what needs to be done. Here and now, gently move forward. Lift yourself from anything that is weighing heavily on your heart and mind so you can soar to great heights. You are powerful. You are able. You can, and you will. You are full of life. You are healed. You are complete. You are beyond space and time. You are the life force.

Reclaim your divine truth. Accept and love yourself. Forgive yourself. Welcome peace in your heart and mind. Your inner freedom shifts all your life experiences. You can alter the way you respond to everything, and this gives you strength and hope that all is okay. Believe in yourself. Dream.

Day 12

I am a resilient soul.

It can test you, but it can't break you. You're solid, you're resilient, and you're unstoppable. You've won many silent battles. You believed it through. You have great purpose. You already know how strong you truly are. Remind yourself that it is in your spirit to thrive, to be resilient, and to make it through. You've done it many times before. You can do it again.

Repeat Daily:

I always make it through.

I can't be stopped.

There's a bigger mission for my life.

I only get better every single day.

I thrive in uncertain situations. I bounce back from challenges. I break free from cycles. I am resilient. I am unstoppable. I have what it takes. The unknown doesn't scare me. I trust the dark moments. I am flourishing, blooming, and coming out on top. I am radiating, glowing, and becoming more energized daily. I have the power. I am the power. I claim a new reality. I am done judging myself. I am on a winning team. I am a winner and a strong spirit. I am supported in every way. My light is growing. I am starting to shine so brightly, everyone feels it. I can't explain my natural gift. It's so special. It's so supernatural. I accept myself. Anything that doesn't evolve me and grow me is a lie and an illusion. I stop going against myself today. I begin right now to become my own cheerleader. I have what it takes. The entire universe supports me, because why else was I created? The source did not make a mistake. It's all perfect. I affirm that. I believe. I live a divine life, and it's all magical. I am so grateful to be alive, to have a chance, and to do what I love. I am following my heart starting today. I am trusting myself and the signs right now. I am thankful!

Day 13

I choose to be consistent with myself.

You're going to start seeing more results, outcomes, and manifestations for all the work you've been doing. There will be a flow of energy that works in your favor on a consistent basis. You'll be celebrating a lot of success and feeling grateful that you made it! You made the choice to get better for a reason. Don't go backward into habits and situations that weren't helping you evolve. You have to keep reminding yourself why you even decided to move forward. Stay positive about what's to come by being consistent with your change now.

Repeat Daily:

I always keep moving forward.
I never give up on myself.
I know it will all be worth it.
My consistency pays off.

Be consistent right now. Keep the visualizations going. Keep your affirmations going. Stay positive about everything. Every moment counts. Don't judge yourself or even the timing of anything. Enter a state of gratitude, celebration, and completion of your manifestations. Everything is already yours: what you think about now belongs to you, what you feel is making its way towards you, what you want wants you. Everything you give your energy to grows and amplifies in your awareness. Stay focused with intention. Let what go of what wants to go. Let what comes enter. Just keep speaking, thinking, and feeling power over your life.

Nothing is complicated when you learn to breathe, believe, and trust that everything is already happening for you. You just need to keep shining from within and keep being patient with yourself. Be loving to yourself. You are very special, and you being here right now shows that your life means so much more than what you can understand sometimes. Start noticing the beauty of your existence—the small things, like your aliveness, your energy, your mind, your abilities, the billion things happening for you every second that don't require your conscious attention. You are being supported to feel lighter today. Feel the warmth and the love. Feel energized to become the greatest expression of yourself by recognizing it and allowing it now. Keep going.

Day 14

This, too, shall pass.

Nothing is set in stone. There are so many chances for you to recreate yourself, to reinvent what it means to be who you are, and to become all that you have always wanted to be. One moment when something went wrong doesn't mean that it will always be that way. If you look back at your life, in most of the things you have gone through or experienced, you have overcome. Events and feelings always pass, and we always get better. Remember to remind yourself of that.

Repeat Daily:

Life is filled with new beginnings.

My story starts over at every moment.

I give myself the chance to overcome it.

I am free to choose a new version of myself.

Stay positive about everything, no matter how it appears. See beyond the shortcomings and challenges. Soon, you'll look back at this moment and feel grateful you didn't give up! It will all be worth it! It's all going according to your divine intention and timing. The unfolding is magical, and the process is in your favor. Be patient with yourself. You might be feeling many different changes happening in your life. You might be feeling like everything is coming together for you, but at the same time, so many things are not the same.

Mentally, physically, spiritually, and emotionally, you are being renewed! Your light is growing brighter, and you're remembering to love yourself, trust who you are, and live your truth. You're remembering that you deserve better and that you can actually have it. This feeling empowers and frees you from any thoughts or emotions that try to limit you. You're now seeing beyond the illusions and awakening to your divine state, which is filled with love and blessings. You're accepting yourself and learning to receive what's always naturally been yours. The universe works in your favor and loves you. Everything is okay, and the more you accept that, the more you will see miracles unfolding for you. Recognizing your blessings is the beginning of seeing your truth. You are extremely blessed! You have a great purpose! Trust your heart and be loving to yourself.

Day 15

This is a powerful time for my soul.

You can feel in your soul that you're being prepared for something special. A new era of your life is beginning: one that fulfills you. Take care of your heart. Protect your happiness, energy, and mind. Focus on what makes your soul feel good.

Repeat Daily:

This is the most transformative time of my life.

I am becoming one with my highest self.

The secrets within me are being revealed.

I am celebrating my life daily, and I am forever grateful.

This is a powerful time for your soul. You are rising into your greatness and seeing actual manifestations happen for you. You're finally breaking free from habits, patterns, and states of being you have outgrown. You're fully operating in your power now. You're no longer delaying what's meant for you due to fear of success and what's possible for you. You're being spiritually liberated, which means many of your innate powers will be activated.

There will be more progress and change in a shorter amount of time. People and events will instantly respond to your thoughts, state of being, what you believe, and how you feel. Accountability will be a major theme for you now, so be bold, direct, and very consistent. Believe that a miracle can happen for you. Trust that a sudden break-through will occur. Feel that high energy of change and accept it. You're about to manifest in a major way.

There's great power in believing in what you can envision in your mind rather than what's happening in front of you in the physical world. Everything that can happen for you starts with a single thought. You have to believe in it until it shows up. The more you believe in that thought, the more you will feel it. The more you feel it, the more quickly it will manifest into your reality.

Trust in the greater power that is constantly aligning everything for you through your visions and inner state of being. Your story isn't over…it's actually just beginning. You've been developing yourself and getting better. Start intending for your new life. Start speaking power over everything. This is a time of great mental and spiritual shifts. Those who have empowered themselves spiritually, in the light, are now in power. Those standing strong and believing in themselves will impact reality. Be bold when you speak! Be bold when you take action! Great things are coming through you.

17

ONE HUNDRED THOUGHT ACCESS AFFIRMATIONS

Thought Access affirmations are supercharged with real energy that is meant to alter the reader's life. Every word, and the way every affirmation is put together, functions as a transformational elixir that activates power in your energy field, biological system, and soul, which alchemizes it for the highest possible use.

These affirmations are meant to create practical change in your life. Every time you read them, you will feel a strong energy current entering your field and accelerating your life forward. The 100 affirmations are divided up into ten sections, all of which encompass support for the insights shared within this book. You can read each affirmation when you want, and repeat it as often as you want. I have realized that when I write and go back to read these affirmations, I take a moment with each one so I can feel it, connect with it, and see it starting to work in my life. I didn't write these to just be read in a mechanized way, only to move on to the next one. Each affirmation should be treasured, reviewed, revisited, and felt.

When you are working with higher energy states, you have to give yourself time to integrate them so they can be part of your life, not just a momentary thought. In this way, you will see results from everything you have been reading here, and quite often, they are very profound. Use the words and concepts in this book as a format for visualizing and speaking goodness over your life. Carry them within your heart. Know that the words are at work for you, renewing you, altering your energy state, optimizing your mind and body, and helping you see beyond the world of limitation. These affirmations are designed to expand your consciousness, give you direct connections to solutions, and assist you in breaking free from any kind of negative mindset. The only place from which we can directly and instantly change is our minds. With supporting affirmations that build us up from within, we can chart the path to experience the unknown fearlessly, spiritually, and boldly, with great trust that something more magical is at work.

You will remember more of who you really are when reading these affirmations because they have been intended in that way. Any form of access to greater consciousness begins with some kind of insight, revelation, or exposure to an experience that takes you there. As your mental state begins to adjust to being spiritually empowered, you will start to see that the freshness of a lifelong abundance of unstoppable flow begins to pour into you. These affirmations are portals into the mental world. Each word opens up a connection to guide you to start embodying it. *Being* it is more important than trying to become anything. As you speak it, feel it, and connect with it, you recognize it within your being as a normal and natural state. You don't have to do anything special…just own who you are.

I believe that once you are connected, there is an unstoppable force behind everything you do. To generate energy in this way, you need to start living your most honorable life. This is why I dedicate myself to sharing these magnificent energies—so the link and the access are available for everyone to explore.

Another thing you can do is see which affirmation connects with you the most. Just as we do with anything else in life, we experience a gravitational pull toward certain things, and words are no different. There will be times when you read something and experience a profound *wow* or feel a deep transformation or rush of inspiration. This means it has activated something within you that you needed to be exposed to. This can also serve as a reminder that you can remove a block, carry on with your adventure, or find the answer to something.

When you sense more in the affirmations, take a moment and close your eyes to feel it. This will help you get more out of it than simply moving on to the next one. My goal is for you to deeply benefit from my book, and for your mind, body, and soul to be profoundly transformed by my work. I want your life to change in the most miraculous way because something turned on within you. This is what everything is all about—helping more people tap into their potential and greatness in life. Enjoy these affirmations in gratitude for all they will bring into your life.

Affirmations for Inner Power

Inner-power affirmations should be used to awaken inner strength, resilience, confidence, knowing, and a new level of self-belief. You will be powered by your own soul and guided by the rise of this new energy within you. Accessing inner power is the most crucial step in managing your life in the physical world. Without inner power, you can fall victim to external circumstances trying to tell you who you are or what you are worth. When you have inner power, you gain a sense of empowerment that can only come out of you, not into you. Hold this kind of energy in your body—the strength of its force depends on the way you harness and maneuver it through your mind.

These affirmations will awaken a memory of your inner power so you can use it to get back to yourself, lift yourself higher, and let your own soul shine through. Without a strong sense of self-awareness, you could find yourself at the whim of a merciless world that only continues to respond to your lack of awareness. Inner power is a crucial theme right now to help humanity to move forward into the next phase of personal development. More people need to know their own strength, their unlimited reservoir of energy, and the ways they can express their most creative state. Inner power is a feeling that inspires your life and accelerates you in all ways. You will be unstoppable, determined, deeply moved, and more centered than you have ever been. Your inner power is ready to be turned on fully!

1. I am remembering my inner power, who I am, and who I have always been. I am a timeless being. I have all the ancient codes to activate my greatness within me. I draw energy from the invisible world and feel it in every area of my life. I am all that has been, all that is, and all that will be. My core energy, where all my inner power comes from, has nothing to do with anything external. It's free energy. It's pure energy. It's a state of potential. I utilize it by remembering my inner power, feeling my inner power, and living from a state of pure empowerment.

2. I reclaim my inner power. I acknowledge who I am. I give my attention and energy to what I want to see happen instead of what appears to be happening to me. I boldly create from within. I know my mind can do it. I know that I can do it. Every time I believe in myself, I welcome more energy into my body, mind, and creations. When I own my truth, I live my truth. Everything starts within me.

3. I seek from within. I know that my body and soul are highly intelligent. There's wisdom buried within me. There's more I can tap into when I acknowledge who I am and what I am made of. It's no coincidence that I have discovered this inner secret. I just had to be myself so my inner power could be activated. I had to just believe that there's a source of guidance within me. This is what makes me stronger, more creative, and more myself. I am filled and fulfilled by this inner energy that has awakened within me. My strength has doubled, my ambition has increased, and my self-awareness has multiplied. Everything I do shows signs that I have discovered my inner power. People feel it, the world

responds to it, the universe gives to it. My self-proclamation has been the secret to my new life, my new path, and all the success I am experiencing and receiving. It feels so good to finally be tapped into this never-ending energy within me. I am grateful to know and blessed to be in it now.

4. I take this moment to feel my sense of aliveness. I feel my heart beating. I feel the air flowing through my lungs. I know how perfectly my blood is circulating throughout my entire body. This is inner power at work. This is nonstop energy at work. This is what I am connected to. I must see myself from a microscopic level to understand that I am made of sacred energy. I generate real energy out of my body, and this is what sustains me. If I keep my focus on these states, I remember everything that deeply supports me, all of which is unseen. My life is grander than all these little moments, which are fleeting. I have always been from somewhere far beyond, and knowing this will assist me in seeing the macrocosm as an interconnected space. Nothing is random; my existence alone is a sign of that. I will walk with so much confidence, honor, and self-trust, knowing that I have legions sustaining me, guiding me, and assisting me. I bring this insight into my day-to-day life, and I treat myself with the utmost respect and love.

5. My mindset has changed as of right now. I finally understand what it feels like to be whole. I have left the world of fragmentation behind. I have gained access to my higher truths. I feel an undeniable energy of balance. I sense harmony coming through me and rippling out into the world. This all feels so electrical, so real, and so close to my heart. My whole life, I have waited for this moment, and now I have arrived. My reunion with myself has given me a surge of inner power that connects me back to what I know is meant to be. I always knew there was more to my life, and for the first time, I know what it looks like and feels like. I have so much clarity of purpose and I will express myself freely, moving forward. This is the beginning of the life I

was destined to live, and it is me narrating, writing, and creating every moment along the way.

6. My inner power saves me from discordance, chaos, and confusion. Having inner power helps me to own my truth, trust myself, and live according to what my intuition and body collectively sense. The more I have tapped into my inner power, the more I have connected to who I am. It's like the answers have always been there, and finally, I am tuned into it and listening. All I had to do was silence the excess noise and distractions to hear myself again. I am so grateful that I have arrived.

7. I empower the world with all the inner power I have discovered. I do this through my kindness, my creativity, and my energy of just being who I am. All I ever really needed to do was just be myself. Finally, I am able to let go of thinking about becoming anything specific, and I have found my place of deep rest as the embodiment of greater. I represent the universe, the creative intelligence, the source within me. All that I am is felt, seen, and translated into every aspect of myself. The tiniest particle of the greatest cosmic structure known to humankind carries the same unique essence. The more I accept my own inner power, the more this interconnection with greater is recognized by me. My ability to see and know this means that I have realized my strength, and through this realization, I have discovered the magic of life.

8. I imagine my inner power as a portal within me that constantly and continuously generates energy into my mind and body. I always feel that I am overflowing with this giving energy from the universe. It just gives and gives to me. There's no end to its giving. I am finally awakening to the truth that I have always been receiving. This helps me get out of past thoughts of survival, lack, limitation, and fear associated with ideas of scarcity. There is abundance already here, and it is within me. This is what I have just discovered. I can only receive, and the truth is, everyone must remember that they can receive, too. When my mind remembers my own treasure, I start to see richness, abundance,

and overflowing energy all around me. My perception is being adjusted to see more of my own inner power and to know what I am really connected to. It was all in my mind, and now it surrounds me accordingly.

9. I am so grateful to be who I am. I am so grateful for my discoveries. I am so grateful for this wisdom. I am so grateful for all the life force and energy I have. I am so grateful for how positively my life has changed. I am so grateful to know my own inner power. I am so grateful for the sudden rise in my energy, growth in my mindset, and peace in my heart. I am so grateful for all the new opportunities that I am now receiving, and for knowing all of this. I am so grateful for the many lives I will impact by living my truth. I am so grateful for all the people I will meet, the love I will share, and the places I will visit. I am so grateful for all the good that is coming my way. I am grateful for myself and how I kept going, kept believing, and kept trusting the process. I am so grateful for everything I am now receiving.

10. My inner power is officially activated. There's nothing that can get in my way; not thoughts, people, the past, fears, or any form of negativity. Once I am activated at this level, I have advanced from the slumber state of not knowing, not feeling, and not seeing who I really am. I have officially arrived. I am here now, knowing who I am and what is inside of me. I can only go forward from here. I can only become greater from here. I can only receive more of myself from here. What took place before is put to rest. Who I am, what is, and what will be is coming to rise. Now that I know my inner power, nothing will ever be done unconsciously or unintentionally. My life begins now.

Affirmations for Dreamers

All dreamers need to know that they are working with real creative energy that is similar to the unseen forces that come into physical manifestation. Dreamers live on sacred ground, which is the world of imagination. These affirmations for dreamers are here to support those going into the unknown territory of creating their dreams, inventing ideas, bringing a vision to life, trusting the process, or simply doing something they believe they were meant to do.

These affirmations are your support system in the mental world, and they represent real energy that will bring you guidance, hope, and encouragement to actually go for it. Every dream is a seed from the cosmos that wants to live through you. Those who answer the calling of a dream are in direct communication and connection with the higher forces of the world of imagination.

What you desire is possible; it is a reality in an invisible state. These affirmations give you that extra push to go forward toward the dreams you're currently working on, those you have set aside, and ones you still have buried in your heart. These affirmations will awaken a dreamer in you. It is all real energy that ignites the imagination, fires the soul, and inspires you to just go for it. You will realize many dreams by reading these affirmations, and you will begin to feel like you can do just about anything you want. You are going to realize all of your wildest dreams!

11. My dreams are real. My dreams are possible. My dreams are my reality. I am in a realized mental state in which my dreams have manifested. In my mental world, I have seen the end results, I have seen the construction, and I have seen everything as already complete. My imagination is a real place that is invisible to physical eyes. It is the place where I create, and it is where the original blueprint is located. Knowing that my creations are coming to life now, I follow the inspired action my mind gives me. I follow the clear signs the universe presents to me. I treat them like flowing energy and allow them to come out of me and into the physical world. I am every part of the process, and I am the culmination of a creation that started in my mind long ago. I know that creation happens in the unseen and comes into the visible realm in every

aspect of the natural world. I am connected to that process, which is why I live in unwavering faith.

12. I have been given this dream for a reason. It is not by coincidence or chance that the Source has put this into my heart and mind. I have been given the Thought Access to see my vision, and I will see it through. I have left the world of needing to convince others of anything. I will live on the fringes of societal constructs so that I can follow my true calling. That which is born from me won't initially make sense to people who only see the world from a limited point of view. This is normal, because I am a dreamer who sees through my imagination. This is why I am not convincing anyone of my truth. Instead, I am showing up as an example of what is possible by following my own calling. I am the one who will show that miracles are real, that life is filled with magic, that supernatural things can happen in natural ways, and that anything is possible. I focus all of my energy on where I am headed instead of worrying about who sees it, who is coming, or who will realize or understand it. I am the one who must do all of this by uniting myself with my soul's purpose, passion, and creative energy. My life will change forever according to my dreams.

13. I am a master dreamer. I use my visualization to paint the world the way I want to see it. In my mind, I alter the physical world to my liking. When I experience things in the physical world, they feel so similar to what I have imagined, dreamed up, and made into reality. I notice that everything responds to my mental images, and this is why I choose to see clear pictures in my mind of what I want to experience, see, and feel all around me. I am a master mental world-builder. I am the architect. I am the engineer. I am the designer. I do all of this in my mind, and see things become what I imagine them to be. This is why I end up living my dream—not only in the ultimate way, but in my ordinary, day-to-day life, as well. I see it all coming together so beautifully, and I know I am the one behind bringing it to life. I do this by initiating a desire, putting up an image, feeling the experience mentally, and following all the inspiration to be where

I need to be, do what I must do, and allow what I am supposed to allow.

14. As a dreamer, my most powerful tools are knowing, trusting, understanding, being patient, surrendering, and letting it all come to me. I must always see everything as already here, and see it being magnetized to me. I am the ultimate receiver. My work is in the mental world and making sure that I have the highest confidence in my dreams, in my ability to create the life I want, and in allowing the space needed for my creations to come to life.

15. My life seems so magical to everyone because I have tapped into my imagination. There is something I have discovered, and the truth is, I have just found myself. I finally got to know my mind. I activated my inner world to become the center of my own creations. This has given me so much energy to do what I love and live the way I want. I am forever grateful for all of this insight.

16. One thing I have learned about life is that dreams eventually manifest. I have seen it many times in my own life, and I know the dreams I am having now will come to pass; they always do.

17. My dreams are becoming my reality. Soon, I will find myself living out my dreams. I will be the example to everyone (even my own self) that what is imagined eventually becomes real. I have claimed a new life, a new reality, and a new state of being for myself, and now I am arriving where I am meant to be. The success and blessings that are coming my way are so life-changing that they will inspire many to dream even bigger and believe in themselves.

18. All inventors are dreamers. All creators are dreamers. Anyone who has ever done magnificent things in the world started with a single dream, and the process for that dream to come to life had to be held so dearly by the dreamer until it manifested in the world. I am one of these great minds, because greatness is a mental state and a state of awareness. When I know who and what I am,

Thought Access

I receive many visions, dreams, ideas, and insights from the unseen world. Knowing that I am connected to all the great minds that have ever existed is knowing that I am a timeless, multidimensional being. In this mental state, so much gets poured into me, and I utilize these powerful revelations to create a better world in some way. Even if my dream means I am in the healthiest and most balanced state, that is good enough. If it means I have the best relationships, that is also great. If it means I create revolutionary change for humanity, that is wonderful, as well. Anything is possible for me—and for all who remember themselves. The gift of dreaming is born from the knower; the rest returns to the universe.

19. I operate in timelessness, where I give myself the space to create. I don't rush my creativity or put timelines on it. I don't create from competition or try to prove a point. I do things my way. I do things the divine way. I live according to a higher expression of order, and I allow things to flow through me so precisely that they come together as they should, when they should. I work with my imagination to pour endlessly into myself, and I express that daily in my life. I am already at one with my dream. As I give that energy and attention to my visions, it is nurtured and brought to life. This helps me to create more freely and at my own natural pace.

20. One day, I will look back at this book, these words, and these insights and remember who I have become and all that I have manifested. Literally all of my dreams have happened, and I speak that over my life right now. I am the future version of myself in this moment, and I am the one who is unfolding. I am headed in the right direction. My entire life is a dream, from the beginning of conception to the full manifestation of this creation. I was born out of the unseen, and I shall return to the unseen to embrace all of its secrets. This never-ending energy I have for life will always be in my soul, and no matter where I am, what I am doing, or who I am with, I shall express it in the highest way possible. I am the biggest dream realized, and

because I understand all it takes to uphold me, I know that I am always supported to give birth to new dreams and new experiences. I am forever grateful for discovering myself, my dreams, and this level of insight.

Affirmations for Your Soul

When one is inspired from their soul, a different kind of energy and illumination enters the mind and body. This set of affirmations is designed to bring inner balance, warmth, understanding, connection, inner union, deep inspiration, guidance, hope, love, and something eternal. The soul is timeless and lives outside the limitations and confinement of worldly affairs, which tend to occupy our consciousness. We swim in the sea of expansion when we remember all that we are.

These affirmations will lift your consciousness to see more, feel more, and sense more of all that you are and all that is around you. You will feel revigorated by every single word, and they will replenish your energy with an abundance of love. You will feel like you have the support you need to go forward in all ways. There will be an obvious connection that you didn't sense before. You will become more content and at peace while entering a place of restfulness with these affirmations. Your mind and body will sense a deeper kind of ease, which means you are in resonance with your own soul.

These affirmations of the soul also have to do with healing the heart, the mind, and the body from discordance and imbalance. Every word will unify you, restore you, and expand you so you can be all that you were meant to be. Many emotions might come up, many tears might be shed, or smiles and happiness might come over you. Everyone feels what they need to feel, and they receive what they were meant to receive from it. I hope you gain yourself out of this, and I hope you feel the expansive power of your soul in every word.

21. My soul is meant for so much more. I am not what has

happened to me. I am not circumstances or situations. I am not hardships or endings. I am all things in life. I am the beginning and the birth of the new. I am the life force that moves everything and lives unbothered and undisturbed by current events alone. My soul is so much more, and the more I remember this energy state, the more I can be pulled into the higher perceptions of life that show me that I am making it through, I have a bigger purpose, and a single phase of my life is no more than a moment of transition. I am always becoming. I am a beautiful unfoldment, and my growth shows that it only goes upward from here.

22. I am now being exposed to the power of my soul. There's so much healing taking place within me. I don't even need to understand or use words to describe the upgrades I am feeling in my mind and body. I know the time has come for me to receive, and now the energy is in an unstoppable flow. My soul is showing my light to me. I am feeling from my heart again. There's this well of joy pouring out from the center of my body. I feel bliss pouring in from the top of my head. I feel a burst of energy in my heart. There's unconditional love present within me. I can't explain it. I can't describe it. I am just in it, and it feels so good to be at home within myself. I am so fulfilled. I am so balanced. My entire body is experiencing healing, and my emotions are being cleared out so I can allow higher expression to flow through me.

23. I have become the illumination of what it means for my soul to be working in my life. I radiate in a new way. I share beautiful energy by just being who I am. I have learned how to be at one with myself, and this has created balance in my entire system as well as all parts of me that are unseen. Something has turned on that can't be described, but can be felt. People see a difference in me. I see a new light over my life. My abundance has multiplied, my health is thriving, my relationships have gotten stronger, my creativity is increasing, and there really is a presence of peace in every area of my life. I can feel that all of this has to do with my

inner connection, my union with my soul, and accepting who I am fully.

24. I keep my heart open for love to flow through me and for love to come into me. I make peace with everything and everyone from my past so I can release it all to let my soul fly high. I let go so easily these days because this allows the energy in my body to circulate and move instead of remaining blocked off and stagnant. I am the energy of love. Love is within my soul, and when I am operating from that state, I manifest higher love and greater peace.

25. I forgive myself for every single thing that doesn't represent my highest expression. I forgive my past self, who didn't know. I forgive every part of me so I can allow new energy to flourish within me. I am making space for myself to come out and shine my light. I am choosing to free myself from all forms of attachment so I can walk my new path lighter, more balanced, and more in tune with myself.

26. My life begins at this moment. Every second means that there is an opportunity for new beginnings, greater possibilities, and more enriching experiences. Life gets better because I believe it will. Life changes because I believe that it can. I am aware of my impact on all things because my mind by aligned with my inner self. The more inner energy I have, the more I can express it into the world. I am the beginning of my change, and I am the one who initiates this from my soul.

27. I am beginning to listen to my own inner voice and guidance. My soul is taking me higher and revealing to me what is necessary for my adventure. Every intuition or sense of more leads me toward all that is meant for me. I trust myself more than ever. I follow these callings, inner glimpses, and sparks that are igniting within me. The stronger my inner relationship with my own inner voice, the better my life gets.

28. I take care of my soul, my happiness, my peace of mind, and

my energy. I do what is necessary to be there for myself so I can live life fully from an authentically balanced state. I have learned how not to internalize everything so I can always have a clear perspective. I am becoming more mentally and emotionally aware. I know how things affect me and the way I respond to them. The most important thing for peace in my life is knowing how to create harmonious experiences and how to manage uncertain moments with grace and confidence. I give myself time to always make better choices from a place of understanding and awareness.

29. My soul has stood powerfully strong. No matter what tested me, what came my way, what did or didn't happen, I am still here, still believing, and still moving forward. I know how resilient I have been, and this shows me that there is more to who I am. I am not the things that have happened to me; I am the one who moves through, grows through, and creates better. I am becoming good at using my mind to create the life I want. Every situation makes me realize my gift all along was in discovering myself, changing my mindset, and continuing my life adventure. Everything will always be just a moment, and I have now decided to cherish every single experience in the knowledge that I am unstoppable, untouchable, and unbreakable. I only rise toward my ultimate greatness.

30. I can feel it in my soul that I am being prepared for something very special. It's a strong feeling that something wonderful and magnificent will happen in my life. I can already feel that the energy has entered. I can feel my own life changing, and blessings are getting ready to happen. My soul has been giving me signs. I have been feeling a massive change within me, and I know this is connected to a manifestation that is about to come into my life. I have been preparing myself for this moment, and now is the perfect time to allow myself to open my mind, heart, and arms to receive. I welcome this beautiful energy into my life. I welcome my manifestations. I welcome higher thoughts, energies, and

experiences. I welcome results. I welcome answers. I allow my soul to work through me and lift me higher at every moment so I can find the vision and faith to see it all through.

Affirmations for Receiving Out of Thin Air

Receiving out of thin air is a natural and normal thing. We call it a miracle when it happens and say things that associate it with the supernatural, because we can't explain how this occurs. These things usually manifest when someone is energetically open or feels like they really need something to happen—and an instant breakthrough occurs. We are naturally hardwired to receive. I discuss this in the "Chapter 12: Thoughts Materialize." Our minds start to open up again, and we play with the field to work outside of the limiting constructs of time and the stillness of matter. We supercharge real miracles into our own lives by initiating their creation.

These affirmations will help you to take your power back and loosen up so you can allow yourself to receive. You will also feel an incredible sense of connection to something sublime, divine, and timeless. You will feel at one with life and the field of creation, and you will know you are being supported. Many things will begin to happen now for you out of thin air. The truth is, these affirmations will open your mind and you will start receiving out of thin air. Through our minds, all things are possible.

31. I always receive out of thin air. Things just have a way of happening for me, and I let them. I trust this. I accept it. I don't need to know how, when, or why. I just know that it will take place, and it happens. My faith has gotten so much stronger since I started releasing all my mental and emotional concerns about how things can happen for me. What I know is that things have a very natural, yet powerful way of happening. I can't even begin to fathom the energetic alignments, the invisible support, the fact

that I am where I am supposed to be, and the timing of everything. I just happen to receive, and it just happens to unfold in the best possible way. All I did was create the desire, feel it, imagine it, and know that it is where I am supposed to be. I initiate all my inspired action and follow where I am called to go. This is all just a part of receiving what I have spoken, intended, and prayed for.

32. Everything is energy. I am energy. My mind sends out real energy currents, and I interact with all things around me through my inner world. My mind has great power to make things manifest out of thin air. This is what faith is all about. It is an inner knowing that something will happen...and it does. I know things are happening for me. I believe in myself, my visions, where I am headed, and what is getting ready to manifest for me. Life is very mystical and mysterious. I am part of a vast network of linked possibilities, and it is all connected to my consciousness. The more I let go of trying to control things, the easier it becomes for me to see more clearly who I am, what I am connected to, and what everything is. My entire life becomes one of revelations, guidance, and power from God. I see everything in its true state, so receiving out of thin air has become second nature to me.

33. My mind is changing. I am seeing the world from an energetic perspective. I am seeing how everything is created out of thin air. I am born out of thin air. I enter the world from the unknown, and I am birthed into my true form. This is the energy with which everything is imbued. When I think of what can happen in my life, I don't think of things as merely solid; I see them as energy, and this gives me the understanding that I am already connected to what is being created in the physical form. The more I keep my mindset in higher awareness, the more that I can see the magic all around me. Life is so much more, and through acceptance of more, I get to see, feel, and create more. I am ready for all of that now, and I know there is no way to

explain it. It just is, and it always has been.

34. When I think of something, it comes into my life. Sometimes it happens so instantly that it surprises me. Even though I know it can happen this way, I am still in awe of the magnificence of creation. I no longer concern myself with *how* or *when*. I just know that it is all in perfect order.

35. My thoughts instantly materialize. When I think of someone, they contact me. When I speak of something, it comes into my life. I have seen my thoughts materialize many, many times, so I should be very comfortable by now with what I want to materialize out of thin air. It used to happen randomly, but now I am intentionally doing it. As I consciously create my own experience, I am very vigilant in terms of what I let into my mind, what stays in my mental world, and the emotions I allow. I feel so much more aware of myself. Things no longer are stagnant in my life, and there is no prolongation of unwanted states. I move forward with the awareness that I am materializing my experience at every moment.

36. My life has accelerated now. Ever since I started viewing life from the mindset of receiving out of thin air, I have seen miraculous and supernatural things happen. What used to take a long time because of my previous way of seeing things has now accelerated, simply because I have accepted this new mindset as my truth. Things happening out of thin air is a natural and normal occurrence for me. The welcoming of these kinds of thoughts speeds up my experience, not just in terms of time, but in terms of my own acceptance of my power to influence the things happening all around me. I have stopped living as a bystander to timelines being created through unaware responses. I have started creating things around me through my thoughts and a high level of self-belief. I am a master at receiving out of thin air.

37. People all around me are sensing my energy now. They can feel that I have tapped into myself. They want to know what I

have done or discovered. People know when someone is operating in their true state, and with that kind of energy, I attract to me the people who are meant for me. I receive many new opportunities, I build wonderful and enriching relationships, and I remind people that anything is possible by embodying the example.

38. Before I ask anyone for anything, I put it out to the universe. I consult my inner self to show me the way. I start to awaken the part of myself that brings positive things into my life and aligns me with what I am ready to receive. When I send a signal from within, it has greater reach and stronger alignment. It creates experiences that are deeply connected to my vision. Nothing about my path is random if I go within and ask. When this form of guidance is activated, I never feel alone, disconnected, or uncertain. I just know intuitively that the way is being made.

39. I am a receiver always. I pleasantly receive out of thin air. I allow things to happen for me instead of trying to force them to happen. I know when I am supposed to complete what I am inspired to create because there is a natural ease, pull, and outcome magnetized toward it. Anything worth it in my life always happens in the most magical way. The next moment is no different. I choose to live in a world where I believe I am connected to something primordial that has always wanted to give to me. This is why I have always received in some kind of way. It is the energy of life giving back to itself.

40. Receiving out of thin air is in my DNA. I am just now remembering that I can receive out of thin air. I am not learning a technique or trying to understand it. It is just a truth. It is just life itself. It is all here now, and all that needs to happen is for few molecules to align. The rest becomes my life story. I am the one rejoicing in my creations, dancing through the process, laughing along the way, and finding moments to just celebrate the incredible nature of it all. I never get caught up in one state. I

transmute it, transition from it, and transform myself into greater. I know life has all kinds of interesting experiences to offer, and the way I choose to see everything is more important than what is happening externally. This is why I have chosen to live my life supernaturally and operate from my divine state. I make peace with it all and I settle into myself, knowing that everything will always magically work out.

Affirmations from Your Future

These affirmations are written in a style that will make you feel like they are a message from your future self, talking directly to you right now. Anytime you want to enter a desired state and feel like you're already there, use these affirmations. Every single word will put you in that mindset, mood, and energy, and you will feel this as your truth now. You will feel electrical and connected to your manifestations.

These words are energetically charged with real energy to create a vortex in your mind to pull you into the world of your dreams. Yes, it is *absolutely* possible for you to have anything you want in this life. Most of the work is believing you can. The rest is following the inspired action that guides you to your ultimate vision.

Some things will occur out of thin air for you, and others will feel like you arrived at your vision in the most supernatural way. You are starting to live the magical life, and your future will represent what it means to be a master creator. Speak these words over your life daily. You will begin to magnetize everything you want to yourself.

41. It all worked out. I made it through. I am the happiest I have ever been. I have my manifestations now. I have my blessings now. I have received all that I have currently been praying for. My story had a few twists and turns, but that was all part of the plan to bring me where I belong. My soul was guiding me the

entire time. I trusted, I believed, and I kept going. Congratulations to me!

42. I finally am living the life of my dreams with the one I love. I have the healthiest, most harmonious relationship. I am the one who attracted all of this. There was a time when I was praying for a connection like this. This is the exact person of my dreams. It feels so good to share so much love and to be so open in my heart and mind to welcome this level of deep attraction. There's so much respect, admiration, understanding, care, and unity in my partnership. I am discovering more of myself in this beautiful union. I am so grateful that I am experiencing every single thing I imagined in someone else. I had no idea this was even possible before, but having it all now, I can say how incredible it all is. I am so glad everything happened for me, and as a matter of fact, it is far greater than I could ever have imagined. This has shown me that anything is possible. Love is here!

43. My body is the heathiest it has ever been. I feel a sense of balance, deep love, and honor for my own self. I am finally at a place where I feel healed mentally, emotionally, and spiritually. It is as if all parts of me have come together, and I feel a higher energetic expression taking place in my body. There's a natural energy flow going on, and I have cleared out so many emotional blocks. This has led to a healthier mind and more emotional balance. I now know that my physical health isn't just about nutrition alone, but the overall wholistic health of my mind, emotions, self-perception, self-love, self-awareness, and liberation from the past. I am healed now because I have discovered myself. I am an energy being first, and I make sure I am good within so I can be excellent in all areas of my life. This all naturally happened for me after I realized that I can have wellness, I can live a magnificent life, and I deserve it all. I live from a place of vast possibility where I can tap into endless expressions and versions of myself.

44. I wish someone had told my past self that I would be living my dreams and that I should stop worrying and overthinking everything. I made it through. I overcame it. I have finally arrived. I feel the happiest I have ever been because I did it all through my mind and trusting myself. I am now sending that message back to my current self: It is done because I have made it here. This is the insight I am telepathically receiving. Through these words, I am communicating with the future version of myself who has manifested it all. For my physical well-being most of all, I know that it is already done. This will save me time and energy because no matter what the situation or how things seem to me now, I have already arrived. This is just a message from my future. I choose to smile about it and let it bring ease into my heart and mind now.

45. My future is bright. I have created so much new energy in my life. People who support me are abundant in my life. I have received so many opportunities, and I am now the one who is making all the decisions about what is best for me. I just have so many options available to me, and every choice I make serves the path for my greatness to further expand. Many of the things I was unsure about before have resolved. Every part of my experience has become so illuminated and filled with so much life that all I do now is share the abundance of joy with others.

46. With deep kindness and understanding, I am almost laughing about my previous life. I can't believe I was so uncertain and so scared of the unknown. I am so glad my past self knows that the future isn't a scary place. It is where all my dreams are lived out, and I get to see how everything ended up unfolding. My future is actually promising, and in this moment, I have the wisdom of knowing that my past, future, and current states are always in communication. Each time I release the past, I tell my future and current self that I am ready for a better life. Each time I trust in the future, I tell my current self and my past self that we are making it through. Every time I become more aware of

my optimal state now, I tell my future self and my past self that it is done. Everything that once seemed challenging now feels like a distant memory. I am so glad my current self knows that my future is greater than my past.

47. My future deeply depends upon me believing in myself right now.

48. It all seems so surreal, but my life has all worked out. That one opportunity I was waiting for came to be. My business is flourishing. My new ideas are taking off. I have really entered my future now, and I feel blessed to know that life only keeps getting better. I am fully tapped in.

49. The future version of me is so proud that I am currently strong, resilient, and trusting of my path.

50. I have entered a portal that transforms me into my future self, just like a scene out of a movie. I see what I am doing, how I feel, and the way I am living. I see myself laughing with those I love, smiling from ear to ear. I peek into the energetic part of myself, and I notice my aura is glowing and my energy field is so strong. This shows me that I am just as happy within as I am on the outside. I see a beautiful golden hue radiating from my heart, and it fills every part of my body. This brings tears to my eyes as I pick up on all that energy and take it back to my current self. I feel revitalized, inspired, and deeply moved by what I just witnessed. I have realized that it is all okay forever, and that life will always be just fine.

Affirmations to Have Spiritual Authority

Spiritual authority is standing in your own power, your own truth, and your own energy. You have a connection with yourself that empowers you, nourishes you, and guides you. This set of affirmations will bring the spiritual authority within you to life. You will start thinking, speaking, and feeling from a place of divinity. You will know what you need to know for yourself.

This section encourages your inner rise to take place. Almost everything in life requires inner awareness to make the best choices for your highest ultimate good. When you pull all your energy back into your own body, it reawakens that beautiful being within you who is awaiting resurrection. This is when you start to have spiritual authority over your life. This next set of affirmations will assist you in doing just that.

51. My willpower is strong. When I say I will do something, I do it. My spiritual authority over my will is strong. If my mind decides something, it is already done. I build this momentum within myself so my body can get used to my mind's commands. The way I test this is to see if I have followed through with what I say I will do. This shows me that I am in primary spiritual authority over my life.

52. I live my truth by listening to my own soul's guidance. There is a unique gift I have, and to be able to tap into that, I need to start utilizing spiritual authority over my life. I have to know that I am a multidimensional being. My power to express myself flows through me to be shared with the external world. I acknowledge that I was born with this power as an innate gift. I return to reclaim it by remembering that everything starts within me.

53. I have been given all the secrets, codes, insights, and revelations already. I have opened myself up to receive, and through my spiritual authority, I step into my divine power to become the embodiment of this incredible energy. I understand that what I need to know comes through me first. I reestablish that contact rather than constantly seeking. I rest within my own self and allow all of this to come through me.

54. I am no longer going to play the game of fear and worry. I completely banish that energy signature from my field by stepping into my spiritual authority of limitless energy, fearlessness, trust,

faith, and deep inner knowing. I am taking control over my life by recognizing who I am, what I am made of, and my level of connection. I am finally going to stand in my truth, live authentically, and follow my own intuition. I am breaking free from something bigger than I can imagine right now, and through these words, I have the freedom to liberate myself mentally, emotionally, physically, and spiritually so that I can see clearly all that I am. I will start to witness how expansive my energy is. I will see that everything is connected to my state of being. Transforming myself gives me greater access to this field. I am so grateful to have discovered my own spiritual authority and how to walk my path consciously and intentionally.

55. From this moment on, I know that I will live my life in full awareness of my spiritual nature. I can no longer remain in the unknown about all that I am. This discovery will free me, my family, and my bloodline. I am the one who completely restores my ancient connection and starts living the way that was destined for me. I return to my original blueprint by operating in my spiritual authority, honoring myself, following my instincts, listening to my soul's guidance, expressing myself freely, and doing what is best for my highest good. I am the one who changes everything. I start with my mindset, my actions, and the world I accept or create around me. I am okay with rebuilding, if necessary. I am okay with change, and most of all, I welcome everything that illuminates my soul.

56. I am now commanding everything in my life. It feels like I have awakened to myself. Now, when I use my voice power, it happens. When I think something, it happens. When I want something, it comes into my life. When I imagine something, it manifests. When I ask for answers, I receive. Everything now responds to me as it naturally should. Since I live from a place of spiritual authority, I am a different person energetically. It is as if everything around me honors me for awakening to my truth.

57. I am the original blueprint of a lineage of great spiritual power. I carry deep codes within my soul. My bloodline goes beyond the physical. The reason many things seem so familiar to me (signs, synchronicities, intuitive insights, and unexplainable occurrences) is because I am remembering who I have always been and what was always meant to be for me. The way the external world communicates with me reminds me to reclaim my spiritual authority and walk in my power. I choose to honor myself in the greatest way possible and be grateful for all the revelations God has shown me.

58. A lot of major changes are happening in my life, the most important being my spiritual rise. My original self wants to shake off all these limitations, false concepts, illusions, distractions, and fears. I know I am destined for greater, so I have to move forward with this mindset. This is a powerful time for my spiritual awakening. I am feeling an increase in my own ability to really see clearly what is going on within me and all around me. I have so much spiritual intelligence and awareness now. I am ready for everything good that I deserve.

59. I choose to walk in my power. I choose to take spiritual authority over my life. Every decision and choice I make is access I have unlocked toward a whole new path.

60. I now radiate magnetic spiritual energy. Everything responds instantly to my energy field. I am constantly receiving in all ways. I get what I want. I don't even have to try hard or force anything. There has just been a natural flow ever since I stepped into my spiritual power. I know that I have always been meant to discover all of this. I am now in a spiritually divine state of being, and I see just how important it is for everyone to start walking in their own spiritual power. It is the greatest gift one can receive.

Affirmations for Healing, Self-Love, and Peace of Mind

Every state is available for you to experience right now. Your

Thought Access

natural state is one of health, love, and peace. Things can happen that push you outside of that equilibrium. These affirmations will serve as a support system to always bring you right back into harmony when you need it. Healing is a mindset first. The body accepts and starts to represent that energy within you. This is why, when you overcome something or work through things, you feel healed, aligned, and balanced in your life. What is happening is that you remove stagnant energy from your mind and body by accepting a greater nature for yourself. Anytime you know things can get better, they do. Self-love supports this. So does being naturally good to yourself, taking care of who you are, and honoring your temple: mind, body, and soul. Every time you read these affirmations, you will shift into a mental state that manifests your desired physical state. You will feel instant peace, energy pouring into you, and the warm embrace of being understood.

61. I release from my mind and body all stagnation. I create a golden aura around my body that protects me from external influences that are not for my highest good. I am surrounded by a great force that repels anything and anyone that doesn't wish the best for me. I am free from limiting habits. I am free from limiting thoughts. I am free from limiting experiences. My mindset has already changed, and now I turn to the subtle nature of my energy field to create a powerful protection and attraction that assists me in my awareness of what I need to know. I can feel my life transforming as I become emotionally open again, expanding the connection with the universe through my heart. I let myself be completely free again.

62. I love every part of who I am. I look into my eyes and tell myself that I am worthy, highly valuable, deeply connected, energetically supported, and always loved. I am the seed of something greater. My life is worthwhile. I can feel it in my core that I am destined for greater in every way. My soul is eternal. I have nothing to worry about. I let my body and energy be

expansive. I acknowledge the wonders of my existence, the resiliency of my body, how patient the universe is with me, and the vast expanse of support I receive. I choose to love myself for simply being me. There's nothing extra I have to do or try to do in order to love who I am. I am already everything. I remember this, embrace it, and live in this way. I am the embodiment of love because I am made of that energy.

63. This is a powerful time for my soul. I can feel myself being healed from everything. This is the closure I needed to finally say that I am healed. I am okay. I am where I need to be right now to understand this insight. Something has shifted within me. It's like a sudden realization that I have always been okay underneath all those thoughts, feelings, and ways of looking at life. I am the one who stopped replaying what has now ended. I am the one who stepped back and looked at things from a greater perspective so I could see more clearly. I have forgiven myself for not knowing that I could have been free anytime I wanted. It was all really a choice. I don't have to be afraid of my own alchemical transformation. My soul is rising, and it wants to be free from where I have kept it. I do all of this not just through mental changes, but also through illumination and insight. A sudden spark of healing has occurred, and I have rearranged the way I distribute my own energy. I am so grateful for these realizations because I am now fully accepting the abundance of energy that brings unlimited healing, love, reassurance, care, and support.

64. My peace of mind isn't connected to an external response to feel peace. My peace of mind is a state I enter as I observe the external experience with a sense of knowing that this, too, shall pass. With every single thing I have been through, no matter how emotional my reaction at the time or how much of my energy I wasted worrying, I have always made it through. I am so much more aware now, and I feel a natural ease that is undisturbed by circumstances. I have learned how to recalibrate myself by studying past habits and seeing what they did to my energy. I am

mentally more powerful now, so I can use lessons from my past to see that there was never anything to worry about. Today, I know better and with this insight. I can properly navigate my inner world to avoid restriction of my energy or blockage of solutions due to my being overly charged up or reacting to whatever is occurring now. I have risen to understand myself emotionally, and I view everything that comes up not from a place of reaction, but from self-observation. The better I become at understanding myself, the easier things get for me. Everything starts within me.

65. I forgive myself for all the times I was unaware. Life has gotten better ever since I have awakened to my truth. In this new world I inhabit, I take full responsibility for my energy, mindset, attractions, and creations. I feel more empowered than I have ever felt in my life because I know that I am a powerful soul. I know that I am forever, and I don't ever have to fear life or death. I am a vital part of humanity. All this new energy I feel happening in my body and my life is a sign that I am ready to live fully, authentically, and supernaturally.

66. I am experiencing more peace, love, restfulness, tranquility, and bliss now. Warm energy surrounds my heart and revitalizes me. I am entering a new path filled with blessings, good energy, positive experiences, higher thoughts, and spiritual wellness. I welcome all of this right now.

67. I have the power, strength, will, and choice to change my life. I am dynamic and multidimensional. I am supernatural and superhuman. I have vast abilities and capabilities. I materialize my visions. I watch everything I speak materialize instantly. I am the source and the connection. I receive in ways I can't even try to fathom or imagine right now. The way the universe is working in my life requires me to trust without needing to know how or when. I just embody it, feel it, and see it all happening as it should.

68. I am valuable just as I am. I am worthy and deserving of the best life has to offer. I feel this way about myself, and the world

sees me this way, too. Self-appreciation gets me further. Self-acceptance attracts new opportunities to me. Self-love gives me back the inner power to be free of it all.

69. I embrace all aspects of my energy, no matter what mood I am in. I can still manifest, because every emotion is real energy that can bring about change. My inner state isn't defined by good or bad. It just is, and I just am. I remove the impulse to try to categorize everything. This helps me avoid forcing things and trying to control everything. Without constantly labeling every state, I don't have to feel like I am not ready when I am ready, no matter what I might be feeling or what is going on. I don't try to get into a positive mood in order to make something happen. I just do it, knowing that this energy state is also a form of creation at work. I am everything, and at every moment, I can shapeshift into any state without the effort of thinking that only one mood manifests things. All things come to life because some form of energy exists behind them. Accepting this greater understanding helps me rest my mind, go back to into my natural flow, and allow everything to be.

70. I operate in my own timing instead of trying to rush everything based on what is happening for other people. I am in my own inner universe, and the more I focus on it, nurture it, and cultivate it, the more it produces for me.

Thought Access

Affirmations for Expanded Consciousness

You are going to receive entry to more of yourself through these affirmations. Expanded consciousness means your awareness of who you are. It activates your abilities, amplifying what is possible and everything that can happen for you. It is a glimpse into a vast world containing unlimited, untapped energy that you can utilize. It is what you can transform yourself into through your inner knowledge that it is there. Every time you discover more about yourself, you are expanding your consciousness. Every time you experience something profound and life-changing, you are in a state of expanded consciousness. This set of affirmations will help you awaken that awareness, tap into that energy, and move in a new way. You are ready for magical things to happen!

71. My mind has opened. I now see through everything. My awareness and experiences are showing me that anything is really possible. I feel a connection that flows energetically through me. I am so much more, and there is so much more. I step into a vast awareness that gives me insight into who I really am. I am experiencing high levels of synchronicity in this state.

72. I can't explain it, but I feel a surge of new energy entering in my life. I feel aligned within myself, and have more radiant inner energy now. I know what I need to know. I feel what I need to feel. I see what I need to see. It's like a self-prophesizing experience: the more I get to know who I am, the more I receive what I intend to create. I am so blessed to be expanded in this way.

73. I am living in a new way and with a whole new mindset. I see life from a greater perspective. It constantly provides me with solutions, guidance, and insight to get through any situation. I longer worry or feel overwhelmed about the future. I know that I have the power to change the direction of my life by stepping into a greater consciousness that sees through everything. I am not caught up in small things; I rise above them. I focus on what

can be and what can come out of it.

74. I make empowered decisions now. I communicate with my own inner guidance by listening to my own voice. This inner voice is my soul, which is all-knowing. My path is connected to something far greater, and I must take the time to listen, contemplate, and do the introspection necessary to gain a deeper understanding.

75. The more awareness I have, the more expanded I am. Expansion brings me freedom because I see life as uninfluenced by affairs of the now. Instead, my life is guided by the light of my soul. Being able to see from my inner vision means I can have a healthy attitude toward any situation. I can thrive in uncertainty. I can change anything about myself, and I can create anything I want at any given moment. This state encompasses many variants of what can be, and with that awareness, I know everything can turn out the way I want it to.

76. I am receiving high levels of creative energy. I always feel like I get a new idea and then take action to bring these powerful life-changing ideas into the world. I get solutions not only for myself, but for the world all around me. I am practically turning into an inventor, because I have tapped into the energy from which creative ideas arise. I can be in the middle of enjoying myself, and suddenly, I need to rush to write down all that is flowing through me. I also have dreams that guide me and show me the way on my path. My life has become one interconnected field of unlimited possibilities. All creative geniuses, writers, artists, inventors, and healthy-living people have discovered this surplus of free energy that brings vitality, vibrancy, life force, creative power, and the abundance I am now tapped into. I see it in my lifestyle, my purpose-driven work, my passion, my relationships, and even in my appearance. I have become a changed person. I am radiating inner energy.

77. I tap into healing energy. I am receiving vibrational energy

that scans every part of my body to bring me back into balance and harmony. Anytime I feel anything, I imagine a light similar to the energy of the sun moving through the top of my head and all the way down to my feet. I feel revitalized and rejuvenated. Awakening the process of healing is a mental process that begets inspiration to make physical changes that align with my new body. I can turn my life around right now. I can turn my health around right now. I align myself from within, get back into balance, and become harmonious with nature's frequencies. I return to the homeostasis of health.

78. My life has become supernatural. I have taken every-thing back into my own hands by being intentional, present, observant, and connected to something more. I am expanded consciousness now. I have Thought Access now. I have a stronger connection now. What I used to pray for and hope would happen one day has now started to happen every single day. I have turned my life into my own dream by linking up with messages from the dreamtime, tapping into my expanded consciousness and opening myself to the mystery of life. Nothing is weird or unusual. What I have access to is literally my mindset and the fact that I am now open to more. If I am expanded in my thinking, so is everything that takes place in my life. I now go beyond identity, day-to-day living, and limiting my own scope to just a few thoughts or emotions. I go beyond all of that as needed and tap into more so I don't get caught up in one timeline or phase of life. We are always moving forward, and I choose to go with the current that guides me to a higher level of living and seeing the world.

79. My expanded consciousness is activated in me.

80. Everything around me now has more vibrancy, hope, and beautiful energy because I see the world differently now. I don't allow external things to paint a picture in my fertile creative ground or use me to co-create unwanted things in the world. Instead, I stand in my power to intentionally and consciously

create the world I want to see. I am living fully and committed to higher ideals while taking the reigns over my own mental world. I don't unconsciously agree to negative narratives or allow myself to be programmed by external influences. I see what is going on, and I step back to recalibrate my own inner state so I can project what I want to see. Everything is energy, moving and looking for a host in which to thrive. I now make conscious choices about the narrative I spread by observing the intentions of the energy behind them.

Affirmations for Mental Health

These mental health affirmations are written to support your emotional healing. They are not only for recovery, but also for strengthening your self-perception so you can feel whole and united within yourself. Mental health means so much to me, as I know how powerful people are when they are free in their inner world. These affirmations will help you gain inner confidence, overcome just about any mental state, discover your own inner strength, and consciously uplift yourself using voice power, mind power, and self-awareness.

81. My mindset is getting better every single day. I am realizing that my mental health has to do with how I perceive things and the way I process what is happening to me. I don't need to identify what is happening as a personal thing. I look at it from the perspective of observation and seeing where it guides me. Nothing is permanent. No situation lasts forever. Everything gradually gets better, so I choose to release everything out of my energy field, mindset, body, and state of being. I am liberated.

82. I have the power to change how I feel and how I think. I don't have to accept one state forever; I can do something about it. I can think better thoughts about myself and my situation. I can choose to believe that my life will get better. I can break free of the hypnotic trance that creates negativity in my life. I don't have

to identify myself as someone who is going through something. I change up my storyline intentionally. All of this impacts my mental health, which, in turn, creates a better life for me.

83. I love myself. I take care of myself. I do what is necessary to make sure that I am whole, balanced, and in harmony with my truth. The healthier I am, the more I can express my life force in the world. The more balanced my mental state, the more I can live in my own inner bliss. The most honorable thing I can do is love my body, love myself, and be kind to my inner self. When I am patient with myself, divine intervention occurs. When I trust myself, I am letting the universe know that I believe. When I respect myself, I am sending the signals to be respected. All I need to do is get my inner affairs in order and bring brightness back to myself by choosing to radiate from within first. Everything else will naturally respond to my new energy.

84. Things always have a way of getting better. Just because I lived one moment where things went a certain way doesn't mean I have to live in that space mentally. I am a new person today, with new thoughts and a new way of seeing life. I don't have to be confined to the past self that people associate me with. I know I can transform, shapeshift, and recreate myself. I keep getting better because it is in my DNA. I am designed and created to always evolve, learn new things, and overcome mental states. With all this insight, I am breaking free and overcoming the links that used to confine me to the ways people see me and what they think. What's important is how I see myself and what I think. I am becoming more empowered and stronger every moment.

85. I heal from heartbreak, mental struggles, and external influences by knowing that my Earth journey is momentary. I don't have to harbor old feelings or live in the biochemistry of the body's signaling of fearful thoughts or previous experiences. I know everything keeps repeating in a loop via thought and emotion, and as I advance in my awareness, I know that it's just

a memory triggering the process. I can put a stop to it right now. I don't have to be pulled into hypnotic trance of my past self or previous connections. I can heal from it all. I can release it. I can give myself the chance to have a heathier mind, a more loving heart, and a more open spirit. In this way, I will manifest new experiences. I know life is filled with limitless possibilities, and the more comfortable I get with my inner freedom to alter my own mind and emotions, the more I can experience acceleration of my awareness and everything I attract into my life. I become a creator by becoming liberated mentally.

86. I am transcending all mental states that no longer serve me. I am rising up into my truth, my greatness, and my higher self.

87. As my awareness increases, so does my mental health. I feel empowered spiritually, and this helps bring ease to my mind, allowing me to overcome just about anything. Change happens first within myself. I alter my own perspective intentionally, and I see a better outcome by believing that anything is possible for me. My results come from remaining conscious on my path. This assists me in being the observer of my thoughts and what is happening externally so I never identify with things outside myself or become consumed by them.

88. I am seeing wonderful results already. My mindset has shifted, and so has everything I feel and see all around me. I am no longer struggling with negative thoughts or self-image issues. I am confident because I have discovered the power of my soul. I am a spirit first, and the energy flowing from my essence uplifts my body and brings me back into harmony so I can access ease in all ways. I have discovered that the secret of mental health is my own awareness of my spiritual nature and how life goes on. I am eternal, and I am free from all things that make me forget who I am. When I stand in my spiritual power and own my truth, I naturally have healthier thoughts and feel uplifted to experience breakthroughs and miracles. My life is a beautiful

adventure, and I will remain on my path as I unfold in my own light and greatness. I feel whole, connected, and united within myself. I am forever grateful for this.

89. I choose to be mindful of my conversations, associations, and ways I spend my energy. I know how much influence is happening all around me, and I steer clear of being pulled in by bad news or misfortune. I choose to see the world in a higher way, by thinking of solutions, imagining greater possibilities, and spreading kindness. I am responsible for my energy, what I tune into, what I focus on, and what I allow to continue. When I see that something isn't helping my mental health or overall wellness, I make the conscious decision to move forward from it. I will do my very best to always communicate in a loving way, and I will be purposeful in my time, creation, lifestyle, and state of being.

90. Every day, I see results that demonstrate how much better I am becoming as a person. I can tell that I have evolved so much. I have become so openminded, that it has shifted my path toward a greater life. All of this has happened because I have decided to become aware and boldly walk my path. I have decided to finally do something about it instead of remaining stuck or labeling myself as someone who is always "going through it." I am not a victim. I know that my narrative and my story are written by me. I know that I can say kind things about myself, understanding that it creates energy all around me and within me. I won't allow pressures or people's self-created limitations to infiltrate my mind. What someone believes and thinks has nothing to do with my life path. I am aware of how thought viruses are spread, and I choose to become immune to them by acting deliberately in the transmissions taking place via my mindset. I don't take on other people's energy. Instead, I strengthen my own, and this allows me to become liberated from previous limitations while pulling my energy higher to attract greater. I am so glad all of this has happened for me. I finally feel in control of my own mental health and overall wellness.

One Hundred Thought Access Affirmations

Affirmations for More Energy and Reigniting Your Spirit

Life force energy is what helps you to be creative, inspired, imaginative, openminded, and naturally very expressive. In this way, more energy can activate you, and most of this comes from your spirit. Through awareness, you can truly transform to awaken to the world around you. Your body is an energy system, and your life force comes from your own essence. The more you are aware of your own multidimensional nature, the less you allow the physical world to create mental limitations within you. This set of affirmations is meant to support the expansiveness of your sprit so you can use certain words to create a ripple of change in your own consciousness. Every word will activate something within you that draws more energy into your body. You will feel like you can do anything, and you actually will. A small amount of energy from your spirit is equivalent to months (even years) of trying to get energy from external things. You can reignite your own purpose, and this is how I will be supporting you. I will provide the insight for you to reignite your own spirit. Be prepared for massive changes and bioelectric upgrades.

91. I am feeling that there is more to who I am, and I am choosing to listen to the guidance of that feeling. The more I go within and follow my own instincts, the more energy I pull into myself. This happens because I am a self-sustaining system. When I believe in myself, I feel a surge of energy in my body that revitalizes me. I feel more energy come into my life when I am openminded, daring to believe in the unseen and the unknown. I am always provided for by higher forces, which work within me and all around me. Everything is connected, and the more I think this way, the more energy comes into my life.

92. The environment around me is filled with so much energy. I breathe in electric energy and feel it circulating throughout my body. I feel connected to nature, the sun, the ocean, the animals, and everything that represents natural life. When I get back to

the basics of real life, I feel even more connected and enriched spiritually. Everything has to do with magnetism and energy, which is harmonious in the natural world. Just as I am surrounded by all these powerful currents, I am also an energy grid that is alive and active. The natural flow of my own energy begins in the openness of my mind, my heart, and my spirit. The more I know who I am, the more energy I receive. Just being myself also provides me with more energy. I let go of all resistance and contradictory thought or actions.

93. Being true to what is in my heart helps me rejuvenate my own physical body's energy. When I am honest about what I want, who I am, and the direction I see myself going, I get more energy to help me break free from stagnation.

94. I have access to unlimited energy and life force right now. When I look at how I am being sustained and provided for every single moment, I can grow even further by feeling grateful for the surplus of energy I am continuously receiving. I am thankful that I have more energy to do what I love and impact the world around me in a positive way.

95. Starting with this moment, I remove anything that zaps my energy or drains me. I have to start being honest with myself about my habits, behaviors, and how I use my life force. When I face myself, I make a bold move to overcome anything negative. When I do something different, I make a fresh choice to alter my life path. My destiny is created by me through the choices I make daily, the actions I take, and the way I feel about myself. When my body is healthy, so are the high levels of energy that flow in. When I make a healthy space to receive more, I get more. Everything is obvious when I am truthful with myself about my personal changes. I live authentically because it frees up so much energy instead of trying to conceal who I am.

96. My spirit holds great secrets, and the revelation has started. I am now receiving insight that rejuvenates me, reenergizes me,

and reignites me. I can feel my passion turning on and my purpose beginning. I can tell this will be a life-changing time for me because I am coming alive to my own potential. As I make this discovery, I can see clearly everything I have access to.

97. My existence is beyond the physical. There's a subtle nature to who I am, and this part of me is what is sustaining me and giving me life. As I bring my attention to all that I am, I get more energy to do what I came here to do. I feel the most creative I have ever felt. I can tell my imagination is expanding further because I can see things that were once unseen to me. The blessing of recognizing my spirit is that I release all sorts of fears, worries, and things that made me take life so seriously. I feel a sense of calm, ease, and trust in myself and the higher nature of who I am. I know my every step is guided. I know my way has been made. All I need to do is acknowledge myself and know that I am a supernatural being in an energetic world. All things are possible for me as the creator of my experience.

98. I feel a rush of energy entering my life: good people, great experiences, blessings filled with abundance, opportunities, health, and lots of prosperity. There's just so much good happening in my life, all because I opened my heart and mind to my spiritual nature and my own truth. I feel deeply connected, transformed, and loved for eternity.

99. I am transcending all limitations, past selves, fears, and illusions that were stealing my energy. I call all of my energy back to me by releasing myself from any bondage that formerly blocked my path. I initiate my own freedom by breaking energetic patterns, connections, and habits. All of these endings free me and allow me to gain access to a new version of myself. This gives me more energy to recreate who I was always meant to be.

100. I now have the access to higher energy, and my spirit is fully reignited. Everything I do from this moment on will be blessed

and supported. I will always have everything I need. My life will represent real spiritual power.

These 100 affirmations will play a crucial role in your life as they pour real power and energy into you. Every single word has been written in a way that will allow you to feel actual energetic increase in your physical body and state of mind. Each affirmation will be a real natural high for elevating your way of being, how you think, and the way you feel about yourself. You can tap into any section at any time to remind yourself of the power that is flowing through you. You can speak your affirmations out loud, do them in front of the mirror, or just read them to yourself. The words will have a prolonged and lasting effect as you see everything around you morph into your new mindset. Everything in your life will literally turn into your own dream world. Be ready for radical changes, unexplainable miracles, supernatural encounters, out-of-thin-air manifestations, a high level of self-confidence, being your healthiest self, and the ability to attract anything to you while receiving what you need, right when you need it. Enjoy the blessings that come from these affirmations.

18

EMBODIMENT: REPRESENTING YOUR THOUGHT WORLD

The time has come for everyone to start representing their thought world. Your physical reality is the embodiment of your inner world. You are your own self-creation. There's no more space for masks, acting, pretending, or hiding behind a limited perception of self. You are felt before you are seen. Your energy is constantly molding in the minds all around you the way you see yourself, how you feel, what you think, and what you believe. This can be your own self-worth, what you value, the things you allow, and how you define yourself as a person.

We don't realize just how profoundly we impact the energy field and how the point of creation begins within us. People don't really have their own perceptions of you; they sense within themselves what you feel about yourself. This is a real signal that picks up on your inner state, allowing the other person to respond accordingly.

The goal for me in this chapter is to bring awareness back to real empowerment of the self, facilitate expansion of your own self-perception, and ignite real power within every soul reading this book. For too long, people have lived their external lives without real, true awareness that everything they are creates their lived experience. You can change this not only through inspirational thinking, but also at the level of your core self, which has adapted beliefs about what it means to be who you are.

Many people have experienced discordance between the image they project and who they actually are. We have been trained to overvalue what people think of us and modulate that perception through external representation of self, even if we create a false representation that doesn't match the way we actually feel internally. Over time, we are trained to be "good enough" for so and so, to be validated by family members, and to be accepted by society's ideas of who we should be. This has created internal imbalance and misrepresentation of the self. Under extreme circumstances, it creates a person with irrational fears, anxiety, disassociation, depression, and self-judgment. It also creates a false concept of limitation. The person, who naturally was born free, has now become hidden in an inner shell.

You must find yourself again. You must get to know who you are to finally shed the false layers put upon you. This is the most important time for your soul to come alive again. When you had no idea what was happening, you lived life day in and day out without awareness of where to actually begin. You just assumed that this was the way life was meant to be. It isn't. As we are pushed to focus solely upon the external, our minds begin to depend on external results, approval, and acceptance to gauge if we are even good enough. This tactic of fear is spread in subconscious ways when people are discouraged from following their own heart and listening to their own inner voice. The collective embodiment state will be a powerful movement in which many will return to themselves, their soul's truth, and awakening of their own potential.

This chapter will teach you how to authentically represent your own soul's blueprint and what it means to be a super being in this current timeline. You will learn how to identify hidden tricks of the psyche that play on fear, ways to banish false systems that depend on your weakness, and techniques for rehearnessing

Thought Access

all of your energy to chart a new path, a new life, and a new world—all through your own body.

You are a super being, and to feel exactly what that means will be the most important experience on your Earth journey. You have experienced parts of your super beingness in states of bliss, love, signs, synchronicities, connections, miracles, instant manifestations, high levels of mental clarity, being at one with the field, expansiveness, increased bioenergy, and openness of the heart. Everyone, at one point or another in their life, has experienced access to more of who they are. We naturally know that we are more than we appear to be, but most people have a way of rationalizing the supernatural experiences they experience as coincidental. This is just a way to feel in control of the "fact" that things are predictable and provable. Since the mind is conditioned to think in this way, most of what people experience on the day-to-day level has to do with how safely they can live in a state of mental confinement. This breaks down to what they can control and change, and is all a part of the external projection that identifies with the physical self alone.

When you know you are multidimensional, you can start to see the world from an energetic perspective. You can start to see yourself as an energy being. This allows flexibility in your thinking, confidence in your attitude, and a high-level of self-belief that anything is possible. When the mind is open, so are the many possibilities of the universe.

> *You don't have to settle or accept what doesn't resonate with your own potential.*

This is the time to be real with yourself. You can no longer do things that create disharmony or imbalance in your life. You can't settle out of fear or live a life you don't agree with. Your chance to make real change is right now. Move forward by accurately representing your thought world. Before you do that, look at where self-doubt and powerlessness originate. To become the embodiment of your true self, build up the inner representative of your new thought world. Purge the false narratives, fears, and insecurities that keep you in a cycle of self-limitation.

We tend to believe our current thought parameters are all that exists. What you need to know is that your current thoughts are not your final thoughts, and they are by no means all there is to life. They are *barriers* to thought; filters through which we sometimes operate, whether from familiarity or exposure. This is why they say knowledge is power. Learning something new will expand the barriers of your mind to believe in more. What you declare to be your self-awareness is really your true power, because it encourages you to understand who you are and to uncover all the abilities hidden in your own consciousness. This begins when we stop confining ourselves to a few limiting thoughts or ways of seeing life that keep us the same. What follows is an open sea of endless possibilities; and as many times as someone might tell you this, you will really only know it when you experience it for yourself.

You are going to start building your inner world up first by overriding all forms of negativity, self-doubt, fear, and limitation by exposing them. Don't treat negative thoughts kindly or think that is just who you are. Get into the seat of your own kingdom by banishing unwanted thoughts, replacing them instantly, and directly confronting their place of origin. When someone has become accustomed to thinking a certain way all their life or the majority of the time, they assume that this is just part of their thought process. The truth is, none of that is who you are. You get to actually pick and choose what you allow to continue. When there is no awareness, we don't think we have the option to pick, choose, or replace willingly.

To start becoming the embodiment of the greatness you are, begin by weeding out the unwanted thoughts currently creating your reality. Lack of self-awareness or unconsciously recreating what is taking place in your external life are not issues to be taken lightly. Everyone needs to know the power of their mind, the power of their soul, and the power of their intentions. It all begins when you stop identifying with any sort of lack or limitation. You have to denounce anything that tries to weaken you.

The mental world is a vast space, constantly communicating with everyone and everything. When you feel confident, love yourself, know who you are, and take care of yourself, it ripples out into the world, sending signals that align with your inner state. It creates people, experiences, and things out of nowhere that match your new self-perception. It even lifts your mood and the way you see the world.

A person who is truly happy within themselves cannot be brought down or bothered. This is energy protection and a form of invisible strength that overrides problems, sees real solutions, and keeps you tuned into your own true frequency. These are real, actual, living experiences we are creating. They are more than just energy shields to create protection against mental viruses trying to corrupt our system through fear, worry, and hopelessness. When we step into our own power, we step into an energy *grid* of power. This is why you feel stronger, healthier, more connected, and truly aligned within yourself.

Take accountability for your thoughts, actions, and feelings. The rest will align.

Everyone needs to start taking accountability for the energy they are representing and the thoughts they are spreading. In the past, many people were still unaware of what was going on, but now, we have awakened to our real power. We will know when someone or something is trying to discourage us with mental viruses. As more people begin to embody their truth and walk in their power, they will eventually change what was once deemed acceptable as a way of thinking. They will become carriers of a stronger mindset that will provide hope, support, love, and a way into a new and more meaningful life. Nobody will settle anymore. Everyone will know what it means to be who they are through exploration and discovery of their own soul.

The external world depends on your mind to interface with it. If the mind lacks the proper tools to maneuver its own path using its own inner compass in the highest way possible, it will cause misunderstanding, missed opportunities in terms of your desired creation, and manifestation of unwanted experiences. You have to know that you are a super being who creates everything in your life. Returning to an awareness of the inner world will give you a stronger relationship with yourself. You will learn to listen to your own voice again, trust yourself, and tap into reservoirs of insight within you.

Creating Your Mental World Intentionally

Start creating the kinds of thoughts you want. It may never occur to us that thoughts are also created, just as things are created. Mentally influence yourself by choosing the thoughts you want to entertain. We tend to assume that our thoughts are random and uncontrollable. The truth is, you can create thoughts that actually support your mental world.

To represent your thought world and embody the power of your own greatness, make sure your inner world's affairs are in order. It is as easy as training yourself to predominantly think the thoughts you want, use words that create the thoughts you want more of, and bring into your awareness the inner state you desire. This building-up of your inner self will naturally turn into everything you wish to manifest.

Since we don't normally focus on *how* we design our mental world, we tend to deal with it only partially by using positivity and inspiration on the go instead of manifesting who we truly are. This is what embodiment is all about. You don't have to set aside a time to be positive or do things for a short period of time to feel inspired. You can generate this energy in your own body by creating your mental world intentionally. You notice that you always have thoughts that favor you, support you, encourage you, and open your mind.

> *Your mental world belongs to you. Choose what stays in your private inner sanctuary.*

The first thing you should do is see what is running in your mental world. When you pay attention to what is taking place, you can smile, knowing that it can easily be changed. You don't really have to do anything special or be afraid of your thoughts. You can dissipate them with your mind power.

Thoughts are energy, just as your mind is energy. The thing is, your mind is stronger and more powerful than anything, which is why thoughts easily fade when you awaken from the slumber of feeling small and afraid in your own inner kingdom. You can take the seat on your own throne and start banishing, one by one, thoughts that are no longer serving your mental kingdom. You'll be surprised at how easy it is, and you will feel inspired to revamp your inner world. As you gain momentum cultivating a stronger self, you will notice everything around you changing, as well. All the emotions, people, things, and experiences associated with your past self will be removed. This mental change initiates a spiritual purge and revitalization of your own body. Many energy blocks that kept you stuck will burst open and clear out, all because you changed the thought patterns that were running your life.

Identifying the Tricks of Fear

Powerlessness is part of the fear that weakens our own ability to see beyond the thoughts, creations, and projections the world has attempted to put on us. Some people don't even realize that many of the emotions they are going through do not belong to them. These creations can be traced back to fear or some kind of mental trick that has caused them to believe that they are "less than."

The reason I repeat that you are powerful multiple times in my book (and in all of my work) is to deeply awaken that true sense of self within you. I know people are pure beings with vast potential underneath the layers of life and the many thoughts, beliefs, and outlooks they have adopted. My goal is to guide you back to yourself so you can have the full access that has always been there.

I know you can do it. You are peeling it all back to unravel yourself. The trick of fear can come up in many ways that naturally cause you to think that you are in that state. One trick I have picked up on is the forceful conditioning and negative experiences that have convinced people that they need to protect themselves from others in a way that closes off their energy for love and life. We don't think about our words when we say, "My circle is small" or "I only trust a few people." This can literally *create* untrust-worthy people in our lives while reaffirming your original belief system about people, perhaps even convincing you to use energy protection to disguise and cover fear, which only keeps you more closed off.

There's nothing to fear. It's all mental.

Powerlessness is anything that makes you overthink, worry, avoid change, stay in the same habits, repeat the same negative thoughts, or feel "not good enough." None of these are who you are. They are just states picked up over time that masquerade as part of something you *think* you are. Anytime you feel like you are in a mental battle with yourself, it is very important to make the best decision for yourself according to your gut feeling. This is the best way to start breaking free from the tricks of fear.

Thought Access

Instead of remaining fragmented, indecisive, confused, or unsure of whether or not you should start, just act in your highest good. Do the best you feel you can do in that moment. This will give you enough of a push to start moving forward.

That resistant feeling of not wanting to do what you know is good for you has to do with the trick of fear working to keep you the same. This is all psychological. You think of doing something about it, but another thought makes you think it's okay to avoid change. The excess back-and-forth in your mental space creates a weakening of the will to just go for it. The beautiful thing is that when you finally follow that calling and decide for yourself to make a change, you feel like an unstoppable force is supporting you. This is when you get your power back. This is when things awaken within you and clear everything out of your way. A new energy comes into your life that makes you feel like you can do anything you dream of.

> *Most of what you need to change won't make sense, initially. It jolts the foundation of what you've been used to doing, and that state puts you in an unfamiliar territory of mind, emotions, and outlook. The desire for predictability chains you to fear of the unknown. Don't be afraid to go forward. Magic awaits.*

Breaking free from fear will show you that there's really nothing to be afraid of. There's nothing standing in your way. People and things aren't against you. All of these are just tricks of fear to close you off and confine you, keeping you limited and disconnected. They make you forget that this is your one life, and you need to fully live it out to the best of your energetic capacity. If you were to leave your physical life today, all of the obsessive thoughts or worries would seem so futile to you. You would wish that you hadn't taken everything so seriously. You would wish that you had owned your power so you could be all you were destined to be in this lifetime. You would wish you had shared more love, taken it easy on yourself, and not allowed things to take you over in mind and body.

This is your opportunity to set yourself free. Live life like you know this moment is all you have. Share yourself to the fullest capacity, be open in your heart so your flow moves unrestricted, and be free in your mindset so the burdens of self-judgment, pessimism, and negativity perish from your field. What will now be restored in you is true power beyond the physical world. Today, you will bring into your mind and body all of your greatest possibilities from your future self as well as the powerful timeline of your past potential. This new energy you are welcoming will amplify your energetic field, get you out of the slumber of chaos and confusion, and reactivate your heart to once again feel what it is to embody greatness.

Reigning in Your Inner Kingdom

As your spiritual energy strengthens and your body's natural energy expands, you will start to notice a magnetic energy pulling everything to you. You will become the ultimate receiver of the universe, all because you decided to reign in your inner kingdom. Everyone must be individually empowered and show signs themselves of running their lives in sync with the abundance, health, vitality, and energy of the universe. You will start to live in resonance and in alignment with your highest thoughts, intentions, values, and creations. You will walk this Earth knowing who you are, living in your authenticity, and letting energy move freely through you and all around you. The person you once were will seem so unfamiliar to your current self. You will feel so alive to know that you are one hundred percent yourself. You are the embodiment of a powerful force, and this energy helps you be at your greatest. When your inner world is in order, you can start to integrate that energy throughout your mind and body.

The first thing that will happen is you will feel an increase in energy; this can be a sudden surge or a constant stream. The reason for this is that when we are in resistance, we block our own energy field. With the high awareness you are receiving as you read this book, you can now experience sudden bursts of energy and the removal of blocks from your mind and body. This is intentional, as I know that a higher sense of understanding and awareness gives you greater energy-field access, which liberates you completely. Sudden increases in energy can result in higher creativity for some people. Others may feel unending bliss. Everyone responds to it differently based upon what they need. Someone people will need to rest to integrate, and others will need to express all the newfound energy in order to process it. When you go deeper in, breaking bonds in the energy field that have kept you unaware for so long, you feel like you have gained a new view on life. You see beyond what appears to be happening, piercing through the veil to get a glimpse of all that you are. It is a very special time for you, and this is just the start as you work with your own mind and body to understand your inner kingdom.

Keep It Simple

The blessing you receive by embodying your own greatness and light is the knowledge that you don't have to do anything specific to become who you already are. Most of the changes are just getting out of old programs, thought patterns, habits, and conditioning that stand in the way of the pure self within. Every habit you quit, and everything you end up giving up, only brings you back to yourself. It actually takes so much effort to *not* be your true self. The reality is, your mind and body are always trying to bring you back to your own soul awareness. This reminds you that you just are. Simply being you assists you in freeing yourself of all the excess of becoming, doing, trying so hard, and forcing things out of a need to control change.

When you settle into your own home within yourself, the world of beauty, simplicity, and understanding opens. Feeling like the latest technique or the next big movement is something you're missing out on is the illusion that tries to make you feel like you don't have the access yourself. Some will try very hard to become what the world has told them to become and feel like they are still lost. This sense of being lost stems from forgetting yourself. When you overconsume content that tries to tell you who you are, you lose the simplicity of uniting with your soul's needs, intelligence, and insights, which are curated just for you. You do have the answers. You *are* the one. You are everything. This is how simple it is, and sometimes, returning to that truth is what people call the process of becoming. You are naturally doing a lot of unlearning when you surrender to your own greater guidance. You need to be able to hear your own voice, use your own intuition, and listen to your own heart.

When something external does all the thinking for you by telling you who you should be, you overcomplicate the personal connection you already have. You then have to filter that outside information and match it up against what your soul is trying to communicate with you. People sometimes forget what it's like to have heard their own inner voice, and truly feel empowered when they reignite that connection. This is the time for the self to arise and return to who you really are. It starts with discovering what is standing in your way as the layers you have built up over time are removed. Knowing how to identify your own authentic behaviors, thought patterns, and beliefs will help liberate you toward the path of simplicity.

Find moments throughout the day to count your blessings. This simple act of conscious gratitude changes your mental and emotional state from lack to abundance. Your shift in perspective will lift you higher, giving you an inner state of peace in the knowledge that it's all good right now.

You are very special being, a gift crafted by the highest source. You were given everything, and as time went on, you may have lost yourself in the noise or become caught up in unwanted habits. That doesn't mean you aren't still a powerful being. One thing for certain is that we can never lose ourselves, even if we get lost momentarily. The ability to instantly recognize this will create a feeling of expansion within you. You will embrace not only your path, but also what it means to be endless, timeless, and continuous for eternity. You are forever, and to see outside of your own perspective right now requires you to return to your observer state to oversee things playing out. From this greater view, you will know how to manage what is taking place in your life without getting caught up. You will know how to maneuver difficult paths without identifying with anything negative. You will know how to create what is to come without feeling like you need to know how or when.

Lastly, you will operate as a superbeing. You never limit yourself, fall for illusions, get trapped by fear, or personalize the events of life. You return to simplicity while still managing the complexities of life. Things that once wore you out because of the way you responded to them energetically will now feel like they don't even phase you at all. This natural shift in how you see life provides powerful energetic protection that doesn't drain your energy. Never again will you lose or compromise that protection.

It's Not Your Responsibility

You're not under any obligation to make someone else see

something they are not ready to see. You can't force anyone to awaken to their potential. You can't try to make someone see life from a certain perspective they are not ready for. People often ask me why someone won't take care of their mental health or do things that will help them break free from certain relationships or habits, understanding that there are greater possibilities for them. This is all a personal journey, and usually, people who realize how much better life gets when they work on themselves and take care of their mind, body, and soul also realize how beautiful, peaceful, and bright everything becomes. At this stage, they want to extend what they have captured within themselves to others in some way. This can create oversharing of their own energy when the other person is not ready.

When this happens, the person overextending the unwanted help begins to feel energetically depleted, overwhelmed, or even resentful at times. This all is taking place because we want to project greater into the world by playing the role of healer or trying to save others from themselves. This is unnatural, as everything is an energy exchange. There is literal cause and effect taking place within every single person's mind—actual signals that create one's experience. You can't do it for them, and they can't do it until they are ready to do it for themselves. The generator of the signal alters it for themselves, which then changes their life.

People sometimes want to feel good momentarily with new insights or information, but don't plan to actually change. Perhaps it wasn't their time to get out of the field in which they've found themselves. This is why I suggest that it is not your responsibility to help manage someone else's energy, what they focus on, the choices they make, the habits in which they partake, or the outcomes they manifest.

Do what feels right for you. Don't lose yourself in other people's stories or paths. Stay focused on

Thought Access

your gift, your vision, and what you possess within you. The unique concoction of your essence happens only once in all of time. If you embrace yourself, the world responds accordingly. Stay tuned within.

We can only hope for better. As we begin to respect other people's paths, we stop overburdening ourselves, wasting our own time, and slowing down our own evolution so others can match us where we are. We can only do so much until we ourselves get sucked into their energy. What is meant for someone will happen, and sometimes, they aren't fully ready to go on their inner journey or uproot the dissonances running rampant. The real help comes when you just embody your greatness, creating a strong force field and putting your creative energy into what you love. The most valuable thing is standing strong, firm, and confident in your own path, because that is what changes the world.

We don't make changes by trying to alter people, but instead by becoming our own greatest self so we can open our energy to the experiences we deserve. Your life force is no longer lost to unwanted encounters, forced relationships, toxic habits, or connections that weaken you. It's all about people restoring their own healthy energy fields, reconnecting with their soul's personal blueprint, emitting radiant energy, embodying thought power, and loving life unconditionally. Life only gets better as *we* get better and start to see with our inner eye the richness, the magic, and the possibilities surrounding us.

Don't let your past keep you away from your greatness today. Regret only lives in the mind. Release it all; you are renewed every second. You can recreate yourself. You can become greater. You can do better. You are so much more than anything or anyone that tries to limit you. Rise above it all.

Humans have the supernatural ability to break free from any habit and completely change their lives. A person who was once in deep despair can turn things around to become their healthiest and happiest. It is never over for anyone. With that said, the person in question needs to realize this and awaken to the truth themselves. Sometimes, people need to hit rock bottom to want to change. Maybe there is something good in that.

If we just look at one part of a person's story and judge it, we assume it will always be that way. Sometimes, tough love helps, too, or being clear and direct. You don't have to play a role. You don't need to even get caught up in it or keep offering advice. The power of the soul is something we can't imagine, and people can activate that change when they need to do so. Step back from it all and take care of yourself. You have been hero enough in the past, constantly trying to save everyone. Now is the time to play in the field of equilibrium alignment, where you energetically match up with what is meant for you. The core energy of sending out signals that you are going to save people, save the world, or force awakening only attracts more of that energy to you, to play out a designed reality you feel is necessary to in order to be fulfilled yourself. You have to think about what your path will look like if that is the common energy you are projecting. This is completely a different energy from people who are showing up ready.

> *Don't use past thoughts to assume future outcomes. Every situation can change in a positive way. Sometimes, a limiting thought linked to fear continues to recreate itself until you choose to acknowledge and operate according to possibilities and potentialities.*

When someone is already doing their own inner work or making an effort to get better, this is a sign that they want to receive what they are searching for. There is no need to go into the streets with a loudspeaker and preach or force a thought pattern onto others. We have to alter the paths in our own minds. If you wish the best for someone, see them in that state in your imagination...if that is the energy effort you want to invest. Sometimes, this might be a loved one, and people will do anything for someone they care about. I would suggest you pray for them, see them in a better light, and imagine them healed, whole, and healthy. Our minds are really powerful in creating what we imagine. This is no different than someone else praying for you. It sends good energy and powerful thoughts to assist them in the mental realm to gain momentum, strength, and support, which helps them break free.

We can do so much in the mental world before we try to speak change upon someone who isn't ready. Encouragement comes through prayer, positive thoughts, and empowering energy sent to that person's mind. Always check in with yourself when it comes to how that feels for you when you are sending positive thoughts and prayers. Always trust if something feels right or off. Usually, your body will let you know when something feels uncomfort-able, or when you feel like it is empowering you to be of energetic assistance. Just know that your energy is very precious, and it is your choice what you do with it. Nothing is your responsibility, and you have the freedom to do as you wish.

Activating Your Soul's Blueprint

You are an ancient being. Your DNA has been around for lifetimes, passed on through generations within your family and spanning back to the beginning of humanity. You are of the original people, not by genetics, but by remembrance,

EMBODIMENT: REPRESENTING YOUR THOUGHT WORLD

embodiment, and owning your truth. Your soul has come alive in this lifetime because you were ready to carry on what it means to hold that kind of energy in your body. If your parents or grandparents didn't have the chance for full expression of self, just know that you do now. We have waited for a long time to own our personal power of thought. This represents the highest honor and grace of who we are, what we are, and what we can do.

To fully activate your abilities means you must own all that you are. This creates a powerful ripple that reminds you of what you came here to do. The most important part of activating your soul's blueprint is unstoppable self-trust, a high level of self-knowledge, a deep connection with your own body's intelligence, understanding that you are a spiritual being, honoring the access available through your awareness, and acknowledging the revelations that surround you in everyday life. Seeing your interconnection with nature and everything around you shows your sensitivity to preexisting higher energies. If nothing in your life feels the same as the years pass, it is because you are rising from the slumber of the unknown self. You are starting to see yourself, feel yourself, and respect yourself. You are no longer settling or doing things that go against your own true path. You are honoring what it means to be alive, to be more, and to know yourself.

> *You have always been a master of the realms, a seer beyond and near. Your treasure has been unlocked. Your command to claim your power has been heard. You are becoming all that you have always been destined to be. It is time to see it for yourself.*

Things that once made you compromise yourself are no longer even a thought. Many of your past ways now look entirely

Thought Access

unfamiliar because you are moving into a new wave of energy. If you were confined before, imagine the burst of new energy now running through you. This only means you have arrived to express more, unrestricted and unrestrained energetically. You will start looking at yourself in a new way, not because you have to, but because you are now being urged to.

This is why nothing feels or looks the same. Before, you may not have had a clue about who you were, and just kept living life completely disconnected from your own body's technology, emotional intelligence, awareness, and what was available to you. That past may have been filled with fears, self-judgement, insecurities, uncertainties, confusion, and habits that didn't represent your greatness. You could have been in a cycle or a loop simply because it was familiar until the change happened to you. One day, you woke up and wanted something different. You were fed up and done with how things were. The time had come for you to rise out of unawareness and see for yourself what it meant to be lucid for your experience.

This was all meant to be. You had to make a change that day. You had to finally break free. This is part of your soul's blueprint. This was when you started to remember all that you are. It made you change a lot about yourself because you attained greater access. With limited awareness in the past, your mind couldn't know anything of which it wasn't yet aware. As you receive what you need for yourself, your changes will be natural. This could even be happening to you right now. It can test your strength or make you question what is happening to you. When we move from limitation and fear into our pure, natural state of expansiveness, we go through a process of releasing, unblocking energies, and healing our minds, all because our soul initiated the transformation. In my book *Inner Glimpse*, I discuss the spiritual realization phase and what that feels like for anyone wanting to know how to integrate the energetic changes. This book goes a step further, welcoming you into your soul's blueprint by reminding you of all that you are.

You are a supernatural being. Allow yourself to be transformed. You know what to do.

Everything gets better because you are no longer afraid of what it means to have vast abilities and to be a superbeing. You are going to see yourself becoming a part of humanity's rise toward greatness, and you will lead the way by owning your own energy field. The energy now supports everyone who is ready and willing. Before, you could have avoided your change, but now it feels unbearable, as it is confronting you daily. Even one small change pushes you into a new path, new opportunities, new experiences, and new outcomes you could only have dreamed of previously. This change will be multiplied with many blessings because it is encouraging you to keep going.

As you are being restored and renewed, you will be drawn to everything that feels real. There will be a period during which your sensations will awaken and start to repulse artificial things that lack real life energy. Part of your rise will be to stop playing with your own health or doing things that are detrimental to your mindset. You will discontinue all forms of self-sabotage. Your body will naturally know what isn't working, what it no longer wants, and what is no longer enjoyable. This sharpens your senses so you can detect what isn't vital or what is lacking in life force. The more you shed these layers of the past, the more you allow your own soul to be activated in the highest way possible. This will look like natural openness of the heart, proactive thinking, a healthy mindset, being content with yourself, being at peace for no reason, being blissful, curious, creative, loving, expressive, balanced, and in harmony with your own energy flow. You will also have greater abilities. Naturally, you will know what you need to know, feel things out, receive many revelations, and perform in optimal ways that once seemed impossible.

Thought Access

Repeat to yourself to accelerate this energy right now:

My soul is timeless. My lineage is strong. I am an ancient being. I am beyond the physical. I am energetically activated. My soul is rising up. I can feel the burning fire to be reborn, to be who I am meant to be, and to pave my own path. I am liberated like never before. I have freedom that is untold and unheard of. I have awakened to my pure state. I am supported by higher forces. I am intentional on my path. I choose the life I want. I am the embodiment of my highest self. I am everything already. I am complete. I have the commanding power to raise positive energy and move humanity forward. I am making the decision right now to step into my power, to be fearless in all ways, and to chart the unknown with great seership. My soul's blueprint is activated.

Key Points to Remember

- *The time has come for everyone to start representing their thought world. Your physical reality is the embodiment of your inner world. You are your own self-creation. There's no longer space for masks, acting, pretending, or hiding behind a limited perception of self.*

- *The embodiment state will be a powerful movement during which many will want to return to themselves and their soul's truth while awakening their own potential.*

- *You are a super being, and to feel what this means will be the most important experience on your Earth journey.*

- *This is the time to be real with yourself. You can no longer do things that create disharmony or imbalances in your life. You can't settle out of fear or live a life you don't agree with. Your chance to make real change is* right now. Go forward in representing your thought world. In order to do this, you must look at where self-doubt and powerlessness originate.

- *Everyone needs to know the power of their mind, the power of their soul, and the power of their intentions. It all begins when you stop identifying with any sort of lack or limitation. You have to denounce anything that tries to weaken you.*

- *When we step into our own power, we step into an actual energy grid. This is why you feel stronger, healthier, more connected, and more aligned within yourself.*

- *Powerlessness arises from the type of fear that weakens someone's own ability to see beyond the thoughts, creations, and projections the world has put on them.*

- *Breaking free from fear will show you that there's really nothing to be afraid of. There's nothing standing in your way. There aren't people or things against you. All of these are just the tricks of fear, designed to close you off and confine you, keeping you limited and disconnected. They cause you to forget that this is your one life, and you need to fully live it out to the best of your energetic capacity.*

- *As your spiritual energy becomes stronger and your body's natural energy expands, you will start to notice a magnetic energy pulling everything positive toward you.*

- *This new energy will amplify your energy field, get you out of the slumber of chaos and confusion, and reactivate your heart to once again feel what it is to embody greatness.*

- *You're not under any obligation to make anyone see*

Thought Access

something they are not ready to see. You can't force anyone to awaken to their potential. You can't try to make someone see life from a certain perspective they are not ready for.

- *Humans have the supernatural ability to break free from any habit and completely change their lives. A person who was once in deep despair can transmute energy to become their healthiest and happiest. It is never over for anyone; however, the person involved needs to realize this and awaken to the truth themselves.*

- *Everything gets better, because you are no longer afraid of what it means to have vast abilities as a superbeing. You are going to see yourself as a part of humanity's rise toward greatness, and you will lead the way by owning your own energy field. The energy now supports everyone who is ready and willing.*

19

YOU NOW HAVE THOUGHT ACCESS

Congratulations to you on completing this book and gaining access to a higher state of awareness, a lifetime of insight, and great guidance to empower you every single day of your life's adventure. This book is more than just a book. It has its own powerful energy field because of the words it contains and the energy put into it. It is intended to accelerate every reader's life to the next level. It will provide healing, bring the highest clarity, move you onto new paths, help you break free, assist you toward your own soul reconnection, remove blocks, magnetize powerful energy to you, support your mental health, help you manifest out of thin air, turn you into a super-believer, expose you to your own supernatural state, activate you to see the blessings all around you, propel massive changes in your life, give you more confidence, and elevate you spiritually.

Every person has in them a treasure that is filled and abundantly overflowing. It is my duty in this lifetime to expose that golden treasure in every single person I encounter and everyone who reads my books. Writing *Thought Access* meant so much to me because I wanted to go deeper with my readers and touch upon states that aren't normally discussed with simplicity. I know many are searching, and during these great times of human energy transition, we are looking for new meaning, new ways, and new understanding to offer a solid and timeless foundation. *Thought Access* isn't just lessons, information, and teachings; it is energy guidance, a powerful activation tool, and a guaranteed profound inner/outer shift inducer. I wrote this book not just to bring revelations into your life, but to allow you to see for yourself all that is possible for you. This is a guide to return to yourself and witness the treasure you hold.

You are a super being, and *Thought Access* projects that energy back into you. It is like a mirror of your greatest self that communicates with you to rise up, be all you were meant to be, and own your divine power. Only greatness is welcomed here, and only greater is magnified in every reader. Access to greater thought means that you have linked up with a mind that is moving through uncharted realms of the mental world. It opens up direct links to possibilities so others can see what is available outside of conditioned thoughts that try to keep you in a limited scope of awareness. *Thought Access* is a bridge to your own explorations, discoveries, and understandings. It helps you to peel back the layers so you can get back to the potential brewing within you. Everyone has a calling now to step it up and go for it. This is your calling. This is your time.

We are all being upgraded energetically. Every cell in our bodies has intelligence and is constantly inter-connected with our state of mind, the way we feel, the way we see ourselves, and the truth we hold. We are one big unified system. When our mind is right, so is every part of our body.

I see things from an energetic perspective. I see words as energy at work, moving at great speed within the body and all around us. I see thoughts as signals being sent out and received by every part of us. I see us as energy fields that have an expansive connection to everything in the universe. As we become empowered, stronger, healthier, and more content within ourselves, we become more in sync energetically. I wanted to introduce that energy awareness as a basis of life, as we are multidimensional and beyond the physical.

If I ever want to change something in my life, no matter

Thought Access

which state it seems to be happening in, I alter the energy state first. Momentum, when created through our mind and inner world, has a powerful way of supporting lasting change. It helps us break free from the hypnotic trance of negative energy that wants to persist. Everything is in oscillation, and sending the energy where it needs to go mirrors the way you direct your own energy. Sometimes, we assume that preexisting states need to be given energy in order to be overcome, when in reality, a new inner design directs your life force in a greater way to help you break free. This is all happening on the subtle level, and you will feel that the battle isn't as hard as it once was when you were confronted with repeating energy states that wanted to persist as they had always done.

This is a great guide for anyone who wants to over-come just about anything. There's no limit to the ways *Thought Access* can be used. It can be the biggest supporter of cultivating a new life and new energy for someone who wants to rebuild themselves. I believe all habits are just energetic conditioning that has been repeated enough times that it turned into something the person assumes to be in their best interest, even if it is not good for them. I expose the subtle nature of thought processes so you can be liberated at will. Many people will be liberated, freed, and restored by *Thought Access*. All habits you once thought you couldn't escape will be energetically released from your field. All procrastination, doubt, harmful thoughts, unwanted states of mind, lack, limitation, fear, and lower natures that keep you consciously distracted will be wiped from your mind and body now.

Thought Access works in the subtle fields of your life so you can have a chance at actually recognizing what is taking place; so you can intentionally make the right choices for yourself. How else will you change for the better, if you don't know where the discordance and imbalance stems from? This book is all about getting real with the causes so the effects naturally start to produce themselves. Everyone deserves to live the life of their dreams and to have the chance to know more of who they truly are.

You don't always have to be barely getting by or barely at peace. You don't have to try to force things or be concerned with the way things will happen. You will know once and for all what it means to stable, centered, content, trusting, open, and connected. You will know that everything is naturally perfect by seeing the way it is all being orchestrated. You can tell that divine power is at work all the time. My experiences during the writing of this book were so heartfelt and profoundly moving that I now feel a surge of energy flowing through me in the knowledge that every single reader of this book will be deeply transformed. I rejoice in the fact that everyone will have radiant energy to lead their glorious lives. Onward and upward for all.

Thought Access was written to be studied, re-read, explored, and integrated over time. It is the kind of book you can just open up to any page and receive what you need. Every chapter is unique in what it provides, and the reader has the choice to dive deeper into chapters that resonate with their soul. I believe *Thought Access* is a guide for the new direction in which humanity is heading. Everyone needs to be individually empowered so they can contribute to collective change. Stronger, healthier minds create stronger relationships, families, communities, nations, and humans who are willing to bypass ways that no longer work—not by force or coercion, but by transcendence of the limited perception of the self. Motivation will be inspired by abundance, natural energy, the heart, solutions from the soul, and health in mind and body instead of scarcity, survivalism, lack, limitation, negativity, or discord. We are moving into a higher state, and I believe *Thought Access* is the key and preparation for this rebirth and reconnection with something primordial and ancient.

I wish for everyone greater self-understanding, unification, awareness, and self-love. I know that within everyone, there are unlimited variations of the ultimate life that are possible to explore. I know anyone can change. I know anyone can turn their life around. This isn't a race or a rush to arrive somewhere. There isn't a moment that can't be captured. We are all living through forever, eternity, and continuous flow as days pass and new moments arise. We are moving forward, always. We can either be held back by what has ended or be inspired by what is to come.

The best days of your life have yet to be lived, and as you gravitate toward better, you can explore many wondrous and wonderful things with the knowledge of how to be resilient through everything and anything that comes your way. *Thought Access* will be a powerful force of change in your life, producing many new ideas, giving you an abundance of energy, helping you believe in yourself at a higher level, giving you access to greater self-perception, and pushing you to get things done that once seemed to take forever. You'll find yourself in a healthier mental, emotional, and physical state. You will attract better opportunities, relationships, and people who are meant to support your path as well as experiences that heighten your own inner vision of the world. You will experience an increase in mind power, intelligence, awareness, and inner knowing that you can. Nothing will feel forced; rather, everything will feel meant to be.

Don't be shocked or surprised if your energy field gets so strong that it attracts many wonderful things to you, even from a distance. You will feel as though you are at one with everything, without even having to try or do anything special. This is the power of *Thought Access*. It increases your self-awareness so you can do everything through your own mind. Not only will things get easier, but your responses will arise from an optimistic place and the belief that everything will naturally work itself out. You will officially leave the state of being at the mercy of an unpredictable ebb and flow, instead becoming the observer of unwarranted changes or things that suddenly and unexpectedly come up. Before, you may have been sucked in, altered emotionally, or drained energetically, forgetting that you are not what is happening; but now, you simply observe all that is taking place. This encourages you to stay grounded so you can receive spiritual guidance and solutions for anything that comes up.

I want everyone to be in their power and to know that when things go wrong, you can change your perception, positioning your response and the way you see things so you can remain open to peak-level awareness that guides you when you need a breakthrough. Usually, miraculous changes happen when we step back from things and let solutions flow into our minds about the kind of inspired action we would like to take. When we are in the emotion of the moment or reactive, we get pulled into the problem to the point that we lose all control—even losing ourselves —to what appears to be taking place. In situations like these, we close off higher channels of guidance and support while getting caught up…until we settle again and gain greater perspective on what needs to be solved. *Thought Access* reinforces the many ways you can remain the observer and calculate probable solutions for just about anything.

One of the major things you'll notice upon finishing this book is how you feel about yourself and how the world responds to you. You will appear to have discovered a secret or a newfound abundance of energy that revitalizes and rejuvenates you. You will be energetically illuminated and radiant. Something will change about you that is taking place on another level, and everyone will detect it energetically. There's no way to explain what has happened, but the fact that you have become the embodiment of a super being will speak for itself. When you are in harmony, aware, connected, and balanced, your body secretes a certain kind of biochemical elixir that activates your nervous system to produce radiant energy. This makes you electromagnetically attractive. It gravitates everything to you without any effort on your part. Just being who you are is all you need.

Thought Access

Thought Access teaches you mental health, emotional wellness, and spiritual activation so you can remove all kinds of energetic blocks and resistance and open your mind to more. The goal is to bring you back into alignment so you can shine your brightest and be your greatest. I know people aren't their storylines, what has happened to them, the perceptions of others, or the circumstances in which they find themselves. They are able to be more and do more, all because they have gained Thought Access. I know your life will never be the same because you are operating on a new wavelength. Everything about you is different now: how you move, think, see the world, and operate as a powerful spiritual being. You will become an inspiration to many, showing others what it means to live life as a multidimensional being. You won't wait for the end to fully appreciate everything along the way. You will live in gratitude for your physical life experience and you will be at peace, knowing that you have done what you came here to do. You will forgive yourself, love yourself, and be at peace with yourself through it all.

Allow yourself to start taking everything to the next level. Don't be timid about who you are. You will naturally lose any insecurities that previously caused you to overthink or judge yourself. You will have worked through that by now. I deeply believe that with *Thought Access*, many, many people will heal from limiting past self-perceptions, fear, self-image problems, not feeling good enough, or confusion about their place in life. They will stop working against themselves by entertaining false narratives that don't encompass all that they are.

This is the time blossom and bloom. I know that you will become all that you were divinely created to be. I know you will see for yourself the treasure within you. I know your life will have a supernatural touch now. I know your mind will be expanded beyond imagination, and your world will turn into a magnificent dream that you are alive to experience. Enjoy every moment of the goodness this will bring.

You Now Have Thought Access

You now hold the key to *Thought Access,* and you officially have *Entry to More!*

YOU ARE NOW ACTIVATED!

www.ingramcontent.com/pod-product-compliance
Lightning Source LLC
Chambersburg PA
CBHW060545080526
44585CB00013B/455